Modern Full-Stack Web Development with ASP.NET Core

A project-based guide to building web applications with
ASP.NET Core 9 and JavaScript frameworks

Alexandre Malavasi

Modern Full-Stack Web Development with ASP.NET Core

Group Product Manager: Kaustubh Manglurkar
Senior Publishing Product Manager: Suman Sen
Book Project Manager: Aparna Nair
Senior Editor: Adrija Mitra
Technical Editor: Simran Ali
Copy Editor: Safis Editing
Indexer: Hemangini Bari
Production Designer: Aparna Bhagat
Senior DevRel Marketing Executive: Priyadarshini Sharma

First published: February 2025

Production reference: 3311025

Published by Packt Publishing Ltd.
Grosvenor House
11 St Paul's Square
Birmingham
B3 1RB, UK.

ISBN 978-1-78913-278-6

www.packtpub.com

To my mother, Marli, for her unwavering love and sacrifices that shaped me. To my daughter, Myla, for inspiring me with her boundless curiosity and joy. And to my wife, Paula, for being my steadfast partner and the heart of our shared journey.

—Alexandre Malavasi

Contributors

About the author

Alexandre Malavasi, CTO at MARELO and 4x Microsoft MVP, is a speaker at international conferences and the author of global books on .NET. With 16 years of software development experience, he has led complex projects across Brazil, Europe, and the United States. Alexandre excels in managing projects within the Microsoft stack. He holds multiple certifications and two postgraduate degrees in software engineering. His expertise and contributions to the field, coupled with his leadership in large-scale projects, have established him as a thought leader and an expert in his domain.

I would like to first and foremost thank my loving and supportive wife Paula and my daughter Myla for their endless encouragement throughout this journey. A special thanks also to my business partners, Joaquim and Jacque, at MARELO for their collaboration and unwavering support, which have been instrumental in making this project a reality.

About the reviewers

Rodrigo Lobenwein is a full-stack developer with a rich background in business management and sales, having transitioned to software development after over 15 years of experience in these fields. Since 2021, he has focused on building and optimizing applications using .NET and React, leveraging his business acumen to deliver efficient, user-focused software solutions. He uses his background to deeply understand users' needs while maintaining a strategic view of the business, always prioritizing process improvement and client satisfaction. Passionate about technology and committed to continuous learning, he loves to understand the core of problems and find effective solutions, always eager to expand his knowledge and skill set.

Alex Tjahjana is a seasoned digital transformation leader with over 25 years of expertise in software development, cloud, AI transformation, and DevOps. He consistently delivers innovative, reliable, and efficient solutions across a range of industries. His leadership has driven high-impact initiatives, including New Zealand's largest multi-cloud deployment and AI-powered system transformations. Alex also advises clients on digital transformation strategies to optimize their business outcomes. He is passionate about leading teams, staying at the forefront of technology, and mentoring IT talent. He holds multiple certifications, including Azure Expert Architect, AWS Architect Professional, Cybersecurity Expert, DevOps Engineer, Scrum Master, and ITIL.

Learn more on Discord

To join the Discord community for this book – where you can share feedback, ask questions to the author, and learn about new releases – follow the QR code below:

`https://packt.link/aspdotnet9projects`

Table of Contents

Part 1: Core Web Development with ASP.NET Core and Blazor

1

2

3

Middleware and Dependency Injection   43

4

Configuration and Security   67

5

Introduction to Blazor   95

Part 2: Advanced Integration and Application Development

6

Advanced Blazor Development   121

7

Advanced Component Architecture in Blazor   145

8

RESTful Services with ASP.NET Core – Part 1   167

9

RESTful Services with ASP.NET Core – Part 2   191

10

Introduction to JavaScript Frameworks   205

11

Exploring Vue.js and Comparing Frameworks   227

12

Integrating Vue.js with ASP.NET Core   259

13

Integrating Angular with ASP.NET Core   285

14

Integrating React with ASP.NET Core   331

Part 3: Good Practices for Full-Stack Projects

15

Planning and Structuring Full-Stack Projects   377

16

Performance, Deployment, and Maintenance   393

17

Unlock Your Exclusive Benefits   407

Preface

Hello there! Full-stack web development combines the strengths of server-side technologies with modern JavaScript frameworks, creating dynamic, high-performance applications. ASP.NET Core, with its flexibility and scalability, is a leading framework for building enterprise-grade applications, and when paired with frameworks such as Angular, React, or Vue.js, it offers endless possibilities for crafting full-stack solutions.

This book is designed to help you navigate the complexities of full-stack development by bridging the gap between frontend and backend technologies. Throughout this journey, we will focus on three key pillars:

- Mastering server-side development with ASP.NET Core
- Seamlessly integrating JavaScript frameworks into your projects
- Implementing performance, security, and best practices for full-stack applications

While many resources introduce these technologies individually, this book provides a project-based approach to full-stack development, emphasizing the integration of ASP.NET Core with leading JavaScript frameworks.

Drawing from my extensive experience in the industry, I will guide you through real-world examples and practical insights, equipping you with the tools to create scalable, robust web applications.

As full-stack development continues to evolve, mastering the integration of frontend and backend technologies will be a key skill. This book will empower you to excel in building modern, efficient web solutions using ASP.NET Core and the JavaScript frameworks that best fit your projects.

Who this book is for

This book is ideal for beginners in web development who are eager to learn how to build full-stack applications using ASP.NET Core and modern JavaScript frameworks such as Angular, React, and Vue.js. Whether you are just getting started with web technologies or have basic experience with either frontend or backend development, this book offers a structured and hands-on approach to mastering full-stack development from the ground up.

Three key groups will benefit from this book:

- **Aspiring full-stack developers**: Individuals who are new to full-stack development and want to learn how to build complete web applications by combining ASP.NET Core for the server side and popular JavaScript frameworks for the client side

- **Beginner backend developers**: Those with a basic understanding of backend development who want to expand their knowledge and learn how to create user-friendly, dynamic interfaces using Angular, React, or Vue.js

- **Frontend developers**: Frontend developers who are familiar with HTML, CSS, and JavaScript and are now looking to gain experience in building scalable server-side applications using ASP. NET Core

With clear explanations, practical examples, and real-world projects, this book is a perfect starting point for anyone who wants to dive into full-stack development and build robust, scalable applications from scratch.

What this book covers

Chapter 1, Introduction to ASP.NET Core, covers the basics of ASP.NET Core, exploring its architecture, key features, and available project templates. By the end, you'll understand its history and build a simple web application, preparing you for more advanced topics in the following chapters.

Chapter 2, Setting Up and Building Basic Applications, guides you through setting up your ASP.NET Core development environment and creating your first web application. You'll learn the essentials of the **Model-View-Controller** (**MVC**) architecture, as well as routing and controllers, which are fundamental to building and navigating applications. By the end, you will have a functional ASP.NET Core app and a solid foundation for future development.

Chapter 3, Middleware and Dependency Injection, explores two core concepts of ASP.NET Core: middleware and dependency injection. You'll learn how to implement middleware to customize the request pipeline and manage services efficiently using dependency injection. By the end, you'll be equipped to build adaptable, maintainable applications with clean and scalable code.

Chapter 4, Configuration and Security, covers the essentials of configuring ASP.NET Core applications across different environments, ensuring flexibility and reliability. You'll also dive into authentication and authorization, learning to secure your applications against unauthorized access. Additionally, you will explore secure data handling practices and implement SSL to protect data in transit. By the end, you'll have the skills to build secure, adaptable applications that are ready for modern web challenges.

Chapter 5, Introduction to Blazor, explores Blazor, a framework that allows you to build interactive web UIs using C#. You'll learn how to create a basic Blazor WebAssembly application and discover the differences between client-side and server-side Blazor. Additionally, you'll dive into Blazor's component architecture and data binding, equipping you to build dynamic, responsive web applications.

Chapter 6, Advanced Blazor Development, dives into advanced Blazor topics, including component architecture and lifecycle. You'll also learn how to handle events in Blazor to create responsive UIs, and master state management techniques to ensure your applications maintain smooth and consistent functionality. By the end, you'll be equipped to build more complex, high-performing Blazor applications.

Chapter 7, Advanced Component Architecture in Blazor, explores advanced Blazor component architecture. You'll learn to create dynamic components, manage complex UIs, and handle advanced routing with parameters. You'll also dive into JavaScript interoperability, allowing you to integrate JavaScript libraries with Blazor. Finally, you'll discover the new render modes in Blazor (.NET 8), optimizing performance and user experience in your applications.

Chapter 8, RESTful Services with ASP.NET Core – Part 1, introduces the foundational concepts of RESTful services and guides you through building basic REST APIs using ASP.NET Core. You'll learn the principles of REST, how to create and configure APIs, handle requests and responses, and implement versioning and documentation. By the end, you'll have the skills to build well-structured, maintainable REST APIs.

Chapter 9, RESTful Services with ASP.NET Core – Part 2, delves into more advanced aspects of REST API development, focusing on complex routing techniques and performance optimization. You'll learn how to create flexible API endpoints and apply strategies such as caching and asynchronous programming to improve API efficiency. By the end, you'll have the skills to build scalable, high-performing APIs using ASP.NET Core.

Chapter 10, Introduction to JavaScript Frameworks, provides an introduction to the three most popular JavaScript frameworks: Angular, React, and Vue.js. You'll learn the foundational principles of each framework, explore their key features, and understand their use cases. By the end, you'll be equipped to start working with these frameworks and apply them to simple web projects.

Chapter 11, Exploring Vue.js and Comparing Frameworks, takes a deeper look at Vue.js, covering advanced features such as state management, routing, and navigation. You'll gain practical skills for building more complex Vue.js applications while exploring how Vue.js compares to Angular and React. By the end, you'll be well-equipped to build scalable Vue.js applications and choose the best JavaScript framework for your projects.

Chapter 12, Integrating Vue.js with ASP.NET Core, focuses on integrating Vue.js with ASP.NET Core to build full-stack applications. You'll learn how to manage data flow between the frontend and backend, implement secure authentication and authorization, and optimize your application's performance. By the end, you'll be ready to create efficient, scalable full-stack applications using these two powerful technologies.

Chapter 13, Integrating Angular with ASP.NET Core, guides you through integrating Angular with ASP.NET Core to create scalable full-stack applications. You'll learn how to set up both frameworks, implement secure API communication, and optimize performance. By the end, you'll be equipped to build dynamic, high-performance applications using Angular for the frontend and ASP.NET Core for the backend.

Chapter 14, Integrating React with ASP.NET Core, walks you through integrating React with ASP.NET Core to build dynamic, scalable full-stack applications. You'll learn how to configure both technologies, establish efficient data communication, and optimize performance for a seamless user experience. By the end, you'll have the skills to create high-performing full-stack applications using React for the frontend and ASP.NET Core for the backend.

Chapter 15, Planning and Structuring Full-Stack Projects, focuses on planning and organizing full-stack web projects to ensure both frontend and backend components work seamlessly. You'll learn how to set project objectives, design scalable architectures, and apply version control strategies. Additionally, we'll cover Agile methodologies for team collaboration, ensuring efficient project management from planning to deployment.

Chapter 16, Performance, Deployment, and Maintenance, explores critical strategies for optimizing the performance of full-stack applications, from backend efficiency to frontend responsiveness. You'll learn deployment techniques to ensure smooth launches and post-deployment monitoring and maintenance practices to keep applications running at peak performance. The chapter also covers scaling applications to handle high traffic, ensuring long-term stability and growth.

To get the most out of this book

To fully benefit from this book, basic knowledge of web development, including HTML, CSS, JavaScript, and C#, is helpful. Familiarity with setting up a development environment and using Git will also make it easier to follow along.

Software/hardware covered in the book	Operating system requirements
Visual Studio 2022	Windows, macOS, or Linux
Visual Studio Code	
Node 21.x	
.NET 9	

If you are using the digital version of this book, we advise you to type the code yourself or access the code from the book's GitHub repository (a link is available in the next section). Doing so will help you avoid any potential errors related to the copying and pasting of code.

After reading this book, I encourage you to take on real-world projects, contribute to open source communities, or explore more advanced topics related to software architecture and advanced concepts of C# and ASP.NET Core. Applying the concepts from this book will solidify your knowledge of full-stack development and help you stay ahead in your career.

Download the example code files

You can download the example code files for this book from GitHub at `https://github.com/PacktPublishing/Modern-Full-Stack-Web-Development-with-ASP.NET-Core`. If there's an update to the code, it will be updated in the GitHub repository.

We also have other code bundles from our rich catalog of books and videos available at `https://github.com/PacktPublishing/`. Check them out!

Conventions used

There are a number of text conventions used throughout this book.

`Code in text`: Indicates code words in text, database table names, folder names, filenames, file extensions, pathnames, dummy URLs, user input, and Twitter handles. Here is an example: "In this folder structure, the `node_modules` directory contains all the necessary dependencies and packages required by your application."

A block of code is set as follows:

```
import React from 'react';

function MyComponent() {
  return (
    <div className="my-component">
      <h2>This is my first React component!</h2>
      <p>Congratulations for your first component.</p>
    </div>
  );
}

export default MyComponent;
```

When we wish to draw your attention to a particular part of a code block, the relevant lines or items are set in bold:

```
<h1>Hello, {{ title }}</h1>
      <p>Congratulations! Your app is running. 🎉</p>
      <br>
      <p>
        <app-my-component></app-my-component>
      </p>
```

Any command-line input or output is written as follows:

```
ng generate component my-component --standalone
```

Bold: Indicates a new term, an important word, or words that you see onscreen. For instance, words in menus or dialog boxes appear in **bold**. Here is an example: "If you open the application in your browser, you'll see the component's content being displayed alongside the message specified in the title property – that is, **My first Angular component**."

> **Tips or important notes**
> Appear like this.

Get in touch

Feedback from our readers is always welcome.

General feedback: If you have questions about any aspect of this book, email us at `customercare@packtpub.com` and mention the book title in the subject of your message.

Errata: Although we have taken every care to ensure the accuracy of our content, mistakes do happen. If you have found a mistake in this book, we would be grateful if you would report this to us. Please visit `www.packtpub.com/support/errata` and fill in the form.

Piracy: If you come across any illegal copies of our works in any form on the internet, we would be grateful if you would provide us with the location address or website name. Please contact us at `copyright@packt.com` with a link to the material.

If you are interested in becoming an author: If there is a topic that you have expertise in and you are interested in either writing or contributing to a book, please visit `authors.packtpub.com`.

Share Your Thoughts

Once you've read *Modern Full-Stack Web Development with ASP.NET Core*, we'd love to hear your thoughts! Scan the QR code below to go straight to the Amazon review page for this book and share your feedback.

`https://packt.link/r/1789132789`

Your review is important to us and the tech community and will help us make sure we're delivering excellent quality content.

Free Benefits with Your Book

This book comes with free benefits to support your learning. Activate them now for instant access (see the "*How to Unlock*" section for instructions).

Here's a quick overview of what you can instantly unlock with your purchase:

PDF and ePub Copies

Next-Gen Web-Based Reader

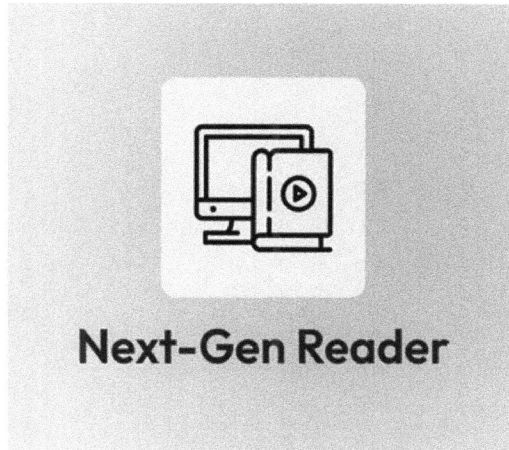

Access a DRM-free PDF copy of this book to read anywhere, on any device.

Use a DRM-free ePub version with your favorite e-reader.

Multi-device progress sync: Pick up where you left off, on any device.

Highlighting and notetaking: Capture ideas and turn reading into lasting knowledge.

Bookmarking: Save and revisit key sections whenever you need them.

Dark mode: Reduce eye strain by switching to dark or sepia themes

How to Unlock

UNLOCK NOW

Scan the QR code (or go to `packtpub.com/unlock`). Search for this book by name, confirm the edition, and then follow the steps on the page.

Note: Keep your invoice handly. Purchase made directly from packt don't require one.

Part 1: Core Web Development with ASP.NET Core and Blazor

In this part, you will be introduced to the core concepts of ASP.NET Core and Blazor, two essential frameworks for modern full-stack development. You will explore the architecture and features of ASP. NET Core, set up your development environment, and build your first web application. Additionally, you will dive into Blazor, understanding how it enables building interactive web UIs using C#.

This part includes the following chapters:

- *Chapter 1, Introduction to ASP.NET Core*
- *Chapter 2, Setting up and Building Basic Applications*
- *Chapter 3, Middleware and Dependency Injection*
- *Chapter 4, Configuration and Security*
- *Chapter 5, Introduction to Blazor*

1

Introduction to ASP.NET Core

Welcome to *Modern Full-Stack Web Development with ASP.NET Core*, an essential guide designed to kickstart your journey into one of the most popular and robust web development frameworks available today. ASP.NET Core is a modern, open-source, cross-platform framework for building web-based, internet-connected applications.

In this chapter, we'll delve into the core components of ASP.NET Core, providing you with a comprehensive understanding of its architecture, functionalities, and how to harness its capabilities for building efficient web applications.

By engaging with the upcoming lessons and activities, you'll gain hands-on experience in setting up your development environment, creating a basic web application, and exploring the essential building blocks of ASP.NET Core, such as **Model-View-Controller** (**MVC**) patterns, **dependency injection** (**DI**), middleware, and more. You'll learn not just the theory but also apply the concepts in practical tasks, enabling you to build and deploy a simple yet functional web application by the end of this chapter.

Understanding ASP.NET Core is invaluable for any web developer aiming to create robust, scalable, and maintainable web applications. By mastering the fundamentals outlined in this chapter, you'll be equipped with the knowledge and skills to explore more advanced features and best practices in subsequent chapters.

In this chapter, we're going to cover the following main topics:

- Introduction to ASP.NET Core – understanding the framework and its advantages
- Understanding the main project templates available for ASP.NET Core
- Exploring the ASP.NET Core architecture and its features
- History of ASP.NET Core

This structured approach will enable you to navigate this chapter efficiently and focus on sections that are most relevant to your learning path.

> **Free Benefits with Your Book**
>
> Your purchase includes a free PDF copy of this book along with other exclusive benefits. Check the *Free Benefits with Your Book* section in the Preface to unlock them instantly and maximize your learning experience.

Technical requirements

Before diving into the hands-on exercises for ASP.NET Core in this book, it's crucial to establish the technical foundation that's required to follow the upcoming chapters effectively. This section outlines the necessary technologies and installations you'll need to maximize your learning experience and engage with the practical exercises provided efficiently:

- **.NET 9 framework**: At the core of your development environment should be the .NET 9 framework. This latest version is essential for leveraging the new and improved features offered in ASP.NET Core. It provides a comprehensive and consistent programming model that's crucial for building high-performance web applications. Ensure that you have .NET 9 installed on your system so that you can work through the examples and projects in this book seamlessly.

- **ASP.NET Core (latest version)**: Alongside .NET 9, having the latest version of ASP.NET Core installed is imperative. This version is specifically designed to integrate with .NET 9, offering a powerful and efficient platform for web development. It's the framework you'll be interacting with throughout this book, so having it updated will ensure you have access to the latest tools and features.

- **Development environment**: For an optimal development experience, this book recommends using either Visual Studio or Visual Studio Code, depending on your preference:

  - **Visual Studio (latest version)**: Known for its comprehensive suite of development tools, Visual Studio is an excellent choice for ASP.NET Core development. It provides an integrated environment where you can write, debug, and deploy your applications efficiently. Ensure you have the latest version installed to benefit from the integrated support for .NET 9 and ASP.NET Core.

  - **Visual Studio Code (latest version)**: If you prefer a lighter yet powerful editor, Visual Studio Code is your go-to option. It supports a wide range of programming languages and frameworks, including C# and .NET, making it suitable for ASP.NET Core development. With its robust ecosystem of extensions, you can tailor the editor to your specific needs, enhancing your productivity and development experience.

By preparing your environment with these technical requirements, you'll be well-equipped to tackle the ASP.NET Core projects and examples presented in this book, ensuring a smooth and effective learning journey.

Understanding ASP.NET Core – exploring the framework and its benefits

Before we start our journey into ASP.NET Core, you must understand the details of the path that you'll be walking in this book.

ASP.NET Core stands as a groundbreaking development framework in the market for web development, offering a versatile and high-performance framework that caters to modern application needs. It has provided constant updates year after year for the last two decades. This section delves into the nature of ASP.NET Core, elucidating its core components, architectural advantages, and the benefits it brings to the development table.

ASP.NET Core is an open source, cross-platform framework for building modern, cloud-enabled, internet-connected applications. At its heart, it's a redesign of classic ASP.NET, but with a modular, more efficient, and cross-platform runtime. This modern framework allows developers to build applications that can run on Windows, Linux, and macOS, thereby broadening the potential user base and deployment environments.

The framework's inception was driven by the need to create a more modern web development platform that could address the evolving challenges and leverage the latest computing environments. ASP.NET Core's architecture is lean and composable, providing developers with the flexibility to include only the necessary components in their applications. This optimizes performance and reduces resource consumption by helping them choose the correct and appropriate project templates.

Key features and architectural benefits

ASP.NET Core distinguishes itself in the web development domain with its exceptional **cross-platform** support, enabling developers to design and deploy applications across various operating systems, such as Windows, Linux, and macOS, without substantial code alterations. This flexibility not only expands the applications' reach across diverse environments but also aligns with the modern trend toward platform-agnostic development, ensuring applications can cater to a wider audience, irrespective of their platform preferences.

The *performance metrics* of ASP.NET Core are equally impressive, showcasing significant enhancements over its forerunners. Its ability to deliver quick response times and minimize latency is crucial for applications that are expected to handle high loads efficiently. This performance edge is attributed to the framework's optimized, lightweight architecture, which streamlines processes and reduces unnecessary overhead, ensuring applications remain agile and responsive under various operational conditions.

Modularity is another cornerstone of ASP.NET Core's architecture, offering developers the flexibility to incorporate only the essential components needed for their applications. This not only reduces the overall size but also optimizes performance. Such modularity is invaluable for maintenance and updates, allowing for individual component enhancements without the need for broad, systemic revisions, thus keeping applications up to date and secure with minimal disruption.

Security is outstanding in ASP.NET Core, which fortifies applications with robust, built-in features safeguarding against prevalent web threats. Developers benefit from integrated support for critical security measures such as data protection, authentication, authorization, and **cross-origin resource sharing (CORS)** defenses, enabling them to build secure, reliable applications by default.

Integrating MVC and a Web API into a cohesive framework demonstrates ASP.NET Core's streamlined and unified approach to web application and service development. This integration simplifies the development workflow, reducing the learning curve and fostering a more intuitive environment for developers, particularly those new to the platform.

Expanding its horizon, ASP.NET Core embraces modern web development trends with Blazor, a groundbreaking framework that allows developers to build interactive web user interfaces using C# instead of JavaScript. This innovative approach provides a seamless development experience, enabling the use of a single language across both client-side and server-side code, thus streamlining the development process and enhancing productivity.

Moreover, ASP.NET Core's ability to integrate seamlessly with various JavaScript frameworks amplifies its versatility. This interoperability is crucial for developers leveraging the unique strengths of JavaScript frameworks such as Angular, React, and Vue.js alongside ASP.NET Core, facilitating the creation of rich, interactive, and highly responsive user experiences. The synergy between ASP.NET Core and these JavaScript ecosystems enables a more comprehensive development strategy that accommodates a wide array of project requirements and enhances the overall capability to deliver sophisticated, modern web applications.

Development experience and ecosystem

ASP.NET Core offers a superior development experience with its integration into the .NET ecosystem, providing access to a vast array of libraries and tools. Developers can leverage the powerful features of Visual Studio, Visual Studio Code, or any other editor of their choice and benefit from features such as IntelliSense, debugging, and unit testing.

The community and ecosystem around ASP.NET Core are vibrant and continuously evolving. Developers have access to a plethora of resources, including documentation, tutorials, forums, and third-party libraries, which facilitate the development process and encourage innovation.

Real-world applications and scalability

ASP.NET Core is designed to handle the demands of modern web applications, from small-scale projects to large, enterprise-level solutions. Its scalability is one of its strongest suits, enabling applications to grow in terms of users and functionality with minimal changes having to be made to the core architecture.

Companies and developers adopt ASP.NET Core for various applications, including web applications, mobile backends, IoT applications, and microservices. The framework's versatility and performance make it suitable for a wide range of industries, including finance, healthcare, education, and e-commerce.

Continuous innovation and community support

The future of ASP.NET Core is promising, with continuous enhancements and updates being rolled out by Microsoft and the community. The framework is open source, which encourages community contributions and feedback, driving its evolution and ensuring it remains at the forefront of web development technologies.

In conclusion, ASP.NET Core is a powerful, modern framework that's designed to meet the challenges of today's web development landscape. Its benefits, including cross-platform support, performance, modularity, security, and scalability, make it an excellent choice for developers looking to build robust, maintainable, and efficient web applications.

Having explored the numerous advantages of utilizing ASP.NET, let's progress to the subsequent section, where we'll delve into the various project templates available for ASP.NET Core.

Understanding the main project templates available for ASP.NET Core

ASP.NET Core's versatility is encapsulated in its range of project templates, each designed to cater to different web development needs. These templates not only offer a jumpstart for your projects but also integrate best practices, guiding you toward a structured and efficient development process. In this section, we'll delve deeper into each primary template, offering a richer perspective to aid you in selecting the most fitting template for your specific project requirements.

MVC

The MVC template in ASP.NET Core serves as a robust foundation for building web applications that are scalable, maintainable, and testable. This in-depth exploration will unpack the MVC architecture, elucidating how each component operates within the framework and how this architecture facilitates a clean separation of concerns – a principle that's vital for complex application development.

The MVC pattern is a well-established design paradigm in web application development that's not only used by the .NET platform but by other technologies as well. ASP.NET Core's MVC template forces the implementation of a clear pattern for web development that helps teams build complex applications while retaining simplicity and consistency in terms of software architecture. Understanding the roles and responsibilities of each component in this architectural pattern is crucial for leveraging its full potential:

- **Model**: In MVC, the **Model** represents the application's domain. It encapsulates the data and the business rules that govern access to and modifications of this data. In ASP.NET Core, models are typically implemented as classes with properties and methods. They can include data validation rules to enforce business logic, ensuring data integrity and consistency. Models aren't just data structures; they embody the business logic of the application, making decisions and performing calculations based on the rules defined within them.

- **View:** The **View** is responsible for rendering the user interface in an MVC application. It displays data from the model to the user and sends user commands to the controller. In ASP.NET Core, views are often created using the Razor view engine, which allows developers to write HTML with embedded C# code. Razor views are dynamic and can react to the model data they receive, enabling the creation of interactive and data-driven user interfaces. This separation of UI rendering from business logic and input handling makes the views manageable and modular.

- **Controller:** A **Controller** is a coordinator in the MVC pattern. Controllers handle user input, work with the model to perform necessary actions or calculations, and determine which view should be rendered. In ASP.NET Core, controllers are C# classes that can contain multiple actions. These actions are methods that respond to different HTTP requests, invoking changes in the model and selecting views for response. Therefore, controllers act as an intermediary, translating user inputs into actions on the model and selecting views based on the outcomes of those actions.

The MVC template is particularly advantageous for developers looking to build applications with a clear separation of concerns, thereby facilitating easier testing, maintenance, and scaling. It comes pre-configured with essential features such as routing, authentication, and authorization, allowing you to focus on developing unique application features rather than boilerplate code. This project template has the following benefits:

- **Separation of concerns:** By dividing the application into three interconnected components, MVC naturally promotes a clean separation of concerns. This separation enhances the maintainability of the application as developers can work on models, views, or controllers independently without significant overlap in functionality.

- **Testability:** The clear delineation of responsibilities in the MVC pattern facilitates more straightforward testing. Models can be tested independently of user interfaces, controllers can be tested for correct routing and response, and views can be verified to render correctly given a model. ASP.NET Core further supports this testability with features such as DI, which can be used to inject mock implementations for testing.

- **Modularity and flexibility:** The MVC template's compartmentalized structure allows for modular development and flexibility. Developers can iterate on the design, presentation, and business logic layers separately, adapting to new requirements or design changes with minimal impact on the overall code base.

- **A rich ecosystem and community support:** Given its popularity, MVC benefits from extensive community support, a wealth of documentation, tutorials, and a plethora of libraries that can be leveraged to add functionality to your application. ASP.NET Core's MVC framework is no exception, with strong support from Microsoft and a vibrant community, ensuring developers have access to a wealth of resources and best practices.

The MVC template in ASP.NET Core is a powerful choice for developers looking to build web applications with a proven architecture that promotes clean coding practices, testability, and separation of concerns. Its structure is conducive to developing applications that aren't only robust and scalable but also adaptable to evolving business requirements. By understanding and utilizing the MVC architecture to its full potential, developers can create dynamic, efficient, and maintainable web applications that stand the test of time. In the next few chapters of this book, you'll have the opportunity to experience how to create applications using the MVC architecture while following a hands-on approach.

ASP.NET Core Web API

The API project template in ASP.NET Core is meticulously designed to streamline the creation of RESTful web services. This template is a boon for developers focusing on the backend services that power web and mobile applications, IoT devices, and more. Here, we'll delve deeper into the components and features that make the API project template a go-to choice for building high-performance and scalable APIs. The following points clarify the main features of the ASP.NET Core Web API project template:

- **Foundation for RESTful services**: The API project template lays the groundwork for adhering to REST principles, which emphasize stateless communication, resource identification through URIs, and the use of standard HTTP methods (GET, POST, PUT, and DELETE). This adherence simplifies the design of your API and aligns it with web standards, making it intuitive and straightforward to consume.

- **Controller-based architecture**: At the heart of the API template is the controller-based architecture. Controllers in ASP.NET Core serve as the entry point for handling HTTP requests and responding with data or status codes. Each controller is typically associated with a specific resource or a related group of resources, encapsulating the logic required to process incoming requests and generate responses.

- **Routing and URL mapping**: The API template configures routing to ensure that HTTP requests are directed to the appropriate controllers and actions. ASP.NET Core's routing engine is capable of handling complex URL patterns and can be customized to fit the needs of your API, enabling you to define clear and descriptive routes that reflect your API's resource hierarchy.

- **Content negotiation and serialization**: ASP.NET Core's built-in support for content negotiation allows your API to serve data in various formats (such as JSON or XML) based on the client's preferences or request headers. The framework automatically handles the serialization and deserialization of data, ensuring that your API can communicate effectively with different clients and systems.

- **Model binding and validation**: The API project template leverages ASP.NET Core's model binding and validation features to streamline data processing. Model binding automatically maps data from HTTP requests to action method parameters, while applying validation attributes to your models helps ensure that incoming data meets your business rules before your application processes it.

- **Error handling**: Robust error handling is crucial for maintaining a reliable API. The API project template includes basic error handling mechanisms that you can extend to create a comprehensive error response strategy. This ensures that your API can gracefully handle and respond to various error conditions, providing meaningful feedback to the client.

- **Testability**: Just like other ASP.NET Core applications, APIs built using the API project template are highly testable. The framework's support for DI, combined with the separation of concerns inherent in the controller-based architecture, allows you to write unit and integration tests that cover your business logic, routing, and response generation.

- **Swagger integration**: Developers often enhance APIs built with this template by integrating Swagger (OpenAPI), which provides interactive documentation, client SDK generation, and API discoverability. Although not included in the template by default, adding Swagger support is straightforward and significantly improves the developer experience when you're working with your API.

By leveraging the API project template in ASP.NET Core, developers can create well-structured, performant, and scalable web services. This template not only provides the scaffolding necessary for RESTful API development but also ensures that the APIs are maintainable, testable, and compliant with industry standards, laying a solid foundation for any application's backend services.

Razor Pages

Razor Pages, introduced in ASP.NET Core as an alternative to the MVC template, offers a streamlined approach to building web applications, emphasizing page-focused scenarios. This framework simplifies web development by integrating the server-side logic directly within the page markup, offering a more intuitive and productive way to construct dynamic web content. Let's embark on a detailed exploration of Razor Pages, highlighting its architecture, advantages, and how it differentiates itself within the ASP.NET Core suite:

- **Page-based programming model**: Razor Pages centers around a page-based programming model that's a departure from the controller and view-based MVC model. Each Razor Page is a self-contained unit consisting of a `.cshtml` file (which combines HTML markup with Razor syntax) and a code-behind file. This structure allows developers to encapsulate the page's UI and business logic cohesively, promoting a high degree of modularity and maintainability.

- **Code-behind model**: The code-behind file in Razor Pages, typically a `.cshtml.cs` file, contains the server-side logic to handle user actions, data access, and other server-side operations. This separation keeps the markup clean and focused on presentation while maintaining a close association with the page's logic. Developers can handle events, such as form submissions, directly within the page model, streamlining the development process.

- **Razor syntax**: Razor syntax is a powerful feature within Razor Pages that allows developers to embed C# code directly into their HTML markup. This syntax is intuitive and designed to work seamlessly with HTML, providing a robust way to dynamically generate content, control page flow, and interact with data. Razor's syntax simplifies many common tasks, such as iterating over data collections, conditionally rendering content, and handling form inputs.

- **Strongly typed data models**: Razor Pages supports strongly typed data models, enabling developers to work with well-defined C# classes within their pages. This strong typing enhances code clarity, compile-time checks, and IntelliSense support in IDEs, reducing errors and improving developer productivity.

- **Tag Helpers**: Razor Pages leverages Tag Helpers to enable server-side code to participate in creating and rendering HTML elements in Razor files. Tag Helpers are a more readable and HTML-friendly way to define server-side logic compared to traditional MVC helpers. They can be used to easily bind form elements to data models, generate links, create forms, and more, all while maintaining a clear separation between HTML and C#.

- **Routing and URL generation**: Razor Pages introduces a simplified routing system that's based on the file structure of the Pages folder. By default, the URL of a Razor Page corresponds to its location within the Pages directory. This convention-based routing reduces the complexity of defining routes and makes URL generation more intuitive.

- **Built-in security features**: Razor Pages come with built-in security features, such as request verification and **cross-site scripting** (**XSS**) protection, that safeguard the application against common web vulnerabilities. The framework enforces best practices such as automatically encoding output and validating request tokens to prevent CSRF attacks.

- **Extensibility and customization**: While Razor Pages provides a streamlined development experience out of the box, it also offers extensive options for customization and extensibility. Developers can create custom Tag Helpers, filters, and middleware to enhance functionality or integrate third-party libraries to extend the capabilities of their Razor Pages applications.

In conclusion, Razor Pages in ASP.NET Core presents a highly productive, page-focused framework for building web applications. Its integration of a UI and business logic within individual pages, support for Razor syntax and Tag Helpers, and a simplified routing model make it an attractive choice for developers seeking an alternative to the traditional MVC approach. Razor Pages strikes a balance between simplicity and power, offering a compelling model for constructing interactive, data-driven web applications.

A deep dive into Blazor Server and Blazor WebAssembly

Blazor is a groundbreaking project type in ASP.NET Core that fundamentally changes how interactive web applications can be built using the .NET ecosystem. With the introduction of .NET 9, Blazor has matured even further, offering new features and enhancements that bolster its performance, ease of development, and functionality. This deep dive explores both Blazor Server and Blazor WebAssembly, elucidating their architectures, key features, and the enhancements brought by .NET 9.

Blazor Server

Blazor Server allows you to build interactive web applications where the application logic and state management are handled on the server side. User interactions are managed through a SignalR connection, providing a robust, real-time communication channel between the client and server. The following points illuminate the key features of the Blazor Server project type and the advancements introduced in .NET 9:

- **SignalR-based state management**: In Blazor Server, the client's UI state is maintained in the server's memory. When a user interacts with the UI, the event is sent to the server over a SignalR connection and processed, after which the required UI updates are sent back to the browser. This architecture minimizes the amount of data that's transferred over the network and leverages the server's capabilities for heavy lifting.

- **.NET 9 enhancements**: With the advent of .NET 9, Blazor Server has seen improvements in performance and development experience. Enhancements in SignalR and rendering efficiencies reduce latency and improve the responsiveness of Blazor Server applications. Furthermore, improved hot reload capabilities in .NET 9 enhanced the developer experience, making UI adjustments and debugging more intuitive and faster.

Blazor WebAssembly

Blazor WebAssembly is the client-side counterpart of Blazor that enables running C# code directly in the browser using a WebAssembly-based .NET runtime. This model is akin to JavaScript frameworks but leverages the full power of .NET. The following points illuminate the key features of the Blazor WebAssembly project type and the advancements introduced in .NET 9:

- **WebAssembly runtime**: The Blazor WebAssembly model downloads the .NET runtime, your application, and its dependencies to the browser, executing the application directly in the browser's sandbox. This allows for rich interactive experiences without server roundtrips, something that's ideal for offline-capable applications, complex client-side computations, and reduced server load.

- **.NET 9 enhancements**: Blazor WebAssembly with .NET 9 introduces performance optimizations, smaller download sizes, and faster startup times. The runtime and tooling improvements in .NET 9 have made Blazor WebAssembly applications more efficient and quicker to load, enhancing the user experience, especially in resource-constrained environments.

Common features and improvements – Blazor Server and Blazor WebAssembly

The following are some common features and improvements that can be found in both Blazor Server and Blazor WebAssembly:

- **Component model**: Both Blazor Server and Blazor WebAssembly utilize a component-based architecture that promotes reusability and maintainability. Components are the building blocks of Blazor applications and encapsulate markup, logic, and styling. They can be nested, reused, and shared between projects, fostering a modular development approach.

- **JavaScript interoperability**: Blazor provides extensive interoperability with JavaScript, allowing developers to leverage existing JavaScript libraries and frameworks. This interoperability is crucial for accessing browser APIs not exposed through Blazor and for integrating with third-party JavaScript-based UI libraries.

- **.NET 9-specific features**: .NET 9 introduces more granular control over component rendering, improved error handling, and enhanced component life cycle methods. These features provide developers with more tools to optimize their applications and improve user experience.

- **Mobile Blazor Bindings**: With .NET 9, developers can experiment with Mobile Blazor Bindings, an exciting feature that allows Blazor components to be used to build native mobile applications using web technologies, extending the reach of Blazor beyond web browsers.

- **PWA support**: Blazor WebAssembly supports building **progressive web applications** (**PWAs**) out of the box. This feature enables applications to be installed on a user's device, work offline, and leverage native device features, bridging the gap between web and native applications.

In summary, Blazor in .NET 9 continues to evolve, offering a compelling model for building web applications using C#. Whether you choose Blazor Server for its real-time capabilities and server-side processing or Blazor WebAssembly for its client-side execution and offline support, Blazor provides a robust platform for building modern web applications. The ongoing enhancements in .NET 9 further cement Blazor's position as a versatile, performant, and developer-friendly framework in the .NET ecosystem.

Worker Service

The Worker Service template in ASP.NET Core is a versatile template that's designed to help developers create background services for a variety of applications. These services can run in the background, executing tasks independently of user interfaces or web requests. This exhaustive overview delves into the architecture, key features, and practical applications of Worker Service templates, providing insights into how they can be utilized effectively in your .NET applications. The following points elucidate the main aspects of the Worker Service project type:

- **Core architecture**: At its heart, a Worker Service in ASP.NET Core is a long-running console application that leverages the generic host (`HostBuilder`), which is also used in ASP.NET Core web applications. This shared foundation allows for the use of familiar features such as DI, logging, and configuration systems, making it easier for developers to transition between web and worker services.

- **Background task execution**: The Worker Service template is ideal for executing background tasks such as processing queues, polling databases, or performing timely operations. The template provides a base class, `BackgroundService`, from which you can derive to implement your long-running tasks. This class offers methods such as `ExecuteAsync`, which you can override to define the logic of your background tasks.

- **Integration with hosted services**: A Worker Service template can be registered as a hosted service within the .NET Core generic host. Each hosted service can run in parallel and independently, starting and stopping together with the application. This model provides a clean abstraction for implementing different background tasks that need to run throughout the life of the application.

- **DI and configuration**: Utilizing the built-in DI in ASP.NET Core, Worker Service can easily access configured services and settings, enhancing its modularity and testability. Configuration values can be read from various sources, such as `appsettings.json`, environment variables, or command-line arguments, allowing for flexible deployment and runtime behavior.

- **Logging**: ASP.NET Core's logging infrastructure is fully supported in Worker Service, enabling you to integrate robust logging mechanisms that can log to various outputs, such as the console, files, or external data stores. This is crucial for monitoring the health and performance of your background services.

- **Health checks**: Worker Service can implement health checks, providing insights into the health and performance of the application. This feature is especially important for services running in production as it allows for proactive monitoring and maintenance.

- **Windows services and Linux daemons**: One of the significant advantages of Worker Service is its ability to be hosted as Windows services or Linux daemons. This means that your Worker Service template can run automatically in the background as a system service, without requiring a user to log in.

- **Containerization**: Worker Service is well-suited for containerization with Docker. Running a Worker Service template in a container allows for the creation of lightweight, isolated, and scalable deployments. This is particularly beneficial in microservices architectures, where different components of the application can be deployed and scaled independently.

- **Practical use cases**: Worker Service can be used in a myriad of practical scenarios, such as sending batch emails, file processing, data imports/exports, or interacting with APIs for data synchronization. It's also ideal for microservices that need to perform background work independently of user requests.

In summary, the Worker Service template in ASP.NET Core provides a robust foundation for building background services that can perform a wide range of tasks. Its integration with the broader .NET Core features, such as DI, configuration, and logging, makes it a powerful and flexible choice for developing background processes in your applications. Whether you're processing jobs, polling resources, or performing scheduled tasks, Worker Service offers a structured yet flexible framework to build reliable and scalable background services.

Now that we understand the main aspects of the project templates available for ASP.NET Core projects, let's move on to the next section, where we'll explore the high-level aspects of the ASP.NET Core architecture and its features.

Exploring the ASP.NET Core architecture and its features

ASP.NET Core is a comprehensive framework designed for building modern, cloud-optimized, and internet-connected applications. Its architecture is modular, flexible, and designed to provide an optimized development framework for both web applications and APIs. Let's delve into the ASP.NET Core architecture and its key features to understand what makes it a powerful choice for developers.

ASP.NET Core's architecture is fundamentally modular, allowing applications to include only the necessary components and libraries, thereby reducing the application's footprint and improving performance. This modularity is facilitated by the framework's reliance on NuGet packages, which can be added or removed based on the specific needs of the application.

Startup and middleware in ASP.NET Core

The `Startup` class and middleware are foundational elements in the architecture of ASP.NET Core applications as they orchestrate the application's behavior and its response to incoming HTTP requests. Understanding how these components interact provides insights into the backbone of ASP.NET Core's processing pipeline.

The Startup class

The `Startup` class contains two main methods:

- `ConfigureServices`: This method is where you add and configure services needed by your application. Services such as Entity Framework Core, MVC, Razor Pages, Identity, and others are registered here. DI is a first-class citizen in ASP.NET Core, and `ConfigureServices` is where the DI container is populated. This method allows your application to adhere to the principle of "explicit dependencies," ensuring that components and services declare their dependencies transparently.

- `Configure`: After `ConfigureServices` runs, ASP.NET Core calls the `Configure` method. This is where you build the application's request pipeline using middleware. Each middleware component can perform operations before and after the next component in the pipeline. The order in which middleware components are added is critical and defines the order of their execution for incoming HTTP requests and outgoing responses.

Middleware

Middleware in ASP.NET Core is software that's assembled into an application pipeline to handle requests and responses. Each piece of middleware can perform operations before passing the request on to the next component in the pipeline or performing operations before the response is sent back to the client.

The following points illustrate the main aspects of the concept of middleware in ASP.NET Core projects:

- **Request pipeline**: Middleware components form a chain of request delegates, where each component can perform operations asynchronously and decide whether to pass the request to the next component. If a middleware component doesn't call the next delegate, it can short-circuit the pipeline, and no subsequent middleware is executed.

- **Built-in middleware**: ASP.NET Core comes with a set of built-in middleware components that you can use to enable functionality such as static file serving, routing, authentication, and session state. For example, the static files middleware serves static files and is often one of the first components in the pipeline, ensuring that requests for static files are handled without going through unnecessary processing.

- **Custom middleware**: You can also create custom middleware for more specific or specialized handling. Custom middleware is written by defining a class with an `Invoke` or `InvokeAsync` method that processes the HTTP request and calls the next middleware in the pipeline. This flexibility allows developers to extend the framework to suit their specific needs.

- **Ordering**: The order in which middleware components are added in the `Configure` method defines the order of their execution. This ordering is crucial because it can affect everything from security (ensuring authentication happens early in the pipeline) to functionality (ensuring MVC handling happens after the necessary preprocessing steps).

- **Branching**: The pipeline can be branched to configure different middleware components for different request paths. This can be achieved using the `Map` or `MapWhen` method, which provides fine-grained control over how requests are handled based on paths or conditions.

In summary, the `Startup` class and middleware in ASP.NET Core provide a robust and flexible way to configure how your application behaves and responds to HTTP requests. By understanding and utilizing these components effectively, developers can architect their applications to be modular, efficient, and maintainable, with clear control over the request handling pipeline.

DI in ASP.NET Core

DI is a design pattern that promotes loose coupling between components, making them more modular and testable. ASP.NET Core has built-in support for DI, allowing services to be registered and resolved throughout the application. Understanding how DI works in ASP.NET Core is crucial for developing applications that are easy to maintain and extend.

Core concepts of DI

The first concept we'll cover is **service registration**. In ASP.NET Core, services are registered in the `ConfigureServices` method of the `Startup` class. This registration process maps interfaces or service types to concrete implementations. The framework provides different service lifetimes for registration, including *Singleton*, *Scoped*, and *Transient*, each defining how and when instances of the service are created and shared.

Now, let's learn about **service resolution**. Once services have been registered, they can be injected into components, such as controllers, middleware, or other services, through their constructors. This is known as constructor injection, the most common method of DI in ASP.NET Core. The framework's built-in DI container automatically resolves these services and their dependencies when the component is created.

In ASP.NET Core applications, services can be configured with distinct lifetimes, each defining the scope and duration of their availability within the application's life cycle. These service lifetimes play a crucial role in determining how instances of services are created, shared, and disposed of, thereby impacting the application's behavior, resource management, and overall architecture. The following lifetimes are available for configuration:

- **Singleton**: Singleton services are created once per application lifetime and shared across all requests. This lifetime is suitable for stateless services that don't maintain any state or data specific to a request.

- **Scoped**: Scoped services are created once per client request (an HTTP request in the case of web applications). This is useful for services that need to maintain state or data within the context of a single request.

- **Transient**: Transient services are created each time they're requested from the service container. This lifetime works well for lightweight, stateless services.

In terms of more advanced scenarios, the following configurations can be set:

- **Factory-based registrations**: Sometimes, more control over the creation of services is needed. ASP.NET Core allows for factory-based registrations, where you can provide a factory function to create the service. This approach is useful when the creation of the service requires more logic than simply instantiating a class.

- **Property injection**: While constructor injection is the recommended approach in ASP.NET Core, property injection can be achieved but requires manual intervention. It's less preferred because it can lead to situations where dependencies aren't initialized properly, leading to less reliable and harder-to-maintain code.

- **Third-party containers**: ASP.NET Core's built-in DI container is designed to satisfy the needs of most applications. However, if you require more advanced features, the framework allows you to replace its built-in container with a third-party container, such as Autofac or StructureMap.

The following are good practices that you must follow to avoid issues when using DI and middleware in ASP.NET Core applications:

- **Prefer constructor injection**: Favor constructor injection over property injection for its better enforcement of dependencies, ensuring that your components are always in a valid state.

- **Avoid service locator pattern**: While it's possible to use the service locator pattern by injecting `IServiceProvider` directly and retrieving services, this practice is discouraged as it hides a class's dependencies, making the code harder to understand and maintain.

- **Design for testability**: Leverage DI to design your components to be easily testable. Mocking frameworks can be used in conjunction with DI to provide mock implementations of services when testing.

- **Be mindful of captive dependencies**: Ensure that you don't inadvertently register a service with a lifetime that's longer than the lifetimes of its dependencies. For example, a Singleton service shouldn't depend on a Scoped service.

DI is a powerful feature of ASP.NET Core that, when used effectively, can greatly enhance the maintainability, testability, and modularity of your applications. Understanding how to properly register and resolve services, along with adhering to best practices, will allow you to fully leverage the benefits of DI in your ASP.NET Core applications.

ASP.NET Core's architecture and features represent a significant evolution in web development frameworks, providing developers with a powerful, efficient, and flexible platform for building modern web applications and services. Whether you're building web applications, RESTful APIs, real-time connections, or microservices, ASP.NET Core offers the tools and performance needed to create high-quality, scalable, and maintainable solutions.

Having explored details on DI and middleware for ASP.NET Core projects, let's progress to the next section, where we'll learn about the history of the .NET platform and ASP.NET Core.

The history of ASP.NET Core

The .NET platform, developed by Microsoft, has been a cornerstone in the evolution of software development, particularly in the web domain. Initially introduced as a beta product in 2000, .NET marked a significant milestone with its official 1.0 release in 2002 by bringing the innovative **Common Language Runtime (CLR)**, which allowed developers to use multiple programming languages within a single solution. This feature enhanced reusability and flexibility, setting a foundation for the rich ecosystem that .NET would become.

As the platform matured, the introduction of ASP.NET provided a powerful framework for building dynamic web applications, significantly reducing the code developers needed to write. However, it was the advent of ASP.NET MVC in 2009 that marked a pivotal shift toward more structured and testable web applications. By implementing the MVC pattern, ASP.NET MVC enabled a clean separation of concerns, facilitating better maintainability and scalability of applications. This was a response to the growing complexity of web applications and the need for architectures that could support more agile development and testing practices.

Along with these advancements, the Razor syntax, introduced with ASP.NET MVC 3 in 2011, provided a more intuitive way for developers to embed server-side code within HTML. This streamlined the development process, allowing for a seamless blend of markup and C# code, and paved the way for further innovations in .NET's approach to web development.

This evolution continued with the introduction of Razor Pages in 2017 alongside ASP.NET Core 2.0. Razor Pages simplified the web development process by offering a page-focused framework that was easier to manage and more suited for scenarios where a full MVC framework was unnecessary. This innovation brought a more approachable and efficient way to build web UIs, especially for developers who preferred a less complex structure than MVC.

A significant breakthrough in the .NET ecosystem was the launch of Blazor in 2018 with .NET Core 3.0. Blazor revolutionized web development within the .NET framework by enabling developers to use C# instead of JavaScript to create interactive client-side web UIs. This innovation allowed existing .NET skills to be leveraged for both server-side and client-side development, offering a unified and streamlined development experience. Blazor demonstrated .NET's adaptability and its commitment to staying at the forefront of web development technologies.

Throughout its history, .NET has continuously evolved, embracing new paradigms and technologies to stay relevant in the ever-changing landscape of software development. From its initial release to the introduction of .NET and the various frameworks and syntaxes that have been added over the years, .NET has proven to be a dynamic and versatile platform. It's catered to the needs of developers building enterprise-level applications, modern web applications, and everything in between, ensuring that .NET remains a powerful and popular choice in the software development world.

Summary

This chapter provided a comprehensive introduction to ASP.NET Core, outlining its inception, core components, and the evolution of its various frameworks and technologies. First, we went through the technical requirements for working with ASP.NET Core, recommending the .NET 9 framework and the latest version of ASP.NET Core for optimal development experience. Using Visual Studio or Visual Studio Code was recommended as the development environment to use to leverage the full range of ASP.NET Core's features.

We began by providing an overview of ASP.NET Core as a modern, open source, cross-platform framework for building cloud-based, internet-connected applications. We emphasized the importance of understanding the framework's architecture, functionalities, and the advantages it brings to web development.

Then, we explored the key features and benefits of ASP.NET Core, including its performance, modularity, security, and cross-platform capabilities. We also touched on the integration of MVC and the Web API, the revolutionary Blazor for building interactive web UIs with C#, and the seamless integration with various JavaScript frameworks.

Furthermore, we discussed the structure of ASP.NET Core applications, emphasizing the importance of the startup class and middleware in configuring application behavior and responses to HTTP requests. DI in ASP.NET Core was explained as a design pattern that enhances modularity and testability.

Finally, this chapter delved into the history of ASP.NET Core, tracing its development from the introduction of the .NET platform in 2000 through to innovative advancements such as ASP.NET MVC in 2009, Razor syntax in 2011, Razor Pages in 2017, and the groundbreaking Blazor in 2018. Each of these milestones was discussed in detail, highlighting how they contributed to making ASP.NET Core a versatile and powerful framework for web developers.

In the next chapter, you'll learn how to set up and build basic applications using the project templates mentioned in this chapter. This will give you your first experience with these project types.

Get This Book's PDF Version and Exclusive Extras

UNLOCK NOW

Scan the QR code (or go to packtpub.com/unlock). Search for this book by name, confirm the edition, and then follow the steps on the page.

Note: Keep your invoice handly. Purchase made directly from packt don't require one.

2

Setting Up and Building Basic Applications

In this chapter, we will embark upon a journey to establish the foundation of **ASP.NET Core** development, ensuring that you gain the essential skills and understanding to construct your first web application. By delving into the practical aspects of setting up your development environment and engaging in the hands-on creation of a basic web application, you'll acquire a robust grasp of the core concepts and architectures that define ASP.NET Core development.

I will introduce you to the **model-view-controller** (**MVC**) architecture, a cornerstone of organizing web applications, ensuring you understand its importance and how it can be effectively applied. Furthermore, we'll explore the intricacies of routing and controllers, key elements that facilitate the navigation and functionality of our applications. By the end of this chapter, you'll have not only your first ASP.NET Core application up and running but also a solid comprehension of the underlying principles that will aid in your journey to becoming a proficient ASP.NET Core developer.

These lessons are designed to provide you with practical, hands-on experience, enabling you to see immediate results while building a foundational understanding that will be indispensable to your development career. By mastering these initial steps, you'll set the stage for more advanced topics and applications, enhancing your skills and confidence in navigating the ASP.NET Core landscape.

In this chapter, we're going to cover the following main topics:

- Building your first ASP.NET Core application
- Exploring the project structure
- Developing a simple page
- Understanding MVC architecture
- Understanding the concept of routing

Each section is crafted to guide you step by step, ensuring that you not only learn but also apply the knowledge to achieve tangible outcomes. By the chapter's conclusion, you'll have a clear understanding and practical experience in these critical aspects of ASP.NET Core development, positioning you well for the further chapters of this book.

Technical requirements

You can refer to the *Technical requirements* section of *Chapter 1* for all the necessary installations.

The code files required for you to follow along with this chapter can be found at: `https://github.com/PacktPublishing/Modern-Full-Stack-Web-Development-with-ASP.NET-Core/tree/main/Chapter02`.

Building your first ASP.NET Core application

Building your first ASP.NET Core application is an exciting step that introduces you to the world of modern web development with Microsoft's robust framework. This process encompasses several stages, from project creation to developing, testing, and understanding the core components that make up an ASP.NET Core application. In this section, we will go over a detailed exploration of what this process involves.

Creating a new project in Visual Studio

When starting your journey with ASP.NET Core, one of the first skills you'll need is creating a new project in Visual Studio, Microsoft's **integrated development environment** (**IDE**). Visual Studio streamlines the development process with its comprehensive suite of tools and features, making it a popular choice among .NET developers. This subsection will guide you through the detailed steps of creating an ASP.NET Core project in Visual Studio, ensuring you have a solid foundation on which to build your web applications.

Before following the steps for project creation, ensure you have Visual Studio installed on your machine. You should download Visual Studio from the official Microsoft website, choosing the edition that best fits your needs (**Community**, **Professional**, or **Enterprise**). For ASP.NET Core development, make sure to include the **ASP.NET and web development** workload during the installation process.

When installing Visual Studio, the workload selection for **ASP.NET and web development** should look like this:

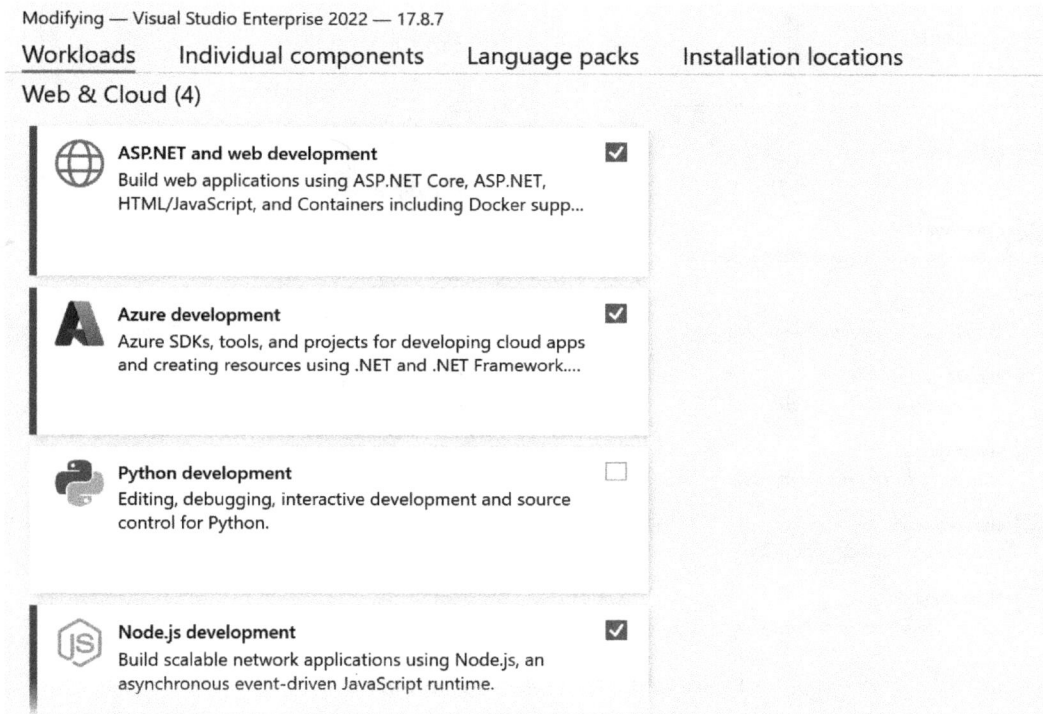

Figure 2.1: ASP.NET and web development workload

After the installation is complete, open Visual Studio from your start menu or desktop shortcut. Upon launching, you'll be greeted with a welcome screen that provides options to open an existing project or create a new one, as seen in *Figure 2.2*:

— ☐ ✕

Visual Studio 2022

Open recent

Blazor| ✕ ▾

🗔	**BlazorApp1.sln**	27/11/2023 20:27
	C:\Users\alexa\source\repos**Blazor**App1	
🗔	**BlazorApp10.sln**	25/11/2023 08:41
	C:\Users\alexa\source\repos**Blazor**App10	
🗔	**BlazorApp11.sln**	25/11/2023 08:43
	C:\Users\alexa\source\repos**Blazor**App11	
🗔	**BlazorApp12.sln**	25/11/2023 08:46
	C:\Users\alexa\source\repos**Blazor**App12	
🗔	**BlazorApp2.sln**	27/11/2023 20:50
	C:\Users\alexa\source\repos**Blazor**App2	
🗔	**BlazorApp3.sln**	27/11/2023 20:57
	C:\Users\alexa\source\repos**Blazor**App3	
🗔	**BlazorApp4.sln**	25/11/2023 06:04
	C:\Users\alexa\source\repos**Blazor**App4	

Get started

⬇ **Clone a repository**
Get code from an online repository like GitHub
or Azure DevOps

🗗 **Open a project or solution**
Open a local Visual Studio project or .sln file

📂 **Open a local folder**
Navigate and edit code within any folder

🗔 **Create a new project**
Choose a project template with code scaffolding
to get started

Continue without code →

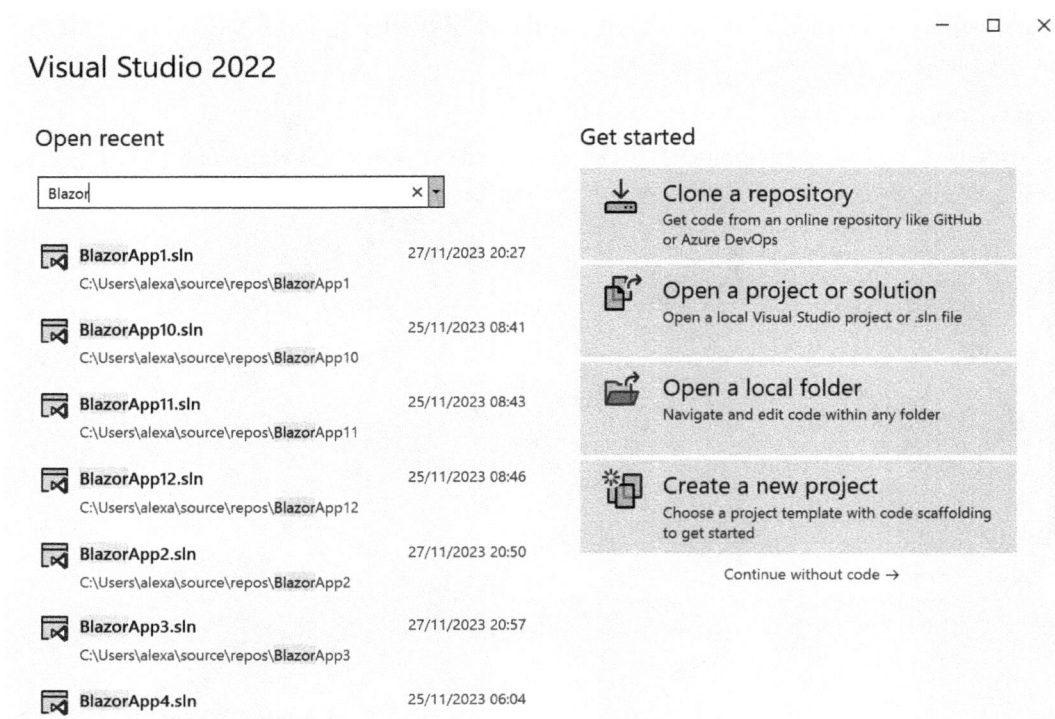

Figure 2.2: Initial screen – Visual Studio

Click on the **Create a new project** option. This action brings up a window showcasing various project templates. Visual Studio offers a range of templates for different programming languages and application types, but you'll want to focus on the ASP.NET Core web application template. In the search bar within the new project window, type Asp.Net Core to filter out unrelated templates:

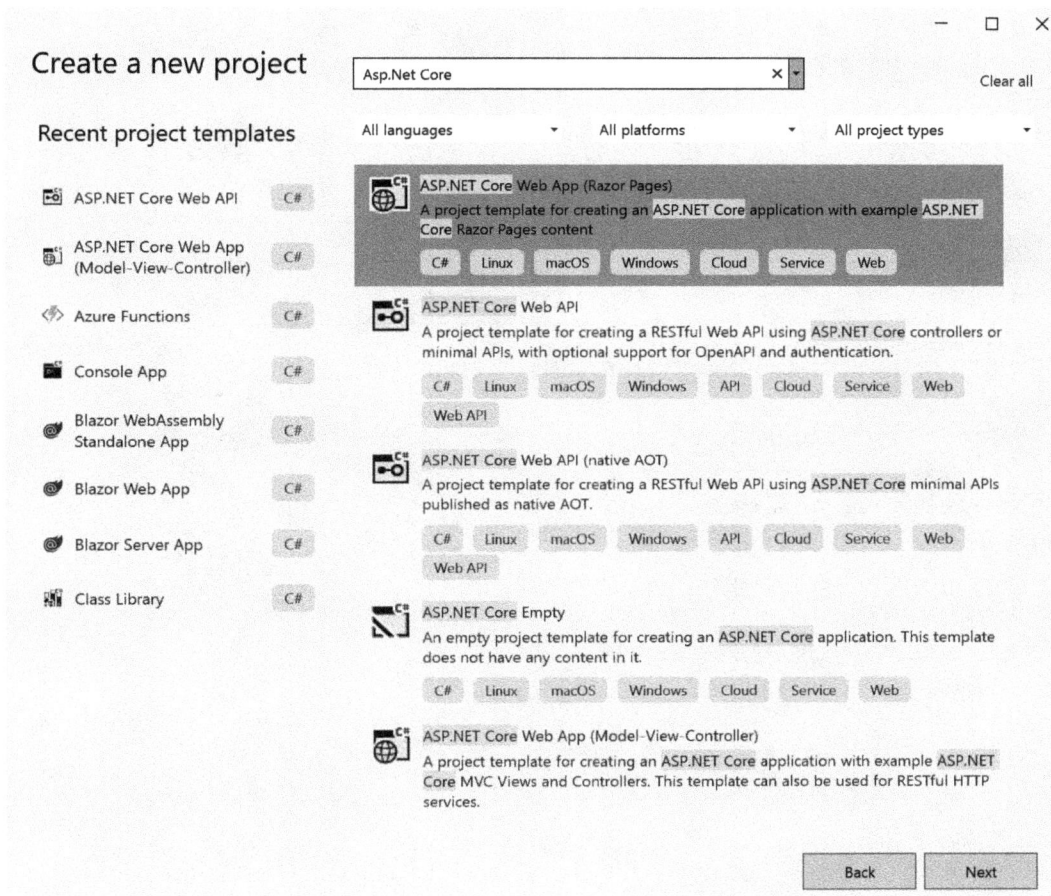

Figure 2.3: Project templates in Visual Studio

Select **ASP.NET Core Web App (Model-View-Controller)** from the list and click **Next**. After selecting the template, you'll need to configure your new project. This step involves naming your project and choosing the location where your project files will be stored. It's crucial to pick a meaningful name and an organized directory structure to manage your projects effectively, as seen in *Figure 2.4*:

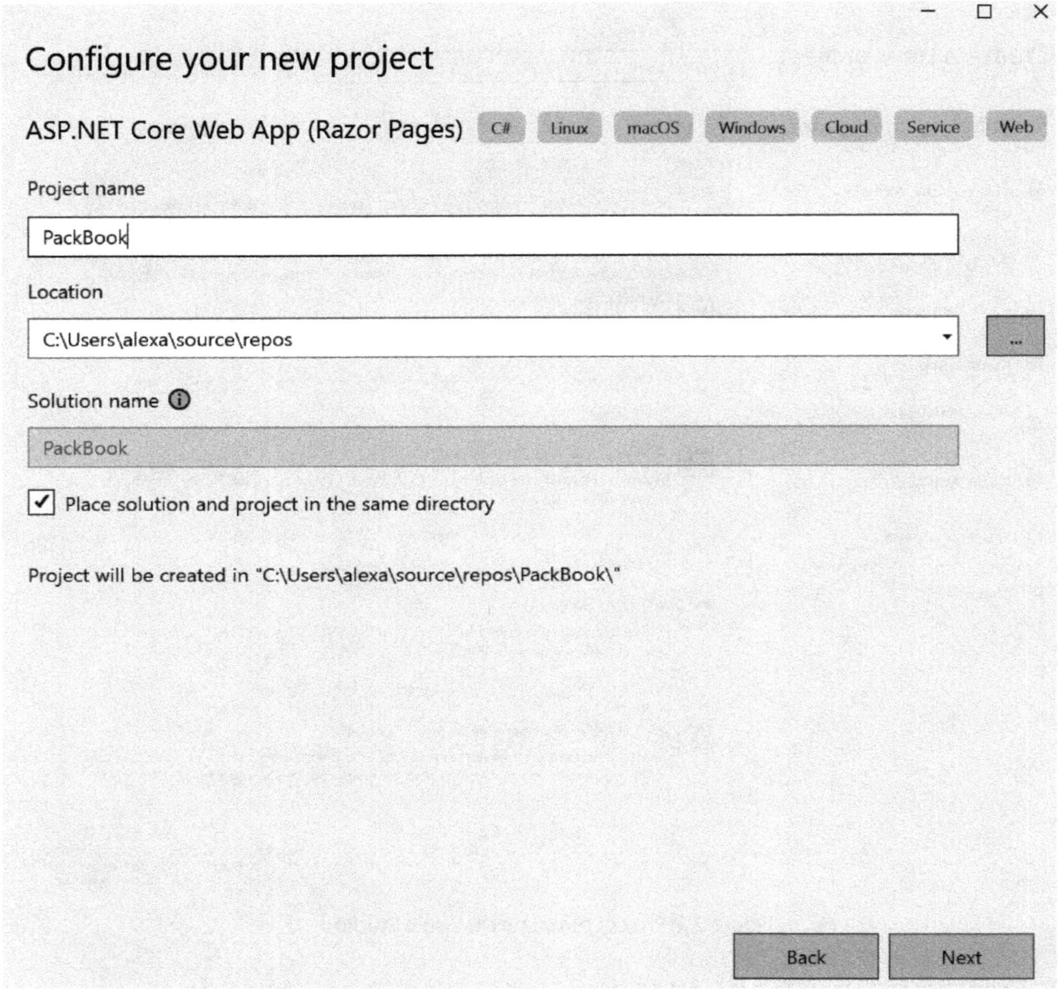

Figure 2.4: Project name – ASP.NET Core

Enter your project name in the **Project name** field. This name will be used as the default namespace and can impact the naming of various project components. Choose a location for your project files. After filling the appropriate fields, click on **Next**.

Each template comes with its preconfigured settings and files, tailored to the type of application you're building. For instance, the MVC template will include default controller, view, and model directories, along with sample files to get you started. Each template also requires choosing specific configurations for the project, such as the .NET **Framework** version, **Authentication type**, and **HTTP** protocol, as seen in *Figure 2.5*:

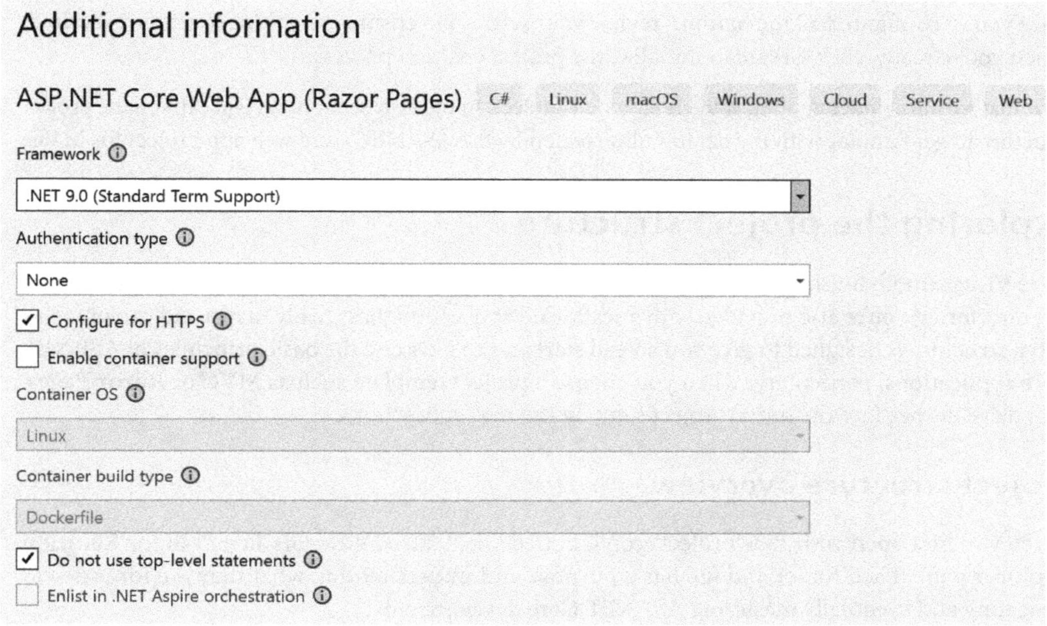

Additional information

ASP.NET Core Web App (Razor Pages)   C#   Linux   macOS   Windows   Cloud   Service   Web

Framework ⓘ

.NET 9.0 (Standard Term Support) ▾

Authentication type ⓘ

None ▾

☑ Configure for HTTPS ⓘ

☐ Enable container support ⓘ

Container OS ⓘ

Linux ▾

Container build type ⓘ

Dockerfile ▾

☑ Do not use top-level statements ⓘ

☐ Enlist in .NET Aspire orchestration ⓘ

Figure 2.5: Template configuration

If your application requires user authentication, Visual Studio provides options to configure this during project creation. You can choose from **No Authentication**, **Individual User Accounts**, or **Work or School Accounts**, depending on your application's needs.

Here's a brief explanation of each option:

- **No Authentication**: This option is suitable for applications that do not require any user login or identity management. It is often used for public-facing websites where authentication is not necessary.

- **Individual User Accounts**: This option allows users to register and log in using their email addresses. It is ideal for applications where users need to manage their own accounts, such as social media platforms or e-commerce sites.

- **Work or School Accounts**: This option integrates with Azure Active Directory, enabling users to sign in with their organizational accounts. It is commonly used in enterprise environments where access needs to be restricted to employees or members of a specific organization.

In addition to the basic settings, there are advanced configuration options available, such as enabling Docker support and configuring HTTPS. **Docker** is a platform that simplifies the process of packaging, distributing, and managing applications within lightweight, portable containers. **HTTPS**, or **Hypertext Transfer Protocol Secure**, is a protocol used to secure communications over a computer network by encrypting data exchanged between the user's browser and the website. These options can be tailored based on the specific needs of your project and can be adjusted as your application evolves.

Once you've configured all the options, review your settings to ensure everything is set up as desired. When you're ready, click **Create** to initialize the project creation process.

Now that we have understood how to create a new project, in the next section, we will explore the project structure to get familiar with the default files created by the ASP.NET Core web app project for MVC.

Exploring the project structure

Once Visual Studio finishes creating your ASP.NET Core project, you're not just left with a set of files and directories; you're also provided with a scaffolded application that's ready to run and explore. This initial structure is designed to give you a head start and to illustrate the basic principles of ASP.NET Core applications, particularly when you choose a project template such as MVC or **Razor Pages**. Let's delve deeper into the initial project setup in the next subsections.

Project structure overview

When you first open your new project, you'll notice a structured directory layout in the **Solution Explorer** pane. Each folder and file has a purpose and understanding what they are for is key to navigating and eventually mastering ASP.NET Core development.

Key directories include `Controllers`, `Views`, `Models` (for MVC projects), and `Pages` (for Razor Pages projects). The `wwwroot` directory houses static assets such as **JavaScript**, **CSS**, and image files:

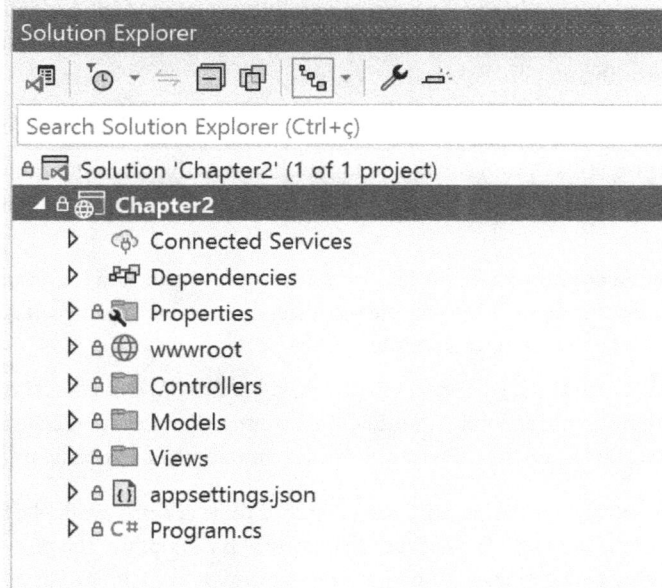

Figure 2.6: Solution Explorer

Let's keep exploring this project structure and understand these folders, except the Models folder, which will be explained and demonstrated along with coding samples in this chapter.

The Controllers folder

The Controllers folder is where you'll find your controller classes. Controllers are responsible for handling incoming HTTP requests and returning responses. Explore the default controller provided in your template and note how actions within the controller correspond to different parts of your application. The project templates come with HomeController by default with the index, privacy, and error endpoints, as seen in the following code:

```
using PacktBook.Models;
using Microsoft.AspNetCore.Mvc;
using System.Diagnostics;

namespace PacktBook.Controllers
{
    public class HomeController : Controller
    {
        private readonly ILogger<HomeController> _logger;

        public HomeController(
            ILogger<HomeController> logger)
        {
            _logger = logger;
        }

        public IActionResult Index()
        {
            return View();
        }

        public IActionResult Privacy()
        {
            return View();
        }

        [ResponseCache(
            Duration = 0,
            Location = ResponseCacheLocation.None,
            NoStore = true
        )]
        public IActionResult Error()
```

```
        {
            return View(new ErrorViewModel {
                RequestId = Activity.Current?.Id ??
                HttpContext.TraceIdentifier
            });
        }
    }
}
```

Each endpoint usually refers to a corresponding Razor page of the same name, as we will see in the next section.

Views and Razor Pages folders

In MVC projects, the Views folder contains Razor view files, which are responsible for generating the HTML content sent to the client's browser. Each view corresponds to an action in a controller.

If you're using a Razor Pages project, you'll see a Pages folder instead, where each Razor page includes both the markup and the associated page model in one file or a pair of files.

Take a moment to open a view or Razor page and examine the Razor syntax, which allows C# code and HTML to intermingle for dynamic content generation, as seen in the following code:

```
@{
    ViewData["Title"] = "Home Page";

    <h1>@ViewBag.Message</h1>
    <p>
        Today's date is:
        @ViewBag.CurrentDate.ToShortDateString()
    </p>
}

<div class="text-center">
    <h1 class="display-4">Welcome</h1>
    <p>
        Learn about
        <a href="https://learn.microsoft.com/aspnet/core">
        building Web apps with ASP.NET Core</a>.
    </p>
</div>
```

Razor syntax is pivotal in creating dynamic web content. You can recognize the Razor code by the @ symbol followed by some C# code. For example, `@DateTime.Now.ToString()` in a view would render the current date and time.

Razor views can use model objects passed from controllers, allowing for data-driven content. For example, `@Model.Name` would display a name property of the model object.

In combination with Razor pages, you can use layouts, partials, and view components. Layouts in Razor provide a way to define a common site template (such as a master page) that can be inherited across multiple views, promoting code reuse and consistency.

Partial views are reusable view snippets that can be embedded in multiple other views, ideal for rendering common **user interface** (UI) segments.

View components are more powerful and reusable than partial views, encapsulating rendering logic and data fetching in one unit, which can then be invoked across different views.

In the next section, we will explore `ViewBag`, `ViewData`, and `TempData`, which are great features in ASP.NET Core for passing data between the server and the client.

ViewBag, ViewData, and TempData

These are dynamic properties used to pass data from a controller to a view. While `ViewBag` and `ViewData` are great for passing data that doesn't fit within the model, `TempData` is particularly useful for passing data between requests, such as redirects.

`ViewBag` is a dynamic property that allows us to pass data from a controller to a Razor page or view without necessarily using models or strongly typed objects. This approach provides a more flexible way to pass data to the views than others as it does not require casting objects.

Here's an example of how you can set `ViewBag` in a controller action:

```
public IActionResult Index()
{
    ViewBag.Message = "Welcome to your first ViewBag";
    ViewBag.CurrentDate = DateTime.UtcNow;
    return View();
}
```

In this case, a dynamic property called `Message` is set with a string content and a property called `CurrentDate` is set with the current UTC time.

In the corresponding view (`Index.cshtml`), you can access these properties as follows:

```
<h1>@ViewBag.Message</h1>
<p>
    Today's date is:
    @ViewBag.CurrentDate.ToShortDateString()
</p>
```

Here, `ViewBag.Message` passes a string and `ViewBag.CurrentDate` passes a `DateTime` object from the controller to the view.

On the other hand, `ViewData` is a dictionary object that stores data as key-value pairs. Different from `ViewBag`, this approach requires casting when you try to use the data in the view. Here's how you can use `ViewData` in a controller action:

```
public IActionResult ShipmentDetails()
{
    ViewData["Title"] = "Shipment Details";
    ViewData["Value"] = 100000.00;
    return View();
}
```

In this case, the `Title` and `Value` properties are added to the `ViewData` object with their corresponding values. Here's how you can retrieve the values in your view:

```
@{
    <h1>@ViewData["Title"]</h1>
    <p>Value: $@ViewData["Value"]</p>
}
```

While very similar to `ViewBag`, `ViewData` is helpful in scenarios where you need or prefer to work with a dictionary or need to pass data to another method in the view.

Finally, `TempData` is useful for passing data between different requests in cases where you need to redirect from one controller action to another and still need to keep the data state preserved on these exchanges. Once you access `TempData`, the data is removed from the memory.

Here's how you can use `TempData` in your controller:

```
public IActionResult SubmitForm()
{
    TempData["SuccessMessage"] =
        "The information was successfully saved!";
```

```
        return RedirectToAction("Confirmation");
}

public IActionResult Confirmation()
{
        return View();
}
```

In this case, the `Confirmation` view can use the `TempData["SuccessMessage"]` data to display the message.

By exploring and understanding these aspects of views and Razor Pages, you equip yourself with the knowledge to craft dynamic and interactive web interfaces for your ASP.NET Core applications. These elements are central to how your application presents data and interacts with users, making them key areas of focus as you develop and enhance your web development skills.

In the next section, we will delve into the creation of a simple page that will demonstrate how to get familiar with Razor syntax and the main aspects of views and controllers.

Developing a simple page

Developing a simple page in ASP.NET Core, whether in an MVC or Razor Pages application, is a foundational skill that demonstrates how you can render content and accept user input. In this section, we'll explore how to create and modify a simple page, including code samples to illustrate the process in both MVC and Razor Pages contexts.

In an MVC application, developing a simple page involves creating a view and a controller action that returns the view. Here's a step-by-step guide to developing a basic **Hello World** page.

Adding a controller

To create a new controller, follow these steps:

1. Go to **Solution Explorer**, right-click on the `Controllers` folder, then click on the **Add** option and choose **Controller...**, as seen in *Figure 2.7*:

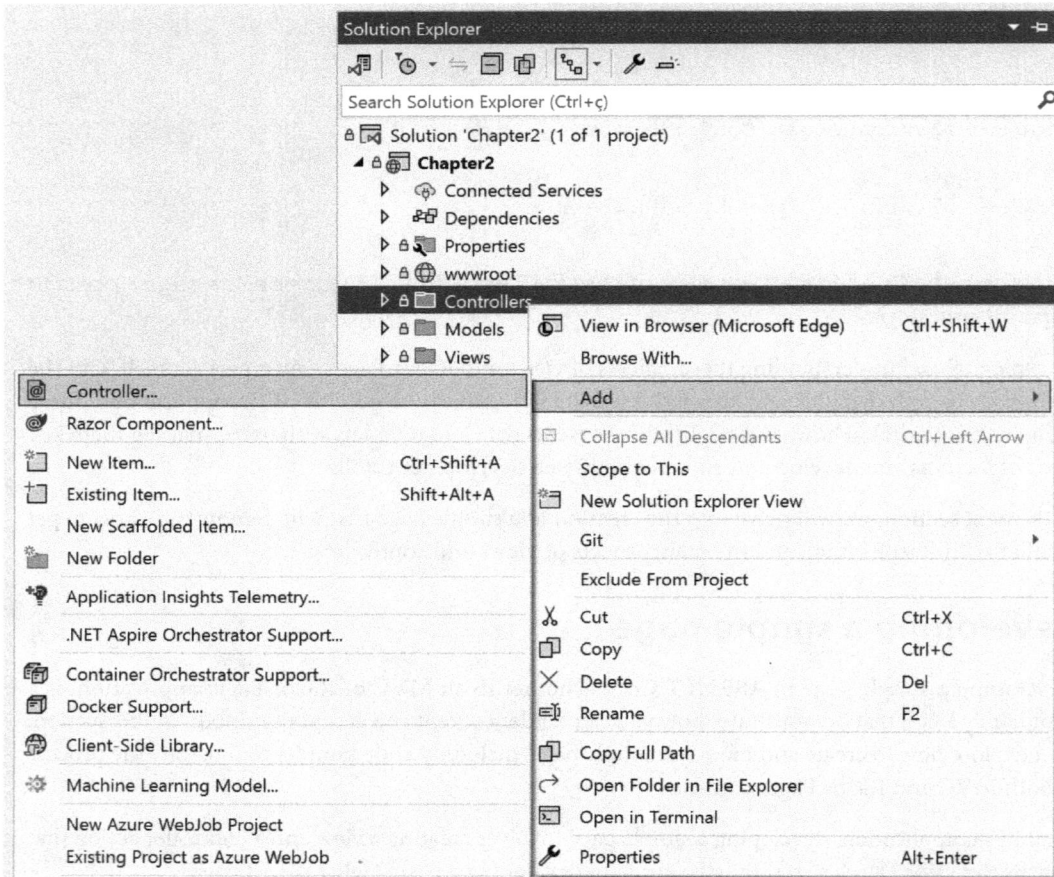

Figure 2.7: Adding a new controller

2. You will be redirected to a list of options for how you want to create the controller. In the context of this chapter, we will be creating an empty controller, so choose the **MVC Controller – Empty** option and click on **Add**, as seen in *Figure 2.8*:

×

Add New Scaffolded Item

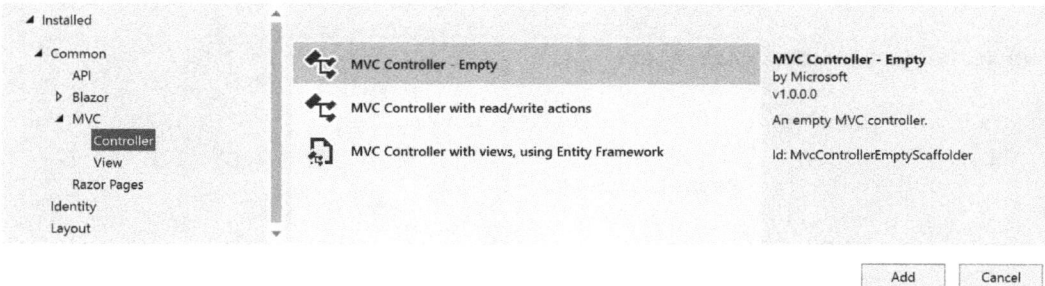

Figure 2.8: MVC Controller – Empty

3. After clicking on the **Add** button, you will need to give the controller a name. It is a good practice to follow the convention where all controllers have the `Controller` suffix in the name. In this example, we will call the controller `HelloWorldController`, as seen in *Figure 2.9*:

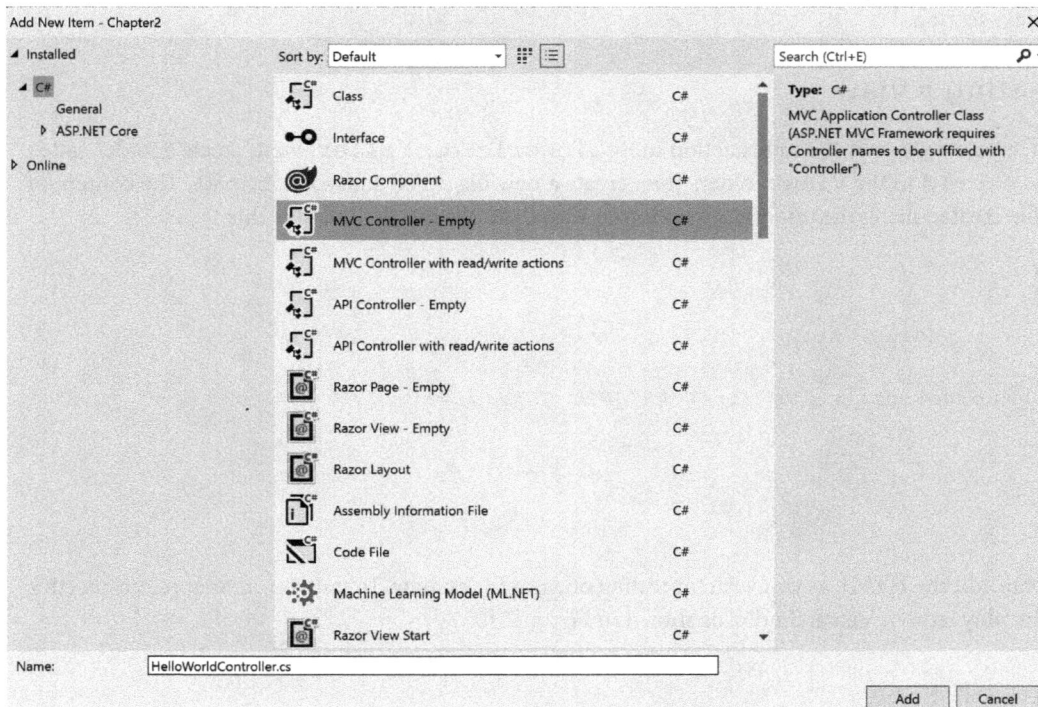

Figure 2.9: HelloWorldController

After confirming the creation of the controller, the underlying file content should look like this:

```
using Microsoft.AspNetCore.Mvc;

namespace PacktBook.Controllers
{
    public class HelloWorldController : Controller
    {
        public IActionResult Index()
        {

            return View();

        }
    }

}
```

In this case, the controller has an index action method that returns a view, which will be created in the next section.

Creating a view

Next, create a view for the index action in `HelloWorldController`. First, create a folder called `HelloWorld` in the `Views` folder. Then create a new file called `Index.cshtml`. The content of the file created using the underlying option in Visual Studio should look like this:

```
@{

    <h1>Hello, World!</h1>

    <p>Welcome to my first ASP.NET Core View!</p>

    <br />

}
```

You can edit the HTML as you wish for testing on your index view. To test your new application, click on the **play** icon in Visual Studio, as shown in *Figure 2.10*:

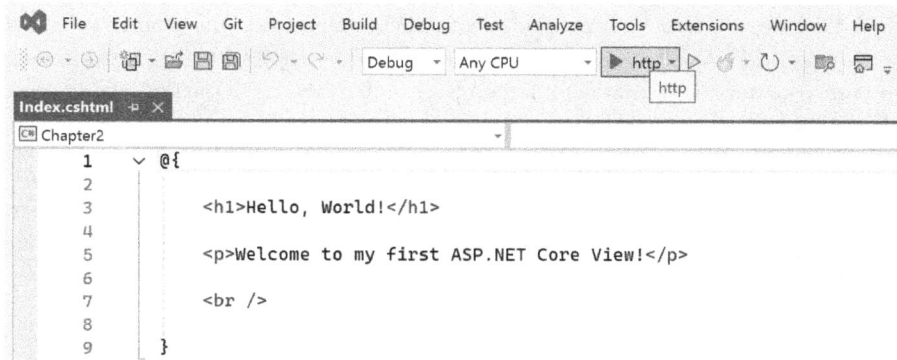

Figure 2.10: Running the application

In this case, as we are running the application in a local environment, the HTTP option will be used and not HTTPS. Visual Studio will launch the web browser with the initial page of the ASP.NET Core MVC template, as seen in *Figure 2.11*:

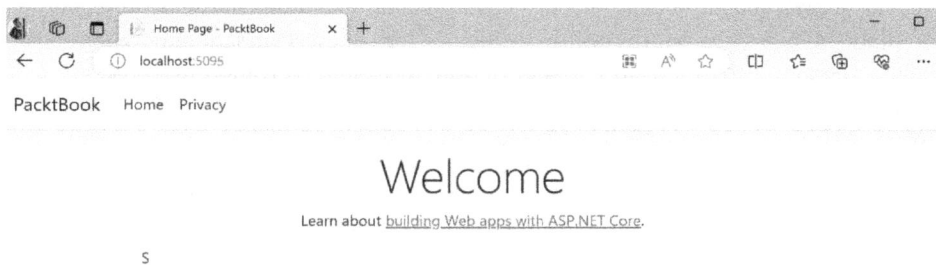

Figure 2.11: Initial page

To test your `HelloWorld` controller and the new index view, execute the URL in the browser with the underlying route, which will be the prefix of the controller (`HelloWorld`), and execute it. The application will render the HTML of the index view present in the `HelloWorld` folder, as seen in *Figure 2.12*:

Figure 2.12: HelloWorld page

Having explored the steps to create a simple view in an MVC application, you've taken your first step into the practical world of ASP.NET Core development. You've seen how controllers interact with views. As you move forward, it's essential to deepen your understanding of the underlying principles that make these interactions possible.

In the next section, we will peel back the layers of MVC to reveal its core components: **models**, **views**, and **controllers**. You'll learn how they collaborate to create a dynamic and responsive web application, providing a foundation that will enhance your ability to build more sophisticated and robust applications with ASP.NET Core MVC.

Understanding MVC architecture

MVC architecture is a time-tested design pattern that originated in the 1970s at Xerox PARC, gaining prominence through its use in the Smalltalk programming language. Initially devised for desktop computing environments, MVC's core principles proved universally applicable and beneficial, leading to its widespread adoption in web application development. Its enduring relevance stems from its ability to compartmentalize different aspects of software applications, making them more manageable and adaptable to change.

At the heart of the MVC pattern is the model component, which encapsulates the application's business logic and data. The model is responsible for responding to requests for information about its state and instructions to change state. It is the central component that directly manages the data, logic, and rules of the application, ensuring data integrity and consistency.

The view component, in contrast, is responsible for presenting the model's data to the user. It is a visual representation of the model, rendering data and providing the UI. In a web application, the view is typically comprised of **HTML**, CSS, and JavaScript, forming the layout and structure that users interact with. The view observes the model and gets updated whenever there is a change in the model's data, maintaining a reflective representation of the current state.

The controller acts as an intermediary between the model and the view, processing incoming requests, manipulating models, and deciding which view to render based on the user interactions and the outcome of the model manipulations. It interprets the user inputs that are converted into actions to be performed by the model. After the model updates its state, the controller selects an appropriate view for response rendering.

This separation of concerns facilitates a modular approach to application development. Developers can work on the model, view, and controller independently, provided they adhere to the agreed contract on how these components interact. This modularity not only enhances the maintainability and scalability of applications but also supports collaborative development environments where different teams or developers focus on specific aspects of the application.

Moreover, the MVC pattern promotes the development of testable applications. By segregating the business logic, UI, and input handling, developers can write unit tests for individual components without reliance on the others. For instance, models can be tested independently of the UI, and controllers can be tested separately from the views.

In web development, particularly with frameworks such as ASP.NET Core, MVC provides a structured approach to building applications. It offers clear pathways for handling requests, managing business logic, and presenting data, all while maintaining a clean separation between the server-side operations and the client-side presentation.

The adaptability of the MVC pattern also means it can be tailored to the specific needs of an application. For instance, in complex applications, the controller can delegate tasks to multiple models or decide between multiple views based on the logic. Similarly, a single model might be represented in various views, each designed for a different user interaction context.

In conclusion, understanding the underlying design principles of MVC architecture provides a foundational framework upon which robust, maintainable, and scalable web applications can be built. As developers delve deeper into each component of MVC, they gain the ability to craft sophisticated and responsive applications that stand the test of time in the ever-evolving landscape of web development.

In the next section, we will explore basic concepts of routing for ASP.NET Core applications.

Understanding the concept of routing

Routing in ASP.NET Core is achieved through a middleware component that analyzes the incoming URL and decides which controller and action method to execute. Thus, understanding and configuring routing correctly is essential for building effective MVC applications. When you start a new MVC project in ASP.NET Core, the routing configuration is set up in the `Program.cs` file, typically in the `Configure` method.

In the default configuration, ASP.NET Core uses a routing approach known as convention-based routing. This setup defines routes based on patterns established in the startup configuration. A typical pattern might look like `/controller/action/id`, where each segment of the URL corresponds to a specific aspect of the routing logic – the controller name, the action method, and an optional parameter, often used as an identifier.

For example, consider the convention-based routing setup defined in `Program.cs` that is seen in the following code:

```
app.MapControllerRoute(
    name: "default",
    pattern: "{controller=Home}/{action=Index}/{id?}"
);

app.Run();
```

This code snippet establishes a default route pattern for the application. If a user visits `http://yourwebsite.com/Products/Details/5`, the routing system interprets this URL to call the `Details` action method of the `Products` controller, passing in 5 as an ID parameter.

However, convention-based routing is not the only option in ASP.NET Core. The framework also supports **attribute routing**, which allows for more granular control by defining routes directly on controllers and actions. With attribute routing, you can specify the route for each controller or action method using attributes.

For instance, you can define a route on a controller like this:

```
using Microsoft.AspNetCore.Mvc;

namespace PacketBook.Controllers
{
    [Route("products")]
    public class ProductsController : Controller
    {
        [Route("")]

        public IActionResult Index()
        {

            return View();

        }

        [Route("{id}")]
        public IActionResult Details(int id)
        {
            return View();
        }
    }
}
```

This example demonstrates how attribute routing provides clear and precise control over the URLs that each action responds to. It's particularly beneficial in scenarios where you need to define custom routes that don't fit the default pattern.

Moreover, routing in ASP.NET Core is extendable and supports the creation of custom routes. For more complex routing requirements, developers can define their own route handlers and even extend the routing framework to create sophisticated routing logic tailored to specific application needs.

Routing also plays a critical role in generating URLs within your application. For instance, when you use the `Url.Action()` helper in a view, ASP.NET Core utilizes routing information to generate the correct URL based on your routing configuration.

Consider the following example, where the `Url.Action()` helper is used in a Razor view:

```
@{
    <h1>Hello, World!</h1>
    <p>Welcome to ASP.NET Core MVC!</p>
    <br />
    <a
        href="@Url.Action(
            "Details",
            "Products",
            new { id = 5}
        )">
        View Product
    </a>
}
```

This helper method generates a URL that matches the routing configuration, ensuring that links within your application are correctly formed and navigable.

Another critical aspect of routing is its impact on **Search Engine Optimization** (**SEO**)and user-friendliness. Well-defined routes contribute to clearer, more memorable URLs, improving the usability and discoverability of your application. From an **SEO** perspective, structured and descriptive routes help search engines better understand the content and hierarchy of your application. They also enable better indexing by search engines, as they can interpret the structure and content of your application more effectively.

Additionally, routing in ASP.NET Core supports the generation of outbound URLs in your application code, facilitating the creation of links that adhere to your routing patterns. This is particularly useful for generating links in emails, notifications, or any external communication, ensuring consistency and reliability in how your application's URLs are represented.

Error handling is another area where routing plays a vital role. By defining specific routes for error pages, you can provide a better user experience during application failures or incorrect URL accesses. For example, you can set up a route to handle 404 errors, directing users to a custom **Page Not Found** page.

In conclusion, routing is a powerful feature of ASP.NET Core that serves as the backbone of how your application responds to HTTP requests. By configuring routing effectively, you can ensure that your application is structured, maintainable, and user friendly. As you continue to build and enhance your ASP.NET Core applications, a deep understanding of routing will enable you to design more intuitive and responsive user interactions, ultimately leading to a more successful and engaging application.

Summary

In this chapter, we have navigated through the essential steps of setting up and developing basic applications using ASP.NET Core. You've been guided through the process of configuring your development environment, an essential foundation that enables you to leverage the full capabilities of ASP.NET Core efficiently. The creation of your first web application served as a practical introduction to the framework, reinforcing the concepts with hands-on experience.

We delved into MVC architecture, a critical structure that organizes web applications into three distinct components, each with a specific responsibility. By breaking down MVC, we aimed to clarify its function and demonstrate its application within ASP.NET Core. This exploration is intended to deepen your understanding of how ASP.NET Core applications are structured and executed.

Routing in ASP.NET Core was another focal point of this chapter, where we examined how the framework processes and directs incoming web requests. Understanding routing is crucial for building applications that respond correctly to user actions and browser requests. Through examples, we illustrated both convention-based and attribute routing, providing you with the knowledge to implement more controlled and sophisticated routing behaviors in your applications.

Throughout the chapter, the emphasis was on applying the discussed concepts practically. By engaging with the material through the creation of a project and exploring its structure, you gained insights into the inner workings of ASP.NET Core applications. This practical approach aimed to reinforce your learning and enable you to visualize how the components of ASP.NET Core interact in a live environment.

As we conclude this chapter, you should now have a foundational understanding of setting up your development environment, MVC architecture, and routing in ASP.NET Core. These elements are crucial to your journey ahead in ASP.NET Core development, providing the groundwork upon which you can build more complex and feature-rich web applications.

In the next chapter, you will learn how to use middleware and dependency injection in ASP.Net Core projects, gaining a first glance at making web applications configurable and testable, and establishing a good foundation for following good practices of software development.

Get This Book's PDF Version and Exclusive Extras

UNLOCK NOW

Scan the QR code (or go to `packtpub.com/unlock`). Search for this book by name, confirm the edition, and then follow the steps on the page.

Note: Keep your invoice handly. Purchase made directly from packt don't require one.

3
Middleware and Dependency Injection

In the realm of web development, mastering the inner workings of ASP.NET Core not only enhances your skill set but also equips you with the tools necessary to construct robust and dynamic web applications. This chapter ventures into two indispensable pillars of ASP.NET Core: middleware and dependency injection. These concepts are not merely theoretical but serve as the bedrock for developing adaptable and maintainable applications.

Through the upcoming lessons, you'll be engaged in a hands-on journey to explore and implement middleware in ASP.NET Core, allowing you to customize the request pipeline to suit your application's needs precisely. You'll learn how to create, configure, and inject middleware components, understanding their pivotal role in your applications. Concurrently, you'll dive deep into the world of dependency injection, a design pattern integral to managing application dependencies efficiently and elegantly. By mastering dependency injection, you'll enhance your ability to maintain and scale ASP.NET Core applications, all while keeping your code base clean and modular.

The knowledge and skills you will acquire here are immensely practical and applicable, preparing you to tackle real-world challenges with confidence. By the end of this chapter, you will be adept at implementing middleware to handle HTTP requests and responses flexibly and using dependency injection to manage dependencies in a decoupled and testable manner.

In this chapter, we're going to cover the following main topics:

- Understanding and implementing middleware
- Fundamentals of dependency injection
- Troubleshooting common issues in DI for ASP.NET Core
- DI best practices in ASP.NET Core

This structured exploration will empower you to elevate your ASP.NET Core applications, making them more responsive, maintainable, and scalable.

Technical requirements

You can refer to the *Technical requirements* section of *Chapter 1* for all the necessary installations.

The code files required for you to follow along with this chapter can be found at: `https://github.com/PacktPublishing/Modern-Full-Stack-Web-Development-with-ASP.NET-Core/tree/main/Chapter03`.

Understanding and implementing middleware in ASP.NET Core

Middleware in ASP.NET Core is software assembled into an application pipeline to handle requests and responses. Each component chooses whether to pass the request to the next component in the pipeline and can perform certain actions before and after the next component is invoked.

At its core, middleware is a construct that is executed on every request in an ASP.NET Core application. It's responsible for the logic that controls how the application responds to **HTTP** requests. Each piece of middleware can process the incoming request, pass it on to the next middleware in the pipeline, and then process the outgoing response.

Middleware components are executed in the order in which they are added to the application pipeline, and this order is critical for security, performance, and functionality.

Configuring middleware

The new minimal hosting model in .NET 9 further streamlines middleware configuration by using `Program.cs` for setup. Here's a simple example showing how middleware components can be registered:

```
public static void Main(string[] args)
{
    var builder = WebApplication.CreateBuilder(args);

    builder.Services.AddControllersWithViews();

    var app = builder.Build();

    if (!app.Environment.IsDevelopment())
    {
        app.UseExceptionHandler("/Home/Error");
    }

    app.UseStaticFiles();
```

```
    app.UseRouting();

    app.UseAuthorization();

    app.MapControllerRoute(
        name: "default",
        pattern:
            "{controller=Home}/{action=Index}/{id?}"
    );

    app.Run();
}
```

In this setup, middleware components such as the use of **Single Page Application (SPA) static files** and authorization are configured with the app instance.

Custom middleware in .NET 9 follows a similar pattern as in previous versions but is integrated within Program.cs. The next section shows how to use custom middleware.

Creating custom middleware

You define your middleware by creating a class that has an InvokeAsync method, following these steps:

1. In **Solution Explorer**, right-click on the project name.
2. Select the **Add...** option.
3. Click on **Folder** and name it Middlewares.
4. Right-click on the Middlewares folder, then select **Add and Class**.
5. Name the class CustomLoggingMiddleware and add the code shown in the following code snippet:

    ```
    namespace PacktBook.Middlewares
    {
        public class CustomLoggingMiddleware
        {
            private readonly RequestDelegate _next;

            public CustomLoggingMiddleware(
                RequestDelegate next)
            {
                _next = next;
            }
    ```

```
        public async Task InvokeAsync(
            HttpContext context)
        {
            // Log the request path
            Console.WriteLine($"Request URL:
                {context.Request.Path.Value}");
            await _next(context);
        }
    }

}
```

This method should accept `HttpContext` and return `Task`.

6. You can now register this middleware in the request processing pipeline in `Program.cs`, as highlighted in the following code:

```
public static void Main(string[] args)
{
    var builder = WebApplication.CreateBuilder(args);

    builder.Services.AddControllersWithViews();

    var app = builder.Build();

    if (!app.Environment.IsDevelopment())
    {
        app.UseExceptionHandler("/Home/Error");
    }

    app.UseStaticFiles();

    app.UseRouting();

    app.UseMiddleware<CustomLoggingMiddleware>();

    app.UseAuthorization();

    app.MapControllerRoute(
        name: "default",
        pattern:
            "{controller=Home}/{action=Index}/{id?}"
    );

    app.Run();
}
```

To test the custom middleware, you can run the application using Visual Studio and navigate across different pages of the ASP.NET MVC app. The console logs should show the information that is configured to be printed by the custom logging class, as seen in *Figure 3.1*:

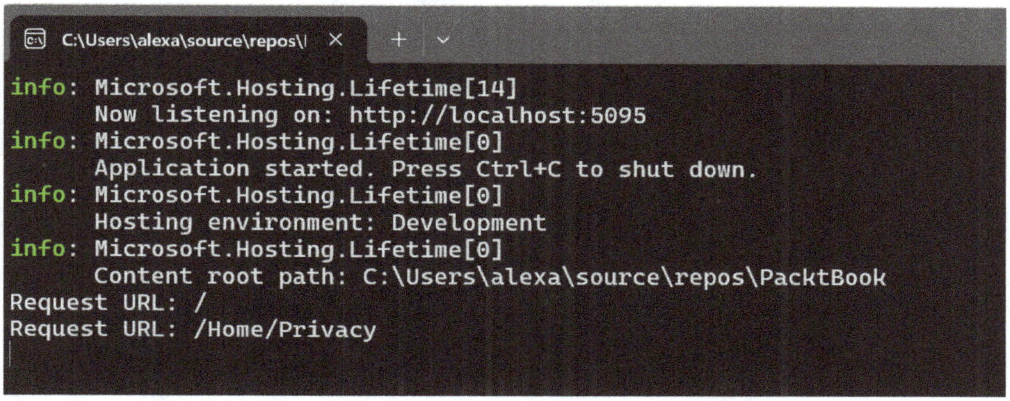

Figure 3.1 – Custom middleware logs

In the next section, you will learn how to create a custom middleware for error handling.

Middleware for error handling

Handling errors gracefully is vital for any application. Here's how you can implement a simple error-handling middleware in .NET 9. Create a class for the middleware, as seen in the following code:

```
namespace PacktBook.Middlewares
{
    public class ErrorHandlingMiddleware
    {
        private readonly RequestDelegate _next;

        public ErrorHandlingMiddleware(
            RequestDelegate next)
        {
            _next = next;
        }

        public async Task InvokeAsync(HttpContext context)
        {
            try
            {
                await _next(context);
```

```
            }
            catch (Exception ex)
            {
                context.Response.StatusCode = 500;
                await context.Response.WriteAsync("An
                    unexpected error occurred.");
                // Log the exception details here
            }
        }
    }
}
```

Include the middleware early in the pipeline to catch subsequent exceptions, as highlighted in the following code:

```
public static void Main(string[] args)
{
    var builder = WebApplication.CreateBuilder(args);
    builder.Services.AddControllersWithViews();

    var app = builder.Build();

    if (!app.Environment.IsDevelopment())
    {
        app.UseExceptionHandler("/Home/Error");
    }

    app.UseStaticFiles();
    app.UseRouting();
    app.UseMiddleware<CustomLoggingMiddleware>();
    app.UseMiddleware<ErrorHandlingMiddleware>();
    app.UseAuthorization();
    app.MapControllerRoute(
        name: "default",
        pattern:
            "{controller=Home}/{action=Index}/{id?}"
    );

    app.Run();
}
```

To test the middleware, you can create a controller that throws an exception, creating a test controller, as seen in the following code:

```
using Microsoft.AspNetCore.Mvc;

namespace PacktBook.Controllers
{
    [ApiController]
    [Route("[controller]")]
    public class TestController : ControllerBase
    {
        [HttpGet]
        public IActionResult Get()
        {
            throw new InvalidOperationException("This is a
                test exception.");
        }
    }
}
```

When you access this endpoint, the middleware should catch the exception, log it, and return a generic error response, as shown in *Figure 3.2*:

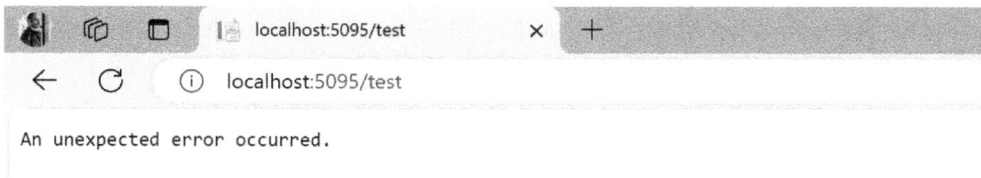

Figure 3.2 – Test controller execution

When you access the /test endpoint, you should not see the specific exception message. Instead, you should receive the generic error message defined in HandleExceptionAsync. In your logging store (console, file, database, etc.), you should see the detailed exception logged by the middleware.

This custom error-handling middleware enhances the resilience of your ASP.NET Core application by centralizing exception handling and response formatting. It hides sensitive error details from the client, helping to prevent potential security vulnerabilities, and provides a consistent error-handling strategy across your application.

In the next section, you will understand the importance of respecting the correct order of middleware registrations in ASP.NET Core to avoid issues in complex applications.

Middleware ordering

Middleware ordering in ASP.NET Core is a critical aspect of the application's request processing pipeline. The order in which middleware components are registered in the pipeline determines how requests and responses are handled and manipulated. Since middleware components can perform operations before and after the next component in the pipeline, their sequence can significantly affect the application's behavior, security, and performance.

When a request is made to an ASP.NET Core application, it travels through the middleware pipeline in the order in which the middleware components were added to the `Program.cs` file. After reaching the end of the pipeline or being handled by a middleware (not passed to the next middleware), the response travels back through the same middleware in reverse order, allowing each middleware to perform post-processing on the response.

Here are some key points regarding middleware ordering:

- **Security middleware**: Security-related middleware, such as authentication (`UseAuthentication`) and authorization (`UseAuthorization`), usually comes early in the pipeline. This ensures that requests are authenticated and authorized before reaching the business logic or endpoint processing middleware, which might depend on the identity of the user.

- **Static files middleware**: The static files middleware (`UseStaticFiles`) is typically placed before components that process requests and generate responses. This is because serving a static file is a terminal operation—if a matching file is found, no further processing is needed, which can save resources.

- **Error handling middleware**: Middleware for error handling, such as exception handling middleware (`UseExceptionHandler`), is often registered at the beginning of the pipeline. This ensures that it can catch exceptions thrown by any subsequent middleware or application code.

- **Routing middleware**: Routing middleware (`UseRouting`) should be placed before any middleware that depends on routing to select an endpoint, such as authorization middleware. However, it comes after error handling and security middleware to ensure requests are valid and authorized before being routed.

- **Endpoint middleware**: Endpoint-related middleware (`UseEndpoints`) is placed toward the end of the pipeline. It maps the incoming request to a specific endpoint (e.g., controller action) based on the routing data.

Here's a simplified example demonstrating middleware ordering in a .NET 9 application:

```
public static void Main(string[] args)
{
    var builder = WebApplication.CreateBuilder(args);
```

```
    builder.Services.AddControllersWithViews();

    var app = builder.Build();

    if (!app.Environment.IsDevelopment())
    {
        app.UseExceptionHandler("/Home/Error");
    }

    app.UseStaticFiles();

    app.UseRouting();

    app.UseMiddleware<CustomLoggingMiddleware>();

    app.UseMiddleware<ErrorHandlingMiddleware>();


    app.UseAuthorization();

    app.MapControllerRoute(
        name: "default",
        pattern:
            "{controller=Home}/{action=Index}/{id?}"
    );

    app.Run();
}
```

In the preceding code snippet, the security middleware configuration is called before the controllers are mapped, making sure all the controllers loaded in the application will have authorization applied. Therefore, keeping the correct ordering enforces the expected result.

Incorrect middleware ordering can lead to various issues, such as the following:

- **Security vulnerabilities**: For example, if the authorization middleware is placed after the endpoint middleware, unauthorized requests could access protected resources.

- **Performance inefficiencies**: Serving static files after processing heavy middleware or endpoints wastes resources since those operations could be bypassed if a static file is requested.

- **Functionality errors**: Certain middleware depend on the outcomes of previous ones (e.g., endpoint data from routing). Incorrect ordering can cause runtime errors or incorrect behavior.

Middleware ordering is essential for the correct functioning of ASP.NET Core applications. It affects how requests are processed, impacts security and performance, and ensures that middleware dependencies are resolved correctly. By carefully considering the role and dependencies of each middleware component, developers can architect efficient, secure, and functional web applications.

In conclusion, middleware in ASP.NET Core serves as the backbone for managing HTTP requests and responses, ensuring error handling, security, and integration with other services and components. By understanding how to implement and leverage middleware, you can significantly enhance the robustness, security, and functionality of your ASP.NET Core applications. Whether it's creating custom middleware for specific tasks, securing your app, or integrating with third-party tools, middleware offers the flexibility and power to tailor your application precisely to your requirements.

In the next section, we will walk through the concepts of dependency injection in ASP.NET Core applications and you will get to know good practices of testability and other benefits of a correct approach in terms of reusability in .NET.

Fundamentals of dependency injection in ASP.NET Core

Dependency injection (**DI**) is a design pattern that promotes loose coupling and enhances testability and maintainability of applications. ASP.NET Core has built-in support for DI, making it an integral part of the framework. This section will explore the fundamentals of DI in ASP.NET Core, providing a comprehensive understanding through definitions, benefits, implementation strategies, and practical examples.

DI is a technique where one object supplies the dependencies of another object. It decouples the usage of an object from its creation, promoting loose coupling, easier testing, and better code organization.

The concept of DI has evolved significantly over the years, becoming a fundamental aspect of modern software development. Understanding its historical context helps in appreciating its importance and the problems it solves.

In the early days of software development, applications were often designed with tightly coupled components. This tight coupling meant that changes in one part of the application could lead to a cascade of required changes in other parts, making maintenance and testing difficult. It was challenging to isolate components for unit testing, as each component was heavily reliant on other components' implementations.

The need for a better architecture led to the development of the DI pattern, which aims to decouple components by removing their direct dependencies on concrete implementations.

The term *dependency injection* is often attributed to Martin Fowler, who described it in his 2004 article, *Inversion of Control Containers and the Dependency Injection Pattern*. However, the principles of DI were applied even before the term was popularized. The concept stems from the broader principle of **Inversion of Control** (**IoC**), where the control flow of a program is inverted compared to traditional procedural programming.

DI became a specialized form of IoC, where dependencies are provided to an object rather than created by the object. This approach significantly improved modularity and testability, allowing developers to replace and mock dependencies easily.

Evolution with frameworks and languages

The rise of object-oriented programming languages and frameworks significantly contributed to the DI pattern's popularity. Frameworks such as Spring for Java and Microsoft's .NET Framework started to offer built-in support for DI, making it more accessible to developers and promoting its adoption.

In Java, the Spring framework was one of the pioneers in adopting DI, providing a rich set of features for managing dependencies. Similarly, in the .NET world, the introduction of Unity, Autofac, and eventually, built-in DI support in ASP.NET Core highlighted the growing importance of DI in application development.

DI in modern development

With the advent of ASP.NET Core, Microsoft provided first-class support for DI, embedding it into the heart of the framework. This move was a testament to the pattern's importance, acknowledging that modern applications require a flexible, testable, and maintainable architecture.

Now, DI is not just a pattern but a fundamental feature expected in modern frameworks. It supports the development of loosely coupled components, which are essential for creating scalable, maintainable, and testable applications.

The future of DI

As software development continues to evolve, the principles behind DI are likely to remain vital. The increasing complexity of applications and the shift toward microservices and cloud-native architectures further underscore the need for patterns such as DI that promote decoupling and flexibility.

In conclusion, the historical evolution of DI reflects a broader shift in software development toward more modular, testable, and maintainable design patterns. As we continue to build more complex and distributed systems, the principles of DI are likely to remain central to software design and architecture, adapting to new paradigms and technologies in the software development landscape.

How DI promotes loose coupling

In traditional tightly coupled systems, components often directly instantiate and manage the life cycle of their dependencies. This approach leads to a high degree of interdependence, making it challenging to modify or replace components without affecting others.

DI addresses this by decoupling the creation of an object from its consumption. Rather than allowing a component to create its dependencies, DI requires that dependencies are provided from the outside, typically by a DI container or framework. This IoC means that the consuming component does not need to know the details of how its dependencies are constructed or where they come from.

Consider a simple application where NotificationService is used by UserController to send notifications, such as the representation in the following code:

```
namespace PacktBook.Services
{

    public class NotificationService
    {
        public void SendNotification(string message)
        {
            // Code to send notification
        }
    }

    public class UserController
    {
        private readonly
            NotificationService _notificationService;

        public UserController(
            NotificationService notificationService)
        {
            _notificationService = notificationService;
        }

        public void UpdateUser(User user)
        {
            // Code to update the user
            _notificationService.SendNotification("User
                updated");
        }
    }


}
```

In this example, UserController directly creates and uses NotificationService. If we decide to change the notification logic or replace NotificationService with a different implementation, we must modify UserController, violating the open/closed principle.

Now, let's refactor the preceding example using DI, starting with the changes proposed in the following code:

```
namespace PacktBook.Services
{

    public interface INotificationService
    {
        void SendNotification(string message);
    }

    public class NotificationService : INotificationService
    {
        public void SendNotification(string message)
        {
            // Code to send notification
        }
    }

    public class UserController
    {
        private readonly
            INotificationService _notificationService;

        public UserController(INotificationService
            notificationService)
        {
            _notificationService = notificationService;
        }

        public void UpdateUser(User user)
        {
            // Code to update the user
            _notificationService.SendNotification("User
                updated");
        }
    }

}
```

In the DI-enabled version, `UserController` depends on an `INotificationService` interface, not a concrete implementation. The dependency (`NotificationService`) is injected into `UserController`, often by a DI container. This approach allows us to change or replace `NotificationService` without modifying `UserController`. For example, during testing, we can inject a mock or stub implementation of `INotificationService`. The loose coupling through DI has a lot of benefits, as explained in the following points:

- **Enhanced testability**: With DI, it's easier to replace dependencies with mocks or stubs in unit tests, leading to more isolated and reliable tests

- **Improved maintainability**: Changes in the implementation details of dependencies do not affect the consuming components, reducing the risk of breaking changes

- **Increased flexibility**: It's simpler to introduce new functionality or change existing behavior by substituting implementations without altering dependent components

- **Scalability**: Loosely coupled architecture supports more scalable applications, as components can be developed, tested, and deployed independently

DI is a powerful pattern for achieving loose coupling in software design. By decoupling the creation and binding of dependencies, DI enables developers to build systems that are more flexible, maintainable, and testable. Through illustrative examples, we've seen how DI facilitates loose coupling and why it is a preferred approach in modern application development, particularly in frameworks such as ASP.NET Core.

Deep dive into service registration

Service registration is a fundamental aspect of working with DI in ASP.NET Core. It is the process where you define how and which services are available to be injected into your components. This registration phase is critical because it tells the DI container what implementations to provide when an interface or class is requested. Let's delve into the details of service registration in ASP.NET Core.

At the core of DI is the concept that your components should not be responsible for creating their own dependencies. Instead, these dependencies should be provided to them. Service registration is the step where you map these dependencies, typically interfaces, to their concrete implementations.

This mapping is done in the `Program.cs` file (or `Startup.cs` in .NET 5 and earlier versions) of an ASP.NET Core application, using `IServiceProvider`, a built-in service. The `WebApplicationBuilder` instance is used to configure and register services. The `builder.Services` property provides an `IServiceCollection` instance, which is used to register services with their respective lifetimes.

When you register a service, you essentially tell the DI container what implementation to return when a specific interface or service type is requested. Here is the general guide to register services:

- **Identify dependencies**: Determine what services or components your application needs. These can be repositories, utilities, or any custom business logic classes.

- **Define interfaces**: It's a good practice to define interfaces for your services. This promotes a loosely coupled architecture, making it easier to replace implementations or mock them during testing.

- **Register services**: Use IServiceCollection provided in WebApplicationBuilder to add your services.

Here's an example of service registration in ASP.NET Core, in the Program.cs file:

```
builder.Services.AddSingleton<ILoggingService,
FileLoggingService>();


builder.Services.AddScoped<IUserService, UserService>();

builder.Services.AddTransient<IEmailSender, EmailSender>();
```

Let's understand the preceding example:

- ILoggingService is registered with a Singleton lifetime using FileLoggingService as its implementation

- IUserService is registered as Scoped, meaning a new UserService will be created for each user session or request

- IEmailSender is registered as Transient, with a new EmailSender instance provided on each request

In the next section, we will understand the details of service lifetimes in ASP.NET Core applications.

Service lifetimes

Service lifetimes in ASP.NET Core's DI framework are crucial concepts that dictate how instances of services are created, shared, and destroyed. There are three primary service lifetimes: Singleton, Scoped, and Transient. Understanding these lifetimes is essential for designing and maintaining a robust and efficient ASP.NET Core application.

Singleton

When you register a service as Singleton, the DI container creates a single instance of the service the first time it's requested and then reuses that instance for all subsequent requests throughout the application's lifetime. Here's an example of the use of the Singleton scope in service registration:

```
builder.Services.AddSingleton<ILoggingService,
FileLoggingService>();
```

In this case, a single instance of `FileLoggingService` will be injected into all classes in which this is configured to be injected. The entire application will share the same instance of the `FileLoggingService` object, with the exact same state.

`Singleton` services are ideal for shared resources or services that are thread-safe and don't maintain stateful information between requests. For instance, a logging service that writes to a file or a console can be a `Singleton` service since it's typically stateless and used across the entire application.

However, using `Singleton` for a service that maintains user-specific data or depends on request-specific data can lead to incorrect data sharing across different requests and users.

Scoped

`Scoped` lifetime services are created once per client request (in web applications, per HTTP request). A new instance is generated for each request but shared across the request, ensuring that all components involved in processing the request have access to the same service instance. Here's an example of the use of the `Scoped` lifetime in service registration:

```
builder.Services.AddScoped<IUserService, UserService>();
```

A user service that needs to provide user-specific data during an HTTP request is a perfect example of a `Scoped` service. It ensures that the user data is consistent and isolated across different HTTP requests but shared throughout a single request, making it ideal for scenarios such as user authentication or data retrieval operations within a request's scope.

Transient

`Transient` services are created each time they are requested from the service container. This ensures that a new instance is provided to every component or service that requires it. Here's an example of the use of the `Transient` lifetime in service registration:

```
builder.Services.AddTransient<IEmailSender, EmailSender>();
```

`Transient` services are suitable for lightweight, stateless services. For instance, an email sender service that sends emails but doesn't retain any state information between sends can be registered as `Transient`.

Using a `Transient` service ensures that each component gets its own instance, which is essential for services that maintain a state or are not thread-safe. This isolation prevents conflicts and ensures that the service's state is not shared across different components or requests.

Understanding the differences between `Singleton`, `Scoped`, and `Transient` lifetimes in ASP. NET Core's DI container is fundamental for building efficient, robust, and bug-free applications. Choosing the correct lifetime depends on the service's design and the intended use case, significantly impacting the application's behavior, performance, and thread safety.

In the next section, we will walk through registering complex dependencies in ASP.NET Core.

Registering and configuring complex dependencies

Registering and configuring complex dependencies in ASP.NET Core involves dealing with scenarios where dependencies themselves have further dependencies or require specific configuration to work correctly. These situations often arise with advanced service configurations, third-party library integrations, or when setting up options patterns for configuration values. Let's delve into how you can handle these more intricate dependency registration and configuration cases with appropriate code snippets.

Sometimes, a service might depend on other services or configuration settings that need to be injected into it. Let's consider a scenario where you have a service that requires a configuration object and another service.

First, define your services and any configuration classes they might depend on, as in the example in the following code:

```
using Microsoft.Extensions.Options;

namespace PacktBook.Services
{
    public class ComplexService : IComplexService
    {
        private readonly IAnotherService _anotherService;
        private readonly ServiceConfig _config;

        public ComplexService(
            IAnotherService anotherService,
            IOptions<ServiceConfig> options
        )
        {
            _anotherService = anotherService;
            _config = options.Value;
        }

        public void PerformAction()
        {
            // Use _anotherService and _config to perform
            // actions
        }
    }

    public class AnotherService : IAnotherService
    {
        public void AnotherAction()
```

```
        {
            // Implementation
        }
    }

    public interface IAnotherService
    {
        void AnotherAction();
    }

    public class ServiceConfig
    {
        public string Url { get; set; }
        public int Timeout { get; set; }
    }

}
```

When you register ComplexService, you also need to ensure that all its dependencies are correctly registered in the DI container. Additionally, you need to configure the ServiceConfig class with values, typically loaded from your application settings, as shown in the following code:

```
builder.Services.Configure<AnotherService>(
    builder.Configuration.GetSection("ServiceConfig")
);
builder.Services.AddScoped<IComplexService,
    ComplexService>();
```

In this example, ComplexService depends on IAnotherService and ServiceConfig. IAnotherService is registered as a scoped service, and ServiceConfig is configured using the IOptions pattern, pulling settings from the application's configuration (e.g., appsettings.json).

There might be cases where you need to create a service with more complex logic than simple constructor injection allows. For this, you can use factory methods during registration.

Consider a scenario where ComplexService requires a runtime value or a service resolved at runtime to be passed to its constructor, as in the following:

```
builder.Services.AddScoped<IAnotherService,
AnotherService>();

builder.Services.AddScoped<IComplexService>(provider =>
{
    var anotherService =
        provider.GetRequiredService<IAnotherService>();
```

```
        var config = provider.GetRequiredService<IOptions<
            ServiceConfig
        >>();
        return new ComplexService(anotherService, config);
});
```

This factory approach allows you to include any logic necessary to instantiate `ComplexService`, providing a flexible way to handle complex dependency chains or runtime values.

Registering and configuring complex dependencies in ASP.NET Core is a powerful feature that supports advanced scenarios in application development. By understanding how to effectively manage complex service registrations, including using configuration objects and factory methods, you can build more flexible, robust, and maintainable ASP.NET Core applications.

As we saw throughout this section, DI in ASP.NET Core is a design pattern that decouples the creation of dependencies from their usage, enhancing code modularity, testability, and maintainability. Historically, DI evolved from the need to manage tightly coupled components, leading to frameworks such as Spring for Java and built-in support in ASP.NET Core. Key benefits include improved testability, maintainability, flexibility, and scalability. DI in ASP.NET Core involves service registration with lifetimes such as `Singleton`, `Scoped`, and `Transient`, with each serving different purposes. Advanced scenarios include configuring complex dependencies using factory methods and configuration objects, crucial for building robust and maintainable applications.

In the next section, we will understand how to troubleshoot common issues in DI for ASP.NET Core applications.

Troubleshooting common issues in DI for ASP.NET Core

While DI is a powerful feature in ASP.NET Core, developers might encounter specific issues that can lead to application errors or unexpected behavior. Understanding how to troubleshoot these common DI-related issues is crucial for maintaining a healthy and robust application. This section will cover troubleshooting strategies for common problems such as issues with service lifetimes, circular dependencies, and improper service registrations.

Issues related to service lifetimes

Service lifetime issues can lead to problems such as unexpected object instances, memory leaks, or instances not being disposed of correctly. Here's how to troubleshoot them:

- **Singleton services referencing Scoped/Transient services**: A singleton service should not depend on scoped or transient services. This dependency can cause the scoped or transient services to behave like singletons, leading to inconsistent data and memory leaks. To resolve this, ensure that singletons only depend on other singleton services.

- **Scoped service lifetimes**: Scoped services should not be resolved in a singleton's constructor or method not scoped to a request. Doing so can cause the application to throw `InvalidOperationException`. Make sure to resolve scoped services within the scope they are meant for, typically within an HTTP request.

- **Disposal of services**: Transient and scoped services that implement `IDisposable` should be carefully managed to ensure they are properly disposed of. Monitor your application for memory leaks, which could indicate that instances are not being disposed of correctly.

Resolving circular dependencies

Circular dependencies occur when two or more services depend on each other, causing the DI container to throw an exception because it cannot construct the services. To troubleshoot and resolve circular dependencies, you can do the following:

- **Refactor code**: The best way to resolve circular dependencies is to refactor your code. This might involve redesigning your service classes so they don't depend on each other directly or introducing an intermediary service to break the cycle.

- **Property injection**: While not a recommended practice, as a last resort, you can use property injection instead of constructor injection for one of the dependent services. However, this should be avoided if possible because it hides the service's dependencies rather than resolving the underlying design issue.

Improper service registrations

Mistakes in service registration can lead to issues where the expected implementation is not available, resulting in exceptions at runtime. To troubleshoot, follow these suggestions:

- **Review registrations**: Ensure all necessary services are registered in the `ConfigureServices` method of your `Program.cs` file. Each service used should have a corresponding registration.

- **Correct implementation**: Verify that the correct implementation is registered for each service interface. Mismatched interfaces and implementations can cause runtime errors.

- **Ambiguous interfaces**: If a service has multiple implementations, ensure that the correct one is being injected where necessary. This might involve qualifying the service injection with attributes or names to differentiate between the available implementations.

- **Configuration errors**: Sometimes, the issue might not be with the service itself but with its configuration. Ensure that any service that depends on configuration settings is receiving the correct values.

Troubleshooting DI issues in ASP.NET Core requires a systematic approach to identify and resolve potential problems. By understanding common issues related to service lifetimes, circular dependencies, and improper registrations, developers can ensure that their applications are robust, maintainable, and error-free. When faced with a DI-related issue, reviewing your DI configurations, understanding the underlying cause, and applying best practices for DI design can help you resolve issues efficiently and effectively.

In the next and final section about DI in this chapter, we will learn about the best practices of DI for ASP.NET Core applications.

DI best practices in ASP.NET Core

DI is a key feature of ASP.NET Core, promoting cleaner, more modular, and testable code. Adhering to best practices in DI not only enhances code quality and maintainability but also helps prevent common issues that can arise in application development. In the upcoming subsections, we delve deeper into some of the crucial best practices for utilizing DI in ASP.NET Core effectively.

Prefer constructor injection

Constructor injection is the recommended way to implement DI in ASP.NET Core. It involves providing the required dependencies through the class's constructor, ensuring that the class is always in a fully initialized and valid state, and following these practices:

- **Explicit dependencies**: Constructor injection makes the dependencies of a class explicit and clear. It documents what is needed for the class to function correctly, improving code readability and maintainability.

- **Immutability**: By using constructor injection, the dependencies are often set as read-only, which ensures that they cannot be altered after the object's construction, adding to the robustness of the application.

- **Testing**: It simplifies unit testing by allowing easy substitution of the class's dependencies with mocks or stubs, facilitating isolated testing.

Avoid the service locator pattern

The service locator pattern can introduce hidden dependencies and make your code harder to understand and maintain. It effectively bypasses the advantages of using DI by fetching dependencies directly from the service container. Hence, you should follow these practices:

- **Transparency**: Avoiding the service locator pattern maintains the transparency of your class's dependencies, ensuring they are explicitly declared and provided through the constructor or properties

- **Testability**: It improves testability by preventing hidden dependencies and ensuring that all required services are provided, allowing for more isolated and controlled tests

Be mindful of lifetimes

Understanding and respecting the lifetimes of services in DI is crucial. It's particularly important to avoid resolving a scoped service from a singleton, as this can lead to unexpected behavior and application errors. These are the practices that must be avoided:

- **Scoped within singleton**: A common mistake is to inject a scoped service into a singleton service, which can cause the scoped service to behave incorrectly, similar to a singleton, leading to issues such as stale data and concurrency bugs
- **Disposal and resource management**: Ensure that services with managed resources are registered with appropriate lifetimes to avoid memory leaks and ensure proper resource cleanup

Use interfaces

Interfaces play a central role in the DI pattern, making your application more modular, testable, and maintainable, and hence you should follow these practices:

- **Loose coupling**: Interfaces help in achieving loose coupling between components, making it easier to swap out implementations without affecting dependent code
- **Testability**: Using interfaces allows for easy mocking in unit tests, ensuring that tests are not reliant on the details of concrete implementations
- **Abstraction**: They provide an abstraction layer over concrete implementations, allowing for more flexible and adaptable code

Additional best practices

The following are some additional practices that you can follow:

- **Avoid optional dependencies**: Try not to use optional dependencies in your classes. If a class requires a dependency, it should be explicitly required. Optional dependencies can introduce ambiguity and make the code harder to understand and maintain.
- **Design for DI**: Design your classes with DI in mind from the start. This means considering how they will be instantiated and ensuring that all dependencies can be injected.
- **Centralize DI configuration**: Keep your DI configurations centralized and organized, ideally within the `ConfigureServices` method in `Program.cs`, to maintain a clear overview of your application's service architecture.

By following these best practices, developers can leverage the full benefits of DI in ASP.NET Core, leading to a more maintainable, testable, and robust application architecture.

Summary

In this chapter, we delved deep into the crucial aspects of middleware and DI within ASP.NET Core, providing a comprehensive guide on how to effectively implement and utilize these features. The chapter started by introducing the concepts of middleware and DI, laying a solid foundation for understanding their roles in the ASP.NET Core framework.

The discussion on middleware focused on its pivotal role in the ASP.NET Core request pipeline, demonstrating how it can be used to customize and control the flow of requests and responses in an application. The chapter provided practical examples and step-by-step instructions on implementing and customizing middleware, ensuring that you gain hands-on experience and a clear understanding of how middleware functions within the ASP.NET Core ecosystem.

Moving on to DI, the chapter elucidated this powerful technique's fundamental principles, demonstrating its importance in achieving loosely coupled, maintainable, and testable code. By exploring the service container, service lifetimes, and service registrations, you were equipped with the knowledge to effectively manage and inject dependencies in your ASP.NET Core applications.

Throughout the chapter, coding examples accompanied the theoretical discussions, enabling you to apply what you learned directly to real-world scenarios. You now have a thorough understanding of how to implement and leverage middleware and DI in your ASP.NET Core projects, enhancing your development skills and the quality of your applications.

By focusing on these areas, the chapter aimed to provide a comprehensive guide that not only taught the theoretical aspects of middleware and DI but also provided practical insights and examples, empowering you to apply these concepts effectively in your own ASP.NET Core projects.

In the next chapter, you will learn how to handle configuration and security in ASP.NET Core projects, giving a first glance at making web applications configurable and secure, following good practices of compliance established in the market.

Get This Book's PDF Version and Exclusive Extras

UNLOCK NOW

Scan the QR code (or go to `packtpub.com/unlock`). Search for this book by name, confirm the edition, and then follow the steps on the page.

Note: Keep your invoice handly. Purchase made directly from packt don't require one.

4
Configuration and Security

In the dynamic and ever-evolving world of web development, mastering the art of configuration and security within ASP.NET Core applications stands as a critical skill set for any developer. This chapter delves deep into the robust configuration system of ASP.NET Core, guiding you through the nuances of managing diverse environments and settings to ensure your application runs smoothly across different scenarios. We'll explore how to tailor your app's behavior to development, testing, and production environments, ensuring flexibility and reliability.

Transitioning from configuration to the cornerstone of any web application—security—we pivot our focus to the mechanisms of authentication and authorization. Understanding these layers is paramount in safeguarding your applications against unauthorized access and ensuring that users are who they claim to be. We'll walk you through implementing various authentication schemes and setting up authorization policies to protect your resources effectively.

Moreover, we'll address the imperative of secure data handling, emphasizing practices that prevent data breaches and ensure the confidentiality and integrity of your users' data. To complement this, we'll delve into the application of **Secure Sockets Layer** (**SSL**), a fundamental technology for encrypting network traffic and reinforcing the security of data in transit.

By the end of this chapter, you'll not only have grasped the theoretical underpinnings but will also have gained hands-on experience in configuring ASP.NET Core applications, implementing robust security mechanisms, and adopting best practices for data protection. Whether you're building enterprise-level solutions or personal projects, the skills learned here will elevate the security and resilience of your applications.

In this chapter, we're going to cover the following main topics:

- Importance of configuration and security in ASP.NET Core
- Configuration in ASP.NET Core
- Implementing authentication and authorization in ASP.NET Core
- Secure data handling and SSL in ASP.NET Core

Armed with this knowledge, you'll be well equipped to craft secure and adaptable ASP.NET Core applications, ready to face the challenges of the modern web landscape.

Technical requirements

You can refer to the *Technical requirements* section of *Chapter 1* for all the necessary installations.

The code files required for you to follow along with this chapter can be found at: `https://github.com/PacktPublishing/Modern-Full-Stack-Web-Development-with-ASP.NET-Core/tree/main/Chapter04`.

Importance of configuration and security in ASP.NET Core

In the context of modern web development, particularly with ASP.NET Core, understanding and implementing robust configuration and security measures is not just beneficial—it's essential. These two facets form the backbone of any reliable and resilient web application, ensuring both flexibility in deployment and protection against ever-evolving security threats.

In terms of configuration, ASP.NET Core is designed to be highly flexible and adaptable, allowing developers to manage application behavior across different environments—development, staging, and production—without changing the code. This adaptability is crucial for applications that need to scale and evolve over time. By externalizing settings such as database connections, API keys, and feature toggles into configuration files or environment variables, developers can adjust an application's behavior without needing to redeploy or alter the application's core logic.

This level of configurability supports the DevOps practices of **continuous integration and continuous deployment (CI/CD)**, facilitating a smoother workflow from development to production. Moreover, it enables the practice of **multi-factor authentication (MFA)** methodology, particularly in configuring applications for various environments, enhancing the app's portability and resilience.

When it comes to security, ASP.NET Core provides an integrated, well-thought-out framework to protect applications from common vulnerabilities and attacks. Security is not just a feature but a fundamental aspect that is woven into the development life cycle of an application. It encompasses various layers, including authentication, authorization, data protection, and secure communication, including the following aspects:

- **Authentication and authorization**: ASP.NET Core allows for a robust and customizable authentication and authorization system. It ensures that only authenticated users can access certain resources and that they have the proper permissions to perform specific actions. This segregation of access is vital for maintaining user data privacy and safeguarding sensitive information from unauthorized access.

- **Data protection**: ASP.NET Core includes a built-in data protection stack that helps safeguard and encrypt sensitive data, both at rest and in transit. This is particularly crucial in a world where data breaches can have far-reaching consequences on privacy and trust.

- **Secure communication**: With the rising prevalence of cyber threats, secure communication becomes paramount. ASP.NET Core's support for SSL/**Transport Layer Security** (**TLS**) is a testament to its commitment to secure data exchange, ensuring that data transmitted over the network is encrypted and shielded from eavesdroppers.

In essence, the configuration and security features in ASP.NET Core are not just about preventing unauthorized access or data leaks; they are about building a foundation of trust with users. By ensuring that applications are flexible, adaptable, and secure, developers can create digital experiences that users can rely on, fostering confidence and loyalty in the digital landscape.

Considering the importance of configuration and security for ASP.NET Core, by the end of this chapter, you will have gained a comprehensive understanding and practical experience in several key areas. Also, you will not only have a theoretical understanding of these concepts but also practical experience in applying them. You'll be equipped with the knowledge and skills to configure ASP.NET Core applications for various environments, implement sophisticated authentication and authorization strategies, handle data securely, and apply SSL for secure communications. These competencies will empower you to develop robust, secure, and flexible ASP.NET Core applications, ready to meet the demands of the modern web ecosystem.

In the next section, we will walk through all the necessary information about configuration for ASP.NET Core applications, understanding how you can manage complex scenarios in terms of settings and how to make your applications scalable in terms of configuration.

Configuration in ASP.NET Core

One of the pillars that sustain the robustness and flexibility of an application is its configuration system. ASP.NET Core redefines this cornerstone by offering a sophisticated and adaptable configuration framework, crucial for modern applications that need to thrive in varying environments and conditions.

The configuration system in ASP.NET Core is ingeniously designed to support a dynamic and modular approach. It allows developers to extract application settings from an array of sources, paving the way for applications that can seamlessly transition from development to production without code changes. This system not only caters to the application's need to adapt to different environments but also ensures that sensitive information is securely managed and separated from the code base.

Understanding and implementing the configuration system effectively can vastly improve the maintainability and scalability of applications, providing a solid foundation for building reliable, secure, and adaptable web applications. In the upcoming sections, we will delve into the various facets of this configuration system, exploring its components, usage, and best practices to harness its full potential.

Overview of configuration in ASP.NET Core

ASP.NET Core provides a flexible and extensible framework for managing application settings and behavior based on the environment. Unlike previous versions of ASP.NET, configuration in ASP.NET Core is not based on static files such as web.config. Instead, it utilizes a variety of sources such as JSON files, environment variables, command-line arguments, and more. Configuration in ASP.NET Core contains the following key components:

- **Configuration providers**: These are the various sources from which configuration settings can be loaded. Each provider can read configuration data from different sources.

- **Configuration builder**: This is used to collect configurations from specified providers and build them into a single configuration object that can be accessed throughout the application.

Furthermore, ASP.NET Core supports multiple configuration sources, such as the following:

- **appsettings.json**: The default JSON file for configuration in ASP.NET Core projects

- **Environment variables**: Useful for overriding settings externally, especially in production environments or during deployment

- **Secrets manager**: Utilized during development to store sensitive data safely out of the project tree

A typical usage pattern for configuration in ASP.NET Core involves creating ConfigurationBuilder method adding the necessary configuration providers, and then building an IConfiguration object. This object is then used throughout the application to access configuration values. A practical example can be seen in the following code:

```
using Microsoft.Extensions.Configuration;

namespace Chapter4
{
    internal class Program
    {
        static void Main(string[] args)
        {
            var configBuilder = new ConfigurationBuilder()
                .AddJsonFile(
                    "mysettings.json",
                    optional: true,
                    reloadOnChange: true
                )
                .AddEnvironmentVariables();

            IConfiguration config = configBuilder.Build();
```

```
        Console.WriteLine($"Custom config:
          {config["ExampleSetting"]}");
    }

  }
}
```

In this case, the configuration source is the `appsettings.json` file, which may have different values for different environments such as development, staging, and production. In the next section, we will understand about configuration providers.

Understanding configuration providers

Configuration providers in ASP.NET Core are the components that read configuration data from various sources and make it available to the application at runtime. Each provider can pull configuration data from different types of sources, ensuring that you can maintain settings across a variety of environments and storage formats. This flexibility allows developers to adjust applications easily without changing code, catering to different stages of development, deployment, and production environments.

The following list details the most common types of sources supported by .NET for configuration:

- The **JSON provider** reads settings from JSON files such as `appsettings.json`, a common default in ASP.NET Core that supports hierarchical configurations. Here's again how to use it:

```
using Microsoft.Extensions.Configuration;

namespace Chapter4
{
    internal class Program
    {
        static void Main(string[] args)
        {
            var configBuilder =
                new ConfigurationBuilder()
                .AddJsonFile(
                    "mysettings.json",
                    optional: true,
                    reloadOnChange: true
                )
                .AddEnvironmentVariables();

            IConfiguration config =
                configBuilder.Build();
```

```
                    Console.WriteLine($"ConnectionString:
                        {config["ConnectionStrings:Default"]}"
        );
                }


            }
}
```

- The **environment variable provider** loads configurations from environment variables, ideal for overriding settings securely in production environments. Here's a usage example:

```
using Microsoft.Extensions.Configuration;

namespace Chapter4
{
    internal class Program
    {
        static void Main(string[] args)
        {
            var builder = new ConfigurationBuilder()
                .AddEnvironmentVariables();

            IConfiguration configuration =
                builder.Build();

            Console.WriteLine($"PATH:
                {configuration["PATH"]}");
        }


    }
}
```

The given code uses the AddEnvironmentVariables extension method from ConfigurationBuilder to load the variables from the environment, indicating the actual source.

- The **command-line provider** allows for command-line configuration during application startup, beneficial for development or when launching an application with specific runtime parameters. The following is an example of setting configuration via the command line:

```
static void Main(string[] args)
{

    string[] arguments = {
        "--ConnectionStrings:Default=
```

```
            MyConnectionString"
    };

    var builder = new ConfigurationBuilder()
        .AddCommandLine(arguments);

    IConfiguration config = builder.Build();

    Console.WriteLine($"ConnectionString: {
        config["ConnectionStrings:Default"] }");

}
```

* The **XML provider** supports applications that require configuration through XML files, useful for integrating with legacy systems or external systems that provide XML configurations. Here's how it's implemented:

```
using Microsoft.Extensions.Configuration;

namespace Chapter4
{
    internal class Program
    {
        static void Main(string[] args)
        {
            var builder = new ConfigurationBuilder()
                .AddXmlFile(
                    "appsettings.xml",
                    optional: true,
                    reloadOnChange: true
                );

            var config = builder.Build();

            Console.WriteLine(
                $"LogFilePath: {config["LogSettings:
                LogFilePath"]}"
            );
        }

    }
}
```

The given example uses the AddXmlFile method to load the settings from the appsettings. xml file. Here's a simplified representation of what the appsettings.xml file would look like:

```xml
<?xml version="1.0" encoding="utf-8" ?>
<configuration>
  <appSettings>
    <!-- Application-specific settings -->
    <add key="ApplicationName" value="MyApp" />
    <add key="Version" value="1.0.0" />
  </appSettings>

  <connectionStrings>
    <!-- Database connection string -->
    <add name="DefaultConnection"
        connectionString="Server=myServerAddress;
                          Database=myDataBase;
                          User Id=myUsername;
                          Password=myPassword;"
        providerName="System.Data.SqlClient" />
  </connectionStrings>

  <LogSettings>
    <!-- Log file path setting -->
    <add key="LogFilePath"
        value="C:\Logs\myapp.log"
    />
  </LogSettings>
</configuration>
```

As you can see in the given XML, you can have nested settings such as LogSettings and refer to that in your .NET app when retrieving configuration.

- The **user secrets provider** is used during development to store sensitive data outside the project in a secure manner, ensuring that secrets such as API keys remain out of source control. Here's an example of implementing this provider:

```csharp
using Microsoft.Extensions.Configuration;

namespace Chapter4
{
    internal class Program
    {
        static void Main(string[] args)
        {
            var builder = new ConfigurationBuilder()
```

```
                .AddUserSecrets<Program>();

            var config = builder.Build();

            Console.WriteLine(
                $"APIKey: {config["APIKey"]}"
            );
        }

    }
}
```

- Finally, the **memory provider** is especially useful for tests or when you need to add configuration settings dynamically during application execution. It loads configuration from in-memory collections:

```
using Microsoft.Extensions.Configuration;

namespace Chapter4
{
    internal class Program
    {
        static void Main(string[] args)
        {
            var dict =
                new Dictionary<string, string>()
                {
                    { "RunTimeSettng","Value"}
                };

            var builder = new ConfigurationBuilder()
                .AddInMemoryCollection(dict);

            var config = builder.Build();

            Console.WriteLine(
                $"RunTimeSettng:
                {config["RunTimeSettng"]}"
            );
        }

    }
}
```

Each provider serves specific scenarios, enhancing the flexibility and security of application configuration management in ASP.NET Core. In the next section, we will understand how to create custom configuration providers for ASP.NET Core applications.

Creating custom configuration providers

ASP.NET Core allows developers to extend configuration capabilities by creating custom providers. This is particularly useful when you need to source configuration data from a store not covered by default providers (such as a database or a custom service). To create your own configuration provider, you can follow these steps:

1. **Implement the interface**: Implement IConfigurationProvider for fetching the data and IConfigurationSource for returning an instance of the provider.

2. **Configure and load data**: The provider should connect to the desired data source, fetch data, and transform it into key-value pairs.

3. **Register the provider**: Add the custom provider to the configuration system during application startup.

Let's create a simple custom configuration provider that reads configuration data from a plaintext file where each line is a key-value pair separated by a colon:

1. As a first step, you have to create a class that inherits from the ConfigurationProvider class, as seen in the following code:

```
namespace PacktBook
{
    public class TextFileConfigurationProvider :
        ConfigurationProvider
    {
        public string FilePath { get; }

        public TextFileConfigurationProvider(
            string filePath
        )
        {
            FilePath = filePath;
        }

        public override void Load()
        {
            var data =
                new Dictionary<string, string>();
```

```
        if (!File.Exists(FilePath))
        {
            throw new FileNotFoundException(
                $"Configuration file not found:
                {FilePath}"
            );
        }

        foreach (var line in
            File.ReadAllLines(FilePath))
        {
            var keyValuePair = line.Split(':');
            if (keyValuePair.Length != 2)
            {
                throw new FormatException(
                    "Line must be in the format
                    'key:value'"
                );
            }

            data[keyValuePair[0].Trim()] =
                keyValuePair[1].Trim();
        }

        Data = data;
    }
}

}
```

This code defines a custom configuration provider named TextFileConfigurationProvider, which inherits from ConfigurationProvider. It is designed to load configuration data from a text file specified by FilePath. The Load method is overridden to read each line from the file, expecting each line to contain a key-value pair separated by a colon. It then splits each line into a key and a value, trims any whitespace, and adds them to the internal data dictionary. If the file does not exist or if any line does not meet the expected format, exceptions are thrown to prevent incorrect configurations from being loaded.

2. The next step is to create a **configuration source**, which means a class that is the implementation of the IConfigurationSource interface, as seen in the following code:

```
namespace PacktBook
{
    public class TextFileConfigurationSource :
```

```
        IConfigurationSource
    {
        public string FilePath { get; set; }

        public IConfigurationProvider Build(
            IConfigurationBuilder builder)
        {
            return new
                TextFileConfigurationProvider(FilePath);
        }
    }

    }
```

This snippet defines `TextFileConfigurationSource`, an implementation of the `IConfigurationSource` interface. The primary role of this class is to encapsulate the details of the configuration provider and expose a `Build` method, which is called by `IConfigurationBuilder`. The `Build` method instantiates `TextFileConfigurationProvider` using the `FilePath` property, effectively linking the source and the provider. This setup allows the configuration system to be extended seamlessly, supporting a custom file format for settings.

3. The final step in this example is to register the custom provider for your application, as highlighted in the following code:

```
using Microsoft.Extensions.Configuration;

namespace Chapter4
{
    internal class Program
    {
        static void Main(string[] args)
        {
            var builder = new ConfigurationBuilder()
                .Add(new TextFileConfigurationSource()
                    { FilePath = "config.txt" });

            var config = builder.Build();

            Console.WriteLine($"Example setting:
                {config["ExampleSetting"]}");
        }

    }
}
```

This final piece of code demonstrates how to incorporate the custom configuration provider into an ASP.NET Core application. In the `Main` method of the `Program` class, `ConfigurationBuilder` is created, and the custom `TextFileConfigurationSource` class is added to it. The `FilePath` property is set to `config.txt`, specifying the source file for the configuration settings. Once the configuration is built, it can be used like any other configuration source in ASP.NET Core, allowing you to retrieve settings using standard key indexing. This example fetches and prints a setting named `ExampleSetting` to demonstrate accessing the loaded configuration data.

Through the exploration of configuration in ASP.NET Core, we have seen the powerful and flexible system at the heart of modern application development. The framework's built-in providers, such as JSON, environment variables, and command-line arguments, along with the capability to implement custom providers, equip developers with the tools needed to manage diverse application settings efficiently across different environments. This adaptability ensures that ASP.NET Core applications can be fine-tuned to meet precise operational requirements and environmental constraints.

Custom configuration providers further extend this flexibility, enabling integration with any data source or format. As demonstrated with `TextFileConfigurationProvider`, developers can tailor the configuration process to include legacy systems, unique file formats, or specialized data stores, ensuring that even the most complex or non-standard configurations can be seamlessly incorporated into an ASP.NET Core application.

As we move forward in this chapter, we will shift our focus from configuration to the crucial aspects of security within ASP.NET Core. The upcoming sections will delve into implementing authentication and authorization, secure data handling, and applying SSL, providing you with the knowledge to not only configure but also secure your applications effectively. By understanding these security mechanisms, you will be equipped to protect your applications against common vulnerabilities and ensure data integrity and confidentiality. This progression from configuration to security highlights the comprehensive nature of application development and maintenance within the ASP.NET Core framework, preparing you for the challenges of creating robust, secure, and scalable web applications.

Implementing authentication and authorization in ASP.NET Core

Authentication and **authorization** are fundamental security processes in web development. Authentication verifies the identity of a user trying to access a system, ensuring that the person is who they claim to be. This might involve checking a username and password or verifying a token that the user presents. On the other hand, authorization determines what an authenticated user is allowed to do or see within the system. For instance, a regular user may be able to view data, while an administrator might have permissions to edit it.

ASP.NET Core provides a robust framework to handle both these processes efficiently, enabling developers to secure their applications against unauthorized access and ensuring that users have appropriate access rights.

ASP.NET Core uses a middleware-based approach to handle authentication. **Middleware** components analyze incoming requests and determine the user's identity based on the provided credentials. This process involves the following key components:

- **Authentication schemes**: These are named configurations that describe how authentication should be performed. They can involve cookies, **JSON Web Token (JWT)** tokens, or external login providers such as Google or Facebook.

- **Authentication handlers**: These are responsible for the actual process of authentication. Each handler corresponds to a different authentication scheme.

Here's a simple example to configure cookie-based authentication in `Program.cs`:

```
public static void Main(string[] args)
{
    var builder = WebApplication.CreateBuilder(args);

    builder.Services.AddAuthentication("MyCookieAuth")
        .AddCookie("MyCookieAuth", options =>
    {
        options.Cookie.Name = "UserLoginCookie";
        options.LoginPath = "/Login";

    });
}
```

In this code, `AddAuthentication` adds authentication services to the application. `MyCookieAuth` is the name of the authentication scheme, and `AddCookie` configures the scheme to use cookies. The `options.LoginPath` instance specifies where to redirect users if they need to log in.

In the next section, we will understand briefly how to configure authorization for ASP.NET Core applications.

How authorization works in ASP.NET Core

Once a user is authenticated, the next step is authorization, which checks if the user has the right permissions to perform certain actions. ASP.NET Core handles this through the following:

- **Policies**: Custom rules that specify what requirements must be met for access to be granted. For instance, you might require that users be authenticated and belong to a certain role.

- **Requirements**: Specific conditions that need to be satisfied for a policy to be fulfilled. This could include being a certain age, having a specific claim, or belonging to a role.

- **Handlers**: Pieces of logic that evaluate whether a given requirement has been met.

Here's how you might set up a simple authorization policy in `Program.cs`:

```
public static void Main(string[] args)
{
    var builder = WebApplication.CreateBuilder(args);

    builder.Services.AddAuthentication("MyCookieAuth")
        .AddCookie("MyCookieAuth", options =>
    {
        options.Cookie.Name = "UserLoginCookie";
        options.LoginPath = "/Login";
    });

    builder.Services.AddAuthorization(options =>
    {
        options.AddPolicy(
            "AdminPolicy",
            policy => policy.RequireRole("Admin")
        );
    });
}
```

This code adds an authorization policy named `"AdminPolicy"` that requires the user to be in the `"Admin"` role to access certain resources.

These authorization concepts are applied in the ASP.NET Core pipeline through middleware. Here's how you might configure the middleware in `Program.cs`:

```
public static void Main(string[] args)
{
    var builder = WebApplication.CreateBuilder(args);

    builder.Services.AddAuthentication("MyCookieAuth")
        .AddCookie("MyCookieAuth", options =>
    {
        options.Cookie.Name = "UserLoginCookie";
        options.LoginPath = "/Login";
    });
```

```
builder.Services.AddAuthorization(options =>
{
    options.AddPolicy(
        "AdminPolicy",
        policy => policy.RequireRole("Admin")
    );
});

var app = builder.Build();

app.UseRouting();

app.UseAuthentication();

app.UseAuthorization();
}
```

In this configuration, `UseAuthentication` and `UseAuthorization` are critical: they apply the configured authentication and authorization policies to every incoming HTTP request to your application.

Understanding and implementing these security processes correctly is essential for protecting ASP. NET Core applications. With the built-in tools provided by ASP.NET Core, you can customize how you authenticate and authorize users, making your application both secure and adaptable to various user requirements.

In the next section, we will understand how to work with various authentication schemes in ASP.NET Core.

Implementing various authentication schemes in ASP.NET Core

ASP.NET Core supports multiple authentication schemes to suit various application needs, ranging from traditional forms using cookies to modern token-based systems. This section explores how to implement different types of authentication mechanisms, specifically focusing on cookie-based and token-based (JWT) authentication.

Cookie-based authentication

Cookie-based authentication is a popular method for maintaining session information on the client's browser across multiple requests. When a user logs in, the server creates a session identifier and sends it as a cookie to the user's browser, which sends it back with subsequent requests for session validation.

In `Program.cs`, configure the cookie authentication services and parameters in the `Main` method:

```
public static void Main(string[] args)
{
    var builder = WebApplication.CreateBuilder(args);
```

```
    builder.Services.AddAuthentication(
        CookieAuthenticationDefaults.AuthenticationScheme)
            .AddCookie(options=>
        {
            options.LoginPath = "/Account/Login";
            options.AccessDeniedPath =
                "/Account/AccessDenied";
            options.ExpireTimeSpan = TimeSpan.FromDays(5);
        });
}
```

The next step is to create a login action in your controller to handle user authentication and cookie issuance:

```
[HttpPost]
public async Task<IActionResult> Login(
    string username,
    string password
)
{
    var user = AuthenticateUser(username, password);
    if (user != null)
    {
        var claims = new List<Claim>
{
    new Claim(ClaimTypes.Name, user.Name),
    new Claim(ClaimTypes.Role, user.Role),
};

        var claimsIdentity = new ClaimsIdentity(
            claims,
            CookieAuthenticationDefaults
                .AuthenticationScheme
        );
        var authProperties = new AuthenticationProperties
            { IsPersistent = true };

        await HttpContext.SignInAsync(
            CookieAuthenticationDefaults
                .AuthenticationScheme,
            new ClaimsPrincipal(claimsIdentity),
            authProperties
        );

        return RedirectToAction("Index", "Home");
```

```
    }

    return View();
}
```

The `AuthenticateUser` function is a custom method that you would implement to verify a user's credentials against a database or any other storage system where user information is kept. This function is typically used in scenarios involving forms-based authentication, such as cookie-based authentication, where the user submits a username and password via a form.

In the next section, we will understand how to configure **token-based authentication** in your ASP. NET Core applications.

Token-based authentication

A JWT provides a compact, URL-safe means of representing claims to be transferred between two parties. It allows you to verify the token's authenticity and the user's identity. This authentication method is especially useful in scenarios involving **single-page applications** (**SPAs**), mobile applications, and cross-origin requests where managing cookies might be impractical.

JWTs consist of three parts: the header, the payload, and the signature. The header typically contains the token type and the hashing algorithm being used. The payload includes claims, which are statements about an entity (typically, the user) and additional data. The signature is used to secure the token and verify that the token hasn't been altered. A JWT involves the following:

- **Header**: For example, `{"alg": "HS256", "typ": "JWT"}`
- **Payload**: Contains claims; for example, `{"sub": "1234567890", "name": "John Doe", "iat": 1516239022}`
- **Signature**: A hash of the header, the payload, and a secret, created using the header's specified algorithm

When a user logs in, the server generates a JWT that encapsulates the user's identity and other essential attributes, signs it, and sends it back to the client. The client then includes this token in the HTTP `Authorization` header of subsequent web requests, and the server verifies the token to authorize requests.

To implement JWT authentication in your ASP.NET Core application, follow these steps:

1. **Configuration in Program.cs**: Configure the JWT authentication services in the `Main` method. You will need to install the `Microsoft.AspNetCore.Authentication.JwtBearer` package, and you will need to specify details such as the issuer, audience, and the key used to sign the token:

   ```
   builder.Services.AddAuthentication(
       JwtBearerDefaults.AuthenticationScheme)
   ```

```
.AddJwtBearer(options =>
{
    options.TokenValidationParameters =
        new TokenValidationParameters
    {
        ValidateIssuerSigningKey = true,
        IssuerSigningKey = new
            SymmetricSecurityKey(
                Encoding.UTF8.GetBytes(
                    "YourSecretKeyHere"
                )
            ),
            ValidateIssuer = true,
            ValidateAudience = true,
            ValidIssuer = "YourIssuer",
            ValidAudience = "YourAudience",
            // Reduce default clock skew to
            // immediate
            // token expiration handling
            ClockSkew = TimeSpan.Zero
    };
});
```

2. **Token generation**: Create a method to generate a JWT when a user successfully logs in. This token includes the user's claims and is signed with a secret key:

```
public string GenerateJwtToken(
    string username, List<Claim> claims
)
{
    var securityKey = new SymmetricSecurityKey(
        Encoding.UTF8.GetBytes("YourSecretKeyHere")
    );
    var credentials = new SigningCredentials(
        securityKey,
        SecurityAlgorithms.HmacSha256Signature
    );

    var token = new JwtSecurityToken(
        issuer: "YourIssuer",
        audience: "YourAudience",
        claims: claims,
        expires: DateTime.Now.AddHours(3),
        signingCredentials: credentials
```

```
    );

    return new
        JwtSecurityTokenHandler().WriteToken(token);
}
```

3. **Securing endpoints**: Apply the [Authorize] attribute to controllers or actions where you require user authentication. This ensures that the JWT is validated before the action is executed:

```
[Authorize]
public class SecureController : ControllerBase
{
    public IActionResult GetSecureData()
    {
        return Ok("This is a secure endpoint and you
            have been authenticated.");
    }
}
```

Additionally, it is possible to configure authorization for all controllers by default without explicitly using the Authorize attribute on each controller. It can be achieved by setting authorization in the Program.cs file, as seen in the following code:

```
builder.Services.AddControllersWithViews(options =>
{
    var policy = new AuthorizationPolicyBuilder()
    .RequireAuthenticatedUser()
    .Build();
    options.Filters.Add(new AuthorizeFilter(policy));
});
```

In this example, an Authorization filter is generally applied to all controllers in the application.

Securing endpoints is a critical aspect of safeguarding the resources and functionalities of your ASP. NET Core application. By implementing JWT-based authentication, you not only ensure that each request comes from an authenticated source but also maintain the ability to fine-tune access control with minimal overhead on each transaction. This security measure effectively creates a robust barrier against unauthorized access, providing a clear and manageable way to protect sensitive data and operations.

Using JWTs for securing endpoints offers several advantages:

- **Statelessness and scalability**: Unlike traditional session-based authentication, JWTs are self-contained and include all necessary user information. This statelessness allows your server to validate the token without needing to maintain session information on the server, which is ideal for scaling applications across multiple servers or environments.

- **Flexibility**: JWTs can be easily used across different domains and services, facilitating secure interactions between multiple systems or microservices. This interoperability is particularly beneficial in modern web architectures, which often involve interactions between disparate systems.

- **Fine-grained access control**: By including claims in the JWT, you can implement more granular access control strategies. For instance, you could encode user roles, permissions, or other attributes directly into the token, allowing your application to make authorization decisions based on these claims.

The framework supports best practices such as HTTPS for secure token transmission and provides robust tools for token validation and expiration handling. By adhering to these practices, you significantly reduce the risk of security breaches.

To effectively secure your endpoints, it is crucial to continuously update and refine your authentication and authorization mechanisms in response to evolving security threats. Regular audits, updating cryptographic practices, and adherence to the latest security guidelines are essential steps in maintaining the integrity and security of your application.

In summary, JWT authentication provides a powerful and efficient method for securing endpoints in ASP.NET Core applications. By understanding and implementing this approach, developers can protect their applications from unauthorized access and ensure that their systems are robust, secure, and ready to handle the demands of modern web environments.

In the next section, we will learn how to apply secure data handling and SSL in ASP.NET Core.

Securing data and SSL in ASP.NET Core

Securing data and ensuring secure communications are fundamental aspects of developing a reliable and trustworthy ASP.NET Core application. This section covers best practices for data handling, the application of encryption and secure coding techniques, and the configuration and enforcement of SSL/TLS to protect data in transit.

Ensuring secure data handling practices

Data handling refers to the methods and protocols you use to ensure the integrity and confidentiality of data throughout its life cycle in your application. Secure data handling minimizes the risk of unauthorized access and data breaches. These are the key points:

- **Data validation**: Always validate incoming data to prevent malformed data from causing unintended effects in your application. Use ASP.NET Core's built-in data annotations and validation frameworks to enforce input validation.

- **Data sanitization**: Before processing the data, it's crucial to sanitize it to prevent injection attacks. For example, if you're running SQL commands, use parameterized queries or Entity Framework to avoid SQL injection.

- **Secure data storage**: Encrypt sensitive data before storing it in your database. Consider using column-level encryption for particularly sensitive information such as passwords or personal identifiable information.

- **Least privilege**: Operate with the **principle of least privilege (PoLP)** when accessing data. Ensure that only the parts of your application or users that need access to certain data can obtain it.

Here's an example of an intentional data validation for a user input model:

```
public class UserInputModel
{
    [Required]
    [StringLength(100, MinimumLength = 5)]
    public string Username { get; set; }

    [Required]
    [EmailAddress]
    public string Email { get; set; }

}
```

This example uses data annotations to ensure that the `Username` and `Email` fields meet specific criteria before they're processed by the application. In the next section, we will learn how to apply encryption in ASP.NET Core.

Applying encryption and secure coding techniques

Encryption is a key element in protecting data, making it unreadable without the appropriate decryption key. Secure coding is about developing your application in a way that guards against vulnerabilities, which has the following key elements:

- **Using encryption**: Implement encryption algorithms to protect data at rest and in transit. For sensitive information, use strong encryption standards such as **Advanced Encryption Standard (AES)** with a key size of at least 256 bits.

- **Secure session management**: Use secure methods for session management. Store tokens securely and ensure that they are transmitted only over secure channels.

- **Code reviews and static analysis**: Regularly perform code reviews and use static analysis tools to identify and fix security vulnerabilities.

Here's an example of an implementation for AES encryption in C#:

```
public static string EncryptString(
    string text, string keyString
)
```

```
{
    var key = Encoding.UTF8.GetBytes(keyString);

    using (var aesAlg = Aes.Create())
    {
        using (var encryptor = aesAlg.CreateEncryptor(
            key, aesAlg.IV))
        {
            using (var msEncrypt = new MemoryStream())
            {
                using (var csEncrypt = new CryptoStream(
                    msEncrypt,
                    encryptor,
                    CryptoStreamMode.Write
                ))
                {
                    using (var swEncrypt = new
                        StreamWriter(csEncrypt))
                    {
                        swEncrypt.Write(text);
                    }
                }

                var iv = aesAlg.IV;
                var decryptedContent =
                    msEncrypt.ToArray();
                var result = new byte[iv.Length +
                    decryptedContent.Length];
                Buffer.BlockCopy(iv, 0, result, 0,
                    iv.Length);
                Buffer.BlockCopy(decryptedContent, 0,
                    result, iv.Length,
                    decryptedContent.Length);

                return Convert.ToBase64String(result);
            }
        }
    }
}
```

The provided C# code for implementing AES encryption involves several steps to encrypt a string securely using AES, a widely recognized and robust symmetric encryption algorithm. Here's an explanation of the process:

1. **Key and initialization vector (IV) initialization**: The encryption key is converted from a string to a byte array. AES encryption also uses an IV, which is automatically generated to ensure that the encryption result is unique even if the same data and key are used multiple times.

2. **AES instance creation**: An instance of the AES cryptographic service provider is created. This instance manages all aspects of the encryption process, including the generation of the IV.

3. **Encryptor creation**: Using the AES instance, an `encryptor` object is created. This object is responsible for the actual encryption process, utilizing the provided key and IV.

4. **MemoryStream and CryptoStream setup**: A `MemoryStream` class is used to hold the encrypted data. A `CryptoStream` class is then linked to this `MemoryStream` class. The `CryptoStream` class handles the encryption by writing the data to the `MemoryStream` class through an encryption layer provided by the encryptor.

5. **Writing data for encryption**: The text to be encrypted is written into the `CryptoStream` class using a `StreamWriter` class. As the data is written, the `CryptoStream` class encrypts it before passing it to the `MemoryStream` class.

6. **Output preparation**: After the encryption process is complete, the encrypted data is extracted from the `MemoryStream` class, and along with the IV it is combined into a single-byte array. The IV must be stored along with the encrypted data because it is required for decryption.

7. **Base64 encoding**: The final step involves converting the byte array (which includes the IV and the encrypted data) into a `Base64` string. This encoding is used because it converts binary data into a string format that can be easily stored or transmitted, especially in environments that might not handle binary data well, such as JSON or XML.

This approach to encryption is secure and effective for scenarios where confidentiality of data is paramount, ensuring that the data cannot be read without access to the encryption key and IV.

In the next section, you will learn how to configure and enforce SSL in ASP.NET.

Configuring and enforcing SSL in ASP.NET Core

SSL and its successor, TLS, are cryptographic protocols designed to provide communications security over a computer network. In the context of web applications, **SSL/TLS** encryption ensures that data transmitted between the web server and browser remains private and integral. This section will guide you through configuring and enforcing SSL in ASP.NET Core, detailing essential steps and best practices.

SSL/TLS is crucial for protecting your application from various security threats, including data breaches, eavesdropping, and **man-in-the-middle** (MiTM) attacks. By encrypting data transmitted over the network, SSL/TLS ensures that sensitive information such as passwords, credit card numbers, and personal data are securely exchanged.

ASP.NET Core supports the automatic use of SSL/TLS certificates and can be configured to enforce HTTPS, redirecting all HTTP requests to HTTPS. Here's how to set it up:

1. **HTTPS Redirection Middleware**

   The HTTPS redirection middleware (`UseHttpsRedirection`) automatically redirects HTTP requests to HTTPS. This is one of the simplest and most effective ways to enforce SSL in your application. Here's how to configure it in the `Program.cs` file:

   ```
   var app = builder.Build();

   if (!app.Environment.IsDevelopment())
   {
       app.UseHttpsRedirection();
   }
   ```

   This directive forces the application to always use HTTPS protocol, forcing redirection for all requests.

2. **HTTP Strict Transport Security (HSTS)**

   HSTS is an HTTP header that informs browsers to only use HTTPS to communicate with your server. HSTS helps protect against attacks such as protocol downgrade attacks and cookie hijacking. This is how you can enable HSTS in `Program.cs`:

   ```
   builder.Services.AddHsts(options =>
   {
       options.Preload = true;
       options.IncludeSubDomains = true;
       // Adjust based on your requirements
       options.MaxAge = TimeSpan.FromDays(365);
   });
   ```

> **Note**
>
> It's recommended to enable HSTS in production environments after you are certain that your site will function correctly over HTTPS.

3. **SSL/TLS certificate configuration**

   For SSL/TLS to work, you must have a valid SSL/TLS certificate installed on your server. This can be obtained from a **Certificate Authority** (**CA**). ASP.NET Core can also be configured to use self-signed certificates for development purposes. Here's how to configure Kestrel to use certificates:

   ```
   builder.Services.Configure<KestrelServerOptions>(
       options =>
       {
   ```

```
options.ConfigureHttpsDefaults(httpsOptions =>
    {
        httpsOptions.ServerCertificate =
            LoadCertificate(); // Method to
                               // load your
                               // certificate
    });
});
```

In terms of the use of SSL/TLS configuration, there are a few good practices to follow:

- **Use strong certificates**: Opt for certificates with strong signatures and key exchanges. Avoid outdated protocols such as SSL 3.0 or TLS 1.0.

- **Regularly update certificates**: Keep track of your certificate's expiration dates and renew them before they expire to avoid service interruptions.

- **Use secure cipher suites**: Configure your server to use secure cipher suites to enhance the security of SSL/TLS connections.

- **Monitor and log**: Regularly monitor your SSL/TLS configurations and use logging to detect potential SSL/TLS-related security issues.

By diligently configuring and enforcing SSL/TLS in your ASP.NET Core application, you ensure that all data transmitted between your server and clients is encrypted and secure, maintaining the integrity and confidentiality of sensitive information and building trust with your users.

Summary

Throughout this chapter, we have deeply explored essential concepts and practical implementations of configuration and security within ASP.NET Core. By engaging with these elements, you've equipped yourself with crucial skills to effectively manage application settings and ensure robust security measures. We started with a comprehensive look at the configuration system in ASP.NET Core, demonstrating how to leverage various configuration providers to adapt your application seamlessly across different environments without the need for code changes. This flexibility is vital for maintaining high levels of performance and adaptability in response to different operational requirements and environments.

We then transitioned to discussing the critical aspects of security, focusing on authentication and authorization techniques to protect your applications from unauthorized access. By implementing various authentication schemes, including cookie-based and token-based methods, you learned how to secure user sessions and data transmissions effectively. Additionally, we covered secure data handling practices and the importance of encryption and secure coding techniques, which are fundamental in protecting sensitive data from potential breaches.

Moreover, the chapter detailed the configuration and enforcement of SSL/TLS in ASP.NET Core, ensuring that all data transmitted over the network is encrypted and secure. This step is crucial for defending against various network security threats and for building trust with end users by safeguarding their personal and sensitive data.

By mastering these skills, you are now well prepared to build secure and efficient ASP.NET Core applications that can scale and adapt to meet the demands of modern web environments. These capabilities not only enhance the security and flexibility of your applications but also position you to effectively tackle more advanced topics in web development.

In the next chapter, we will expand upon these foundational skills by exploring Blazor, a cutting-edge framework for building interactive client-side web **user interfaces** (**UIs**) with .NET. This progression into Blazor will introduce you to the powerful capabilities of building robust and dynamic UIs within the ASP.NET Core ecosystem. By integrating server-side logic directly with client-side experiences, you'll learn to create more engaging and responsive applications. This shift will equip you with the tools to seamlessly blend client- and server-side development, preparing you to tackle modern web development challenges effectively.

Get This Book's PDF Version and Exclusive Extras

UNLOCK NOW

Scan the QR code (or go to `packtpub.com/unlock`). Search for this book by name, confirm the edition, and then follow the steps on the page.

Note: Keep your invoice handly. Purchase made directly from packt don't require one.

5

Introduction to Blazor

In this chapter, we start the exploration into web development with Blazor, embarking on a journey to uncover the intricacies of Blazor, a groundbreaking framework that revolutionizes web UI development using the familiar language of C#. This chapter serves as your gateway to mastering the fundamentals of Blazor.

Throughout the upcoming pages, you'll engage in an immersive learning experience designed to equip you with practical skills and insights. We begin by unraveling the essence of Blazor, shedding light on its purpose and potential in the realm of web development. By understanding the core concepts behind Blazor, you'll gain a deeper appreciation for its significance in shaping the future of web applications.

As we progress in this chapter, you will get in touch with hands-on exercises that help you build your very first Blazor **WebAssembly** application. From setting up your development environment to crafting interactive user interfaces, you'll witness firsthand the power and versatility of Blazor in action.

Furthermore, we'll venture into the realm of server-side Blazor, exploring its architecture and advantages over its WebAssembly counterpart. By comprehending the differences between these hosting models, you'll be empowered to make informed decisions when choosing the right approach for your projects.

In addition to hosting models, we'll delve into the heart of Blazor applications: components and data binding. You'll learn how to create reusable components and seamlessly bind data to them, enabling you to construct dynamic and responsive web experiences with ease.

In this chapter, we're going to cover the following main topics:

- What is Blazor?
- Key features of Blazor

By the conclusion of this chapter, you'll emerge with a deep understanding of Blazor and its practical applications in web development. Armed with the ability to create both client-side and server-side Blazor applications, you'll be well-prepared to tackle real-world projects with confidence and efficiency.

Technical requirements

The technical requirements to do all the practices in this chapter are identical to the *Technical requirements* section of *Chapter 1*. Please take a look at that section.

The code files required for you to follow along with this chapter can be found at: `https://github.com/PacktPublishing/Modern-Full-Stack-Web-Development-with-ASP.NET-Core/tree/main/Chapter05`.

What is Blazor?

Blazor is a modern web development framework built by Microsoft that allows developers to build **single-page applications (SPAs)** and standard web applications using **C#, HTML,** and **WebAssembly**. What sets Blazor apart from other frameworks is its unique approach of enabling client-side web development entirely in C#, without requiring any JavaScript. This means that developers can leverage their existing knowledge of C# and **.NET** to create feature-rich web applications, eliminating the need for context-switching between different programming languages.

The significance of Blazor in web development cannot be overstated. Let's look at some of the benefits of using Blazor:

- Traditionally, web development has been dominated by JavaScript frameworks such as Angular, React, and Vue.js. While these frameworks have their strengths, they often require developers to learn new languages and paradigms, leading to increased complexity and potential for errors. Blazor eliminates this friction by allowing developers to use C#, a language that many are already familiar with, for both server-side and client-side development.

- One of the key advantages of Blazor is its ability to share code between the client and server. This is made possible by its integration with the .NET ecosystem, which provides a unified development experience across different platforms. With Blazor, developers can write code once and run it anywhere, whether it's on the client side in the browser or on the server side in a .NET application.

- Furthermore, Blazor promotes code reusability and maintainability through its component-based architecture. Developers can create modular components that encapsulate UI elements and logic, making it easier to manage complex applications. This modular approach also facilitates collaboration among teams, as different developers can work on separate components independently.

- In addition to its technical advantages, Blazor offers practical benefits for businesses and organizations. By enabling developers to leverage their existing skills in C# and .NET, Blazor reduces the learning curve associated with adopting new technologies. This can lead to faster development cycles, lower costs, and increased productivity, ultimately resulting in a more competitive edge in the market.

Overall, Blazor represents an innovation in software development, giving software engineers the possibility of building powerful web applications using familiar tools in the .NET ecosystem. The importance of Blazor is also highlighted by its potential, considering it opens up a vast range of possibilities to build cross-platform applications for desktop, web, and mobile devices in the future, all based on C#, WebAssembly, and HTML.

Blazor's unique approach of using C# for client-side web development

Blazor's unique approach to client-side web development lies in its ability to execute C# code directly in the browser using WebAssembly. **WebAssembly**, or **Wasm** for short, is a binary instruction format that enables running compiled code in web browsers at near-native speeds. This allows Blazor to bring the power and performance of C# to the client side, opening up new possibilities for web development. Here are the key points of the use of C# for client-side development:

- *Use of WebAssembly*: Blazor uses WebAssembly to run .NET code in the browser. When a Blazor application is compiled, the C# and .NET code is translated into WebAssembly instructions, which are then executed by the browser's JavaScript engine. This seamless integration between .NET and WebAssembly enables Blazor to deliver a rich, interactive user experience without relying on traditional client-side technologies like JavaScript.

- *Leverage .NET ecosystem*: One of the key benefits of using C# for client-side development is the ability to leverage the full power of the .NET ecosystem. With Blazor, developers can take advantage of familiar tools and libraries, such as **LINQ**, **Entity Framework**, and **ASP.NET Core**, to build sophisticated web applications. This eliminates the need to learn new languages or frameworks, allowing developers to focus on solving business problems instead of wrestling with technology.

- *Consistency to the development process*: Furthermore, using C# for client-side development brings consistency to the development stack. In traditional web development, developers often have to switch between different languages and frameworks when transitioning from the client to the server. With Blazor, both client-side and server-side code can be written in C#, providing a unified development experience that simplifies code sharing, debugging, and maintenance.

- *Code sharing*: Another advantage of Blazor's approach is its support for code sharing between the client and server. Because both sides of the application are written in C#, developers can easily share code, models, and business logic between the client and server, reducing duplication and ensuring consistency across the application. This promotes a more efficient development workflow and helps to eliminate common sources of bugs and errors.

Summing up, Blazor's unique approach of using C# for client-side web development offers numerous advantages for developers and businesses alike. By leveraging the power and familiarity of the .NET ecosystem, Blazor enables developers to build modern, interactive web applications with ease, while also promoting code reuse, consistency, and maintainability across the entire development stack.

History of Blazor and its evolution

Blazor's journey began in 2017 when Steve Sanderson, a developer at Microsoft, unveiled the experimental project at the NDC Oslo conference. The initial concept behind Blazor was to explore the possibility of running .NET code in the browser using WebAssembly, with the goal of providing a compelling alternative to traditional JavaScript frameworks.

In its early stages, Blazor was purely experimental and lacked many of the features and capabilities that are available today. However, it quickly gained traction within the developer community, thanks to its ambitious vision and potential to revolutionize web development.

Over the next few years, Blazor underwent significant development and refinement, with Microsoft officially announcing Blazor as an experimental project in early 2018. Throughout 2018 and 2019, the Blazor team released several preview versions, each introducing new features and improvements based on community feedback and internal testing.

In April 2019, Microsoft announced the official release of Blazor Server in .NET Core 3.0, marking a major milestone in the project's evolution. Blazor Server introduced a server-side execution model where UI updates are sent to the client over a **SignalR** connection, offering a viable alternative to traditional client-side JavaScript frameworks.

Later that year, in September 2019, Microsoft released Blazor WebAssembly as part of .NET Core 3.1, enabling developers to run .NET code directly in the browser using WebAssembly. This release marked the culmination of years of research and development, bringing Blazor one step closer to its vision of a full-stack web development framework powered by C# and .NET.

Since then, Blazor has continued to gain momentum, with Microsoft investing heavily in its development and adoption. With each new release, Blazor introduces new features, performance improvements, and tooling enhancements, making it an increasingly compelling choice for building modern web applications.

As of the time of writing, Blazor has evolved into a mature and robust framework with a thriving ecosystem of libraries, tools, and resources. It has garnered widespread attention and adoption within the developer community, with many developers and organizations embracing Blazor as their framework of choice for web development.

Looking ahead, the future of Blazor appears bright, with Microsoft committed to its ongoing development and support. With its unique combination of productivity, performance, and flexibility, Blazor is poised to play a significant role in shaping the future of web development for years to come.

Here's a timeline representation of the development of Blazor and its introduction to the .NET ecosystem and its evolution over time:

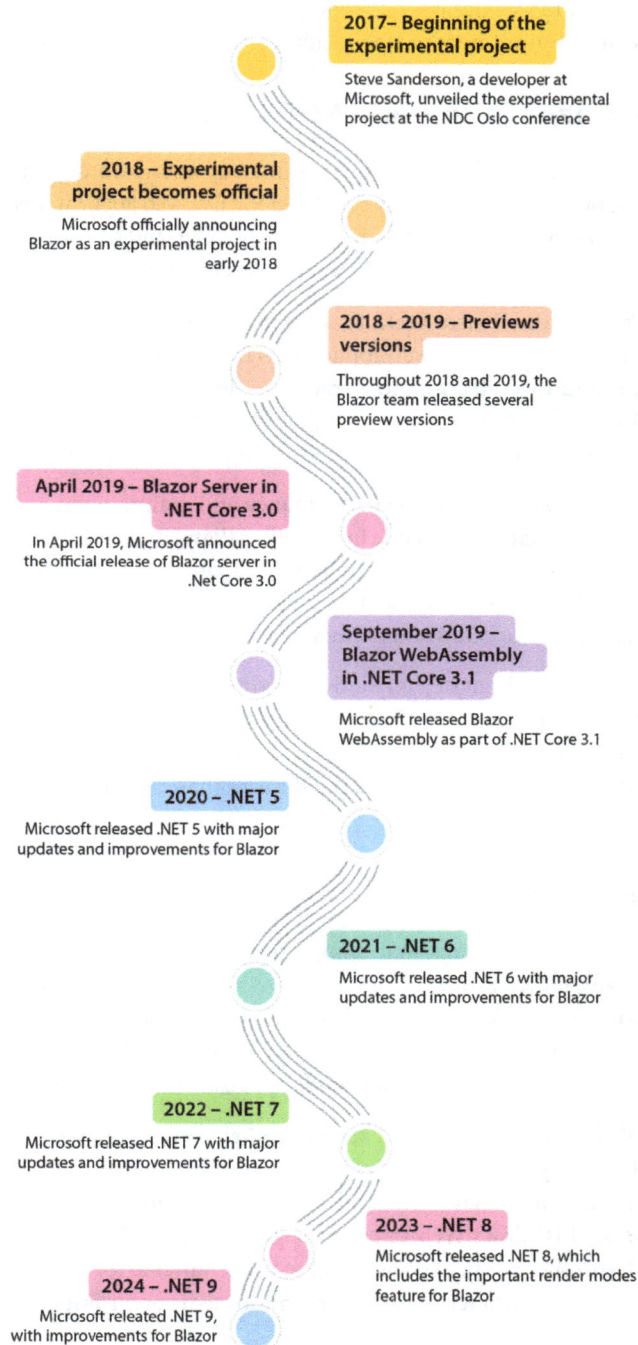

2017– Beginning of the Experimental project

Steve Sanderson, a developer at Microsoft, unveiled the experiemental project at the NDC Oslo conference

2018 – Experimental project becomes official

Microsoft officially announcing Blazor as an experimental project in early 2018

2018 – 2019 – Previews versions

Throughout 2018 and 2019, the Blazor team released several preview versions

April 2019 – Blazor Server in .NET Core 3.0

In April 2019, Microsoft announced the official release of Blazor server in .Net Core 3.0

September 2019 – Blazor WebAssembly in .NET Core 3.1

Microsoft released Blazor WebAssembly as part of .NET Core 3.1

2020 – .NET 5

Microsoft released .NET 5 with major updates and improvements for Blazor

2021 – .NET 6

Microsoft released .NET 6 with major updates and improvements for Blazor

2022 – .NET 7

Microsoft released .NET 7 with major updates and improvements for Blazor

2023 – .NET 8

Microsoft released .NET 8, which includes the important render modes feature for Blazor

2024 – .NET 9

Microsoft releated .NET 9, with improvements for Blazor

Figure 5.1: Blazor timeline

As you can see in *Figure 5.1*, Blazor has been evolving since 2017 with major updates released every year by Microsoft, showing commitment to stabilization and addition of new features.

Significance of Blazor in the ASP.NET Core ecosystem

The motivation behind the creation of Blazor can be summed up in one word: productivity. Microsoft's goal with Blazor is to empower developers to build rich, interactive web applications using the skills and tools they already know and love. By leveraging the power of .NET and C#, Blazor aims to streamline the development process, reduce complexity, and increase developer productivity in web development.

One of the primary problems that Blazor seeks to solve in web development is the fragmentation of technology stacks. Traditionally, building web applications has required developers to juggle multiple languages, frameworks, and tools, leading to a fractured development experience and increased cognitive overhead. With Blazor, Microsoft aims to unify the development stack by enabling developers to use a single language (C#) and framework (.NET) for both client-side and server-side development.

Another problem that Blazor addresses is the performance and maintainability of web applications. By allowing developers to write client-side code in C# rather than JavaScript, Blazor aims to eliminate many of the pain points associated with JavaScript development, such as type safety, tooling support, and debugging. Additionally, Blazor's component-based architecture promotes code reusability and maintainability, making it easier to build and maintain complex web applications over time.

Generally, Blazor represents a significant step forward in web development, offering developers a powerful and productive alternative to traditional JavaScript frameworks. With its seamless integration with the .NET ecosystem and its focus on developer experience, Blazor has the potential to revolutionize the way web applications are built and deployed, making it easier than ever to create modern, interactive experiences for users.

Understanding WebAssembly

WebAssembly (Wasm) is a binary format that allows programming languages to be executed on the client side, more specifically, in web browsers. Introduced as a web standard in 2017, Wasm is designed to complement JavaScript as a low-level, efficient bytecode format that browsers can execute at near-native speeds. In the context of Blazor, WebAssembly plays a crucial role in enabling the execution of .NET code directly in the browser, without the need for plugins or transpilation to JavaScript.

At its core, WebAssembly provides a portable, secure, and efficient execution environment for web applications. Unlike JavaScript, which is a high-level, interpreted language, WebAssembly code is compiled ahead of time into a binary format that can be interpreted and executed by the latest versions of web browsers. This allows WebAssembly applications to achieve performance levels that are comparable to native desktop applications, making them suitable for a wide range of use cases, from games and simulations to productivity tools and multimedia applications.

Here are some of the benefits of using WebAssembly:

- One of the key benefits of using WebAssembly is its ability to execute compiled code in web browsers following high-performance standards. By leveraging low-level optimizations and hardware acceleration features, WebAssembly enables developers to build web applications that deliver exceptional performance and responsiveness, even for computationally intensive tasks.

  This is particularly advantageous for applications that require high performance, such as games, multimedia applications, and scientific simulations.

- Another benefit of WebAssembly is its cross-platform compatibility. Because WebAssembly is supported by the latest versions of browsers for desktop and mobile, including Chrome, Firefox, Safari, and Edge, developers can write code once and run it anywhere, without having to worry about compatibility issues or platform-specific optimizations.

  This allows developers to reach a wider audience with their web applications, regardless of the devices or operating systems their users are using.

- Furthermore, WebAssembly is designed to be secure and sandboxed, ensuring that code running in the browser cannot access sensitive system resources or compromise the user's privacy.

  This makes WebAssembly an ideal choice for running untrusted code, such as third-party libraries or user-generated content, without exposing the underlying system to potential security vulnerabilities.

In summary, WebAssembly is a powerful technology that enables developers to bring high-performance, native-like experiences to the web. By providing a portable, efficient execution environment for compiled code, WebAssembly unlocks new possibilities for building fast, responsive web applications that can run on any device, platform, or browser. In the context of Blazor, WebAssembly serves as the foundation for running .NET code in the browser, allowing developers to harness the full power of C# and .NET for client-side web development.

Blazor hosting models

Blazor offers two distinct hosting models for building web applications: WebAssembly and server-side. Each hosting model has its own unique characteristics, advantages, and use cases, catering to different development scenarios and requirements.

In the **WebAssembly hosting model**, the Blazor application is executed directly in the browser using WebAssembly. When the application is loaded, the browser downloads the compiled .NET assemblies, along with the necessary runtime components, and executes them within a secure sandbox environment. This allows developers to create client-side web applications entirely in C#, without the need for server-side processing or round trips to the server for UI updates.

The **server-side hosting model** uses a constant SignalR connection between the server and the client to update the state of UI components. When the application is loaded in the browser, a connection is established with the server, and the UI updates are streamed to the client as they occur. This allows developers to leverage the full power of the .NET runtime on the server, while still providing a rich, interactive user experience in the browser.

The next sections contain a comparison of both hosting models and suggestions on how to decide which one is the best for specific scenarios.

Architecture

In the WebAssembly model, the entire Blazor application, including the .NET runtime, is downloaded to the client's browser and executed locally. This results in a client-side architecture where the UI logic and rendering are performed in the browser.

Considering this model uses SignalR to apply UI changes based on what happens in the server, this results in a server-centric architecture where the UI logic and rendering are performed on the server.

Performance

Because the entire application is executed in the browser, the WebAssembly model offers better performance for client-side interactions and responsiveness. However, the initial load time may be longer due to the need to download the application and runtime to the client.

The server-side model offers lower latency for UI updates since the processing is performed on the server. However, it may have higher server-side resource usage, especially for applications with a large number of concurrent users.

Use cases

Blazor WebAssembly is well-suited for applications that require rich client-side interactivity, offline support, or the ability to run in environments where server-side processing is limited or unavailable.

Server-side Blazor is ideal for applications that prioritize real-time updates, scalability, or compatibility with existing server-side infrastructure, such as ASP.NET Core middleware or authentication services.

When choosing between Blazor WebAssembly and server-side Blazor for a particular application, several factors should be taken into consideration:

- **Performance requirements**: Evaluate the performance requirements of your application, including factors such as latency, responsiveness, and scalability

- **Network conditions**: Consider the network conditions and bandwidth constraints of your target audience, as well as the potential impact on the initial load time and runtime performance

- **Client-side versus server-side logic**: Determine whether your application requires client-side processing for interactivity or can rely on server-side processing for UI updates

- **Offline support**: Assess whether your application needs to support offline scenarios or can rely on a continuous connection to the server

- **Resource usage**: Consider the server-side resource usage and scalability implications of running Blazor applications on the server, especially for applications with a large number of concurrent users

By carefully weighing these factors and considering the unique requirements of your application, you can choose the hosting model that best aligns with your goals and objectives, ensuring optimal performance, scalability, and user experience.

In the next section, you will have the opportunity to explore, in a hands-on experience, the key features that Blazor has to offer.

Key features of Blazor

Blazor is a feature-rich web development framework that empowers developers to build modern web applications using C# and .NET. Let's dive into some of its key features and capabilities in the subsequent sections.

Component-based architecture

Blazor's component-based architecture is a core feature that allows developers to build reusable, encapsulated UI elements. This architecture based on components makes the development process easier and increases aspects of scalability and flexibility of applications. Components in Blazor are self-contained units of UI and logic, which can be composed to create complex user interfaces. Let's delve deeper into this concept with comprehensive examples and detailed explanations.

Creating a simple component

To understand the basics of a Blazor component, let's start by creating a simple Blazor project using Visual Studio. With Visual Studio open, create a new project using the Blazor Web App project template available by default in Visual Studio. This project template contains two sub-projects: one focused on the server side and another focused on the client side, which contains the `.Client` suffix by default. Go to the server project and, within the `Components` folder, create a `SimpleButton.razor` file, which will become a component that can be reused across the application. Include the following code in the new file:

```
<button @onclick="OnClick">@ButtonText</button>

@code {
    [Parameter] public string ButtonText { get; set; }
    [Parameter] public EventCallback OnClick { get; set; }
}
```

Let's look at this `SimpleButton` component:

- The `ButtonText` parameter allows the button text to be set by the parent component
- The `OnClick` parameter is `EventCallback` that enables the parent component to specify what happens when the button is clicked

This component can be reused in any parent component, providing flexibility and reducing code duplication.

Using the SimpleButton component

Here's how you might use the `SimpleButton` component in a parent component:

```
@page "/parent-simple-button";
<h3>ParentComponentSimpleButton</h3>

<SimpleButton
    ButtonText="Click me" OnClick="ShowMessage"
/>

<p>@Message</p>

@code {
    private string Message;

    private void ShowMessage()
    {
        Message = "Button clicked";
    }
}
```

In this `ParentComponentSimpleButton`, the `SimpleButton` component is used with specific values for `ButtonText` and `OnClick`. When the button is clicked, the `ShowMessage` method is invoked, updating the `message` variable.

Advanced component example – modal dialog

To illustrate a more advanced usage, let's create a modal dialog component that can display any content passed to it. This example includes the full component and its usage in a parent component, as demonstrated in the next example:

```
<div class="modal"
    style="display:@(IsVisible ?
    "block" : "none")">
    <div class="modal-content">
```

```
            <span class="close" @onclick="CloseModal">
                &times;
            </span>
            @ChildContent
        </div>
    </div>

    @code {
        [Parameter] public bool IsVisible { get; set; }
        [Parameter] public EventCallback<bool> OnClose
        {
            get;
            set;
        }
        [Parameter] public RenderFragment ChildContent
        {
            get;
            set;
        }

        private void CloseModal()
        {
            IsVisible = false;
            OnClose.InvokeAsync(IsVisible);
        }
    }
```

The ModalDialog component includes the following:

- An IsVisible parameter to control its visibility

- An OnClose callback to notify the parent component when the modal is closed

- A ChildContent parameter to display any content inside the modal

In the next section, you will understand how you can use the ModalDialog component.

Using the ModalDialog component

ModalDialog can be used across the Blazor application passing the underlying parameters as seen in the following code snippet:

```
@page "/parent-modal"
<button @onclick="ShowModal">Open Modal</button>
<ModalDialog
    IsVisible="@isModalVisible"
```

```
    OnClose="HandleModalClose(false)">
    <b>
        This is content is shown within the
        ModalDialog!!!
    </b>
</ModalDialog>
@code {
    private bool isModalVisible = false;

    private void ShowModal(){
        isModalVisible = true;
    }

    private void HandleModalClose(bool isVisible){
        isModalVisible = isVisible;
    }
}
```

In ParentModalComponent, the modal dialog is controlled by the isModalVisible variable. The ShowModal method sets this variable to true, displaying the modal. The HandleModalClose method updates the visibility state when the modal is closed.

In the next section, you will understand how you can specify nested components in your Blazor application.

Nested components and parameter cascading

Blazor components can be nested, and parameters can be cascaded from parent to child components. This allows for more complex UI structures and shared data contexts. To check this functionality, create a child component with a cascading parameter, as seen in the following code snippet:

```
<p>Shared Data: @SharedData</p>

@code {
    [CascadingParameter]
    public string SharedData { get; set; }
}
```

You can pass data to the child component using CascadingValue, as seen in the following example:

```
@page "/cascading"

<CascadingValue Value="sharedData">
    <ChildComponent />
</CascadingValue>
```

```
@code {
    private string sharedData = "This is shared data";
}
```

In this example, CascadingValue is used to pass sharedData from CascadingParent to ChildComponent. The CascadingParameter attribute in ChildComponent binds this value, allowing it to be used within the component.

Styling components

Components can also include CSS to style their elements. Here's an example of a styled component:

```
<button class="styled-button" @onclick="OnClick">
    @ButtonText
</button>

<style>
    .styled-button {
        background-color: #4CAF50; /* Green */
        border: none;
        color: white;
        padding: 15px 32px;
        text-align: center;
        text-decoration: none;
        display: inline-block;
        font-size: 16px;
        margin: 4px 2px;
        cursor: pointer;
    }
</style>

@code {
    [Parameter] public string ButtonText { get; set; }
    [Parameter] public EventCallback OnClick { get; set; }
```

The StyledButton component includes embedded CSS to style the button. This approach ensures that the component's styles are self-contained and do not affect other parts of the application.

Lifecycle methods

Blazor components have **lifecycle methods** that allow developers to hook into the component's initialization, rendering, and disposal processes. Here's an example:

```
@page "/lifecycle"
<p>Lifecycle Demo</p>
```

```
@code {
    protected override void OnInitialized()
    {
        Console.WriteLine("OnInitialized called");
    }

    protected override void OnParametersSet()
    {
        Console.WriteLine("OnParametersSet called");
    }

    protected override void OnAfterRender(bool firstRender)
    {
        Console.WriteLine("OnAfterRender called");
    }

    public void Dispose()
    {
        Console.WriteLine("Component disposed");
    }
}
```

In LifecycleComponent, several lifecycle methods are overridden to log messages during the component's lifecycle. These messages are displayed in the browser console. This demonstrates how developers can manage component behavior at different stages of its existence.

Component communication

Components can communicate with each other through parameters and events. Here's an example of parent-child communication. Here's the code for a child component:

```
<button @onclick="IncrementCount">Increment</button>
@code {
    [Parameter] public EventCallback<int> OnCountChanged
    {
        get;
        set;
    }
    private int count;

    private async Task IncrementCount()
    {
        count++;
```

```
        await OnCountChanged.InvokeAsync(count);
    }
```

}In this case, the component has a parameter called `OnCountChanged` that can be used by a parent component to override its behavior. In the following example, the parent component triggers an event in the child component:

```
@page "/parent-counter"
<ChildCounter OnCountChanged="HandleCountChanged" />

<p>Current Count: @count</p>

@code {
    private int count;

    private void HandleCountChanged(int newCount)
    {
        count = newCount;
    }
}
```

In this example, `ParentCounter` listens for count changes from `ChildCounter` through the `OnCountChanged` event. `ChildCounter` increments its count and notifies the parent component, which updates its own state accordingly. This component can be used as many times as you want in multiple components, with no limitation, including the possibility of referencing the `<ChildCounter>` component multiple times on the same page.

Blazor's component-based architecture is a powerful feature that promotes reusability, maintainability, and scalability in web applications. By encapsulating the UI and logic into modular components, developers can build complex applications more efficiently. The ability to nest components, cascade parameters, and manage lifecycle events provides a robust framework for developing interactive and dynamic web interfaces.

In the next section, you will understand how data binding works for Blazor applications.

Data binding

Data binding in Blazor is a powerful feature that connects the UI to the data model, allowing for seamless interaction and real-time updates. Blazor supports both one-way and two-way data binding, making it easy to keep the UI and data model in sync. This section will provide a detailed overview of data binding concepts, with comprehensive code samples and explanations.

One-way data binding

One-way data binding in Blazor is used to display data from the model in the UI. Changes to the data in the model will automatically be reflected in the UI. Here's an example:

```
@page "/one-way"
<h3>One-Way Data Binding</h3>
<p>@message</p>

@code {
    private string message = "Hello, Blazor!";
}
```

In this example, the `message` field is bound to the paragraph element. Any changes to the `message` variable in the code will be automatically reflected in the UI.

Two-way data binding

Two-way data binding allows for the synchronization of data between the UI and the data model. This is particularly useful for form inputs where the user can enter data that needs to be reflected in the model. Here's an example:

```
@page "/two-way"
<h3>Two-Way Data Binding</h3>
<input @bind="name" placeholder="Enter your name" />
<p>Hello, @name!</p>

@code {
    private string name;
}
```

In this example, the `input` element is bound to the `name` variable. Any changes in the `input` field will update the `name` variable, and changes to the `name` variable will update the `input` field. The next section will show a more advanced example of data binding for you.

Advanced example – contact form with validation

Let's create a more complex example involving a contact form with data binding and validation. The following steps will demonstrate how to bind form fields to a model and use data annotations for validation:

1. We can start creating the `Contact` class:

    ```
    namespace PacktFullStackDevelopmentDotNet
    {
    ```

```
using System.ComponentModel.DataAnnotations;

public class Contact
{
    [Required(ErrorMessage = "Name is required")]
    [StringLength(
        100,
        ErrorMessage = "Name is too long"
    )]
    public string Name { get; set; }

    [Required(ErrorMessage = "Email is required")]
    [EmailAddress(
        ErrorMessage = "Invalid email address"
    )]
    public string Email { get; set; }

    [StringLength(
        500,
        ErrorMessage = "Message is too long"
    )]
    public string Message { get; set; }
}

}
```

This class defines the Name, Email, and Message properties with data annotations for validation. The [Required] attribute ensures that the field is not left empty, and [StringLength] and [EmailAddress] provide further validation rules.

2. The next step is to create the ContactForm component, as seen in the next example:

```
@page "/contact"
<h3>Contact Form</h3>

<EditForm
    Model="@contact"
    OnValidSubmit="HandleValidSubmit">
    <DataAnnotationsValidator />
    <ValidationSummary />

    <div class="form-group">
        <label>Name:</label>
        <InputText
```

```
                @bind-Value="contact.Name"
                class="form-control" />
        <ValidationMessage
                For="@(() => contact.Name)" />
    </div>

    <div class="form-group">
        <label>Email:</label>
        <InputText
                @bind-Value="contact.Email"
                class="form-control" />
        <ValidationMessage
                For="@(() => contact.Email)" />
    </div>

    <div class="form-group">
        <label>Message:</label>
        <InputTextArea
                @bind-Value="contact.Message"
                class="form-control" />
        <ValidationMessage
                For="@(() => contact.Message)" />
    </div>

    <button type="submit" class="btn btn-primary">
        Submit
    </button>
</EditForm>
@code {
    private Contact contact = new Contact();

    [Parameter] public EventCallback<Contact>
        OnContactAdded { get; set; }

    private async Task HandleValidSubmit()
    {
        await OnContactAdded.InvokeAsync(contact);
        Console.WriteLine("Name: {0}", contact.Name);
        contact = new Contact(); // Reset form
    }
}
```

Here's a detailed explanation of the Contact Form elements:

- EditForm is used to create a form bound to the contact model. The Model attribute specifies the data model, and OnValidSubmit is the event handler for form submission.

- DataAnnotationsValidator and ValidationSummary are used to provide validation feedback.

- The InputText and InputTextArea components are bound to the respective properties of the contact model using the @bind-Value attribute.

- The ValidationMessage components are used to display validation messages for individual fields.

The HandleValidSubmit method is called when the form is successfully validated. It outputs the form data to the console (in a real application, this is where you would handle the form data, such as sending it to a server).

In the next section, you will explore how component interaction works in Blazor.

Component interaction

Blazor components can also interact with each other, passing data and events between them. Here's an example where a parent component interacts with a child component to display a list of contacts:

1. Create a ContactList component with the code demonstrated in the following example:

```
@page "/contactlist"
<h3>Contact List</h3>
<ContactForm OnContactAdded="AddContact" />
<ul>
    @foreach (var contact in contacts)
    {
        <li>
            @contact.Name (@contact.Email):
            @contact.Message
        </li>
    }
</ul>

@code {
    private List<Contact> contacts =
        new List<Contact>();

    private void AddContact(Contact newContact)
    {
        contacts.Add(newContact);
```

```
        }
    }
```

The `ContactList` component contains a reference to the `ContactForm` component to allow users to add new data, and the component also contains logic to display a list of contacts that were added.

2. Adapt the `ContactForm` component with `EventCallback` within the `@code` block:

```
@code {
    private Contact contact = new Contact();

    [Parameter] public EventCallback<Contact>
        OnContactAdded { get; set; }

    private async Task HandleValidSubmit()
    {
        await OnContactAdded.InvokeAsync(contact);
        contact = new Contact(); // Reset form
    }
}
```

Let's break down the preceding code:

*   The `OnContactAdded` parameter is `EventCallback<Contact>` that allows the parent component to handle the event when a new contact is added.

*   The `HandleValidSubmit` method invokes the `OnContactAdded` callback, passing the new contact as an argument, and then resets the form.

*   The `ContactForm` component is used to capture new contacts. When a contact is added, the `AddContact` method is called, which adds the contact to the contacts list. The list of contacts is displayed in an unordered list, with each contact's name, email, and message.

By using these examples, you can see how Blazor's component-based architecture and data-binding capabilities enable the creation of rich, interactive web applications. These concepts, along with the ability to easily handle form validation and component interaction, make Blazor a powerful framework for modern web development.

In the next section, you will understand the basics of routing for Blazor applications.

Routing

Routing is a fundamental aspect of any web application, allowing navigation between different pages or views. In Blazor, routing is handled in a straightforward yet powerful manner, enabling developers to define and manage navigation in a declarative style. This section will provide a detailed exploration of routing in Blazor, including the setup, configuration, advanced routing scenarios, and practical code examples.

Blazor uses the `Router` component to manage routing. The `Router` component is typically defined in the `App.razor` file as follows:

```
<Router AppAssembly="@typeof(App).Assembly">
    <Found Context="routeData">
        <RouteView
            RouteData="routeData"
            DefaultLayout="typeof(MainLayout)" />
        <FocusOnNavigate
            RouteData="routeData"
            Selector="h1" />
    </Found>
    <NotFound>
        <LayoutView Layout="typeof(MainLayout)">
            <p>Sorry, there's nothing at this address.</p>
        </LayoutView>
    </NotFound>
</Router>
```

Here's a brief explanation of each part of the `Router` configuration in the `App.razor` file:

- The `Router` component uses the `AppAssembly` attribute to specify the assembly that contains the routing information
- The `Found` block defines the layout and view to display when a route is matched
- The `NotFound` block defines what to display when no routes are matched

Routes are defined using the `@page` directive in Razor components. Here's an example of defining a few basic routes:

```
@page "/"
<PageTitle>Home</PageTitle>
<h1>Hello, world!</h1>
```

Welcome to your new app.In the preceding code, each component has a `@page` directive that specifies the URL template for the route. When the user navigates to the corresponding URL, the appropriate component is rendered.

Blazor also supports **parameterized routes**, allowing data to be passed through the URL, as seen in the following example:

```
@page "/product/{id:int}"

<h3>Product Details</h3>
<p>Product ID: @Id</p>
```

```
@code {
    [Parameter] public int Id { get; set; }
}
```

In this example, the {id:int} segment in the @page directive specifies a route parameter named id of the int type.

The Id property in the @code block is decorated with the [Parameter] attribute to bind the route parameter.

Additionally, you can define **optional parameters** in routes, as seen in the following code:

```
@page "/user/{name?}"

<h3>User Profile</h3>
<p>Name: @Name</p>

@code {
    [Parameter] public string Name { get; set; } = "Guest";
}
```

The {name?} segment in the @page directive specifies an optional parameter named name. If no name is provided in the URL, the Name property defaults to "Guest".

Furthermore, you can work with **catch-all parameters** to capture the remainder of the URL, as seen in the following example:

```
@page "/search/{*query}"

<h3>Search</h3>
<p>Query: @Query</p>

@code {
    [Parameter] public string Query { get; set; }
}
```

The {*query} segment captures the entire remainder of the URL after /search/ into the Query parameter.

In Blazor, you can also use the following configurations for routes:

- **Route constraints**: Blazor allows developers to enforce specific rules on route parameters, ensuring they meet certain criteria such as type and value ranges. This feature enhances the robustness of the application by validating parameters directly within the route definition.

  For example, parameters can be constrained to integers, minimum values, or even custom patterns, providing a controlled and predictable routing experience.

- **Navigation and navigation with state**: Blazor facilitates both declarative and programmatic navigation using the `NavigationManager` service. This service enables seamless navigation between different pages within a Blazor application.

  Additionally, Blazor supports passing state information during navigation, allowing complex data to be transferred across components. This feature is particularly useful for maintaining context or transferring data that doesn't fit neatly into URL parameters, enhancing the interactivity and functionality of applications.

- **Handling navigation events and nested routing**: Blazor's navigation events allow developers to execute custom logic during navigation changes, such as logging or UI updates, by handling the `LocationChanged` event. This capability ensures dynamic and responsive user experiences.

  Nested routing, another powerful feature, permits the creation of complex layouts by defining sub-routes within parent components. This hierarchical routing structure enables modular design, allowing components to manage their own routing contexts independently, thereby improving code organization and maintainability.

As you can see, Blazor offers a lot of possibilities to configure different types of routes, allowing the development of many features that are based on friendly URLs to improve the user experience.

Summary

In this chapter, we embarked on a journey to explore Blazor, a revolutionary framework that enables web development using C#. We started by understanding what Blazor is and its significance in the realm of web development. This included learning about its unique approach of using C# for client-side development via WebAssembly, which allows developers to leverage their existing C# and .NET skills to build feature-rich web applications. The chapter highlighted the historical evolution of Blazor, tracing its development from an experimental project to a mature and robust framework widely adopted by the developer community.

Throughout the chapter, we engaged in practical exercises that guided us through building Blazor WebAssembly applications. We set up our development environment, created interactive UIs, and explored the differences between Blazor WebAssembly and server-side Blazor. This hands-on approach provided a comprehensive understanding of Blazor's capabilities, including its component-based architecture and data-binding features. We learned how to create reusable components, bind data seamlessly, and implement form validation using data annotations, thus enhancing our ability to develop dynamic and responsive web experiences.

The skills and knowledge gained in this chapter are invaluable for modern web development, as they enable developers to create efficient and maintainable web applications using familiar tools.

In the next chapter, we will build on this foundation by delving into advanced Blazor topics such as state management, authentication, and integrating Blazor with other web technologies. This progression will equip you with the expertise to tackle more complex projects and leverage Blazor's full potential in your web development endeavors.

Get This Book's PDF Version and Exclusive Extras

UNLOCK NOW

Scan the QR code (or go to `packtpub.com/unlock`). Search for this book by name, confirm the edition, and then follow the steps on the page.

Note: Keep your invoice handly. Purchase made directly from packt don't require one.

Part 2:
Advanced Integration and
Application Development

In this part, you will build upon the foundational skills of ASP.NET Core and begin integrating advanced frontend technologies. This part focuses on the seamless integration of modern JavaScript frameworks—Vue.js, React, and Angular—with ASP.NET Core, providing a hands-on approach to creating full-stack applications. You will explore the core principles of these frameworks, understand their differences, and learn how to effectively integrate them into your projects. Additionally, you will dive into advanced Blazor components and RESTful service development, further enhancing your ability to build scalable and maintainable applications.

This part includes the following chapters:

- *Chapter 6, Advanced Blazor Development*
- *Chapter 7, Advanced Component Architecture in Blazor*
- *Chapter 8, RESTful Services with ASP.NET Core – Part 1*
- *Chapter 9, RESTful Services with ASP.NET Core – Part 2*
- *Chapter 10, Introduction to JavaScript Frameworks*
- *Chapter 11, Exploring Vue.js and Comparing Frameworks*
- *Chapter 12, Integrating Vue.js with ASP.NET Core*
- *Chapter 13, Integrating Angular with ASP.NET Core*
- *Chapter 14, Integrating React with ASP.NET Core*

6
Advanced Blazor Development

Welcome to this chapter, where we delve into the advanced aspects of Blazor, a powerful framework for building interactive web UIs with C#. This chapter is designed to take your Blazor skills to the next level, focusing on the intricacies and sophisticated features that will enable you to create more complex and efficient Blazor applications.

In this chapter, we will learn how to develop advanced Blazor components, gaining a deeper understanding of their architecture and lifecycle. We will explore event handling in Blazor, a crucial aspect of creating responsive and dynamic user interfaces. Additionally, we will cover state management techniques that ensure your applications run smoothly and efficiently, maintaining a consistent state across different components and user interactions.

By mastering these advanced Blazor concepts, you will be able to build robust, high-performing applications that provide a seamless user experience. Whether you are developing enterprise-level solutions or innovative personal projects, the skills and knowledge you gain here will be invaluable.

In this chapter, we're going to cover the following main topics:

- Exploring Blazor components and lifecycle
- Deep diving into event handling in Blazor
- State management in Blazor applications

Prepare to enhance your Blazor expertise and unlock new possibilities in your web development endeavors.

Technical requirements

You can refer to the *Technical requirements* section of *Chapter 1* for all the necessary installations.

The code files required for you to follow along with this chapter can be found at:

```
https://github.com/PacktPublishing/Modern-Full-Stack-Web-Development-
with-ASP.NET-Core/tree/main/Chapter06
```

Exploring Blazor components and lifecycle

Blazor components are the building blocks of Blazor applications, enabling developers to create reusable, modular pieces of the UI. In this section, we will explore advanced concepts related to Blazor components, including component parameters, cascading values, and lifecycle methods. By understanding these advanced features, you can build more dynamic and efficient applications. We will start by reviewing aspects of how component parameters work in Blazor.

Component parameters

Component parameters allow you to pass data from a parent component to a child component. In .NET 9, defining component parameters is straightforward using the [Parameter] attribute. Here's a more complex example demonstrating nested components and parameter binding, as seen in the next three code snippets, starting with the following code:

```
<h3>@Title</h3>
<p>@Description</p>
<GrandChildComponent
    @bind-Title="Title"
    OnTitleChanged="OnGrandChildComponentEvent">
</GrandChildComponent>

@code {
    [Parameter]
    public string Title { get; set; }
    [Parameter]
    public string Description { get; set; }
    [Parameter]
    public EventCallback<string> OnTitleChanged { get; set; }

    private async Task OnGrandChildComponentEvent(string
        value)
    {
        await OnTitleChanged.InvokeAsync(value);
    }
}
```

The preceding code defines a Blazor component, which consists of HTML markup and C# code. The <h3>@Title</h3> line displays the value of the Title parameter in an <h3> HTML element. The @Title syntax is used to bind the value of the Title property from the C# code section to the HTML.

The <p>@Description</p> line displays the value of the Description parameter in a <p> (paragraph) HTML element. The @Description syntax binds the value of the Description property from the C# code section to the HTML.

The <GrandChildComponent @bind-Title="Title"
OnTitleChanged="OnGrandChildComponentEvent" /> line renders another Blazor
component named GrandChildComponent. The @bind-Title="Title" attribute binds the
Title property of GrandChildComponent to the Title property of the current component.
This means that any changes to the Title property in either component will automatically update
the other. The OnTitleChanged="OnGrandChildComponentEvent" attribute assigns an
event callback named OnGrandChildComponentEvent to the OnTitleChanged parameter
of GrandChildComponent.

In the C# code section, the [Parameter] attribute is used to define properties that can receive values
from a parent component. The Title property is a parameter that holds a string value representing
the title, and the Description property is a parameter that holds a string value representing the
description. The EventCallback<string> OnTitleChanged property is an event callback
parameter that allows the parent component to be notified when the title changes.

The OnGrandChildComponentEvent method is a private asynchronous method that takes a
string value as a parameter. This method is invoked when the OnTitleChanged event is triggered
in GrandChildComponent. Inside the method, OnTitleChanged.InvokeAsync(value)
is called to notify the parent component of the new title value asynchronously.

The next step to understand how component parameters work is to create GrandChildComponent,
as seen in the following code:

```
<input @bind="Title" />
<button @onclick="HandleClick">Update Title</button>

@code {
    [Parameter]
    public string Title { get; set; }
    [Parameter]
    public EventCallback<string> OnTitleChanged { get; set; }
    private void HandleClick()
    {
        OnTitleChanged.InvokeAsync(Title);
    }
}
```

The preceding code defines a Blazor component with HTML markup and C# code that allows for
two-way binding and event handling. The <input @bind="Title" /> line creates an HTML
input element that is bound to the Title property. The @bind directive sets up two-way data
binding between the input element and the Title property. This means that any changes made
to the input field will update the Title property in the C# code, and any changes to the Title
property will update the value in the input field.

The `<button @onclick="HandleClick">Update Title</button>` line creates a button that, when clicked, triggers the `HandleClick` method defined in the C# code. The `@onclick` directive binds the button's click event to the `HandleClick` method.

In the C# code section, the `[Parameter]` attribute is used to define properties that can receive values from a parent component. The `Title` property is a parameter that holds a string value representing the title.

The `EventCallback<string> OnTitleChanged` property is an event callback parameter that allows the parent component to be notified when the title changes.

The `HandleClick` method is a private method that gets triggered when the button is clicked. Inside this method, `OnTitleChanged.InvokeAsync(Title)` is called to notify the parent component of the new title value. This allows the parent component to react to changes in the `Title` property, facilitating communication between the child and parent components.

The next step is to create `ChildComponent`, as demonstrated in the following code:

```
<h3>@Title</h3>
<p>@Description</p>
<GrandChildComponent
    @bind-Title="Title"
    OnTitleChanged="OnGrandChildComponentEvent">
</GrandChildComponent>

@code {
    [Parameter]
    public string Title { get; set; }
    [Parameter]
    public string Description { get; set; }
    [Parameter]
    public EventCallback<string> OnTitleChanged { get; set; }

    private async Task OnGrandChildComponentEvent(
        string value
    )
    {
        await OnTitleChanged.InvokeAsync(value);
    }
}
```

The preceding code defines a Blazor component that includes HTML markup and C# code. It demonstrates how to bind parameters and handle events between nested components. The `<h3>@Title</h3>` line displays the value of the `Title` parameter inside an `<h3>` HTML element. The `@Title` syntax is used to bind the value of the `Title` property from the C# code section to the HTML markup.

The `<p>@Description</p>` line displays the value of the `Description` parameter inside a `<p>` (paragraph) HTML element. The `@Description` syntax binds the value of the `Description` property from the C# code section to the HTML markup.

The `<GrandChildComponent @bind-Title="Title" OnTitleChanged="OnGrandChildComponentEvent" />` line renders another Blazor component named `GrandChildComponent`. The `@bind-Title="Title"` attribute binds the `Title` property of `GrandChildComponent` to the `Title` property of the current component. This enables two-way data binding, so any changes to the `Title` property in either component will automatically update the other. The `OnTitleChanged="OnGrandChildComponentEvent"` attribute assigns an event callback named `OnGrandChildComponentEvent` to the `OnTitleChanged` parameter of `GrandChildComponent`.

In the C# code section, the `[Parameter]` attribute is used to define properties that can receive values from a parent component. The `Title` property is a parameter that holds a string value representing the title. The `Description` property is a parameter that holds a string value representing the description.

The `EventCallback<string> OnTitleChanged` property is an event callback parameter that allows the parent component to be notified when the title changes. This facilitates communication from the child component back to the parent component.

The `OnGrandChildComponentEvent` method is a private asynchronous method that takes a string value as a parameter. This method is invoked when the `OnTitleChanged` event is triggered in `GrandChildComponent`. Inside the method, `OnTitleChanged.InvokeAsync(value)` is called to notify the parent component of the new `Title` value asynchronously. This allows the parent component to react to changes in the `Title` property, facilitating communication between the child and parent components.

In this example, involving the three components altogether, `ParentComponent` passes parameters to `ChildComponent`, which, in turn, passes a bound parameter and event callback to `GrandChildComponent`. This setup enables nested components to communicate and share data effectively.

In the next section, we will cover the lifecycle methods of Blazor components to manage initialization, state changes, and clean-up tasks.

Lifecycle methods

Understanding the lifecycle methods of Blazor components is crucial for managing initialization, state changes, and clean-up tasks. The key lifecycle methods include `OnInitialized`, `OnParametersSet`, and `OnAfterRender`. Here's a more complex example demonstrating these methods with asynchronous operations and multiple lifecycle methods:

```
<h3>Lifecycle Component</h3>
<p>Data: @data</p>
```

```
<p>Status: @status</p>

@code {
    private string data;
    private string status;
    private Timer _timer;

    protected override async Task OnInitializedAsync()
    {
        status = "Initializing...";
        await LoadDataAsync();
        status = "Initialized";
    }

    protected override void OnParametersSet()
    {
        status = "Parameters Set";
        StartTimer();
    }

    protected override async Task OnAfterRenderAsync(
        bool firstRender
    )
    {
        if (firstRender)
        {
            status = "First Render Completed";
            await PerformPostRenderOperationsAsync();
        }
    }

    private async Task LoadDataAsync()
    {
        await Task.Delay(2000); // Simulate data loading
        data = "Sample Data Loaded";
    }

    private async Task PerformPostRenderOperationsAsync()
    {
        await Task.Delay(1000); // Simulate additional
                                // operations
        status = "Post Render Operations Completed";
```

```
    }

    private void StartTimer()
    {
        _timer = new Timer(Callback, null, 0, 1000);
    }

    private void Callback(object state)
    {
        status = $"Timer tick at {DateTime.Now}";
        InvokeAsync(StateHasChanged);
    }

    public void Dispose()
    {
        _timer?.Dispose();
    }
}
```

The preceding code defines a Blazor component that demonstrates the use of lifecycle methods, asynchronous operations, and periodic updates using a timer.

The <h3>Lifecycle Component</h3> line displays a heading for the component. The <p>Data: @data</p> line displays the value of the data variable inside a <p> (paragraph) HTML element. The @data syntax binds the value of the data property from the C# code section to the HTML markup. The <p>Status: @status</p> line displays the value of the status variable inside a <p> HTML element. The @status syntax binds the value of the status property from the C# code section to the HTML markup. The data and status variables store information that will be displayed in the component. The _timer variable is used to create a timer for periodic updates. The OnInitializedAsync method is called when the component is first initialized. It sets the status to "Initializing...", calls the LoadDataAsync method to load data asynchronously, and then sets the status to "Initialized". The OnParametersSet method is called whenever the component's parameters are set or updated. It sets the status to "Parameters Set" and calls the StartTimer method to start a timer.

A similar operation happens in the other methods. If you run the Blazor application and load the underlying component, you are going to see the effect of how this configuration works and will understand the exact order the methods run. The sequence runs as follows:

1. OnInitializedAsync: This method is called first when the component is initialized. It sets the initial status, loads data asynchronously, and then updates the status to "Initialized".

2. OnParametersSet: This method is called after OnInitializedAsync. It sets the status to "Parameters Set" and starts the timer by calling StartTimer.

3. `OnAfterRenderAsync`: This method is called after the component has been rendered. If this is the first render (`firstRender` is `true`), it sets the status to `"First Render Completed"` and performs post-render operations asynchronously.

4. `Timer Callback (Callback)`: The timer's `Callback` method is called periodically (every 1 second, as set by `StartTimer`). It updates the status with the current time and calls `InvokeAsync(StateHasChanged)` to trigger a re-render of the component.

5. `Dispose`: This method is called when the component is destroyed. It disposes of the timer to release resources.

Therefore, this Blazor component demonstrates the use of lifecycle methods to manage initialization, parameter setting, and post-render operations. It also shows how to use a timer to perform periodic updates and how to handle asynchronous operations within the component's lifecycle. By understanding these concepts, you can create more complex and interactive Blazor applications.

In the next section, we will cover how to enable communication between components.

Enabling component communication

Component communication is essential for building complex applications where different components need to interact. You can achieve this through event callbacks and shared services. To demonstrate communication between components, we need to create a few components first. Here's a more complex example using event callbacks and shared state via a service, starting from `ParentComponent`:

```
@page "/second-parent"
@inject SharedStateService SharedState

<h3>Parent component</h3>
<SiblingComponent
    OnButtonClick="HandleButtonClick">
</ SiblingComponent >

@code {
    private void HandleButtonClick()
    {
        SharedState.Message =
            "Button clicked in child component";
        StateHasChanged();
    }
}
```

In this component, a `SharedStateService` class is used to share the state between components. Here's the code for the `SharedStateService` class:

```
namespace Chapter6
{
    public class SharedStateService
    {
        public string Message { get; set; }
    }
}
```

This `SharedStateService` class must be registered in the `Program.cs` file among other services you might have. You can use the following for this example:

```
var builder = WebApplication.CreateBuilder(args);

builder.Services.AddRazorComponents()
    .AddInteractiveServerComponents()
    .AddInteractiveWebAssemblyComponents();

builder.Services.AddScoped<SharedStateService>();
```

The last component is `SiblingComponent`, which has the following code:

```
@inject SharedStateService SharedState
<h3>Shared Message: @SharedState.Message</h3>

@code {
    protected override void OnInitialized()
    {
        SharedState.Message = "Initial Message";
    }
}
```

In this example, considering the three components, `ParentComponent` uses an event callback to update the shared state via a service (`SharedStateService`), allowing multiple components to share and react to the same state changes. `SiblingComponent` displays the shared message, demonstrating how different components can communicate through a shared state.

In the next section, we will cover advanced component features such as `RenderFragment` and **templated components**.

Advanced component features

Blazor also provides advanced features such as RenderFragment and templated components, which enable more flexible and reusable UI patterns. Here's a more complex example using RenderFragment and a templated component with multiple template parameters:

```
@typeparam TItem
<h3>Render Fragment Component</h3>
@ChildContent(Item)
<FooterContent />

@code {
    [Parameter]
    public TItem Item { get; set; }
    [Parameter]
    public RenderFragment<TItem> ChildContent { get; set; }
    [Parameter]
    public RenderFragment FooterContent { get; set; }
}
```

In a parent component, RenderFragmentComponent is referenced, as seen in the following code:

```
<RenderFragmentComponent TItem="string" Item="sampleItem">
    <ChildContent>
        <div>This is a templated content: @context</div>
    </ChildContent>
    </RenderFragmentComponent>
@code {
    private string sampleItem { get; set; } =
        "Sample Item";
}
```

In this example, RenderFragmentComponent allows the parent component to pass templated content using RenderFragment, with the ability to pass contextual data to the templated content and define a separate footer content.

By understanding and utilizing these advanced Blazor component features, you can build more robust and dynamic web applications. The examples provided illustrate how to implement these features effectively using .NET 9, ensuring your Blazor applications are up to date with the latest advancements in the framework.

In this section, we explored details on component lifecycles and how we can leverage component communication in different ways, by rendering child components as fragments and establishing parameters that can be used to share state and data between components.

In the next section, we will deep dive into the details of **event handling** in Blazor applications.

Deep diving into event handling in Blazor

Event handling is a crucial aspect of building interactive and dynamic web applications. Blazor provides a seamless way to handle events, allowing you to respond to user actions such as button clicks, form submissions, and other interactions. In this section, we will explore various event-handling techniques in Blazor, including standard event handling, custom events, and event callbacks. We will also discuss how to manage event propagation and prevent default behavior, starting from the standard behavior.

Standard event handling

Blazor allows us to handle standard HTML events using the @on{event} directive. Common events include @onclick, @oninput, and @onchange. Here's a basic example of a ClickEventComponent component:

```
<h3>Click Event Component</h3>
<p>Button clicked @count times</p>
<button @onclick="IncrementCount">Click me</button>

@code {
    private int count = 0;

    private void IncrementCount()
    {
        count++;
    }
}
```

In this example, the @onclick directive is used to bind the IncrementCount method to the button's click event. Each time the button is clicked, the IncrementCount method increments the count variable, and the UI is automatically updated.

In the next section, we will cover how to create and handle custom events in Blazor components.

Creating custom events

Blazor also supports custom events, which can be useful for more complex interactions. Here's an example of creating and handling a custom event:

```
<ChildComponent OnCustomEvent="HandleCustomEvent">

</ChildComponent>
@code {
```

```
    private void HandleCustomEvent(string message)
    {
        Console.WriteLine($"Custom event received with
            message {message}");
    }
}
```

To configure a custom event with interactions between parent and child components, you can create a child component, as seen in the following code:

```
<button @onclick="TriggerCustomEvent">
    Trigger Custom Event
</button>
@code {
    [Parameter]
    public EventCallback<string> OnCustomEvent { get; set; }

    private async Task TriggerCustomEvent()
    {
        await OnCustomEvent.InvokeAsync("Hello from Child
            Component");
    }
}
```

In this example, `ChildComponent` defines an `OnCustomEvent` custom event using `EventCallback<string>`. The `TriggerCustomEvent` method is called when the button is clicked, invoking the custom event with a message. The parent component handles this event using the `HandleCustomEvent` method.

In the next section, we will cover how to manage event propagation and prevent default behavior in Blazor components.

Managing event propagation and preventing default behavior

Blazor allows us to manage event propagation and prevent default behavior using the `@on{event}:stopPropagation` and `@on{event}:preventDefault` directives. Here's an example:

```
<h3>Prevent Default Component</h3>
<form @onsubmit="HandleSubmit" @onsubmit:preventDefault>
    <input @bind="inputValue" />
    <button type="submit">Submit</button>
</form>
```

```
@code {
    private string inputValue;

    private void HandleSubmit()
    {
        Console.WriteLine("Form submission prevented. Input
            value: " + inputValue);
    }
}
```

In this example, the @onsubmit:preventDefault directive is used to prevent the default form submission behavior. Instead, the HandleSubmit method is called when the form is submitted. This method logs the input value to the console, demonstrating how you can control form submissions in Blazor.

Blazor also allows you to stop event propagation to parent elements using the @on{event}:stopPropagation directive. Here is an example:

```
<h3>Stop Propagation Component</h3>
<div @onclick="HandleDivClick">
    <button
        @onclick="HandleButtonClick"
        @onclick:stopPropagation>
        Click me
    </button>
</div>

@code {
    private void HandleDivClick()
    {
        Console.WriteLine("Div clicked");
    }

    private void HandleButtonClick()
    {
        Console.WriteLine("Button clicked");
    }
}
```

In this example, the @onclick:stopPropagation directive prevents the click event on the button from propagating to the parent div element. As a result, when the button is clicked, only the HandleButtonClick method is called, and the HandleDivClick method is not triggered.

In the next section, we will cover how to handle multiple events in Blazor components.

Handling multiple events

Blazor components can handle multiple events, either by binding multiple handlers to different events or by handling multiple events within a single method. Here's an example:

```
<h3>Multiple Events Component</h3>
<input
    @oninput="HandleInput"
    @onfocus="HandleFocus"
    @onblur="HandleBlur" />
<p>@message</p>

@code {
    private string message;

    private void HandleInput(ChangeEventArgs e)
    {
        message = "Input changed: " + e.Value;
    }
    private void HandleFocus()
    {
        message = "Input focused";
    }

    private void HandleBlur()
    {
        message = "Input lost focus";
    }
}
```

In this example, the <input> element handles multiple events: @oninput, @onfocus, and @onblur. Each event is handled by a corresponding method in the C# code. The HandleInput method updates the message variable with the new input value, the HandleFocus method updates the message when the input is focused, and the HandleBlur method updates the message when the input loses focus. This demonstrates how you can handle multiple events in Blazor components.

In the next section, we will cover how to implement debouncing and throttling for events in Blazor components.

Debouncing and throttling events

Debouncing and **throttling** are techniques to control the rate at which event handlers are called. This is especially useful for events that fire frequently, such as `oninput`. Here's an example of debouncing an `oninput` event:

```
<h3>Debounce Component</h3>
<input @oninput="HandleInput" />
<p>@debouncedValue</p>

@code {
    private Timer _debounceTimer;
    private string debouncedValue;

    private void HandleInput(ChangeEventArgs e)
    {
        _debounceTimer?.Dispose();
        _debounceTimer = new Timer(
            DebounceCallback,
            e.Value,
            300,
            Timeout.Infinite
        );
    }

    private void DebounceCallback(object state)
    {
        debouncedValue = (string)state;
        InvokeAsync(StateHasChanged);
    }
}
```

In the example, the HTML markup includes an input element (`<input @oninput="HandleInput" />`) where the `oninput` event is bound to a method called `HandleInput`. This means that every time a user types something into the input field, the `HandleInput` method is invoked. Additionally, there is a paragraph element (`<p>@debouncedValue</p>`) that displays the value of the `debouncedValue` variable, which represents the debounced result after the user stops typing for a certain period (300 milliseconds in this example).

Inside the code block defined by the `@code` directive, two private variables are declared: `_debounceTimer` of the `Timer` type, and `debouncedValue` of the `string` type. `_debounceTimer` is used to manage the delay between event triggers. The `HandleInput` method takes `ChangeEventArgs` as a parameter, which provides access to the new input value. When `HandleInput` is called, it first disposes of any existing timer to clear the previous debounce delay.

Then, it initializes a new `Timer` instance, which schedules a callback to the `DebounceCallback` method after a delay of 300 milliseconds. The `Timeout.Infinite` parameter ensures that the timer only runs once.

The `DebounceCallback` method is the actual debounced function that gets called after the delay. It takes an object parameter named `state`, which contains the value passed from the `HandleInput` method. This method assigns the debounced value (`debouncedValue`) to the input received and then calls `InvokeAsync(StateHasChanged)` to notify the Blazor framework that the component needs to be re-rendered. This approach ensures that the UI is updated only after the user has stopped typing for 300 milliseconds, reducing unnecessary updates and improving performance.

In the next section, we will go into more detail on state management in Blazor applications.

State management in Blazor applications

State management is a critical aspect of building robust and efficient Blazor applications. It involves managing the state of various components and ensuring that the UI reflects changes in state accurately and efficiently. In this section, we will explore different state management techniques in Blazor, including component state, cascading values, dependency injection, local storage, and the use of state containers. By understanding these techniques, you can build more responsive and maintainable Blazor applications.

Each Blazor component can manage its own state using local variables and properties. This state is maintained as long as the component is alive. Here's an example that is usually given by the default project template in Visual Studio:

```
<h3>
    Counter component
</h3>
<p>
    Current count: @CurrentCount
</p>
<button onclick="IncrementCount">Increment</button>

@code{
    private int CurrentCount = 0;

    private void IncrementCount(){
        CurrentCount++;
    }
}
```

In this example, `CounterComponent` manages its own state with the `currentCount` variable. Each time the button is clicked, the `IncrementCount` method is called, which updates the state and causes the UI to re-render.

In the next section, we will cover how to share state across multiple components using cascading values.

Cascading values

Cascading values and parameters allow you to share state across multiple components without explicitly passing them through every intermediate component. Here's an example that modifies the `App.razor` file:

```
<CascadingValue Value="theme">
    <MainLayout />
</CascadingValue>

@code {
    private string theme = "dark";
}
```

In the following, you can see an example of configuring a cascading parameter in the `MainLayout` component:

```
@inherits LayoutComponentBase

<div class="page">
    <div>Current theme: @Theme</div>
    <div class="sidebar">
        <NavMenu />
    </div>

    <main>
        <article class="content px-4">
            @Body
        </article>
    </main>
</div>

@code{
    [CascadingParameter]
    public string Theme {get;set;}
}
```

In this example, the App component provides a cascading value theme to all its descendants, including MainLayout and ChildComponent. The MainLayout component accesses this value using the CascadingParameter attribute.

In the next section, we will cover how to manage state using dependency injection in Blazor.

Dependency injection

Dependency injection (**DI**) is a powerful pattern for managing state and dependencies in Blazor applications. You can register services that manage state and inject them into your components. Here's an example:

```
public class CounterService
{
    public int Count { get; private set; }

    public void IncrementCount()
    {
        Count++;
    }
}
```

In the previous code, CounterService is defined to be injected later in another example. This is only a standard counter that increments a number after an action is made.

In the following, you can see how to register CounterService in the Program.cs file:

```
builder.Services.AddRazorComponents()
    .AddInteractiveServerComponents()
    .AddInteractiveWebAssemblyComponents();

builder.Services.AddScoped<CounterService>();
```

In this case, CounterService is registered as a service as AddScoped, which means that the service has a lifecycle scoped to the context of a request.

Use the counter service via DI in components, as shown in the following code:

```
@page "/counter-component"
@inject CounterService CounterService
@rendermode InteractiveServer

<h3>Counter Component</h3>
<p>Current count: @CounterService.Count</p>
<button @onclick="CounterService.IncrementCount">
    Increment
</button>
```

In this example, `CounterService` manages the state of the counter. The service is registered in the `Program.cs` file and then injected into `CounterComponent`. This approach allows for a shared state across multiple components and better separation of concerns.

In the next section, we will cover how to persist state using local storage in Blazor applications.

Local storage

Local storage can be used to persist state across browser sessions. Blazor provides libraries such as `Blazored.LocalStorage` to make working with local storage easy. Here's an example:

```
@page "/localstorage"
@using Blazored.LocalStorage
@inject ILocalStorageService LocalStorage

<h3>Local Storage Component</h3>
<p>Stored value: @storedValue</p>
<button @onclick="SaveToLocalStorage">Save</button>
<button @onclick="LoadFromLocalStorage">Load</button>

@code {
    private string storedValue;

    private async Task SaveToLocalStorage()
    {
        await LocalStorage.SetItemAsync(
            "myValue",
            "Hello, Blazor!"
        );
    }

    private async Task LoadFromLocalStorage()
    {
        storedValue = await
            LocalStorage.GetItemAsync<string>("myValue");
    }
}
```

In this example, `ILocalStorageService` is injected into the component. The `SaveToLocalStorage` method saves a value to local storage, and the `LoadFromLocalStorage` method retrieves it. This allows the state to persist even if the user closes and reopens the browser.

Remember, you have to register the service in the `Program.cs` file, as seen in the following code:

```
builder.Services.AddRazorComponents()
    .AddInteractiveServerComponents()
```

```
        .AddInteractiveWebAssemblyComponents();

builder.Services.AddScoped<CounterService>();

builder.Services.AddBlazoredLocalStorage();
```

In the next section, we will cover how to manage state using state containers in Blazor.

State containers

State containers are used to manage state in a centralized place and make it accessible to any component. This is particularly useful for managing complex state or sharing state between deeply nested components.

First, let's define the StateContainer class. This class will hold the shared state and provide mechanisms to notify components when the state changes, as shown in the following code:

```
namespace Chapter6
{
    public class StateContainer
    {
        public string Property { get; set; }
        public event Action OnChange;

        public void SetProperty(string value)
        {
            Property = value;
            NotifyStateChanged();
        }

        private void NotifyStateChanged() =>
            OnChange?.Invoke();
    }

}
```

In this example, the StateContainer class has Property that holds the state. The SetProperty method updates this property and invokes the OnChange event to notify subscribers about the state change. The NotifyStateChanged method triggers the event.

Next, register the StateContainer service in the DI container so that it can be injected into components, as seen in the following code:

```
builder.Services.AddScoped<CounterService>();
```

```
builder.Services.AddBlazoredLocalStorage();

builder.Services.AddScoped<StateContainer>();
```

This registration ensures that `StateContainer` is available for DI throughout the Blazor application.

Now, let's create `ParentComponent` that uses the `StateContainer` service to manage its state, as shown in the following code:

```
@page "/parent"
@inject StateContainer StateContainer

<h3>Parent Component</h3>
<p>Shared property: @StateContainer.Property</p>
<button @onclick="ChangeProperty">Change Property</button>
<ChildComponent />

@code {
    private void ChangeProperty()
    {
        StateContainer.SetProperty("New Value from
            Parent");
    }
}
```

In `ParentComponent`, the `StateContainer` service is injected and used to display and modify the shared property. The `ChangeProperty` method updates the shared property using the `SetProperty` method of `StateContainer`.

Finally, create `ChildComponent` that also uses the `StateContainer` service to access the shared state, as seen in the following code:

```
@inject StateContainer StateContainer

<h3>Child Component</h3>
<p>Shared property: @StateContainer.Property</p>

@code {
    protected override void OnInitialized()
    {
        StateContainer.OnChange += StateHasChanged;
    }

    public void Dispose()
    {
```

```
            StateContainer.OnChange -= StateHasChanged;
    }
}
```

In ChildComponent, the StateContainer service is injected to access the shared property. The OnInitialized method subscribes to the OnChange event of StateContainer, and the Dispose method unsubscribes from the event when the component is disposed of. This ensures that the component updates its UI whenever the shared state changes.

By using state containers in Blazor, you can manage shared state in a centralized manner, making it easier to maintain and update state across multiple components. This pattern is particularly useful for complex state management scenarios and helps in building more responsive and maintainable Blazor applications. The examples provided illustrate how to define a state container, register it with DI, and use it in both parent and child components to share and react to state changes.

Summary

In this chapter, we delved into the advanced aspects of Blazor development, enhancing our understanding of component architecture, lifecycle methods, event handling, and state management. We learned how to develop complex Blazor components, manage their lifecycles, and implement efficient event-handling techniques to create interactive and dynamic web applications.

By understanding the lifecycle methods, such as OnInitialized, OnParametersSet, and OnAfterRender, we can effectively manage component initialization, state changes, and clean-up tasks. These lifecycle methods are crucial for ensuring that components behave as expected throughout their lifespan, providing a solid foundation for building robust applications. Additionally, we covered how to handle events in Blazor, from simple button clicks to more complex custom events and event callbacks. This knowledge allows us to create responsive and interactive user interfaces that react seamlessly to user interactions.

We explored state management strategies in Blazor, including using local component state, cascading values, DI, local storage, and state containers. These techniques are crucial for building responsive and maintainable applications, allowing for better control and sharing of state across different components. Managing state effectively ensures that our applications remain consistent and reliable, even as they grow in complexity. Using cascading values, we can share state across multiple components without needing to pass data through each component layer. DI allows us to manage services and state in a centralized manner, making our applications more modular and easier to test. Leveraging local storage ensures that the application state can persist across sessions, providing a better user experience. State containers help in managing complex state scenarios by providing a centralized store that any component can access and update.

These skills and lessons are invaluable for any Blazor developer, enabling the creation of robust, high-performing applications that meet various business needs and user expectations. By mastering these advanced techniques, you are well-prepared to tackle more complex Blazor projects, ensuring your applications are both efficient and maintainable.

In the next chapter, we will build upon these advanced concepts by diving into Blazor's advanced component architecture. We will explore routing and navigation, nested components, and JavaScript interoperability to create more complex and interactive user interfaces. This progression will ensure you are well-equipped to handle sophisticated Blazor application scenarios, taking your development skills to the next level.

7

Advanced Component
Architecture in Blazor

Blazor, as a modern web framework, provides a powerful platform for building interactive and dynamic web applications using C#. In this chapter, we will delve into the advanced aspects of Blazor's component architecture, focusing on concepts that will enable you to create more sophisticated and high-performing applications. This chapter is designed to build on the foundational knowledge you have gained in the previous chapters, introducing new techniques and features to enhance your Blazor applications.

We will start by exploring advanced component architecture, where you will learn how to create and manage dynamic components, compose complex UIs from simpler ones, and efficiently handle parameter binding. Next, we will cover advanced routing and navigation, including defining routes with parameters. Understanding these concepts will allow you to build more flexible and scalable applications.

Additionally, we will understand how to integrate JavaScript with Blazor, enabling you to leverage existing JavaScript libraries and APIs to enhance your applications. This section will cover invoking JavaScript functions from Blazor, handling JavaScript events, and ensuring secure and isolated JavaScript interactions.

Finally, we will learn about the new render modes available in Blazor since .NET 9, including static rendering, interactive rendering, and auto rendering. These render modes will allow you to optimize the performance and user experience of your applications by choosing the most appropriate rendering strategy for each scenario.

By the end of this chapter, you will be equipped with the skills to build complex, interactive, and high-performing Blazor applications. You will be able to implement advanced routing, leverage JavaScript for enhanced functionality, and optimize your applications with the new render modes.

In this chapter, we're going to cover the following main topics:

- Exploring advanced component architecture
- Routing and navigation in Blazor
- Implementing JavaScript interoperability in Blazor
- Introducing new render modes in Blazor (.NET 9)

Technical requirements

You can refer to the *Technical requirements* section of *Chapter 1* for all the necessary installations.

The code files required for you to follow along with this chapter can be found at: `https://github.com/PacktPublishing/Modern-Full-Stack-Web-Development-with-ASP.NET-Core/tree/main/Chapter07`.

Exploring advanced component architecture

In this section, we will explore advanced concepts of Blazor's component architecture that will enable us to create more dynamic and sophisticated applications. These concepts include dynamic components, component composition, and advanced parameter binding. By mastering these techniques, you will be able to build more maintainable, reusable, and complex Blazor applications.

Dynamic components

Dynamic components allow you to render components at runtime based on specific conditions or user interactions. This provides flexibility in how components are displayed and interacted with in your application.

Here's an example of how to create and render dynamic components:

1. Create a new Razor component file named `FirstComponent.razor`, as seen in the following code:

```
@code {
    [Parameter] public string Title { get; set; }
}

<div>
    <h4>@Title</h4>
    <p>This is the first component.</p>
</div>
```

2. Similar to the previous component, create another Razor component file named SecondComponent.razor, as seen in the following code:

```
@code {
    [Parameter] public string Title { get; set; }
}

<div>
    <h4>@Title</h4>
    <p>This is the second component.</p>
</div>
```

3. Considering the first two components are already created, here's how to create and render dynamic components in the following code:

```
@page "/dynamic-components"
@using Microsoft.AspNetCore.Components
@rendermode InteractiveServer

<h3>Dynamic Components</h3>

<select @onchange="OnComponentSelectionChanged">
    <option value="">Select a component</option>
    <option value="FirstComponent">
        First Component
    </option>
    <option value="SecondComponent">
        Second Component
    </option>
</select>

@if (selectedComponentType != null)
{
    <DynamicComponent
        Type="@selectedComponentType"
        Parameters="@(new Dictionary<string, object>
        {
            { "Title", "Dynamic Title" }
        })"
    />
}
else
{
    <p>Please select a component to render.</p>
}
```

-

```
@code {
    private Type? selectedComponentType;

    private void OnComponentSelectionChanged(
        ChangeEventArgs e)
    {
        var componentName = e.Value?.ToString();
        selectedComponentType = componentName switch
        {
            "FirstComponent" =>
                typeof(FirstComponent),
            "SecondComponent" =>
                typeof(SecondComponent),
            _ => null
        };
    }
}
```

In this example, we use a drop-down menu to dynamically select and render a component at runtime. The DynamicComponent element is used to render the component type specified by the selectedComponentType variable. When a user selects an option from the dropdown, the OnComponentSelectionChanged method updates selectedComponentType based on the user's choice. This approach allows for flexible and dynamic UI rendering, enabling the application to display different components based on user input or the current state of the application. This technique is particularly useful for scenarios where the UI needs to adapt to varying conditions or user interactions, enhancing the interactivity and responsiveness of the application.

Dynamic components are particularly useful in scenarios where the application needs to render different UI elements based on user actions, application state, or other runtime conditions.

In the next section, we will see how to compose complex components from simpler ones to promote code reuse and modular design.

Component composition

Component composition is the practice of building complex components by combining simpler, reusable components. This promotes code reuse and modular design, making your applications easier to maintain and extend.

In the following code, you can see an example of composing a more complex component from simpler components:

```
@page "/component-composition"

<h3>Component Composition</h3>

<Card Title="Card Title" Subtitle="Card Subtitle">
    <p>This is the content of the card.</p>
</Card>

@code {
    [Parameter] public string Title { get; set; }
    [Parameter] public string Subtitle { get; set; }
    [Parameter] public RenderFragment ChildContent
    {
        get;
        set;
    }
}
```

Next, create the `Card` component, as in the following code:

```
<div class="card">
    <div class="card-header">
        <h4>@Title</h4>
        <h6>@Subtitle</h6>
    </div>
    <div class="card-body">
        @ChildContent
    </div>
</div>
```

In this example, we define a `Card` component that takes the `Title`, `Subtitle`, and `ChildContent` parameters. The `ChildContent` parameter allows us to pass in any additional content to be rendered within the card. This modular approach enables us to build complex UIs by composing smaller, reusable components.

The `Card` component can be used to create various card elements in the application, each with different content but consistent styling and structure.

Here's another example where we compose a list of `Card` components dynamically in the following code:

```
@page "/card-list"

<h3>Card List</h3>

@foreach (var card in cards)
{
    <Card Title="@card.Title" Subtitle="@card.Subtitle">
        <p>@card.Content</p>
    </Card>
}

@code {
    private List<CardModel> cards = new List<CardModel>
    {
        new CardModel
        {
            Title = "Card 1",
            Subtitle = "Subtitle 1",
            Content = "Content for card 1"
        },
        new CardModel
        {
            Title = "Card 2",
            Subtitle = "Subtitle 2",
            Content = "Content for card 2"
        },
        new CardModel
        {
            Title = "Card 3",
            Subtitle = "Subtitle 3",
            Content = "Content for card 3"
        }
    };

    private class CardModel
    {
        public string Title { get; set; }
        public string Subtitle { get; set; }
        public string Content { get; set; }
    }
}
```

In this example, we define a list of `CardModel` objects and render a `Card` component for each item in the list. This demonstrates how component composition and dynamic rendering can be combined to create complex and dynamic UIs.

In the next section, we will see how to implement advanced parameter binding to pass complex data types and manage parameter updates efficiently.

Advanced parameter binding

Advanced parameter binding allows you to pass complex data types and handle parameter updates efficiently. This is crucial for building dynamic and interactive applications where the component state needs to be managed carefully.

Here's an example of binding complex data types to components:

```
@page "/advanced-parameter-binding"

<h3>Advanced Parameter Binding</h3>

<UserProfile User="user" />

@code {
    private User user = new User
    {
        Name = "John Doe",
        Age = 30,
        Address = new Address
        {
            Street = "123 Main St",
            City = "Anytown",
            State = "CA"
        }
    };
}
```

Here's the `UserProfile` component code:

```
@code {
    [Parameter] public User User { get; set; }
}

<div>
    <h4>User Profile</h4>
    <p>Name: @User.Name</p>
    <p>Age: @User.Age</p>
```

```
    <p>
        Address: @User.Address.Street,
        @User.Address.City,
        @User.Address.State
    </p>
</div>
```

In this example, we bind a complex User object to the UserProfile component. This allows the UserProfile component to display detailed information about the user, including nested properties, such as the Address. This approach ensures that your components can handle rich data models effectively.

Advanced parameter binding also involves handling parameter updates efficiently. Let's extend the previous example to include a form that allows the editing of the user's details. Include in your project the component represented in the following code:

```
@page "/edit-user"

<h3>Edit User</h3>
<EditForm Model="user" OnValidSubmit="HandleValidSubmit"
FormName="UserForm">
    <DataAnnotationsValidator />
    <ValidationSummary />

    <div>
        <label>Name: </label>
        <InputText @bind-Value="user.Name" />
    </div>
    <div>
        <label>Age: </label>
        <InputNumber @bind-Value="user.Age" />
    </div>
    <div>
        <label>Street: </label>
        <InputText @bind-Value="user.Address.Street" />
    </div>
    <div>
        <label>City: </label>
        <InputText @bind-Value="user.Address.City" />
    </div>
    <div>
        <label>State: </label>
        <InputText @bind-Value="user.Address.State" />
```

```
    </div>
    <button type="submit">Save</button>
</EditForm>

<UserProfile User="user" />

@code {
    private User user = new User
    {
        Name = "John Doe",
        Age = 30,
        Address = new Address
        {
            Street = "123 Main St",
            City = "Anytown",
            State = "CA"
        }
    };

    private void HandleValidSubmit()
    {
        Console.WriteLine("User details saved
            successfully.");
    }
}
```

In this example, we use EditForm to allow the user to edit their details. The form is bound to the user object, and updates to the form fields are reflected in the user object. When the form is submitted, the HandleValidSubmit method is called to save the user details.

Advanced parameter binding, combined with forms and validation, provides a robust mechanism for handling complex data models and user interactions in Blazor applications.

In the next section, you will see how to implement routing and navigation in Blazor, which is essential for building **single-page applications (SPAs)** with seamless user experiences.

Routing and navigation in Blazor

In this section, we will delve into advanced routing and navigation techniques in Blazor. While basic routing involves defining simple routes and parameters, advanced routing covers more complex scenarios, such as nested routing, route constraints, and dynamic routing. By mastering these advanced techniques, you can create more sophisticated and user-friendly SPAs.

Route constraints

Route constraints allow you to enforce specific rules on route parameters, ensuring they meet certain criteria, such as type or value ranges. This enhances the robustness and reliability of your application by validating routes directly.

Here's an example of route constraints in the following code:

```
@page "/orders/{orderId:int:min(1)}"

<h3>Order Details</h3>

@if (orderId > 0)
{
    <p>Displaying details for order ID: @orderId</p>
}
else
{
    <p>Invalid order ID.</p>
}

@code {
    [Parameter] public int orderId { get; set; }
}
```

In this example, the `orderId` parameter is constrained to be an integer with a minimum value of 1. This ensures that only valid order IDs can be passed to the Order Details page.

In the next section, you will learn how to work with dynamic routes.

Dynamic routing

Dynamic routing enables you to define routes dynamically at runtime. This is useful for applications that need to generate routes based on data or user input. Here's an example of dynamic routing in the following code:

```
@page "/dynamic-routes"
@rendermode InteractiveServer

@inject NavigationManager NavigationManager

<h3>Dynamic Routes</h3>
<input @bind="dynamicRoute" placeholder="Enter a route" />
<button @onclick="NavigateToRoute">Go</button>

@code {
```

```
    private string dynamicRoute;

    private void NavigateToRoute()
    {
        NavigationManager.NavigateTo($"/{dynamicRoute}");
    }
}
```

By using the @inject directive, you inject the NavigationManager service into your component. The NavigateToRoute method then uses NavigationManager to navigate to the route specified in the dynamicRoute variable. With these changes, your component will correctly navigate to the dynamically entered route when the button is clicked.

In the next section, we will understand how to combine JavaScript and Blazor in your enterprise applications.

Implementing JavaScript interoperability in Blazor

Blazor is a powerful framework for building interactive web applications using C# and .NET. One of its standout features is the ability to interoperate with JavaScript, allowing developers to leverage existing JavaScript libraries and frameworks within their Blazor applications. This capability ensures that developers can use the best tool for the job, whether it's C# for most of the application logic or JavaScript for specific client-side interactions. This section provides an in-depth look at JS interop in Blazor, including how to call JavaScript from Blazor and vice versa.

JS interop in Blazor allows Blazor components to call JavaScript functions and JavaScript functions to call Blazor methods. This feature bridges the gap between the .NET world and the JavaScript ecosystem, enabling the use of existing JavaScript libraries and leveraging the power of both languages within a single application.

Calling JavaScript from Blazor

To call JavaScript functions from Blazor, you need to use the IJSRuntime service. This service provides methods to invoke JavaScript functions from .NET code. For instance, if you want to call a JavaScript function that displays an alert message, you can define the function in a .js file or within a <script> tag in your HTML. In your Blazor component, you inject the IJSRuntime service and use it to call the JavaScript function. Here's an example of how to do this:

```
@page "/js-interop-first-example"
@inject IJSRuntime JSRuntime
@rendermode InteractiveServer

<h3>Javascript Interop Example</h3>
```

```
<button @onclick="ShowAlert">Show Alert</button>

<script>
  function ShowAlert(message){
    alert(message);
  }
</script>
@code {
    private async Task ShowAlert()
    {
        await JSRuntime.InvokeVoidAsync(
            "showAlert",
            "Hello from Blazor"
        );
    }
}
```

In this example, the ShowAlert method calls the showAlert JavaScript function, passing a message as an argument. The InvokeVoidAsync method is used when the JavaScript function does not return a value. If the function returns a value, you can use InvokeAsync<T>, where T is the type of the returned value.

Calling Blazor methods from JavaScript

You can also call Blazor methods from JavaScript. This is useful for scenarios where a JavaScript library needs to notify Blazor of certain events or state changes. To achieve this, you define a .NET method in your Blazor component and make it accessible to JavaScript using the DotNetObjectReference class. Here's how you can do it:

```
@page "/js-interop-second-example"
@inject IJSRuntime JSRuntime
@rendermode InteractiveServer

<h3>JavaScript Interop Example</h3>
<button @onclick="InvokeJsFunction">
    Invoke JS Function
</button>
<script>
    function callBlazorMethod(dotNetObject)
    {
        dotNetObject.invokeMethodAsync('BlazorMethod');
    }
</script>
```

```
@code {
    private DotNetObjectReference<JSInteropExample> objRef;

    protected override void OnInitialized()
    {
        objRef = DotNetObjectReference.Create(
            new JSInteropExample()
        );
    }

    private async Task InvokeJsFunction()
    {
        await JSRuntime.InvokeVoidAsync(
            "callBlazorMethod",
            objRef
        );
    }

    public void Dispose()
    {
        objRef?.Dispose();
    }
}

@code{
    private class JSInteropExample
    {
        [JSInvokable]
        public void BlazorMethod()
        {
            Console.WriteLine("Blazor method called from
                JavaScript");
        }
    }
}
```

In this example, the BlazorMethod method in the Blazor component is decorated with the [JSInvokable] attribute, making it callable from JavaScript.

The callBlazorMethod JavaScript function invokes the Blazor method using the dotNetObject. invokeMethodAsync function. In the next section, we will understand how to pass parameters and get returning values.

Handling parameters and return values

Blazor JS interop supports passing parameters and returning values between JavaScript and .NET. When invoking JavaScript functions from .NET, you can pass multiple parameters, and similarly, JavaScript functions can pass parameters to .NET methods. For example, if you have a JavaScript function that adds two numbers and returns the result, you can define it as follows:

```
<script>
    function addNumbers(a, b) {
        return a + b;
    }
</script>
```

You can call this function from your Blazor component and handle the returned value, as seen in the following code:

```
@page "/js-interop-parameters-return-values"
@inject IJSRuntime JSRuntime
@rendermode InteractiveServer

<h3>JavaScript Interop Example</h3>
<button @onclick="AddNumbers">Add Numbers</button>

<script>
    function addNumbers(a, b) {
        return a + b;
    }
</script>

@code {
    private async Task AddNumbers()
    {
        int result = await JSRuntime.InvokeAsync<int>(
            "addNumbers",
            10,
            18
        );
        Console.WriteLine($"Result from JS: {result}");
    }
}
```

In this example, the AddNumbers method in Blazor calls the addNumbers JavaScript function, passing two integers as parameters and receiving the result. In the next section, we will learn how to use JavaScript libraries integrated with Blazor.

Using JavaScript libraries

Blazor's JS interop allows you to utilize existing JavaScript libraries within your Blazor applications. This can be particularly useful for adding rich UI components or leveraging functionality that is not natively available in Blazor. For example, to use a date picker library, you would first include the JavaScript library in your project, either by referencing it in your HTML file or installing it via a package manager such as npm. Then, you can call the library's functions from Blazor using JS interop. Here's how you can initialize a date picker on an input element:

```
<script>
    function initializeDatePicker(elementId) {
        $('#' + elementId).datepicker();
    }
</script>
```

In your Blazor component, you can initialize the date picker as follows:

```
@page "/js-interop-datepicker"
@inject IJSRuntime JSRuntime
@rendermode InteractiveServer

<h3>JavaScript Interop Example</h3>
<input id="datePicker" />
<button @onclick="InitializeDatePicker">
    Initialize Date Picker
</button>

<script>
    function initializeDatePicker(elementId) {
        $('#' + elementId).datepicker();
        $('#' + elementId).focus();
    }
</script>

@code {
    private async Task InitializeDatePicker()
    {
        await JSRuntime.InvokeVoidAsync(
            "initializeDatePicker",
            "datePicker"
        );
    }
}
```

In this example, a date picker library is initialized on an input element when the button is clicked, demonstrating how you can integrate third-party JavaScript libraries into your Blazor applications.

JS interop in Blazor is a powerful feature that enables developers to blend the strengths of both .NET and JavaScript within a single application. By understanding how to call JavaScript from Blazor and vice versa, you can leverage existing JavaScript libraries, create rich interactive experiences, and extend the capabilities of your Blazor applications. This interoperability ensures that you can take advantage of the best tools and frameworks available, creating robust and dynamic web applications.

In the next section, we will get to know the new render modes for Blazor, a new feature introduced in .NET 9.

Introducing new render modes in Blazor (.NET 9)

With the release of .NET 9, Blazor has introduced new render modes that significantly enhance the flexibility and performance of Blazor applications. These new render modes provide developers with more control over how components are rendered, whether on the server or the client, allowing for more sophisticated and responsive web applications. This section will delve into the new render modes in Blazor, explore their benefits, and provide detailed code examples to illustrate their use.

Introduction to render modes

Render modes in Blazor determine how and where components are rendered. In previous versions, Blazor primarily offered two models: **Blazor Server** and **Blazor WebAssembly** (**Wasm**). Blazor Server renders components on the server and updates the UI via SignalR, while Blazor Wasm runs the application entirely in the browser. .NET 9 introduces new render modes that combine the strengths of these approaches, enabling hybrid rendering strategies.

Blazor WebAssembly (Wasm) and Blazor Server – a recap

Before diving into the new render modes, it's essential to understand the basics of Blazor Wasm and Blazor Server:

- **Blazor Wasm**: It runs the application entirely in the client's browser using Wasm. It provides a rich interactive experience with offline capabilities but can have a slower startup time due to the need to download the entire application.

- **Blazor Server**: It executes the application on the server and interacts with the client via **SignalR**. It offers fast initial load times and efficient use of resources but relies on a continuous network connection.

Understanding the differences between these two types of Blazor applications is crucial for a deeper comprehension of the new render modes introduced in .NET 9.

Let's now get into the different types of render modes, but first, create a new project in Visual Studio from the Blazor Web App template, which will be used for the code examples in the next sections.

InteractiveServer

The `InteractiveServer` render mode explicitly uses server-side rendering for the Blazor component. This mode is suitable for applications where server-side processing is preferred, such as when dealing with large datasets or complex operations that benefit from the server's processing power. Server-side rendering also provides a consistent user experience across different client devices, as the rendering logic is handled entirely on the server.

Using `InteractiveServer`, the component maintains a persistent connection to the server via SignalR. This connection allows the server to push updates to the client in real time, ensuring that the UI remains synchronized with the server's state.

Here's an example of how to implement `InteractiveServer` in a Blazor component:

```
@page "/server-component"
@rendermode InteractiveServer

<h3>Server Component</h3>

<p>
    This component is rendered using the InteractiveServer
    render mode.
</p>

<button @onclick="HandleClick">Click Me</button>

@code {
    private void HandleClick()
    {
        Console.WriteLine("Button clicked on the server");
    }
}
```

In this example, the Blazor component is configured to use the `InteractiveServer` mode, ensuring that all rendering and processing occur on the server. This setup is beneficial for scenarios requiring robust server-side processing and real-time updates.

InteractiveWebAssembly

The `InteractiveWebAssembly` render mode explicitly uses Wasm for client-side rendering. This mode is ideal for applications that aim to leverage the client's processing power, providing a more interactive and responsive user experience. Wasm enables the application to run entirely in the browser, reducing the need for constant server communication and allowing for offline capabilities.

Using `InteractiveWebAssembly`, the Blazor component is compiled into Wasm and executed in the client's browser. This approach can significantly improve performance for applications with rich interactive features and complex UI logic, as the client handles most of the processing.

Here's an example of how to implement `InteractiveWebAssembly` in a Blazor component:

```
@page "/webassembly-component"
@rendermode InteractiveWebAssembly

<h3>WebAssembly Component</h3>

<p>
    This component is rendered using the
    InteractiveWebAssembly render mode.
</p>

<button @onclick="HandleClick">Click Me</button>

@code {
    private void HandleClick()
    {
        Console.WriteLine("Button clicked on the client");
    }
}
```

In this example, the Blazor component is configured to use the `InteractiveWebAssembly` mode, ensuring that all rendering and processing occur in the client's browser. This setup is advantageous for scenarios where client-side interactivity and performance are critical.

In the next section, you will learn how to combine render modes in Blazor.

InteractiveAuto

The `InteractiveAuto` render mode automatically selects the most appropriate rendering method based on the environment. This mode dynamically chooses between server-side and client-side rendering, aiming to provide the best possible user experience. It is particularly useful in scenarios where the application needs to adapt to varying network conditions and client capabilities.

When using `InteractiveAuto`, the Blazor framework evaluates the client's environment and decides whether to use server-side rendering or Wasm. By default, if the client supports Wasm, it will be used; otherwise, the application will fall back to server-side rendering. This adaptive behavior ensures that the application remains performant and responsive across different devices and network conditions.

Here's an example of how to implement `InteractiveAuto` in a Blazor component, as seen in the following example:

```
@page "/interactive-auto"
@rendermode InteractiveAuto

<h3>InteractiveAuto Render Mode</h3>

<p>
    This component is rendered using the InteractiveAuto
    render mode.
</p>

<button @onclick="HandleClick">Click Me</button>

@code {
    private void HandleClick()
    {
        Console.WriteLine("Button clicked");
    }
}
```

In this example, the Blazor component is set up to render using the `InteractiveAuto` mode. The framework will decide the best rendering strategy based on the client's capabilities, ensuring optimal performance and user experience. In the next section, we will learn about the `InteractiveServer` mode.

Combining render modes

One of the significant advantages of the new render modes in Blazor .NET 9 is the ability to combine them within a single application. Developers can leverage the strengths of each mode, optimizing different parts of the application based on specific needs. For instance, an application might use `InteractiveServer` for data-intensive components that require robust server-side processing, while employing `InteractiveWebAssembly` for components that benefit from client-side interactivity and responsiveness.

Combining render modes allows for a hybrid approach, ensuring that the application can adapt to varying requirements and provide the best possible user experience. This flexibility is especially beneficial in complex applications with diverse functionality and performance considerations.

Here's an example of a Blazor application that combines different render modes:

```
@page "/hybrid-render-modes"
@rendermode InteractiveAuto


<h3>Hybrid Render Modes</h3>

<div>
    <p>Server-side component:</p>
    <ServerComponent />
</div>
<div>
    <p>WebAssembly component:</p>
    <WebAssemblyComponent />
</div>

@code {
}
```

In this example, the main component references two child components. The child components will use their own specified render modes. ServerComponent uses the InteractiveServer render mode, ensuring that all its processing and rendering occur on the server. WebAssemblyComponent uses the InteractiveWebAssembly render mode, ensuring that all its processing and rendering occur in the client's browser. If you try to reuse the previous ServerComponent and WebAssemblyComponent code samples, you must exclude the @rendermode directives first.

By combining these different render modes, the application can efficiently utilize server resources for data-intensive operations while providing a responsive and interactive user experience through client-side rendering. This hybrid approach allows developers to create sophisticated applications that leverage the best aspects of both server-side and client-side rendering.

Summary

In this, we delved deeply into the advanced aspects of Blazor's component architecture, focusing on creating sophisticated and high-performing applications using Blazor in .NET 9. This chapter is built on the foundational knowledge from previous chapters, introducing new techniques and features to enhance your Blazor applications significantly.

We started by exploring advanced component architecture. We learned how to create and manage dynamic components, compose complex UIs from simpler ones, and efficiently handle parameter binding. These skills are crucial for building modular, maintainable, and scalable applications.

Next, we covered advanced routing and navigation. This section included defining routes with parameters and implementing navigation guards. Mastering these concepts allows us to build more flexible and scalable applications, ensuring users have a seamless and efficient navigation experience.

Additionally, we examined JS interop in Blazor. We discovered how to integrate JavaScript with Blazor, leveraging existing JavaScript libraries and APIs to enhance your applications. This section covered invoking JavaScript functions from Blazor, handling JavaScript events, and ensuring secure and isolated JavaScript interactions. These skills enable you to extend the functionality of your Blazor applications by integrating the vast ecosystem of JavaScript libraries.

We then introduced the new render modes available in Blazor since .NET 9: `InteractiveAuto`, `InteractiveServer`, and `InteractiveWebAssembly`. These render modes allow us to optimize the performance and user experience of our applications by choosing the most appropriate rendering strategy for each scenario. `InteractiveAuto` dynamically selects the best rendering method based on the client's environment, while `InteractiveServer` and `InteractiveWebAssembly` explicitly use server-side or client-side rendering, respectively.

By implementing these new render modes, we can create sophisticated Blazor applications that adapt to varying network conditions and client capabilities, ensuring optimal performance and user experience. The skills learned in this chapter are essential for optimizing application rendering strategies and making informed decisions about when to use server-side or client-side rendering.

In the next chapter, we will transition from Blazor to focus on building RESTful services with ASP. NET Core. We will start with an introduction to RESTful services, outlining their principles and best practices. Then, we will go through building basic REST APIs, handling requests and responses, and implementing API versioning and documentation basics. This progression will provide a solid foundation for integrating robust and scalable RESTful services into our applications, marking the next natural step in your journey.

8
RESTful Services with ASP.NET Core – Part 1

In this chapter, we will delve into the world of RESTful services, a crucial aspect of modern web development. RESTful services enable communication between different software applications over the internet, allowing them to exchange data and perform operations seamlessly. Understanding RESTful principles and implementing them effectively is essential for building robust and scalable web applications.

Throughout this chapter, we will learn about the foundational concepts of RESTful services and how to build and deploy basic **Representational State Transfer (REST)** APIs using ASP.NET Core. We will start with the principles of REST, exploring best practices and guidelines to ensure your APIs are well structured and easy to maintain. We will then learn how to create and configure REST APIs, handle various types of requests and responses, and implement versioning and documentation to keep our APIs organized and user-friendly.

By the end of this chapter, we will have a solid understanding of RESTful services and the skills needed to build and manage basic REST APIs with ASP.NET Core. These skills are invaluable for any developer working on web applications, as they allow for efficient data exchange and interaction between different systems.

In this chapter, we're going to cover the following main topics:

- Understanding RESTful services principles
- Creating Basic REST APIs with ASP.NET Core
- Handling requests and responses
- API versioning and documentation basics

Technical requirements

You can refer to the *Technical requirements* section of *Chapter 1* for all the necessary installations.

The code files required for you to follow along with this chapter can be found at: `https://github.com/PacktPublishing/Modern-Full-Stack-Web-Development-with-ASP.NET-Core/tree/main/Chapter08`.

Understanding RESTful services principles

REST is an architectural style that outlines a set of constraints and best practices for creating web services. It was introduced by Roy Fielding in his doctoral dissertation in 2000 and has since become the standard for designing networked applications. RESTful services use standard HTTP methods and a stateless communication protocol, making them highly scalable, reliable, and easy to integrate.

The core principles of RESTful services revolve around the idea of resources and the actions that can be performed on them. In a RESTful architecture, everything is considered a resource, which can be represented in various formats, such as JSON, XML, or HTML. Resources are identified by **Uniform Resource Identifiers** (**URIs**) and manipulated using standard HTTP methods, such as `GET`, `POST`, `PUT`, `DELETE`, and `PATCH`.

Let's understand the key principles of general RESTful APIs.

Key principles of RESTful services

To effectively design and implement RESTful services, it's crucial to understand the core principles that underpin this architectural style. These principles ensure that services are scalable, maintainable, and efficient, facilitating seamless communication between clients and servers. By adhering to these principles, developers can create APIs that are not only easy to use but also flexible and robust. In this section, we will explore the fundamental concepts that define RESTful services, including statelessness, resource identification, representation, uniform interface, caching strategy, and layered system architecture. Each of these principles plays a vital role in shaping how RESTful services operate and interact, providing a solid foundation for building modern web applications. In the next sections, details of each key principle are explained.

Statelessness

One of the fundamental principles of REST is statelessness. This means that each request from a client to the server must contain all the information needed to understand and process the request. The server does not store any client context between requests. **Statelessness** simplifies the server design and improves scalability, as each request can be processed independently.

For example, when a client makes a request to retrieve a list of products, all the necessary information, such as authentication tokens or query parameters, must be included in the request. The server processes the request and returns the response without retaining any client-specific data.

Resource identification through URIs

In REST, resources are identified using URIs. A resource could be any object or data, such as a user, a product, or an order. The URI acts as a unique identifier for the resource, allowing clients to interact with it using standard HTTP methods.

For instance, a URI such as `https://api.example.com/products/123` might refer to a product with the ID `123`. Clients can perform various actions on this resource, such as retrieving its details (`GET`), updating it (`PUT`), or deleting it (`DELETE`).

In the next section, we are going to learn about the representation of resources in RESTful services, focusing on how resources are represented in different formats, such as JSON or XML, and how these representations are used to exchange data.

Representation of resources

Resources in RESTful services are represented in different formats, commonly JSON or XML. The representation provides the current state of the resource and is transferred between the client and server. Clients can request specific formats using the `Accept` header in the HTTP request.

For example, a `GET` request to `https://api.example.com/products/123` might return a JSON representation of the product, as seen in the following example:

```
{
    "id": 123,
    "name": "Packt Book",
    "price": 29.99
}
```

In the next section, we are going to learn about the uniform interface constraint in RESTful services, which simplifies the interaction between clients and servers through a set of standard methods and conventions.

Uniform interface

RESTful services adhere to a uniform interface, simplifying the interaction between clients and servers. The uniform interface consists of four constraints:

- **Identification of resources**: Resources are identified using URIs

- **Manipulation of resources through representations**: Clients manipulate resources using their representations

- **Self-descriptive messages**: Each message includes enough information to describe how to process it

- **Hypermedia as the engine of application state (HATEOAS)**: Clients navigate the application state through hypermedia links provided dynamically by the server

These constraints decouple the implementation of services from the client and server, promoting scalability and flexibility.

In the next section, we are going to learn about the importance of **cacheability** in RESTful services and how caching can enhance performance and scalability by reducing the need for repeated server interactions.

Cacheability

Caching is a critical feature of RESTful services that enhances performance and scalability. Responses from the server can be explicitly marked as cacheable or non-cacheable using HTTP headers. When a response is cacheable, clients can store and reuse it for subsequent requests, reducing the need for repeated server interactions.

For example, a server can include a `Cache-Control` header in the response to indicate that the data can be cached for a certain period: `Cache-Control: max-age=3600`.

This header tells the client that the response can be cached for one hour (3,600 seconds).

In the next section, we are going to learn about the layered system architecture in RESTful services, which enhances scalability, security, and manageability by structuring the system into multiple layers.

Layered system

A RESTful system can be composed of multiple layers, with each layer providing specific functionality and hiding the complexity of the system beneath it. This layered architecture enhances scalability, security, and manageability.

For example, an intermediate layer, such as a load balancer, can handle incoming requests, distribute them to multiple servers, and cache responses. This approach improves performance and ensures that the system can handle a large number of requests efficiently.

By understanding and applying these key principles, we are now well equipped to design and build RESTful services that are both robust and scalable, laying the groundwork for effective web service development.

In the next section, we will create basic REST APIs with ASP.NET Core with practical examples.

Creating basic REST APIs with ASP.NET Core

Creating a basic REST API with ASP.NET Core involves several steps, from setting up the project to defining the endpoints and handling requests and responses. This section will guide you through the process, providing practical examples and code snippets to help you build a functional REST API. Let's get started.

Setting up the project

To begin, you need to set up an ASP.NET Core project:

1.   Use the .NET CLI or Visual Studio to create a new web API project.

2.   Using the .NET CLI, you can create a new project by running the following command:

```
dotnet new webapi -n MyFirstApi
```

The preceding command creates a new ASP.NET Core web API project named MyFirstApi.

3.   Navigate to the cd MyFirstApi project directory.

4.   Next, open the project in your preferred code editor or IDE.

That's it. In the next section, we are going to configure the project by setting up the necessary middleware components and defining the application's services.

Configuring the project

In .NET 8, the configuration and setup of the project are done in the Program.cs file. Open the Program.cs file and set up the middleware components and services, as shown in the following code:

```
namespace Chapter8
{
    public class Program
    {
        public static void Main(string[] args)
        {
            var builder =
                WebApplication.CreateBuilder(args);

            builder.Services.AddControllers();

            var app = builder.Build();

            app.UseAuthorization();
```

```
                    app.UseDeveloperExceptionPage();
                    app.UseHsts();
                    app.UseHttpsRedirection();
                    app.MapControllers();

                    app.Run();
                }
            }
        }
```

Here's a detailed explanation of each relevant line in the code sample:

- `builder.Services.AddControllers()` adds the services required to use controllers in the application
- `app.UseDeveloperExceptionPage()` enables detailed error information when running in the development environment
- `app.UseHsts()` adds **HTTP Strict Transport Security (HSTS)** headers
- `app.UseHttpsRedirection()` redirects HTTP requests to HTTPS
- `app.MapControllers()` maps controller endpoints using top-level route registrations

In the next section, we will create a controller to handle incoming HTTP requests and generate responses.

Creating a controller

Controllers in ASP.NET Core handle incoming HTTP requests and generate responses. To create a new controller, follow these steps:

1. Add a new class to the `Controllers` folder. Name the class `ProductsController.cs`.
2. Define the `ProductsController` class and the in-memory data store as follows:

```
using Microsoft.AspNetCore.Mvc;

namespace Chapter8.Controllers
{
    [Route("api/[controller]")]
    [ApiController]
    public class ProductsController : ControllerBase
    {
        private static readonly List<Product>
            Products = new List<Product>
        {
            new Product
```

```
            {
                Id = 1,
                Name = "Product 1",
                Price = 10.0
            },
            new Product
            {
                Id = 2,
                Name = "Product 2",
                Price = 20.0
            }
        };

        [HttpGet]
        public ActionResult<
            IEnumerable<Product>> Get()
        {
            return Products;
        }
    }

    public class Product
    {
        public int Id { get; set; }
        public string Name { get; set; }
        public double Price { get; set; }
    }
}
```

Let's understand the preceding code:

- The `ProductsController` class is decorated with `[Route("api/[controller]")]`, which sets the base route to `api/products`
- The `[ApiController]` attribute simplifies model validation and binding
- The `Products` list acts as an in-memory data store for demonstration purposes

3. Next, add the `Get` method to retrieve all products as follows in the following code:

```
public class ProductsV1Controller : ControllerBase
{
    private static readonly List<Product> Products =
        new List<Product>
    {
        new Product
```

```
        {
            Id = 1,
            Name = "Product 1",
            Price = 10.0
        },
        new Product
        {
            Id = 2,
            Name = "Product 2",
            Price = 20.0
        }
    };

    [HttpGet]
    public ActionResult<IEnumerable<Product>> Get()
    {
        return Products;
    }
}
```

This method handles GET requests to api/products and returns the list of all products.

4. Next, add the Get method with an integer parameter to retrieve a product by its ID, as shown in the following example:

```
[HttpGet("{id}")]
public ActionResult<Product> Get(int id)
{
    var product = Products.Find(x=> x.Id == id);

    if(product == null)
    {
        return NotFound();
    }

    return product;
}
```

This method handles GET requests to api/products/{id} and returns the product with the specified ID.

5. Next, add the Post method to create a new product, as shown in the following example:

```
[HttpPost]
public ActionResult<Product> Post(
    [FromBody] Product product)
```

```
{
    product.Id = Products.Count + 1;
    Products.Add(product);

    return CreatedAtAction(nameof(Get), new { id = product.Id },
        product);
}
```

This method handles POST requests to api/products and creates a new product. It returns the created product and its location.

6. Next, add the Put method to update an existing product, as shown in the following code:

```
[HttpPut("{id}")]
public ActionResult Put(
    int id, [FromBody] Product updatedProduct)
{
    var product = Products.Find(x=> x.Id == id);

    if(product == null)
    {
        return NotFound();
    }

    product.Name = updatedProduct.Name;
    product.Price = updatedProduct.Price;

    return NoContent();
}
```

This method handles PUT requests to api/products/{id} and updates the product with the specified ID.

7. Finally, add the Delete method to delete a product, as shown in the following code:

```
[HttpDelete("{id}")]
public ActionResult Delete(int id)
{
    var product = Products.Find(x=> x.Id == id);

    if(product == null)
    {
        return NotFound();
    }

    Products.Remove(product);
```

```
        return NoContent();
    }
```

This method handles DELETE requests to `api/products/{id}` and deletes the product with the specified ID.

Here's the complete `ProductsController` in the following code:

```csharp
using Microsoft.AspNetCore.Mvc;

namespace Chapter8.Controllers
{
    [Route("api/[controller]")]
    [ApiController]
    public class ProductsV1Controller : ControllerBase
    {
        private static readonly List<Product> Products =
            new List<Product>
        {
            new Product
            {
                Id = 1,
                Name = "Product 1",
                Price = 10.0
            },
            new Product
            {
                Id = 2,
                Name = "Product 2",
                Price = 20.0
            }
        };

        [HttpGet]
        public ActionResult<IEnumerable<Product>> Get()
        {
            return Products;
        }

        [HttpGet("{id}")]
        public ActionResult<Product> Get(int id)
        {
            var product = Products.Find(x=> x.Id == id);

            if(product == null)
```

```
    {
        return NotFound();
    }

    return product;
}

[HttpPost]
public ActionResult<Product> Post(
    [FromBody] Product product)
{
    product.Id = Products.Count + 1;
    Products.Add(product);

    return CreatedAtAction(nameof(Products),
        product);
}

[HttpPut("{id}")]
public ActionResult Put(
    int id, [FromBody] Product updatedProduct)
{
    var product = Products.Find(x=> x.Id == id);

    if(product == null)
    {
        return NotFound();
    }

    product.Name = updatedProduct.Name;
    product.Price = updatedProduct.Price;

    return NoContent();
}

[HttpDelete("{id}")]
public ActionResult Delete(int id)
{
    var product = Products.Find(x=> x.Id == id);

    if(product == null)
    {
        return NotFound();
    }
```

```
        Products.Remove(product);

        return NoContent();
    }
}

public class Product
{
    public int Id { get; set; }
    public string Name { get; set; }
    public double Price { get; set; }
}
}
```

In the next section, we will learn how to test and run our ASP.NET Core REST API to ensure it functions correctly.

Testing and running the API

Once you have created your controller, it is time to test and run your API. ASP.NET Core provides a built-in development server called **Kestrel**, which you can use to run your application locally. Additionally, you can use tools such as Postman, cURL, or your browser to test the API endpoints. This section will guide you through the process of running and testing your API.

Running the API

To start the application, run the following command in the terminal from the root directory of your project:

```
dotnet run
```

This command builds and runs your application. You should see output indicating that the application is running and listening on a specific URL, typically https://localhost:5001 for HTTPS and http://localhost:5000 for HTTP.

Testing the API endpoints

You can test the API endpoints using tools such as Postman, cURL, or your web browser. The next bullet points contain examples of how to use cURL to test the different endpoints of your API:

- **Get all products**: To retrieve a list of all products, use the following cURL command:

  ```
  curl -X GET https://localhost:5001/api/products
  ```

  This request retrieves the list of all products from the in-memory data store.

- **Get product by ID**: To retrieve a specific product by its ID, use the following cURL command:

```
curl -X GET https://localhost:5001/api/products/1
```

This request retrieves the product with ID 1 from the in-memory data store.

- **Create a new product**: To create a new product, use a POST request. The following command creates a new product with the name Product 3 and price 30.0:

```
curl -X POST https://localhost:5001/api/products -H "Content-
Type: application/json" -d '{"name":"Product 3","price":30.0}'
```

In this case, the command is doing the following:

- X POST specifies that this is a POST request

- -H "Content-Type: application/json" sets the content type to JSON

- -d '{"name":"Product 3","price":30.0}' provides the data for the new product in JSON format

- **Update a product**: To update an existing product, use a PUT request. The following command updates the product with ID 1 to have the name Updated Product and a price of 15.0:

```
curl -X PUT https://localhost:5001/api/products/1 -H
"Content-Type: application/json" -d '{"name":"Updated
Product","price":15.0}'
```

Let's break this command down:

- -X PUT specifies that this is a PUT request

- -H "Content-Type: application/json" sets the content type to JSON

- -d '{"name":"Updated Product","price":15.0}' provides the updated data for the product in JSON format

- **Delete a product**: To delete a product by its ID, use a DELETE request. The following command deletes the product with ID 1:

```
curl -X DELETE https://localhost:5001/api/products/1
```

In this case, -X DELETE specifies that this is a DELETE request.

In the next section, we will learn about handling requests and responses in more detail, including working with query parameters, headers, and body data.

Handling requests and responses

Handling requests and responses is a crucial part of building RESTful APIs. This section will cover how to manage different types of requests and responses in your ASP.NET Core application, including working with query parameters, headers, and body data. By understanding how to effectively handle these elements, you can create APIs that are flexible, robust, and easy to use.

Let's start by getting to know how to work with parameters in ASP.NET Core.

Working with query parameters

Query parameters are used to filter or modify the data returned by an API. In ASP.NET Core, you can access query parameters using the Request.Query property or by defining parameters in the action method signature. In the following coding example, the [FromQuery] attribute is used to bind query parameters to method parameters. The Get method filters products based on the name and minPrice query parameters. If the name parameter is provided, it filters the products to include only those whose names contain the specified string, ignoring the case. If the minPrice parameter is provided, it filters the products to include only those with a price greater than or equal to the specified value. This allows clients to retrieve a subset of products based on their search criteria:

```
[HttpGet("search")]
public ActionResult<IEnumerable<Product>> Get(
    [FromQuery] string name, [FromQuery] double? minPrice)
{

    var products = Products.AsQueryable();

    if (!string.IsNullOrEmpty(name))
    {
        products = products.Where(x => x.Name.Contains(
            name, StringComparison.OrdinalIgnoreCase
        ));
    }

    if (minPrice.HasValue)
    {
        products = products.Where(
            x => x.Price >= minPrice.Value
        );
    }

    return products.ToList();
}
```

In the next section, we will learn about working with headers in ASP.NET Core, including how to read from and write to HTTP headers.

Working with headers

HTTP headers provide additional information about the request or response. You can access headers using the Request.Headers and Response.Headers properties. In the following code example, the [FromHeader(Name = "X-Custom-Header")] attribute binds a specific header from the request to a method parameter. The Get method reads the value of the X-Custom-Header header from the request and includes it in the response. Additionally, the Get method adds a custom header (X-Response-Header) to the response. This demonstrates how to both read from and write to HTTP headers, allowing for greater flexibility and control over the HTTP communication. Here's an example in the following code:

```
[HttpGet("{id:int}")]
public ActionResult<Product> Get(int id, [FromHeader(
    Name = "X-Custom-Header")] string customHeader)
{
    var product = Products.Find(x=> x.Id == id);

    if(product == null)
    {
        return NotFound();
    }

    Response.Headers.Add(
        "X-Response-Header", "Response value"
    );

    return Ok(new
    {
        Product = product,
        CustomHeaderReceived = customHeader
    });
}
```

In the next section, we will learn about working with body data in ASP.NET Core, focusing on how to bind the request body to a method parameter.

Working with body data

The body of an HTTP request is used to send data to the server, typically in POST, PUT, and DELETE requests. In ASP.NET Core, you can use the [FromBody] attribute to bind the request body to the parameter of the Post method. In the following code example, the [FromBody] attribute binds the request body to the product parameter. The Post method handles POST requests to create a new product. It checks if the product is null and returns a BadRequest response if it is. The product is then added to the in-memory data store, and a CreatedAtAction response is returned with the location of the newly created product, as demonstrated in the following code:

```
[HttpPost]
public ActionResult<Product> Post(
    [FromBody] Product product)
{
    product.Id = Products.Count + 1;
    Products.Add(product);

    return CreatedAtAction(nameof(Products), product);
}
```

In the next section, we will learn about handling different response types in ASP.NET Core, including how to return various status codes and responses.

Handling different response types

ASP.NET Core provides various ways to return responses, including built-in action result types, such as Ok, NotFound, BadRequest, and CreatedAtAction. In the following code example, the Put method handles PUT requests to update an existing product. It checks whether the updatedProduct is null and returns a BadRequest response if it is. If the product with the specified ID is not found, it returns a NotFound response. Otherwise, it updates the product's name and price and returns a NoContent response, indicating the update was successful but there is no content to return. Here's an example in the following code:

```
[HttpPut("{id}")]
public ActionResult Put(
    int id, [FromBody] Product updatedProduct)
{
    var product = Products.Find(x=> x.Id == id);

    if(product == null)
    {
        return NotFound();
    }
```

```
    product.Name = updatedProduct.Name;
    product.Price = updatedProduct.Price;

    return NoContent();
}
```

In the next section, we will learn about API versioning and the basics of documentation for ASP.NET Core web API projects.

API versioning and documentation basics

API versioning and documentation are critical aspects of building robust and maintainable APIs. Versioning ensures that changes to your API can be made without breaking existing clients, while documentation helps developers understand how to use your API effectively. This section will cover the basics of implementing API versioning and creating comprehensive documentation using tools such as Swagger in ASP.NET Core.

API versioning

To set up API versioning in your ASP.NET Core project, you first need to install the Asp. Versioning.Mvc package. This package adds the necessary functionality to manage API versions. After installing the package, configure API versioning in the Program.cs file. In this configuration, the AddApiVersioning method sets up versioning with default settings, specifying the default API version as 1.0. The AssumeDefaultVersionWhenUnspecified option ensures that the default version is used if none is specified in the request, while the ReportApiVersions option includes version information in the response headers. The configuration needs to be done as demonstrated in the following example:

```
builder.Services.AddApiVersioning(options =>
{
    options.DefaultApiVersion = new ApiVersion(1, 0);
    options.AssumeDefaultVersionWhenUnspecified = true;
    options.ReportApiVersions = true;
});
```

The AddApiVersioning method configures API versioning with default settings. DefaultApiVersion sets the default API version. AssumeDefaultVersionWhenUnspecified ensures that the default version is used if none is specified in the request, while ReportApiVersions includes version information in the response headers.

In the next section, we will learn how to create versioned controllers for your project.

Creating versioned controllers

To create versioned controllers, use the `[ApiVersion]` attribute and specify the version in the route. In the example provided in the following code, `ProductsV1Controller` and `ProductsV2Controller` demonstrate how to handle different versions of the same API. The `[ApiVersion("1.0")]` attribute indicates that `ProductsV1Controller` is for version 1.0 of the API, and it uses the `api/v{version:apiVersion}/[controller]` route to include the version in the URL path. Similarly, the `[ApiVersion("2.0")]` attribute specifies that `ProductsV2Controller` is for version 2.0 of the API. These controllers manage different sets of products, allowing clients to interact with either version of the API as needed, as seen in the following example:

```
[ApiVersion("1.0")]
[Route("api/v{version:apiVersion}/[controller]")]
[ApiController]
public class ProductsV1Controller : ControllerBase
{
    private static readonly List<Product> Products =
        new List<Product>
    {
        new Product
        {
            Id = 1,
            Name = "Product 1",
            Price = 10.0
        },
        new Product
        {
            Id = 2,
            Name = "Product 2",
            Price = 20.0
        }
    };

    [HttpGet]
    public ActionResult<IEnumerable<Product>> Get()
    {
        return Products;
    }
}

[ApiVersion("2.0")]
[Route("api/v{version:apiVersion}/[controller]")]
```

```
[ApiController]
public class ProductsV2Controller : ControllerBase
{
    private static readonly List<Product> Products =
        new List<Product>
    {
        new Product
        {
            Id = 1,
            Name = "Product 1",
            Price = 10.0
        },
        new Product
        {
            Id = 2,
            Name = "Product 2",
            Price = 20.0
        },
        new Product
        {
            Id = 3,
            Name = "Product 3",
            Price = 30.0
        }
    };

    [HttpGet]
    public ActionResult<IEnumerable<Product>> Get()
    {
        return Products;
    }
}
```

The [ApiVersion("1.0")] attribute specifies that the ProductsV1Controller is for version 1.0 of the API. The [ApiVersion("2.0")] attribute specifies that ProductsV2Controller is for version 2.0 of the API. The Route attribute includes the version in the URL path, allowing clients to interact with specific versions of the API.

In the next section, we will learn about creating comprehensive API documentation using Swagger.

API documentation with Swagger

Swagger is a popular tool for generating interactive API documentation. It allows developers to explore and test your API endpoints directly from the documentation. ASP.NET Core provides native integration with Swagger through the `Swashbuckle.AspNetCore` package.

To set up Swagger in your ASP.NET Core project, first install the `Swashbuckle.AspNetCore` package. This package adds the necessary functionality to generate Swagger documentation. After installing the package, configure Swagger in the `Program.cs` file. The `AddSwaggerGen` method registers the Swagger generator, and you can configure it to generate documentation for each API version. Additionally, the `IncludeXmlComments` method adds XML comments to the Swagger documentation, enhancing it with detailed descriptions for API endpoints and parameters. Finally, in the development environment, the `UseSwagger` and `UseSwaggerUI` methods set up the Swagger middleware and UI, enabling developers to access the interactive documentation, as highlighted in the following code:

```
using Asp.Versioning;
using Asp.Versioning.ApiExplorer;

namespace Chapter8
{
    public class Program
    {
        public static void Main(string[] args)
        {
            var builder =
                WebApplication.CreateBuilder(args);

            builder.Services.AddControllers();

            builder.Services.AddApiVersioning(options =>
            {
                options.DefaultApiVersion =
                    new ApiVersion(1, 0);
                options.AssumeDefaultVersionWhenUnspecified
                    = true;
                options.ReportApiVersions = true;
            });

            builder.Services.AddEndpointsApiExplorer();
            builder.Services.AddSwaggerGen(options =>
            {
                var provider = builder.Services
                    .BuildServiceProvider()
```

```
                .GetRequiredService<
                    IApiVersionDescriptionProvider>();

            foreach (var description in
                provider.ApiVersionDescriptions)
            {
                options.SwaggerDoc(
                    description.GroupName,
                    new Microsoft
                        .OpenApi.Models.OpenApiInfo
                    {
                        Title = $"My API
                            {description.ApiVersion}",
                        Version = description
                            .ApiVersion
                            .ToString()
                    }
                );
            }

            var xmlFile = $"{System.Reflection.Assembly
                .GetExecutingAssembly()
                .GetName()
                .Name}.xml";
            var xmlPath = System.IO.Path.Combine(
                AppContext.BaseDirectory, xmlFile);
            options.IncludeXmlComments(xmlPath);
});


var app = builder.Build();

if (app.Environment.IsDevelopment())
{
    app.UseDeveloperExceptionPage();

    app.UseSwagger();
    app.UseSwaggerUI(options =>
    {
        var provider = app.Services
            .GetRequiredService<
                IApiVersionDescriptionProvider
```

```
                            >();

        foreach (var description in
            provider.ApiVersionDescriptions)
        {
        options.SwaggerEndpoint(
            $"/swagger/
                {description.GroupName}/
                    swagger.json",
            description
                .GroupName
                .ToUpperInvariant()
            );
        }
    });
}
else
{
    app.UseHsts();
}

app.UseAuthorization();
app.UseHttpsRedirection();
app.MapControllers();

app.Run();
        }
    }
}
```

The `AddSwaggerGen` method registers the Swagger generator, enabling it to create Swagger documentation for your API. The `IncludeXmlComments` method adds XML comments to the Swagger documentation, providing detailed descriptions for API endpoints and parameters. The `UseSwagger` and `UseSwaggerUI` methods set up the Swagger middleware and UI in the development environment, enabling developers to access interactive API documentation.

Summary

In this chapter, we covered the foundational principles and practices for building RESTful services with ASP.NET Core, including understanding RESTful principles, creating basic REST APIs, handling requests and responses, implementing API versioning, and creating comprehensive API documentation with Swagger.

We began by exploring the key principles of RESTful services, such as statelessness, resource identification through URIs, representation of resources, uniform interfaces, cacheability, and layered systems. These principles are crucial for designing scalable, maintainable, and efficient web services that facilitate seamless communication between clients and servers.

Next, we walked through the process of creating a basic REST API with ASP.NET Core. This involved setting up the project, configuring necessary middleware components, and defining controllers to handle HTTP requests. We provided practical examples and code snippets to help you build a functional API, covering methods for retrieving, creating, updating, and deleting resources.

We then delved into handling requests and responses in more detail, including working with query parameters, headers, and body data. Understanding these aspects is essential for creating flexible and robust APIs that can efficiently handle different types of client requests and return appropriate responses.

The chapter also introduced API versioning, which ensures that your API can evolve without breaking existing clients. We demonstrated how to set up API versioning using the `Asp.Versioning.Mvc` package and create versioned controllers. This approach allows us to manage multiple versions of your API, providing backward compatibility and facilitating the introduction of new features.

Finally, we covered API documentation using Swagger, a powerful tool for generating interactive API documentation. By integrating Swagger with ASP.NET Core, we can create detailed, user-friendly documentation that helps developers understand and use your API effectively.

These lessons and skills are useful because they provide a strong foundation for developing RESTful services that are scalable, maintainable, and easy to use. They equip us with the knowledge to build robust APIs that can handle various client requests, evolve over time, and provide clear documentation for developers.

In the next chapter, we will advance to more complex aspects of REST API development, including security measures, advanced routing techniques, and in-depth API documentation. We will also discuss best practices for securing APIs and optimizing their performance. This is the next natural step from what we've just covered, as it will build on the foundational knowledge and skills you've gained to create even more powerful and secure APIs.

9

RESTful Services with ASP.NET Core – Part 2

This chapter is focused on more complex aspects of REST API development with ASP.NET Core, including a deeper understanding of techniques for performance, efficiency, and routing for APIs. As modern web applications become more dependent on external data and integrations in an interconnected environment, the requirement to have robust solutions for APIs becomes essential. Throughout this chapter, we will learn about advanced concepts that will improve your development skills, applying modern concepts of scalability and maintainability.

First, we will explore complex scenarios for routing that will give us the opportunity to create and configure flexible API endpoints, allowing our application to correctly manage many different scenarios in terms of requests that come from multiple clients with different needs. Taking a deeper look at these routing techniques is essential for building robust APIs while maintaining good standards of performance and maintainability.

Next, we will explore ways to increase the performance of APIs, applying strategies regarding caching, compression, and other approaches. We will also learn the basics of asynchronous programming, caching, database optimization techniques, load balancing, and horizontal scaling to provide a seamless user experience in terms of application performance.

In this chapter, we are going to cover the following main topics:

- Exploring advanced routing techniques
- Performance optimization for APIs

By the end of this chapter, you will have gained valuable skills to implement advanced routing techniques, enhance security, create collaborative documentation, and optimize API performance. These competencies will set a solid foundation for building reliable and robust web applications using ASP.NET Core, ensuring your APIs are efficient, scalable, and capable of handling complex routing scenarios with ease.

Technical requirements

You can refer to the *Technical requirements* section of *Chapter 1* for all the necessary installations.

The code files required for you to follow along with this chapter can be found at: `https://github.com/PacktPublishing/Modern-Full-Stack-Web-Development-with-ASP.NET-Core/tree/main/Chapter09`.

Exploring advanced routing techniques

In this section, we will explore ways of configuring advanced routing techniques in ASP.NET Core that will allow us to handle API endpoints for complex scenarios. Routing is a crucial concern for API development, as it determines how API consumers interact with your application. Let's start with exploring attribute routing and jump into more complex scenarios in the following subsection.

Attribute routing

Attribute routing allows you to configure routes in the context of your controller actions, giving great flexibility and control to the routing specification. This type of routing is important when you have to define complex routes that are not simple to express using standard routing techniques. By using attributes to define routes, you can determine a custom URL schema to match the underlying functionality of your API endpoint. Here's how you can define attributes for your controller actions:

```
[Route("api/[controller]")]
[ApiController]
public class ShipmentController : Controller
{
    private readonly List<Shipment> shipments;

    public ShipmentController()
    {
        shipments = new List<Shipment>
        {
            new Shipment { Id = 1, Type = "International",
                Description = "Shipment 1" },
            new Shipment { Id = 2, Type = "Domestic",
                Description = "Shipment 2" }
        };
    }
    [HttpGet("{id:int}")]
    public IActionResult GetShipmentById(int id)
    {
        return Ok();
    }
```

```
    [HttpGet("type/{type}")]
    public IActionResult GetShipmentByType(string type)
    {
        var shipments_result = shipments.Where(x => x.Type == type);
        return Ok(shipments_result);
    }
}
```

In this example, attribute routing is used to define routes for retrieving shipments by ID and type, allowing for more meaningful and friendly URL patterns. In this case, the endpoint that allows the retrieval of a shipment by type would have a URL similar to the following example: `http://localhost/api/shipment/type/international`.

In the next section, we will learn how to work with advanced attribute routing with regular expressions.

Advanced attribute routing with regular expressions

In certain scenarios, you may want to configure more advanced constraints on your endpoint parameters using regular expressions. This technique offers a great way to check dynamically for complex patterns in your routing configuration. Here's an example of how you can do that:

```
[HttpGet("{shipmentId:regex(^SHIPMENT-[[0-7]]{{5}}$)}")]
public IActionResult GetShipmentByCustomNumber(
    string shipmentId)
{
var shipment = shipments.Where(x => x.Id == int.Parse(shipmentId));
return Ok(shipment);
}
```

In this example, the `regex(^SHIPMENT-[0-7]{{5}}$)` regular expression enforces that only custom IDs for shipments that follow the `SHIPMENT-XXXXX` pattern are accepted; otherwise, the request is going to be rejected by the pipeline. This is helpful in removing validation rules from the body of the controller actions, keeping the controllers clean for their real purpose. In the next section, we will learn how to handle multi-tenant routing with subdomains.

Multi-tenant routing with subdomains

Routing configurations based on subdomains is helpful in scenarios where the application follows a multi-tenant architecture with each tenant having their specific domain to access the API endpoints. This approach allows us to apply custom behavior of the controller actions for each tenant and points each client to their specific resources. Here's an example of how you can configure routes per tenant in your controller:

```
[Route("{tenant}.domainexample.com/api/[controller]")]
[ApiController]
```

```
public class TenantShipmentController : Controller
{
    [HttpGet("")]
    public IActionResult GetShipments(string tenant)
    {

        return Ok();
    }
}
```

In this example, the routing focuses the strategy on checking the subdomain, as highlighted in the previous code, allowing `TenantShipmentController` to handle resources or a specific logic for each tenant. This approach makes the handling of requests that come from multiple tenants easier to manage without compromising the logic implementation of the controller actions themselves.

In the next section, we will customize route handlers for dynamic endpoints in ASP.NET Core.

Custom route handlers for dynamic endpoints

The configuration of custom route handlers for ASP.NET Core applications allows us to determine advanced aspects of routing that cannot be set using the regular attributes for routing. This approach is helpful in cases where the routing logic is directly dependent on external resources, such as database configurations or conditions in dynamic environments. Here's an example of how you can create a custom handler for dynamic endpoints:

```
public class CustomRouteHandler: IRouter
{
    private readonly IShipmentService _shipmentService;

    public DynamicRouteHandler(
        IShipmentService shipmentService)
    {
        _shipmentService = shipmentService;
    }

    public async Task RouteAsync(RouteContext context)
    {
        var path = context
            .HttpContext.Request.Path.Value.Trim('/');
        var segments = path.Split('/');

        if (segments.Length == 2 &&
            segments[0] == "shipments")
        {
```

```
            var shipmentId = segments[1];
            if (_shipmentService.ShipmentExists(
                shipmentId))
            {
                context.Handler = async httpContext =>
                {
                    var shipment = await
                        _shipmentService.GetShipment(
                            shipmentId);
                    await httpContext.Response.WriteAsync(
                        JsonConvert.SerializeObject(
                            shipment)
                    );
                };
            }
        }
    }

    public VirtualPathData GetVirtualPath(
        VirtualPathContext context)
    {
        return null;
    }
}
```

In this example, `CustomRouteHandler` contains a custom implementation to handle routing based on the path obtained from the URL. If the path matches the pattern, the custom handler retrieves the underlying shipment data using a service to include it in the response. This technique allows you to configure custom behavior for routing based on the dynamic data that comes from the API request itself.

In the next section, we will explore how to combine versioning with query parameters and headers when working with routes in ASP.NET Core.

Versioning with query parameters and headers

Versioning APIs is crucial for tracking changes and updates to the underlying service provided without breaking the communication between the service itself and clients. It is possible to configure and handle versioning in ASP.NET Core applications using query parameters and headers, giving you an easy way to control the transition between versions.

Here's an example of how you can configure versioning for your API endpoints:

```
public class ShipmentVersioning : Controller
{
    [HttpGet]
    [MapToApiVersion("1.0")]
    public IActionResult GetShipmentsV1()
    {
        return Ok();
    }

    [HttpGet, MapToApiVersion("2.0")]
    public IActionResult GetShipmentsV2()
    {
        return Ok();
    }
}
```

In this example, the MapToApiVersion attribute is used to determine the version of each endpoint. To finalize the configuration for versioning, it is necessary to make changes in the Program.cs file as well, as highlighted in the following code:

```
var builder = WebApplication.CreateBuilder(args);

builder.Services.AddControllers();

builder.Services.AddApiVersioning(options =>
{
    options.DefaultApiVersion = new ApiVersion(1, 0);
    options.AssumeDefaultVersionWhenUnspecified = true;
    options.ReportApiVersions = true;
    options.ApiVersionReader = new
        QueryStringApiVersionReader("v");
});

var app = builder.Build();
```

After applying this configuration, API consumers can specify the underlying API version as part of their requests by using the v parameter. This technique allows you to make updates in your APIs without disrupting clients, allowing a good experience in terms of compatibility.

These advanced routing techniques in ASP.NET Core give you many tools to build dynamic and scalable APIs, allowing you to take advantage of the full flexibility provided by ASP.NET Core in terms of routing, making it possible to address complex business requirements.

In the next section, we are going to discuss aspects of performance optimization for APIs.

Performance optimization for APIs

In modern web applications, user experience is crucial in determining the success of projects, and the performance of APIs is one of the most important factors influencing the user's perception of the velocity, responsiveness, and reliability of applications. As your APIs need to scale and handle a large number of requests, applying techniques for API performance becomes essential to maintain efficiency and reliability. This section covers important strategies that can be used to optimize the performance of your APIs in ASP.NET Core, including database optimization, asynchronous programming, compression, and caching.

Let's start with diving into caching strategies for ASP.NET Core applications.

Caching strategies

Caching is one of the best ways to increase the performance of APIs, as it reduces the amount of direct access to expensive server resources for repeated requests. By storing the response of frequent requests in a caching system, the API can serve subsequent requests without accessing databases and other resources, significantly reducing server load and response time.

Imagine a scenario where you have an API that retrieves shipment details from a database. This data does not change very often, which means that you may want to use caching to avoid querying the database frequently.

Here's an example of how you can use caching in a regular controller in ASP.NET Core:

```
using Chapter9.Interfaces;
using Chapter9.Models;
using Microsoft.AspNetCore.Mvc;
using Microsoft.Extensions.Caching.Memory;

namespace Chapter9.Controllers.Caching
{
    [Route("api/[controller]")]
    [ApiController]
    public class ShipmentController : ControllerBase
    {
        private readonly IMemoryCache _cache;
```

```csharp
public ShipmentController(IMemoryCache cache)
{
    _cache = cache;
}


[HttpGet("{id}")]
public IActionResult GetShipment(int id)
{
    var cacheKey = $"Shipment_{id}";
    if (!_cache.TryGetValue(
        cacheKey, out IShipment shipment))
    {
        shipment = GetShipmentFromDatabase(id);


        var cacheOptions =
            new MemoryCacheEntryOptions
        {
            AbsoluteExpirationRelativeToNow =
                TimeSpan.FromMinutes(10),
            SlidingExpiration =
                TimeSpan.FromMinutes(2)
        };

        _cache.Set(
            cacheKey,
            shipment,
            cacheOptions
        );
    }

    return Ok(shipment);
}

private IShipment GetShipmentFromDatabase(int id)
{
    // Simulate a database call
    return new Shipment();
}
}

}
```

In this example, the `GetShipment` method caches the shipment details in memory using `ImemoryCache`. If the shipment is not found in the cache, it is retrieved from a database source and then stored in the cache for subsequent requests with associated expiration settings. Caching results are usually faster than regular database calls, which can improve the overall performance of your API.

In the next section, we will explore response compression in ASP.NET Core.

Response compression

Using response compression can significantly reduce the payload size transferred between the API and clients via the network. This is crucial when dealing with large JSON responses. ASP.NET Core provides a native mechanism that supports response compression using middleware.

To add response compression to your API, make the following changes in the `Program.cs` file, as highlighted in the following code:

```
using Microsoft.AspNetCore.Mvc.Versioning;
using Microsoft.AspNetCore.Mvc;
using Microsoft.AspNetCore.ResponseCompression;
using System.IO.Compression;

namespace Chapter9
{
    public class Program
    {
        public static void Main(string[] args)
        {
            var builder =
                WebApplication.CreateBuilder(args);

            builder.Services.AddControllers();

            builder.Services.AddApiVersioning(options =>
            {
                options.DefaultApiVersion =
                    new ApiVersion(1, 0);
                options.AssumeDefaultVersionWhenUnspecified
                    = true;
                options.ReportApiVersions = true;
                options.ApiVersionReader =
                    new QueryStringApiVersionReader("v");
            });
```

```
builder.Services.AddResponseCompression(options =>
{
    options.EnableForHttps = true;
    options.Providers
        .Add<BrotliCompressionProvider>();
    options.Providers
        .Add<GzipCompressionProvider>();
});

builder.Services.Configure<
    GzipCompressionProviderOptions>(options =>
{
    options.Level = CompressionLevel.Fastest;
});

var app = builder.Build();

app.UseAuthorization();
app.MapControllers();

app.Run();
        }
    }
}
```

In this example, the `AddResponseCompression` service is added to the pipeline to use the `Brotli` and `Gzip` compression modes. The middleware handles the compression based on the `Accept-Encoding` header present in the requests. By compressing API responses, you can significantly reduce the network traffic between the API and clients and improve the overall speed of operations when large payloads are involved.

Asynchronous programming

Asynchronous programming is an important technique for improving the performance and scalability of APIs in ASP.NET Core, as it can prevent threads on the server from being blocked while waiting for long-running operations to complete, such as external API calls, database queries, and file I/O operations.

In APIs that don't take advantage of asynchronous programming, when a request to the API involves a time-consuming operation, the server blocks the thread until the operation finishes, which means that the server cannot handle other requests in the meantime, resulting in potential bottlenecks and significantly degrading performance.

In ASP.NET Core, you can implement asynchronous methods using the `async` and `await` keywords, which are related to **Task-Based Asynchronous Programming (TAP)**. Here's how you can use asynchronous programming in a regular API controller:

```
using Chapter9.Interfaces;
using Microsoft.AspNetCore.Mvc;

namespace Chapter9.Controllers.Async
{
    [Route("api/[controller]")]
    [ApiController]
    public class ShipmentController : ControllerBase
    {
        private readonly IShipmentService _shipmentService;

        public ShipmentController(
            IShipmentService shipmentService)
        {
            _shipmentService = shipmentService;
        }

        [HttpGet("{id}")]
        public async Task<IActionResult> GetShipment(
            string id)
        {
            var shipment =
                await _shipmentService.GetShipment(id);

            if (shipment == null)
            {
                return NotFound();
            }
            return Ok(shipment);
        }
    }

}
```

In this example, the `GetShipment` method is asynchronous, as indicated by the `async` keyword. The action returns `Task<IActionResult>`, which means that an ongoing operation will eventually produce `IActionResult` when it is complete.

The `await` keyword is used to wait for the completion of the `GetShipment` method, which retrieves the shipment data from the database. During the waiting period, the server where the application is hosted is free to handle other requests in parallel, improving the overall responsiveness of the API.

The same principle applies when the `async` and `await` keywords are used with Entity Framework Core and any other library or framework that supports asynchronous methods.

Asynchronous programming is a powerful approach in the entire .NET ecosystem as it improves performance, providing high scalability in many scenarios for ASP.NET Core APIs.

In the next section, we will explore basic concepts of database optimization for ASP.NET Core applications.

Database optimization techniques

The performance of APIs is highly related to the efficient use of database access in most applications. Problematic database queries and other factors related to how databases are structured can lead to slow response times and bottlenecks. Therefore, optimizing database interactions in your APIs is crucial for achieving great application performance.

Here are some examples of how you can apply practices that will optimize database usage in your APIs:

- **Batch processing**: Combine queries and operations when possible when inserting and updating data for multiple records.

- **Early filter**: Apply filter conditions that will reduce the amount of data returned and take advantage of database indexes in the `WHERE` clause.

- **Reduce joins**: Simplify your queries to use joins only when necessary.

- **Avoid over-fetching**: Avoid fetching more data than you need. For instance, instead of retrieving all columns from a table, select only the columns that are necessary for the API response.

- **Avoid long-lived connections**: Always close connections when an operation is finished to avoid bottlenecks in the database connection.

- **Monitoring**: Take advantage of tools that allow you to monitor query performance to identify slow-running queries. Tools such as Application Insights, SQL Server Profiler, and others can be helpful in determining problematic queries in your application.

Database optimization is an essential factor in API performance. Following good practices will enhance the responsiveness, reliability, and scalability of your APIs. In the next section, we will explore connection pooling for ASP.NET Core applications.

Connection pooling

Connection pooling is helpful in managing database connections with efficiency, mainly in the context of intense usage of heavy-load scenarios. You can significantly reduce the risk of issues in concurrent database access when reusing database connections. Here's an example of how you can implement connection pooling when using Entity Framework Core:

```
builder.Services.AddDbContextPool<SystemContext>(options =>
options.UseSqlServer("YOUR_CONNECTION_STRING"));
```

In this example, the `AddDbContextPool` method is used to configure Entity Framework Core to use a pooled `DbContext`. This approach allows better management of the `DbContext` instances by reusing them in multiple requests instead of creating a new one, improving the performance of your API, especially under high usage conditions.

Summary

In this chapter, we delved into advanced aspects of RESTful API development using ASP.NET Core, focusing on optimizing performance, implementing advanced routing techniques, and ensuring scalability and maintainability of your APIs.

We began by exploring advanced routing techniques, including attribute routing, multi-tenant routing with subdomains, and custom route handlers. These techniques provide the flexibility needed to handle complex scenarios where API endpoints must cater to diverse client needs. Through practical examples, such as using regular expressions for dynamic routing and implementing custom route handlers, we illustrated how to configure routes that respond dynamically to different conditions and external resources.

Next, we examined performance optimization strategies critical for modern web applications. We covered caching strategies to reduce server load, response compression to decrease payload sizes, and asynchronous programming to improve server responsiveness. These techniques ensure that your APIs can handle a high volume of requests efficiently, providing users with a seamless experience. We also discussed database optimization practices, emphasizing the importance of efficient data access, reducing query complexity, and using connection pooling to manage resources effectively.

These lessons and skills are essential for building robust, scalable, and high-performance APIs. They equip you with the tools necessary to address complex business requirements, ensuring that your APIs remain efficient and maintainable as they grow in complexity and usage.

In the next chapter, we will shift our focus to an introduction to JavaScript frameworks. We will explore how these frameworks can complement your API development by enhancing the frontend experience, leading to the creation of dynamic and responsive web applications. This transition builds on the knowledge you've gained in optimizing backend performance, setting the stage for a holistic understanding of full-stack development.

Get This Book's PDF Version and Exclusive Extras

UNLOCK NOW

Scan the QR code (or go to packtpub.com/unlock). Search for this book by name, confirm the edition, and then follow the steps on the page.

Note: Keep your invoice handly. Purchase made directly from packt don't require one.

10

Introduction to JavaScript Frameworks

JavaScript frameworks have become essential in web development, providing mature tools to build efficient, large, and complex frontend applications. There are many frameworks available on the market, each of them with its own characteristics. This chapter aims to provide a basic understanding of the three most popular JavaScript frameworks: Angular, React, and Vue.js. You'll gain basic knowledge of their core principles and use cases, which will help you choose the right framework for the context of the project you'll be working on.

In this chapter, we'll explore the foundational concepts of JavaScript frameworks, highlighting what makes them different from each other. We'll learn how to start working with these frameworks, creating components, and setting up basic structures so that we can delve deeper into the concepts of each later in this book. By the end of this chapter, you'll have a solid knowledge of the key features of these frameworks and will be able to apply the concepts in simple web projects.

In this chapter, we will cover the following main topics:

- Overview of Angular
- Getting started with React
- Understanding the basics of Vue.js

Technical requirements

To study Angular, React, and Vue.js effectively, you'll need the latest version of Node.js installed on your machine as it provides the runtime environment to execute and run your applications. Node.js is also required for package management as it contains tools for managing dependencies and packages required to develop your applications locally. The most recent version of these tools is sufficient to get you ready for the practical examples in this chapter, assuming you've already installed VS Code, which was required in the previous chapters of this book.

The code files required for you to follow along with this chapter can be found at: `https://github.com/PacktPublishing/Modern-Full-Stack-Web-Development-with-ASP.NET-Core/tree/main/Chapter10`

Overview of Angular

Angular is a robust JavaScript framework that's been developed and maintained by Google since 2010. The very first version of Angular was called AngularJS. Due to the framework evolving considerably over the years, the name of the framework changed to Angular to demonstrate to companies, developers, and technical communities that its core had changed so much that a new name was required. Angular is built with TypeScript, which helps developers catch errors early during development. TypeScript enhances JavaScript by adding static typing, enabling developers to find errors during compilation instead of runtime. With a robust type system, TypeScript allows for more reliable and maintainable code, which is especially useful in large-scale, complex applications.

Here are the key features of this powerful JavaScript framework:

- **Component-based architecture**: Angular encourages developers to work with a modular approach to building web applications by heavily using the concept of reusable components.

- **Dependency injection**: Angular uses dependency injection extensively in its core, which promotes good development practices and improves testability and scalability, especially for complex projects.

- **Two-way data binding**: Angular synchronizes data between the model and the UI. This ensures that any changes in the model are automatically reflected in the UI and vice versa, facilitating a better experience for both users and developers.

- **Reactive programming**: Angular utilizes RxJS, a library for reactive programming that allows developers to handle asynchronous data streams. This is particularly useful for dealing with complex scenarios in large applications and elaborate workflows.

- **Broad-ranging tooling**: Angular has a powerful **command-line interface** (**CLI**) that enhances the development experience, assisting with project setup, deployment, and testing.

- **Routing**: Angular has a native routing system that enables navigation between pages in an application with lazy loading, significantly improving the user experience and application performance by loading only the required components when needed.

In the next section, we'll learn how to set up a local environment so that we can work with Angular, enabling you to replicate the code samples in the following sections.

Setting up your Angular environment

Before starting Angular development, you'll need to install the Angular CLI, a command-line tool that aids the development process. To install it, run the following command in your terminal (cmd or a terminal in VS Code):

```
npm install -g @angular/cli
```

This command installs the Angular CLI in your local environment, facilitating the creation and management of Angular projects using the command line.

With this installation, you're all set to create your very first Angular application. In the next section, we'll create components step by step and understand a typical Angular project structure.

Creating your first Angular project

First of all, you need to create the Angular application using the Angular CLI tool using your terminal. You can achieve this by using the following command, where you can also specify the name of your application:

```
ng new angular-chapter-10
```

In this example, the name of the application is angular-chapter-10. The Angular CLI gives you the option to make choices for your application regarding the stylesheet format, as shown in *Figure 10.1*:

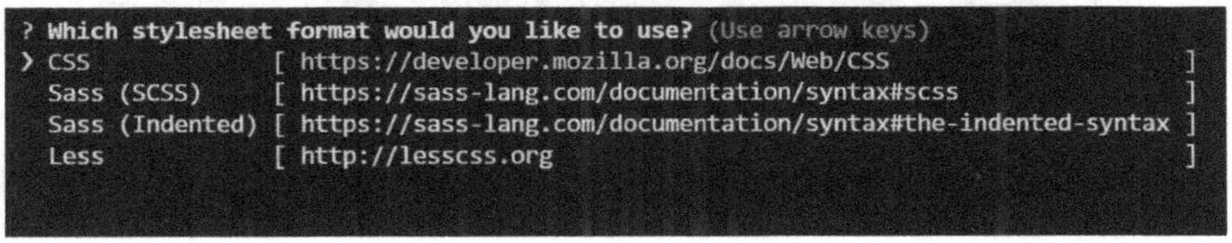

Figure 10.1: Stylesheet format for Angular

In this project example, this chapter uses the first stylesheet option, which is the standard CSS format. Additionally, the Angular CLI will ask if you want to enable **Server-Side Rendering (SSR)** and **Static Site Generation (SSG/Prerendering)**, as shown in *Figure 10.2*:

Figure 10.2: SSR configuration

You can choose No in this case, as we won't be using SSR in this chapter. SSR is an approach where the HTML of the Angular application is generated on the server instead of the client. In this case, when a user requests a page in the browser, the server processes it and returns the fully generated HTML. This technique improves performance based on the nature of the application, is more SEO-friendly, and provides a better user experience as the load is generally faster compared to client-side rendering.

However, SSR can be more complex to configure and requires server infrastructure to serve the requests. Therefore, there are trade-offs to consider when making this decision.

After confirming your choices, the command generates the new project, installing all the necessary files and packages. You can navigate to your newly created project by running the following command, where the second part is the name of your project:

```
cd angular-chapter-10
```

To start and run your application, you can use the `serve` command of the Angular CLI, as shown in the following example:

```
ng serve
```

This command builds the application and makes it available on a default localhost URL to be executed, as shown in *Figure 10.3*:

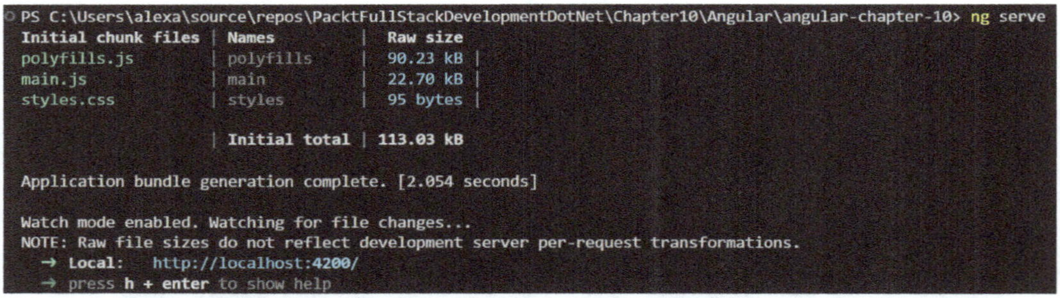

Figure 10.3: Result of the ng serve command

If you open the URL shown in the terminal, the Angular application will launch in the default browser, displaying the default component present in the Angular project, as shown in *Figure 10.4*:

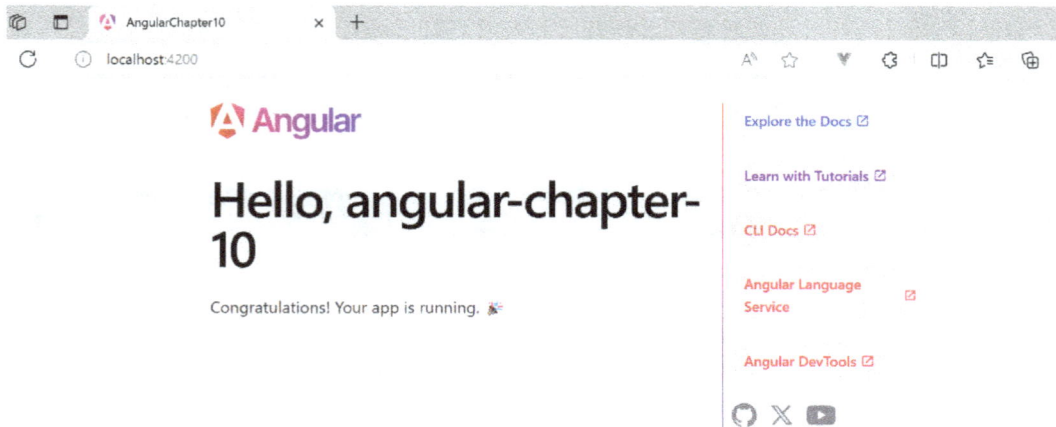

Figure 10.4: Angular application running in the browser

The Angular application comes with a default structure and specific sample components. If you're using the most recent version of Angular CLI, your project structure should look like this:

```
∨ ANGULAR-CHAPTER-10
  > .angular
  > .vscode
  > public
  ∨ src
    ∨ app
      > my-component
      #  app.component.css
      <> app.component.html
      TS app.component.spec.ts
      TS app.component.ts
      TS app.config.ts
      TS app.routes.ts
    <> index.html
    TS main.ts
    #  styles.css
  ⚙ .editorconfig
  ◈ .gitignore
  {} angular.json
  {} package-lock.json
  {} package.json
  ⓘ README.md
  {} tsconfig.app.json
  ▨ tsconfig.json
  {} tsconfig.spec.json
```

Figure 10.5: Angular project structure

When you create an Angular project using the Angular CLI, the structure is organized to help developers follow best practices for Angular applications. The root of the directory contains specific key files and folders.

In this folder structure, the `node_modules` directory contains all the necessary dependencies and packages required by your application. These packages are installed when you execute the `npm install` command or when a new project is created using `create-react-app`. This folder is exclusively managed by NPM. Any manual changes that are made in this folder will be overridden by npm commands. You don't need to make any changes to it.

The `src` folder is crucial as it contains the actual application code. Inside this folder, you'll find the `app` folder, which houses the application components, modules, and underlying services.

The `angular.json` file centralizes the configuration for the Angular CLI, allowing you to determine how the project is built, including environment configurations. The `package.json` file contains all the project dependencies and scripts to automate specific tasks like serving and building the Angular application.

Finally, the `tsconfig.json` file defines the TypeScript settings for your project. Additionally, the project structure includes files such as `.gitignore` and `.editorconfig`, which contain configuration regarding files that shouldn't be tracked by Git and editor settings for Angular, respectively.

In the next section, we'll learn how to create a basic Angular component that contains **HTML**, **CSS**, and logic implementation.

Creating a basic Angular component

Angular uses a component-based architecture, with each component containing the styles, HTML, and logic written in TypeScript. To create a basic Angular component, you can use the Angular CLI, as shown in the following command:

```
ng generate component my-component --standalone
```

In this command, `my-component` is the actual name of the component. After executing it, a new folder is generated under the `app` folder, as shown in *Figure 10.6*:

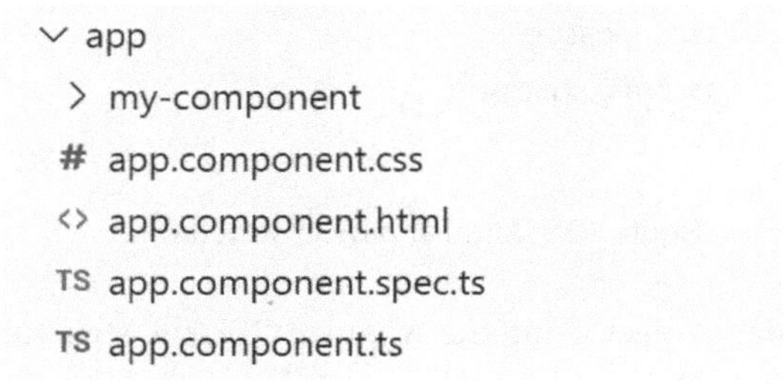

```
∨ app
  › my-component
  # app.component.css
  <> app.component.html
  TS app.component.spec.ts
  TS app.component.ts
```

Figure 10.6: Component structure

It's good practice to separate files for CSS, HTML, logic, and tests for Angular components as this is a practice that's followed by the Angular CLI. By default, all component files have the `component` suffix. After opening the `my-component.component.ts` file, you can include a `title` property and rename the class to `MyComponent`, as demonstrated in the following code:

```
import { Component } from '@angular/core';

@Component({
  selector: 'app-my-component',
  standalone: true,
  imports: [],
  templateUrl: './my-component.component.html',
  styleUrl: './my-component.component.css'
})
export class MyComponent {
  title = "My first Angular component"
}
```

Now that the `title` property has been created, you can reference it in the corresponding HTML file for the component (`my-component.component.html`), as shown in the following code:

```
<p>{{ title }}</p>
```

To use the component across the application and verify that it's working as expected to display the title, you can reference the newly created component in the `app.component.ts` file, as highlighted in the following code:

```
import { Component } from '@angular/core';
import { RouterOutlet } from '@angular/router';
import {
  MyComponent
} from './my-component/my-component.component';


@Component({
  selector: 'app-root',
  standalone: true,
  imports: [RouterOutlet, MyComponent],
  templateUrl: './app.component.html',
  styleUrl: './app.component.css'
})
export class AppComponent {
  title = 'angular-chapter-10';
}
```

In this case, the path for the new component is referenced at the beginning of the file, and the `MyComponent` exported class is referenced in the `imports` property of the `@Component` directive.

Since the new component is already registered in the `app.component.ts` file, you can use the component in the `app.component.html` file, as highlighted in the following code:

```
<h1>Hello, {{ title }}</h1>
<p>Congratulations! Your app is running. 🎉</p>
<br>
<p>
  <app-my-component></app-my-component>
</p>
```

If you open the application in your browser, you'll see the component's content being displayed alongside the message specified in the title property – that is, **My first Angular component** – as shown in *Figure 10.7*:

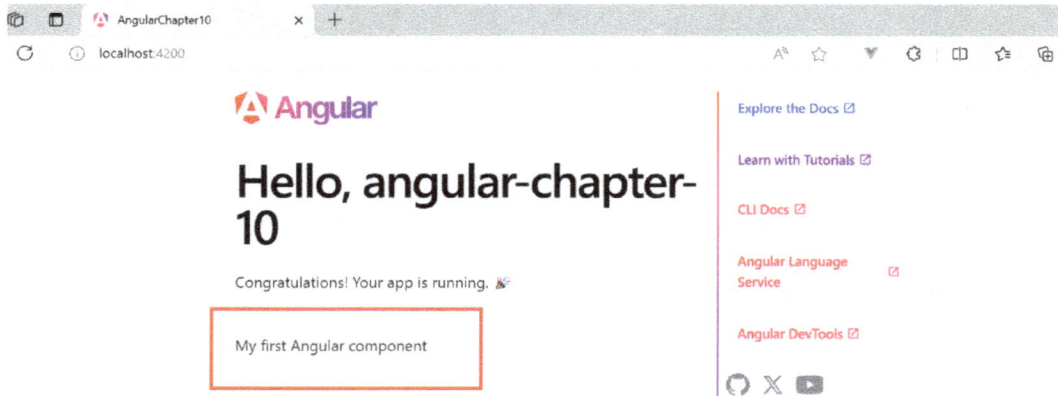

Figure 10.7: The new component being displayed

Angular is a straightforward framework to work with, making it easy for developers to create dynamic web applications. This section aimed to provide a basic overview of Angular. In *Chapter 13*, you'll have the opportunity to explore this powerful framework in more detail, including how to call backend APIs and work with more complex scenarios.

In the next section, we'll learn the basics of React, another popular and powerful JavaScript framework for building modern web applications.

Getting started with React

React is a powerful and popular JavaScript framework for building **single-page applications** (**SPAs**), where the application doesn't need to be fully reloaded when users navigate between pages.

This framework is developed by Facebook with robust and mature features supported by technical communities around the React ecosystem.

The framework has the following key features and benefits:

- **Virtual DOM manipulation**: React uses a virtual DOM to improve performance when rendering visual components. This means that the framework compares the virtual DOM with the actual DOM to determine which updates should be reflected in the browser if the state changes, making the rendering process efficient.

- **Component-based architecture**: Like Angular, React follows the concept of reusable components, with each component encapsulating HTML, CSS, and logic.

- **JavaScript XML (JSX)**: React allows the use of JSX, a syntax pattern that enables HTML-like code within JavaScript code. This feature facilitates the visualization of the HTML structure within the JavaScript code by the developer. It's worth noting that the use of JSX syntax isn't universally agreed upon in the React community, although it's heavily used.

- **Hooks**: React implements the concept of Hooks, which is a way to manage state using functional components. This approach allows for writing more declarative and modular code without explicitly creating class-based components.

- **One-way data flow**: React works with unidirectional data flow, meaning that communication between parent and child components is forced to happen in only one direction. This facilitates state management for complex applications, thereby improving the developer experience when debugging large applications with complicated data flows.

- **React state and reactivity**: In React, state manages dynamic data, enabling interactive and responsive components. With React's reactivity, any state updates cause the affected components to automatically re-render, reflecting the latest data.

In the next section, you'll learn what you'll need to set up your local environment so that you can build React applications.

Setting up the environment for React

To develop React applications, you need to install the `create-react-app` package globally by running the following command:

```
npm install -g create-react-app
```

This command installs the `create-react-app` tool globally on your machine, which facilitates the creation of React applications from anywhere via the terminal.

After running the command, you can verify whether the installation happened correctly. You can check the installation by executing the following command:

```
create-react-app --version
```

This command displays the version of the `create-react-app` package. After this installation, you'll be able to create React applications using the standalone method that the framework provides.

In the next section, we'll explore the basic concepts of React applications by creating a simple application from scratch.

Creating a basic React application

React uses a component-based architecture, with each component containing the necessary styles, HTML, and logic. To create a basic initial React application, you can use the `create-react-app` tool and specify the name of the application, as shown in the following command:

```
create-react-app react-chapter-10
```

In this case, `react-chapter-10` is the name of the application. You can specify your own in your local environment. After executing the command, you can navigate to your project directory by executing the `cd` command along with the name of your project, as shown in the following command:

```
cd react-chapter-10
```

To start the development server for the React application and view the newly created application in the browser, you can use the following command:

```
npm start
```

If you've executed the previous commands correctly, the application should automatically open in the browser, as shown in *Figure 10.8*:

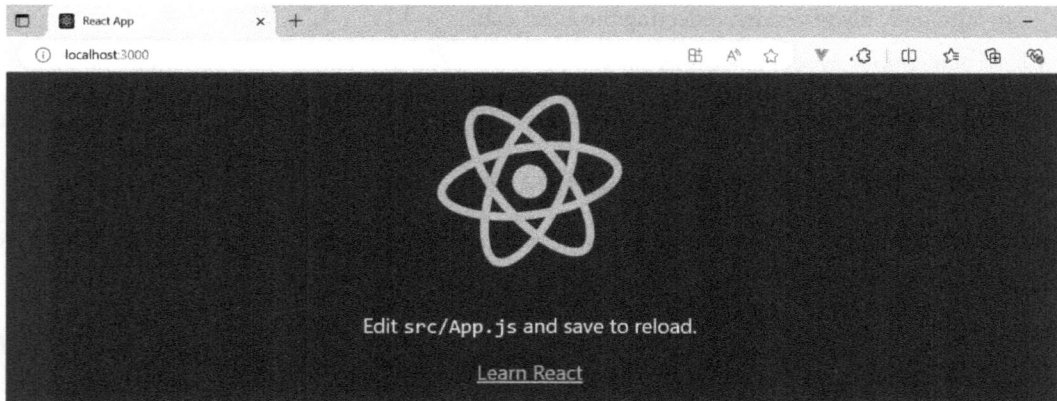

Figure 10.8: React application running

With that, your first React application is running! The `create-react-app` command creates a default folder structure and sample components to help developers by providing examples of how to set up and create other components. The folder structure looks like this:

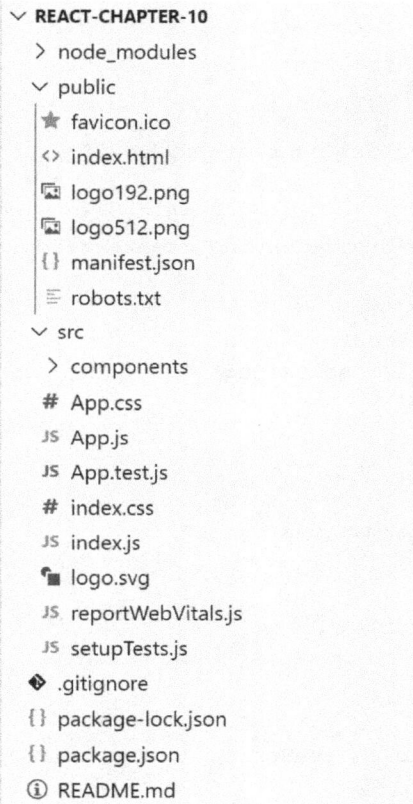

```
∨ REACT-CHAPTER-10
  > node_modules
  ∨ public
    ★ favicon.ico
    <> index.html
    🖼 logo192.png
    🖼 logo512.png
    {} manifest.json
    ≡ robots.txt
  ∨ src
    > components
    # App.css
    JS App.js
    JS App.test.js
    # index.css
    JS index.js
    🔖 logo.svg
    JS reportWebVitals.js
    JS setupTests.js
  ◆ .gitignore
  {} package-lock.json
  {} package.json
  ⓘ README.md
```

Figure 10.9: React application structure

The `public` folder contains all the static assets and the main HTML file for your project. Static files are images, styles, HTML, and any other resources that need to be served by your application and don't need any be processed by the logic of components dynamically.

In the `public` folder, `index.html` is the main HTML file. It acts as a starting point for your React application, with this file being downloaded by the browser in the first request to the application. This file contains references to all the necessary references to CSS, as well as JavaScript files, that are used globally by the application. Also, this file contains a `<div>` element with a "root" ID, as highlighted in the following code snippet:

```
<!DOCTYPE html>
<html lang="en">
```

```
<head>
  <meta charset="utf-8" />
  <link rel="icon" href="%PUBLIC_URL%/favicon.ico" />
  <meta
    name="viewport"
    content="width=device-width,
    initial-scale=1"
  />
  <meta name="theme-color" content="#000000" />
  <meta
    name="description"
    content="Web site created using create-react-app"
  />
  <link
    rel="apple-touch-icon"
    href="%PUBLIC_URL%/logo192.png"
  />

  <link
    rel="manifest"
    href="%PUBLIC_URL%/manifest.json"
  />

  <title>React App</title>
</head>
<body>
  <noscript>
      You need to enable JavaScript to run this app.
  </noscript>
  <div id="root"></div>
</body>
</html>
```

React uses this element to render your application inside. It's a default root element when you create a React application.

The src directory contains the actual source code for your React application. In this folder, the index.js file instructs the React application that the root element should be used to render the application, as shown in the following example:

```
import React from 'react';
import ReactDOM from 'react-dom/client';
import './index.css';
```

```
import App from './App';
import reportWebVitals from './reportWebVitals';

const root =
  ReactDOM.createRoot(document.getElementById('root'));
root.render(
  <React.StrictMode>
    <App />
  </React.StrictMode>
);


reportWebVitals();
```

The App.js file inside the src folder is the entry point for the entire logic in your React application. This is how the file should look in your newly created application:

```
import logo from './logo.svg';
import './App.css';

function App() {
  return (
    <div className="App">
      <header className="App-header">
        <img src={logo} className="App-logo" alt="logo" />
        <p>
          Edit <code>src/App.js</code> and save to reload.
        </p>
        <a
          className="App-link"
          href="https://reactjs.org"
          target="_blank"
          rel="noopener noreferrer"
        >
          Learn React
        </a>
      </header>
    </div>
  );
}

export default App;
```

The package.json file contains all the dependencies and configurations required for your application to run. The .gitignore file tells Git which files and directories should be ignored in version control. Additionally, the src folder contains the global .css files for your application. These files contain base styles that will apply to all components unless they're overridden by other CSS files.

In the next section, you'll learn how to create your very first React component.

Creating React components

As React follows a component-based architecture, it's important to understand the main types of React components available to encapsulate the logic, styling, and structure of your features and reusable code.

Two types of React components can be used by developers:

- **Functional components**: These are JavaScript functions that return JSX. Their structure is more readable, especially when combined with Hooks, which provide an efficient way to manage state and side effects in functional components.

- **Class components**: These components are **ECMAScript 6** classes that inherit from the React. Component type and contain a method to render the UI. It's worth noting that functional components are the most popular way to create components, mainly due to their simplicity and compatibility with Hooks.

In this chapter, we'll focus on functional components as they're the standard way to create components in React applications. To create a new component, follow these steps:

1. Navigate to the src directory in your React project with VS Code and create a components folder to organize and place your components.

2. Next, create a MyComponent.js file inside the components folder in VS Code.

3. Open the new MyComponent.js file and define a functional component, as shown in the following code:

```
import React from 'react';

function MyComponent() {
  return (
    <div className="my-component">
      <h2>This is my first React component!</h2>
      <p>Congratulations for your first component.</p>
    </div>
  );
}

export default MyComponent;
```

In this code, the import statement, `import React from 'react'`, is mandatory for using JSX. Additionally, `function MyComponent {..}` explicitly defines a functional component named `MyComponent`, which returns a JSX component that determines how the UI looks.

To test your new React component, you can import and include it in the `App.js` file, as shown in the following code:

```
import logo from './logo.svg';
import './App.css';
import MyComponent from './components/MyComponent';


function App() {
  return (
    <div className="App">
      <header className="App-header">
        <img src={logo} className="App-logo" alt="logo" />
        <p>
          Edit <code>src/App.js</code> and save to reload.
        </p>
        <a
          className="App-link"
          href="https://reactjs.org"
          target="_blank"
          rel="noopener noreferrer"
        >
          Learn React
        </a>
      </header>
      <main>
        <MyComponent />
      </main>
    </div>
  );
}


export default App;
```

In this `App.js` file, the reference to the component in the `import MyComponent from './components/MyComponent';` line allows the component to be used in the context of App. The content of the App component also includes the `<MyComponent />` reference to render the component's output.

To view your component in your browser, re-run the `npm start` command in the root folder of your application via the terminal. After that, open your browser to the default URL, `http://localhost:3000/`; you should see the content of your component at the bottom of the page, as shown in *Figure 10.9*:

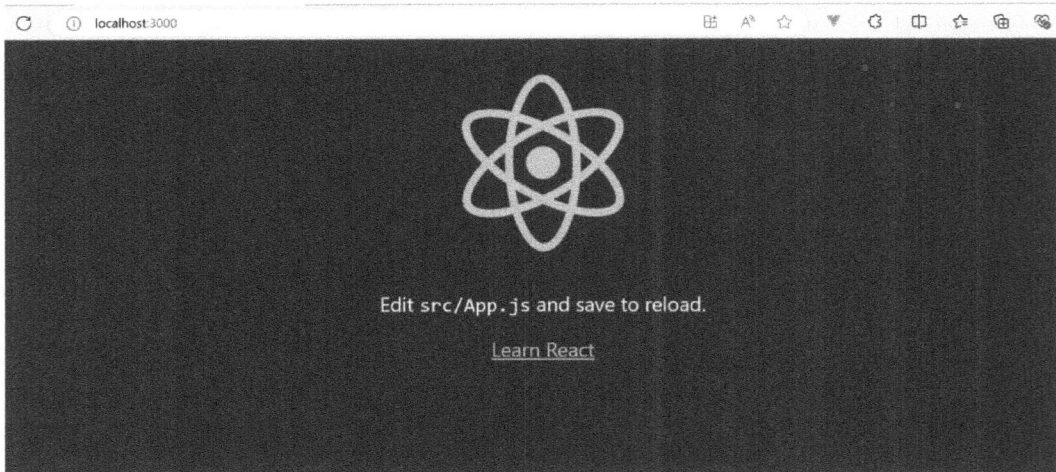

Figure 10.10: View of the React component

React is a very popular library that facilitates the creation of powerful web applications. This section aimed to provide only a basic overview of React. In *Chapter 14*, you'll have the opportunity to explore React in more detail, including how to connect with backend APIs and manage more complex scenarios.

In the next section, we'll learn about **Vue.js**, another very popular JavaScript framework for building SPAs.

Understanding the basics of Vue.js

Vue.js is a very popular JavaScript framework that's known for being a simpler alternative compared to other JavaScript frameworks. This framework was developed by Evan You, a former member of the Angular project's core team. Vue.js is especially useful for building rich user interfaces using the SPA approach. This powerful framework has the following main features:

- **Component-based architecture**: Similar to Angular and React, Vue.js has a component-based architecture, which allows UI elements to be divided into reusable components that encapsulate HTML, logic, and styling.

- **Single-file components**: Vue allows you to create single-file components using the `.vue` extension. This approach allows you to combine HTML, JavaScript, and CSS implementation in a single file in an organized manner.

- **Vue Router**: Vue includes Vue Router as its official tool for navigation and routing. Vue Router allows developers to establish routes, manage dynamic routing, and create an SPA experience by loading views or components without a full page reload. This is beneficial for applications that require structured navigation and seamless transitions between views.

- **Pinia (state management)**: Pinia replaced Vuex as the preferred state management library in Vue 3. It provides a simpler API and is compatible with both the Composition API and the Options API, making state integration across the application easier. Previously, Vuex was used to handle state in Vue, but Pinia's lightweight and modular design has made it the favored choice for modern Vue applications, boosting reactivity and flexibility.

- **Directives**: Vue.js uses standard directives to control the rendering of components. All the directives have the `v-` prefix, such as `v-if` and `v-for`, which allows us to control the DOM more expressively.

To start building applications with Vue.js, you need to set up your local environment by installing the **Vue CLI**, a command-line tool that facilitates the creation of Vue applications. To install it, execute the following command in your terminal:

```
npm install -g @vue/cli
```

This command installs the **Vue CLI** globally, allowing you to run Vue commands anywhere in your environment. Once the Vue CLI has been installed, you can create a new Vue application using the following command:

```
vue create chapter-10-vue-app
```

Additionally, you can install the Vue extension on VS Code for proper syntax highlighting.

In this command, you can specify the name of the application. In this example, its name is `chapter-10-vue-app`. The Vue CLI will display configuration options for you to choose during creation. Select the Vue 3 version, which is the latest one.

After project creation, navigate into the project directory using the following command, and specify your project name:

```
cd chapter-10-vue-app
```

To run your newly created application and view it in your browser, execute the following command:

```
npm run serve
```

This command starts the development server. You can view your application in your browser by accessing the default URL, http://localhost:8080, as shown in *Figure 10.11*:

Figure 10.11: Vue.js application running

In the next section, you'll learn how to create your very first Vue component.

Creating a basic Vue.js component

To create a new Vue component, within VS Code, navigate to the `src/components` directory and create a new file called `MyComponent.vue` with the following content:

```
<template>
  <div class="my-component">
    <h2>{{ title }}</h2>
    <p>{{ description }}</p>
  </div>
</template>

<script>
  export default {
    name: 'MyComponent',
    data() {
      return {
        title: 'My first Vue component!',
        description: 'I am proud of my first component.'
      };
    }
  };
</script>

<style scoped>
  .my-component {
    border: 1px solid black;
    padding: 15px;
    border-radius: 4px;
    background-color: blanchedalmond;
  }
  .my-component h2 {
    color: black;
  }
</style>
```

In this code, the `<template>` block contains the HTML of the component. It's possible to use the `{{ }}` directive to bind data to the UI.

The `<script>` section contains the logic of the component, including methods, events, and data. In this example, the `data` function returns two properties: `title` and `description`. These properties are used in the template block to display data.

The `<style scoped>` block contains the CSS for the component. This is only applicable to the context of the component itself since the `scoped` attribute is being used. This prevents the CSS from affecting other parts of the application.

To display the newly created component, you can edit the `App.vue` file so that it includes the component, as shown in the following code:

```
<template>
  <img alt="Vue logo" src="./assets/logo.png">
  <HelloWorld msg="Welcome to Your Vue.js App"/>
  <br>
  <MyComponent />

</template>

<script>
import HelloWorld from './components/HelloWorld.vue'
import MyComponent from './components/MyComponent.vue';


export default {
  name: 'App',
  components: {
    HelloWorld,
    MyComponent
  }
}
</script>

<style>
#app {
  font-family: Avenir, Helvetica, Arial, sans-serif;
  -webkit-font-smoothing: antialiased;
  -moz-osx-font-smoothing: grayscale;
  text-align: center;
  color: #2c3e50;
  margin-top: 60px;
}
</style>
```

In this code, the component is imported using `import MyComponent from './components/MyComponent.vue';`, making the component available so that it can be used in the context of the App component. It's also necessary to register the component in the `components` property, as highlighted in the previous code. Finally, the `<MyComponent />` tag is used in the template to render the actual content within the App component.

If your application is still running in your browser, you should see your new component displayed at the bottom of the page once you've saved the changes in the related files, as shown in *Figure 10.12*:

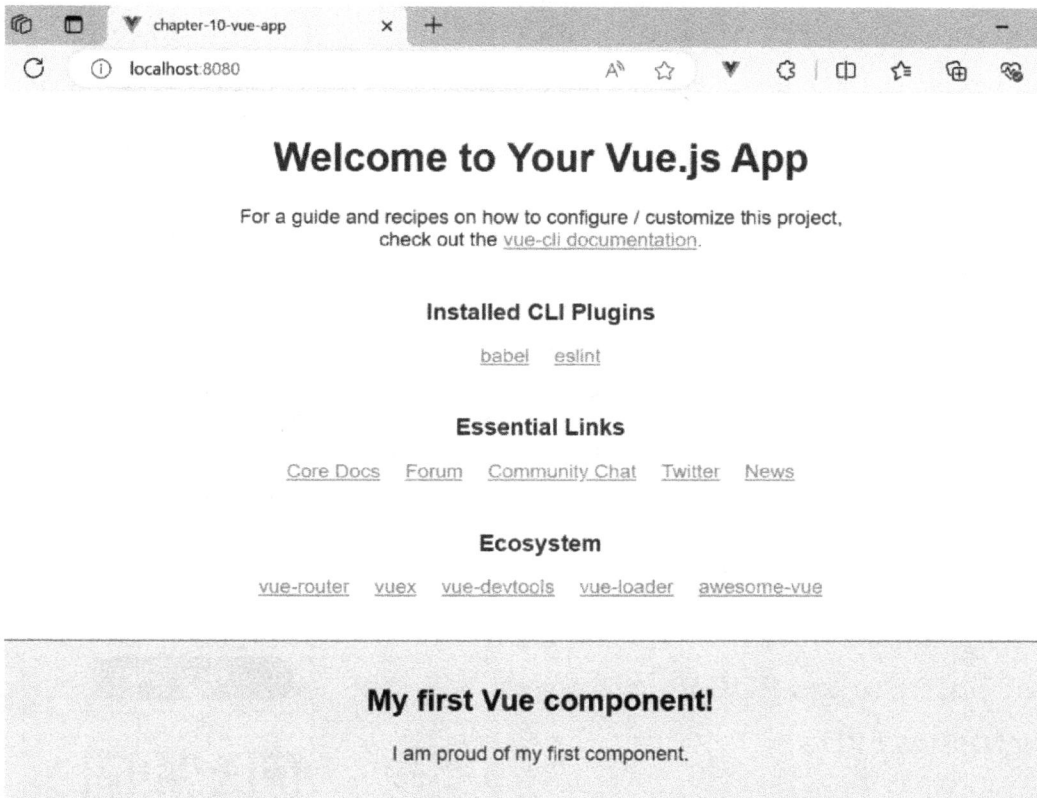

Figure 10.12: Vue application running

Vue.js is a simple and powerful JavaScript framework for building web applications. This section aimed to provide only a basic overview of Vue.js. In *Chapter 11*, we'll learn more advanced concepts regarding this robust framework.

Summary

In this chapter, we explored the basic concepts of the three most popular JavaScript frameworks: Angular, React, and Vue.js. Each of them has characteristics for building robust web applications, and you had the opportunity to explore their main features to help you choose the right tool for your specific development requirements.

We started with Angular, covering key aspects such as component-based architecture, two-way data binding, and comprehensive tooling with the Angular CLI. These features make Angular suitable for complex applications. You also learned how to set up an Angular environment, create a basic component, and explore what the Angular CLI has to offer.

Next, went through the basic concepts of React, emphasizing its component-based structure, JSX syntax, and aspects of component rendering. You gained hands-on experience in setting up your React environment, creating a basic functional component, and using props to make your component dynamic and reusable.

Finally, we explored the Vue.js framework, highlighting its main characteristics, such as single-file components, Vue Router, and Vuex. You learned how to set up your local environment for Vue development, created a basic component, and gained an understanding of the framework's core concepts.

The skills you gained from this chapter are essential so that you can start working with these frameworks, allowing you to scale to more complex cases as you continue your learning journey in the upcoming chapters. Understanding the strengths and basics of each framework enables you to transition to a deeper understanding, allowing you to make informed decisions on which one to use in your projects.

In the next chapter, we'll dive deeper into the Vue.js framework, exploring detailed aspects such as state management, routing, and component hierarchy. We'll conclude by providing a comprehensive comparison of Angular, React, and Vue.js, helping you choose the right framework for specific projects.

11

Exploring Vue.js and Comparing Frameworks

In the previous chapter, we introduced you to the basics of Vue.js, highlighting how to set up your development environment and demonstrating how you can create simple components. Now, in this chapter, we will dive deeper into Vue.js, exploring its more advanced features and ecosystem to give you a solid perspective and understanding of how to build more complex applications with Vue.js. As you progress through this chapter, you will learn about state management in Vue.js, see how to configure routing and navigation, and gain the necessary skills to make well-informed decisions when comparing Vue.js with Angular and React.

By the end of this chapter, you will be able to create more complex Vue components and manage the application state effectively. The practical examples in this chapter will help you build Vue.js applications that are easy to maintain and scale. Furthermore, the chapter provides a perspective on the main differences between Angular, React, and Vue.js, helping you determine which framework will best fit your needs in future professional projects.

In this chapter, we're going to cover the following main topics:

- Deep dive into Vue.js
- Understanding state management in Vue.js
- Routing and navigation in Vue.js
- Framework comparison and selection criteria

The content of this chapter will equip you with the necessary knowledge and tools to build robust Vue.js applications and make sound strategic decisions regarding the JavaScript frameworks you choose for professional projects.

Technical requirements

As mentioned in the previous chapter, to effectively use Vue.js, you need Node.js installed on your machine, as it provides the runtime environment to execute and run your applications. Node.js is also required for package management. Along with Node.js, you need **npm (Node Package Manager)** or Yarn installed, which are tools for managing dependencies and packages required to develop your applications locally. The most recent versions of these tools are sufficient to get you ready for the practical examples in this chapter, assuming you have already installed VS Code, which was required in the previous chapters of this book.

The code files required for you to follow along with this chapter can be found at: `https://github.com/PacktPublishing/Modern-Full-Stack-Web-Development-with-ASP.NET-Core/tree/main/Chapter11`

Deep dive into Vue.js

In this section, we will explore more advanced features of Vue.js, particularly focusing on its reactivity system, computed properties, and the differences between the Composition API and Options API approaches. Understanding these concepts is an important step in building complex and efficient Vue.js applications, making your code easier to maintain and scale. We will begin our deep dive into Vue.js by exploring the Vue.js reactivity system in the next subsection.

Vue.js Reactivity System

Vue.js's reactivity system is one of its most impressive aspects, providing applications with excellent responsiveness by dynamically changing the UI based on changes in the underlying data. Vue.js smartly tracks dependencies as components render, and automatically updates the DOM when the associated data model changes. Its reactivity system gives both end users and developers of Vue.js applications a sense of dynamic and smooth flow.

Let's explore a code example that demonstrates Vue's reactivity system in action. First, create a new Vue.js application using the Vue CLI by executing the following command in the terminal in Visual Studio:

```
vue create chapter-11-reactivity
```

The Vue CLI will display configuration options for you to choose during creation. You should select the Vue 3 version, which is the latest one.

In this case, `chapter-11-reactivity` is the name of the project. You can choose another name if you prefer. Next, navigate to the application folder by executing the following command, but remember to replace the name of the project (after `cd`) if you chose a different one:

```
cd chapter-11-reactivity
```

In the next steps, we will create a simple shipment tracking dashboard for a logistics company, which will give you a good sense of how reactivity works in Vue.js applications. The dashboard will display the statuses of a list of shipments and allow the user to filter the results based on their status.

First, we will set up the component with reactive state, computed properties, and methods. This example will also use the Composition API, which will be explained later in this section. In Visual Studio, create a new file called `ShipmentTrackingDashboard.vue` within the `components` directory. Next, include the code for the `<template>`, `<script>`, and `<style>` sections, as shown in the following code:

```
<template>
  <div class="shipment-tracker">
    <h1>Shipment Tracking Dashboard</h1>

    <div class="filters">
      <label>
        <input
          type="radio"
          value="all"
          v-model="filterStatus"
        />
        All
      </label>
      <label>
        <input
          type="radio"
          value="in-transit"
          v-model="filterStatus"
        />
        In Transit
      </label>
      <label>
        <input
          type="radio"
          value="delivered"
          v-model="filterStatus"
        />
        Delivered
      </label>
      <label>
        <input
          type="radio"
          value="delayed"
          v-model="filterStatus"
```

```
        />
        Delayed
      </label>
    </div>

    <ul>
      <li
        v-for="shipment in filteredShipments"
        :key="shipment.id">
        <strong>
          {{ shipment.id }}
        </strong>:
          {{ shipment.status }}
      </li>
    </ul>

    <p>Total Shipments: {{ shipments.length }}</p>
    <p>
      Displayed Shipments:
      {{ filteredShipments.length }}
    </p>
  </div>
</template>

<script>
import { ref, reactive, computed } from 'vue';

export default {
  setup() {
    const shipments = reactive([
      { id: 'SHP1001', status: 'in-transit' },
      { id: 'SHP1002', status: 'delivered' },
      { id: 'SHP1003', status: 'delayed' },
      { id: 'SHP1004', status: 'in-transit' },
      { id: 'SHP1005', status: 'delivered' },
    ]);

    const filterStatus = ref('all');

    const filteredShipments = computed(() => {
      if (filterStatus.value === 'all') {
        return shipments;
      }
```

```
      return shipments.filter(
        shipment => shipment.status ===
        filterStatus.value
      );
    });

    return {
      shipments,
      filterStatus,
      filteredShipments,
    };
  }
};
</script>

<style scoped>
.shipment-tracker {
  font-family: Arial, sans-serif;
  max-width: 500px;
  margin: auto;
  text-align: left;
}

.filters {
  margin-bottom: 20px;
}

label {
  margin-right: 10px;
}

ul {
  list-style-type: none;
  padding: 0;
}

li {
  margin: 8px 0;
}

li strong {
  color: #2c3e50;
}
</style>
```

In the `<template>` section, there are radio buttons for filtering shipments by status. The `v-model` directive binds the selected radio button to `filterStatus`. The `v-for` directive loops through the `filteredShipments` array to display each shipment that matches the filter criteria. Additionally, the template displays the total number of shipments, and the number of shipments currently displayed after a filter is applied.

In the `<script>` section, the shipments array is a **reactive** object that contains shipment data. Each shipment has an identifier and a status (e.g., *In Transit, Delivered, Delayed*). `filterStatus` is a `ref` that tracks the current filter status selected by the user. The default is `all`, which displays all shipments in the filter results. Everything in Vue.js components that is embedded with `ref` and `reactive` is related to the **reactivity system** provided by Vue.js.

`filteredShipments` is a computed property. Computed properties are used to explicitly tell Vue that a value depends directly on other values. In the given code, `filteredShipments` is derived from the `shipments` array based on the value of `filterStatus`. If `filterStatus` is set to `all` it returns the entire `shipments` array. Otherwise, it filters the shipments based on the selected status.

To use and display the component, you can adapt the App.vue file with the following code:

```
<template>
  <img alt="Vue logo" src="./assets/logo.png">
  <ShipmentTrackingDashboard />
</template>

<script>
import ShipmentTrackingDashboard
  from './components/ShipmentTrackingDashboard.vue'


export default {
  name: 'App',
  components: {
    ShipmentTrackingDashboard
  }
}
</script>

<style>
#app {
  font-family: Avenir, Helvetica, Arial, sans-serif;
  -webkit-font-smoothing: antialiased;
  -moz-osx-font-smoothing: grayscale;
  text-align: center;
  color: #2c3e50;
```

```
    margin-top: 60px;
}
</style>
```

In this code, the `ShipmentTrackingDashboard` component is referenced in the `<script>` block and used in the `<template>`. To view the application running in the browser, run the following command:

```
npm run serve
```

This command builds the Vue application and starts a development server, usually accessible at `http://localhost:8080`. For your local environment, please check the URL displayed in the terminal in Visual Studio Code after running the command. After opening the generated URL, you should see the **Shipment Tracking Dashboard** component, as shown in *Figure 11.1*:

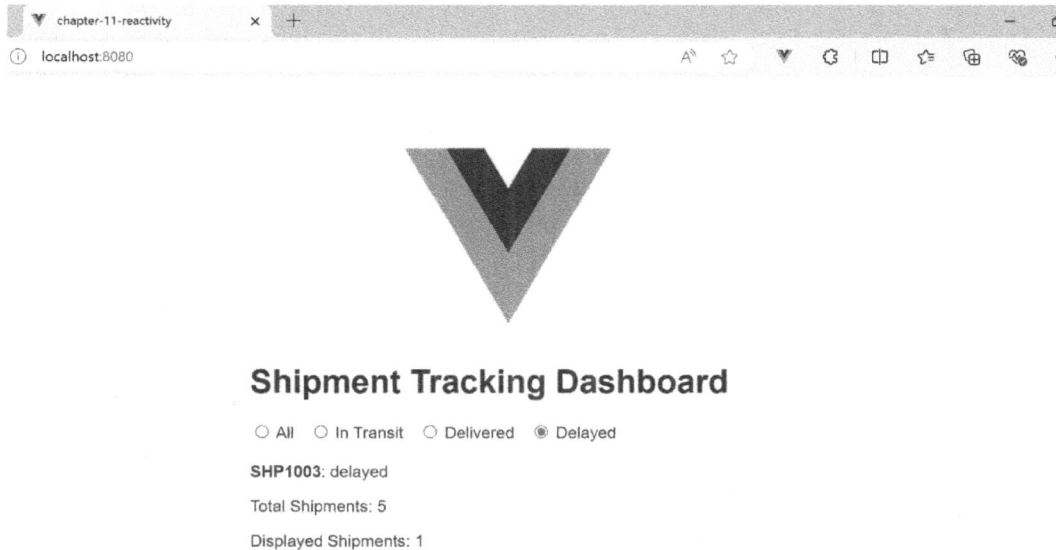

Figure 11.1: Shipment Tracking Dashboard component

This example demonstrates how reactivity works, meaning that if the selected status changes, the list of shipments changes automatically as well. You can adapt this example and create additional behaviors for this component to verify and test reactivity. Additionally, you can create a new component with different requirements that follow similar logic: associating data models to reflect changes in the UI when the state changes.

We used the Composition API to build the Shipment Tracking Dashboard component. It is important for you to understand what the Composition API is, including the main differences between this approach and the Options API, an alternative for organizing component logic in Vue.js applications. More details are provided in the next section.

Difference between the Options API and the Composition API

Vue.js offers two main approaches to define the logic of components: the **Options API** and the **Composition API**. Having a clear understanding of these two ways of handling Vue components is crucial for building Vue.js applications in the long term, especially in cases when an application grows in complexity over time. While the Options API has been the most commonly used method by developers, the Composition API, introduced in **Vue 3**, has quickly become popular among frontend engineers as it provides a more flexible way to organize and reuse code.

The Options API is the approach used by Vue since its first version. It organizes the logic of the component by using specific predefined options, such as `computed`, `data`, and `methods`, and manages the lifecycle hooks, such as `mounted` and `created`. This structure for organizing the logic of a component makes components easy to understand, especially for beginners.

To better understand how the Options API approach works, let's create a new Vue.js project using the following command in Visual Studio Code's terminal:

```
vue create chapter-11-options-api
```

In this case, `chapter-11-options-api` is the name of the project. You can choose another name if you prefer. Next, navigate to the root of your new project by executing the following command:

```
cd chapter-11-options-api
```

In this command, put the name of your project after `cd`. Now, create a new Vue component called `OptionsApiComponent.vue` within the `src/components` folder and place the following code as the content of the file:

```
<template>
<div>
  <span style="font-weight: bold;">
    Current Count:
  </span>
  {{ count }}
  <br><br>
  <b>Count twice: </b> {{ countTwice  }}
  <br><br>
  <button @click="increase()">Increment</button>
  <br>
</div>
```

```
</template>
<script>
export default {
  data() {
    return {
      count: 0,
    };
  },
  methods: {
    increase() {
      this.count++;
    },
  },
  computed: {
    countTwice() {
      return this.count * 2;
    },
  },
  watch: {
    count(newValue) {
      console.log(`Count changed to ${newValue}`);
    },
  },
  mounted() {
    console.log('Component has been mounted.');
  },
};

</script>
```

This code represents a simple counter that demonstrates how the Options API approach works:

- `data` is an option that returns a JavaScript object containing reactive properties for the component. In this example, `count` is the object with an initial value of `0`.

- `methods` defines custom functions created by the developer to be used as event handlers or for other logic implementations for the component. In this case, the code contains a single method called `increase` that increments the value of the `count` object each time the button is clicked.

- `computed` is used to define properties that depend on other properties. Specifically, in this code, it contains a computed property called `countTwice` that changes its value to double the value of the `count` property.

- watch allows you to run a routine in response to changes in specific reactive properties referenced in watch. In this code, it is programmed so that the count property is watched, and every time its value changes, a console log is displayed with the new value.

- mounted is a predefined lifecycle hook in Vue that is executed when the component is mounted in the DOM. In this example, a console log is displayed only once when the component is mounted.

To use and view the component, adapt the App.vue file in your project within the src directory, as shown in the following code:

```
<template>
  <img alt="Vue logo" src="./assets/logo.png">
  <OptionsApiComponent/>
</template>

<script>
import OptionsApiComponent
  from './components/OptionsApiComponent.vue'

export default {
  name: 'App',
  components: {
    OptionsApiComponent
  }
}
</script>

<style>
#app {
  font-family: Avenir, Helvetica, Arial, sans-serif;
  -webkit-font-smoothing: antialiased;
  -moz-osx-font-smoothing: grayscale;
  text-align: center;
  color: #2c3e50;
  margin-top: 60px;
}
</style>
```

In this adapted version of the App.vue component, there is an import of OptionsApiComponent and the usage of the component in the <template> block using <OptionsApiComponent/>.

To view the component working in the Vue app, you can run the following command in Visual Studio Code's terminal:

```
npm run serve
```

Open the browser and navigate to the localhost URL displayed by the output of this command. You will be presented with the main app component featuring the **Increment** button and a display of the **Count** and **Double Count** results. If you press the **Increment** button a few times, you will see the updates, as shown in *Figure 11.2*.

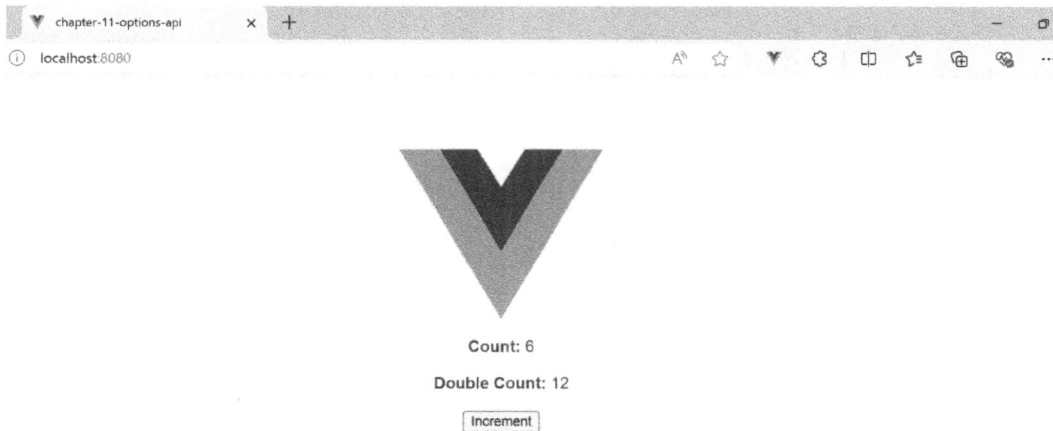

Figure 11.2: OptionsApiComponent in the browser

Remember that the **Count** display refers to the reactive count property. Also, **Double Count** is a computed property that changes every time the value of count changes, multiplying the count value by two.

To view the behavior of the watch and mounted methods, right-click on the page in the browser and choose the **Inspect** option. This will open the browser console and display the console logs specified earlier in the mounted and watch lifecycle methods of the OptionsApiComponent, as shown in *Figure 11.3*:

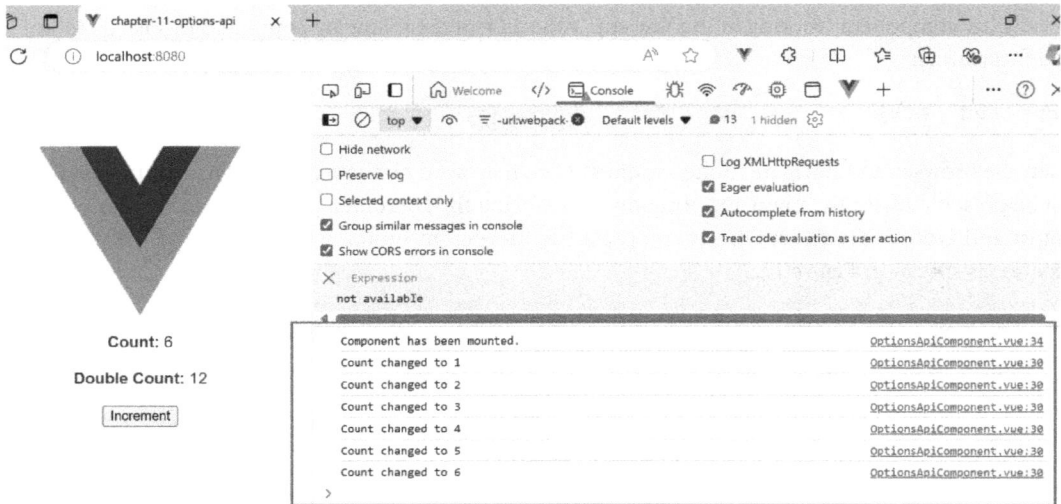

Figure 11.3: Console logs of the OptionsApiComponent

The console logs in the browser show that the `mounted` method was executed only once, as the message **Component has been mounted** appears only once. The `watch` method, configured to watch for changes on the `count` property, was triggered six times, because in this example, the **Increment** button was pressed six times.

This example aimed to demonstrate how the Options API structure works in Vue.js applications. While this approach is straightforward for simple components, it can become a significant challenge to manage large and complex components. When you have multiple features that affect each other in a cascade, it may be quite difficult to manage the code that runs in all the different features, making it hard to follow and maintain.

In the next section, you will learn about the Composition API, a new approach introduced in Vue 3 to address some of the limitations of the Options API.

Composition API

The Composition API started being used in the Vue.js framework in version 3 to address the limitations of the Options API approach, particularly when an application has to handle large and complex components. Instead of having the logical structure of the component separated by options, the Composition API allows you to group logic statements using functions and reactive properties. This approach makes it easier to maintain the code for complex projects and makes the code more modular.

To demonstrate how the Composition API works, create a new Vue.js project from scratch, in a new directory, using the following command in Visual Studio Code's terminal:

```
vue create chapter-11-composition-api
```

In this command, `chapter-11-composition-api` is the name of the project, but you can choose another name if you prefer.

After that, navigate to your newly created project via the terminal using the following command:

```
cd chapter-11-composition-api
```

In this case, after `cd`, put the name of your project. Next, create a new component called `CompositionApiComponent.vue` within the `src/components` directory of your project and write the following code:

```
<template>
  <div>
  <b>Count: </b> {{ count }}
  <br><br>
  <b>Double Count: </b> {{ doubleCount  }}
  <br><br>
  <button @click="increment()">Increment</button>
  <br>
</div>
</template>
<script>
import { ref, computed, watch, onMounted } from 'vue';

export default {
  setup() {
    const count = ref(0);

    const increment = () => {
      count.value++;
    };

    const doubleCount = computed(() => count.value * 2);

    watch(count, (newValue) => {
      console.log(`Count changed to ${newValue}`);
    });

    onMounted(() => {
      console.log('Component has been mounted.');
    });

    return {
      count,
```

```
      increment,
      doubleCount,
    };
  },
};
```

```
</script>
```

This example is identical to the previous one that uses the Options API in terms of user experience. This component displays a **Counter** and a **Double Counter** on the screen, along with a button to increment the counter value. Therefore, the `<template>` block is exactly the same as the previous one, but the code in the `<script>` block has changed completely to use the Composition API approach.

Here's an explanation of the key points in this code that you need to be aware of:

- `ref` is used to define the reactive behavior of the `count` property. Reactive properties can be accessed using the `.value` object property.

- `computed` is a function that determines that `doubleCount` is a computed property based on other reactive values.

- `watch` is used to monitor changes in reactive properties and perform custom actions when their values change.

- `onMounted` is a lifecycle hook function that is executed when the component is `mounted`, an identical feature to the mounted option in the Options API.

The `setup` function is the main method of the Composition API, as it is where you declare the entire logic for the component, including defining computed properties, reactive state, watchers, and lifecycle hooks. The `setup` routine executes before the component is actually created and returns all the methods and properties that need to be exposed to the `<template>` block.

Despite the output in the `<template>` block being identical in the Options API and Composition API approaches, it is important to highlight the key differences between and benefits of Composition API over Options API:

- **Reusability and modularity**: The Options API has limitations in terms of reusability because complex scenarios often require mixins, which can cause naming conflicts, making the code hard to debug and understand. On the other hand, the Composition API provides better ways to separate code into composition functions, making it easier to extract and reuse logic across different components that share custom hooks.

- **TypeScript support**: The Options API allows the use of **TypeScript** but with significant limitations for the `data`, `computed`, and `methods` options, resulting in a poor experience for developers. Alternatively, the Composition API has better compatibility with TypeScript, allowing you to use functions and strongly typed properties directly.

- **Structuring of code**: The Options API organizes the logic of the component into options, which can lead to undesired fragmentation in complex projects. For instance, all the methods for a component are grouped together along with computed properties, resulting in code that is hard to read and maintain. Conversely, the Composition API allows developers more flexibility to group related elements in the code. For instance, the state, methods, and computed properties related to a particular feature can be written together in the main setup function, making the code easier to read and maintain for complex components.

Both options are valid approaches for writing Vue.js components, but the Composition API approach has been the preferred choice for developers since Vue 3, especially for complex projects that require scalability over time. However, understanding both techniques is important for you to decide which one is best for your project requirements.

In the next section, you will be introduced to state management for Vue.js applications, an important topic for creating and managing sustainable Vue.js projects.

Understanding state management in Vue.js

As a Vue.js application grows in complexity and size, state management for components becomes proportionally complex and an essential part of code maintainability. In this context, *state* refers to the data shared across two or more components, such as authentication information, application settings, or any content that needs to be reactive and involves multiple components in an application. Vue.js provides several ways to define the strategy for state management at different levels of the application. This section will explore state management at multiple levels, combining the Composition API and **Vuex**, starting with component-level state management in the following section.

It's worth mentioning **Pinia** as a modern, lightweight alternative to Vuex for state management in Vue.js. Pinia integrates seamlessly with both the Composition and Options APIs and has features such as modular stores, robust TypeScript support, and **SSR** compatibility. These advantages make Pinia a simpler and more flexible choice, ideal for building scalable and maintainable applications.

Component-level state management

For simple projects, managing state at the component level is quite sufficient in most cases. In Vue.js applications, each component can manage its own state. To understand how state management works in practice using the Composition API approach, create a new project in Visual Studio Code via the terminal by executing the following command:

```
vue create chapter-11-state-management
```

In this case, `chapter-11-state-management` is the name of the project, but you can choose another name if you prefer. Next, create a new component `ComponentStateManagement.vue` within the `src/components` folder in your project, and specify the following code:

```
<template>
  <div>
    <h1>{{ title }}</h1>
    <button @click="toggleStatus">
      {{ isActive ? 'Deactivate' : 'Activate' }}
    </button>
  </div>
</template>

<script>
import { ref } from 'vue';

export default {
  setup() {
    const title = ref('Component State Management');
    const isActive = ref(false);

    const toggleStatus = () => {
      isActive.value = !isActive.value;
    };

    return { title, isActive, toggleStatus };
  },
};
</script>
```

In this example, the component manages its own state as the `title` and `isActive` properties are using the `ref` directive to inject reactivity behavior. While this approach works well for small components, it can quickly become difficult to manage when multiple other components need to share and react to the same data managed by this component-level state management definition.

When an application grows in size and complexity, with many components requiring to share the same state, a more scalable approach is needed. This is where Vuex shows its value. **Vuex** is a state management library that provides a centralized store for all the components, facilitating consistent state changes and a more readable data flow for the application. Here are the key concepts of Vuex:

- **State**: This is a central data store maintaining shared information across components
- **Getters**: These are functions that allow you to get and compute state from the centralized store

- **Mutations**: These are synchronous functions that serve as the only way to change state in the store, centralizing the access to modify the data shared across the application

- **Actions**: These are functions that can run asynchronously and commit mutations

- **Modules**: These allow you to separate the store into smaller parts

To use Vuex in the project created in this section, navigate to the root of your project using the `cd` command in the terminal, as demonstrated previously in this chapter. Next, you need to install Vuex by running the following command:

```
npm install vuex@next
```

Once it has been installed, you can configure a basic Vuex store. The following example is of a Vuex store that manages shipment data in a logistics application. Within the `src` directory in your project, create a folder called `store` and a file called `index.js` within this folder with the following code:

```js
import { createStore } from 'vuex';

export default createStore({
  state() {
    return {
      shipments: [
        { id: 'SHP1001', status: 'in-transit' },
        { id: 'SHP1002', status: 'delivered' },
        { id: 'SHP1003', status: 'delayed' },
      ],
    };
  },
  getters: {
    filteredShipments: (state) => (status) => {
      if (status === 'all') {
        return state.shipments;
      }
      return state.shipments.filter(
        shipment => shipment.status === status
      );
    },
  },
  mutations: {
    addShipment(state, payload) {
      state.shipments.push(payload);
    },
    updateShipmentStatus(state, { id, status }) {
      const shipment = state.shipments.find(
```

```
        shipment => shipment.id === id
      );
      if (shipment) {
        shipment.status = status;
      }
    },
  },
  actions: {
    async fetchShipments({ commit }) {
      const data = await new Promise((resolve) => {
        setTimeout(() => {
          resolve([
            { id: 'SHP1004', status: 'in-transit' },
            { id: 'SHP1005', status: 'delayed' },
          ]);
        }, 1000);
      });
      data.forEach(shipment => commit(
        'addShipment', shipment
      ));
    },
  },
});
```

Based on the key features of Vuex, here's the correlation between each feature and the code:

- **State**: The shipments array is specified as the central data store and can now be accessed by any component of the application

- **Getters**: The filteredShipments getter returns a list of shipments filtered by status based on the parameter received

- **Mutations**: The addShipment mutation adds a new shipment to the store, while updateShipmentStatus updates the status of an existing shipment in the centralized store

- **Actions**: The fetchShipments action simulates an asynchronous API call to fetch shipments and places the result in the state

Now, let's integrate this Vuex store into an actual Vue component to manage shipment data. First, create a new component called ShipmentManagement.vue within the src/components directory in the project created earlier in this section, and put the following code in the component:

```
<template>
  <div>
    <h2>Shipment Management</h2>
    <button @click="fetchShipments">
```

```
      Fetch Shipments
    </button>
    <ul>
      <li
        v-for="shipment in filteredShipments('all')"
        :key="shipment.id"
      >
        {{ shipment.id }} - {{ shipment.status }}
        <button
          @click="updateStatus(
            shipment.id, 'delivered'
          )"
        >
          Mark as Delivered
        </button>
      </li>
    </ul>
  </div>
</template>

<script>
import { useStore } from 'vuex';

export default {
  setup() {
    const store = useStore();

    const fetchShipments = () => {
      store.dispatch('fetchShipments');
    };

    const updateStatus = (id, status) => {
      store.commit('updateShipmentStatus', { id, status });
    };

    const filteredShipments = (status) =>
      store.getters.filteredShipments(status);

    return {
      fetchShipments,
      updateStatus,
      filteredShipments,
    };
```

```
    },
  };
  </script>
```

This example explicitly uses Vuex features integrated within the component. Here's an explanation of the main points:

- **State and actions**: The `fetchShipments` method dispatches the `fetchShipments` action to fetch shipment data

- **Mutations**: The `updateStatus` method commits the `updateShipmentStatus` mutation to update a shipment's status

- **Getters**: The `filteredShipments` function uses a Vuex getter to filter shipments based on their status

To fully run this example, you must register the store in the `main.js` file within the `src` directory of your project, as highlighted in the following example:

```
import { createApp } from 'vue'
import App from './App.vue'
import store from './store';

const app = createApp(App);
app.use(store);
app.mount('#app');
```

In this code, the store previously created is imported using the `import store from './store';` directive, and the app is configured to use it with `app.use(store);`. This makes the store available to be used by all components in the application.

Next, you need to adapt the `App.vue` file to use the `ShipmentManagement.vue` component. This can be achieved by modifying the `App` component with the following code:

```
<template>
  <img alt="Vue logo" src="./assets/logo.png">
  <ShipmentManagement />
</template>

<script>
import ShipmentManagement
  from './components/ShipmentManagement.vue'

export default {
  name: 'App',
  components: {
```

```
    ShipmentManagement
  }
}
</script>

<style>
#app {
  font-family: Avenir, Helvetica, Arial, sans-serif;
  -webkit-font-smoothing: antialiased;
  -moz-osx-font-smoothing: grayscale;
  text-align: center;
  color: #2c3e50;
  margin-top: 60px;
}
</style>
```

Now, the `ShipmentManagement.vue` component has been imported into the `App.vue` component. To view the Vuex logic in action, after these adaptations, you can run your application in the browser using the following command, executed in the root of your app directory in Visual Studio Code's terminal:

```
npm run serve
```

Open the URL shown in the terminal. Your application should look like the representation in *Figure 11.4*:

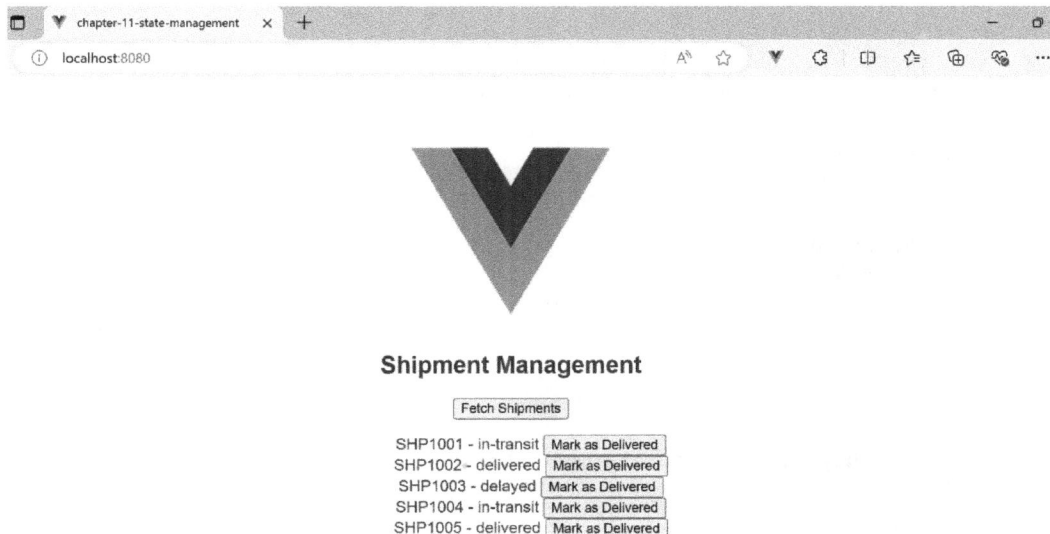

Figure 11.4: Shipment Management component

If you click on the **Fetch Shipments** button, you will see the component retrieving data from the Vuex store. The **Mark as Delivered** button updates the data in the centralized store using the `commit` method from the store.

This setup using Vuex allows a scalable, centralized state management approach where the entire application can keep the data synchronized in a consistent manner. In the next section, you will learn how to handle state management in Vue applications using another approach, utilizing `provide` and `inject` along with the Composition API.

State management with the Composition API

For projects where you want a lightweight approach to state management without using Vuex, Vue 3 provides a simpler way to share state across multiple components using the Composition API with `provide` and `inject`. This approach is helpful for managing state in nested components or small components. To see how `provide` and `inject` work, create a new component called `ParentComponent.vue` within the `src/components` directory in the project created in the previous section. In this new component, replicate the following code:

```
<template>
  <div>
    <h1>Logistics Dashboard</h1>
    <ShipmentList />
  </div>
</template>

<script>
import { reactive, provide } from 'vue';
import ShipmentList from './ShipmentList.vue';

export default {
  components: { ShipmentList },
  setup() {
    const shipmentState = reactive({
      shipments: [
        { id: 'SHP1001', status: 'in-transit' },
        { id: 'SHP1002', status: 'delivered' },
      ],
    });

    provide('shipmentState', shipmentState);

    return {};
  },
};
</script>
```

In this example, the parent component provides the shipmentState object to its child components. To include a child component in your project, create a new component called ShipmentList.vue within the src/components directory, and include the following code in the new component:

```
<template>
  <div>
    <ul>
      <li
        v-for="shipment in shipmentState.shipments"
        :key="shipment.id"
      >
        {{ shipment.id }} - {{ shipment.status }}
      </li>
    </ul>
  </div>
</template>

<script>
  import { inject } from 'vue';

  export default {
    setup() {
      const shipmentState = inject('shipmentState');

      return { shipmentState };
    },
  };
</script>
```

The child component, ShipmentList, uses inject to access the state and display the shipment data. This approach is simpler than the Vuex approach, providing an alternative to share reactive state across components without explicitly passing props between them.

State management is an essential part of any Vue.js application. For simple scenarios, component-level state management might be sufficient for your needs, but as your application grows in size and complexity, centralized state management approaches such as Vuex become more reliable and maintainable. Alternatively, the Composition API's provide and inject methods offer a low-overhead solution for sharing state across components without the need to configure and use a complex state management library.

By understanding and applying these state management techniques, you will be able to create more organized and predictable Vue.js applications that are aligned with the needs of your project.

In the next section, we will explore details on routing and navigation for Vue.js applications.

Routing and navigation in Vue.js

Routing is a core element of **single-page applications** (**SPAs**), allowing users to navigate between different components without having to reload the web page itself, which is a valuable feature for delivering an excellent user experience. Vue.js provides a robust library called **Vue Router** for managing routing and navigation in Vue.js applications. This library integrates seamlessly with Vue.js, allowing you to create advanced navigation patterns and interactive user experiences with ease.

This section will provide details on the essential aspects of Vue Router, such as handling dynamic and nested routes.

To understand in practice how Vue Router works, create a new project in Visual Studio Code, in a new directory, by executing the following command:

```
vue create chapter-11-router
```

In this case, `chapter-11-router` represents the name of the project. You can choose another name if you prefer. After that, navigate to your new project via the terminal using the `cd` command, as demonstrated earlier in this chapter, and install the Vue Router library using the following command:

```
npm install vue-router@4
```

Once it has been installed, create a new directory called `router` within the `src` directory of your new project and create a file called `index.js` within the new folder. This file will contain all the routes for your application. After creating the file, you can replicate the following content in the file:

```
import {
  createRouter, createWebHistory
} from 'vue-router';
import HomeView from '../views/HomeView.vue';
import AboutView from '../views/AboutView.vue';

const routes = [
  { path: '/', name: 'Home', component: HomeView },
  { path: '/about', name: 'About', component: AboutView },
];

const router = createRouter({
  history: createWebHistory(process.env.BASE_URL),
  routes,
});

export default router;
```

The `routes` array defines the mapping between paths and the components that should be rendered when a URL matching the pattern is accessed. Each route object contains the following properties:

- `path`: The URL path associated with the route
- `name`: A unique name for the route, which can be helpful when referring to the routes programmatically
- `component`: The Vue component that should be displayed when the route is matched

In this example, the `/` path maps to the `HomeView` component, and the `/about` path maps to the `AboutView` component. To effectively test this route configuration, you need to create the `HomeView.vue` and `AboutView.vue` components within a folder called `views` that you can create in the `src` directory. Here is an example of the `HomeView.vue` component:

```
<template>
  <div>
      <h1>This is the Home View</h1>
  </div>
</template>
```

This is a simple component that displays the message **This is the Home View** to test the route configuration. Additionally, create the `AboutView` component within the `views` directory as well. Copy the following code for the content of the component:

```
<template>
  <div>
      <h1>This is the About View</h1>
  </div>
</template>
```

This component follows the same pattern as the previous one (`HomeView`), which only displays a message in the `<template>` block. Considering you have now created both components, open the `main.js` file within the `src` directory of your project and apply the following changes:

```
import { createApp } from 'vue'
import App from './App.vue'
import router from './router';


const app = createApp(App);

app.use(router);
app.mount('#app');
```

As a final step, you need to use the `<router-view>` component in the `App.vue` file, an element used by Vue Router to render the content of one component within another. Open the `App.vue` file and modify its content to match the following code exactly:

```
<template>
  <router-view></router-view>
</template>

<script>
export default {
  name: 'App'
}
</script>
```

Now that the basic configuration is complete, you can run your application by executing the following command:

```
npm run serve
```

Access your application using the URL displayed in the terminal output. Then, navigate to the routes by changing the URL to include the respective path. For instance, use `http://localhost:8080/` for the `HomeView` component, which uses only the `/` suffix, and `http://localhost:8080/About`, which complements the URL with the `/About` suffix. In both cases, the respective components will be rendered in the browser, according to the configuration defined in the `router/index.js` file. Here's the output of the `/About` route in *Figure 11.5*:

This is the About View

Figure 11.5: About View component

The Vue Router library allows you to configure routes in a simple and flexible way, determining which components will be rendered when the path of the URL matches the specification on the router. It is important to note that this route configuration does not involve any page refresh when navigating between pages.

In the next section, we will explore defining dynamic routes using Vue Router.

Dynamic routing

Dynamic routing is helpful when your application needs to render views based on dynamic parameters, such as object IDs or other variables. You can define dynamic routes using the : symbol followed by the parameter name in the `path` attribute of the route. Here's an example of defining a route that redirects to a shipment in a logistics application, passing the shipment ID as a parameter. Adapt the `router/index.js` file of your application to include the highlighted route in the following code:

```
import {
  createRouter, createWebHistory
} from 'vue-router';
import HomeView from '../views/HomeView.vue';
import AboutView from '../views/AboutView.vue';
import ShipmentDetailsView
  from '../views/ShipmentDetailsView.vue';


const routes = [
  { path: '/', name: 'Home', component: HomeView },
  { path: '/about', name: 'About', component: AboutView },
  {
    path: '/shipment/:id',
    name: 'ShipmentDetails',
    component: ShipmentDetailsView
  },

];

const router = createRouter({
  history: createWebHistory(process.env.BASE_URL),
  routes,
});


export default router;
```

In this example, a new route is added referencing the `ShipmentDetailsView` component. The `/shipment/:id` route is dynamic. It can match any URL with the pattern `/shipment/123`, where `123` is the dynamic parameter `id`.

Now, create the `ShipmentDetailsView` component within the `src/views` directory of your project, specifying the following code:

```
<template>
  <div>
```

```
    <h1>Shipment Details</h1>
    <p>Shipment ID: {{ shipmentId }}</p>
  </div>
</template>

<script>
import { useRoute } from 'vue-router';

export default {
  setup() {
    const route = useRoute();
    const shipmentId = route.params.id;

    return { shipmentId };
  },
};
</script>
```

This component accesses the parameter ID of the route using `this.$route.params.id` in the Options API or `useRoute()` in the Composition API. With the app running, you can test the dynamic route by opening the following URL: `http://localhost:8080/shipment/123`. The `ShipmentDetailsView` component will be displayed, along with information about the dynamic route parameter, as shown in *Figure 11.6*:

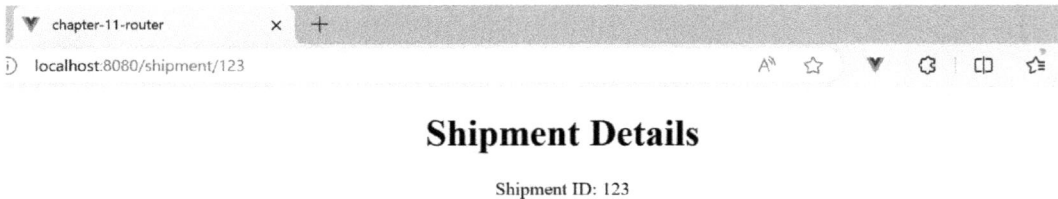

Figure 11.6: Shipment Details route

Routing is a fundamental aspect of every Vue.js application. Vue Router provides a simple way to manage navigation, from very basic routes to more advanced ones like dynamic routes. A solid understanding of Vue Router will allow you to create user-friendly navigation flows for your Vue.js applications, enhancing the overall user experience.

In the next section, we will compare Vue.js and other JavaScript frameworks, such as Angular and React, to help you decide which one is the best for your future project needs.

Framework comparison and selection criteria

Deciding which JavaScript framework is the right one for a project is essential for its long-term plans in terms of maintenance and scalability. Vue.js, Angular, and React are the most popular frameworks on the market, each with strengths, use cases, and characteristics. After providing an overview of each of them in the previous chapter, this section provides a comprehensive comparison of these three robust frameworks, discussing their advantages and potential drawbacks, and helping you select the right framework based on your project's requirements.

The next sections provide an analysis of the key strengths of each framework, along with their potential drawbacks.

React analysis

As mentioned in the previous chapters, **React** is a JavaScript library developed by Facebook for building user interfaces, mainly SPAs. This framework is entirely focused on reusable components and has a robust ecosystem and community involved in its evolution. It uses a declarative approach to write components and features virtual DOM manipulation to optimize UI rendering. Here are the key strengths of React:

- **Rich ecosystem**: The React ecosystem includes several mature libraries, such as React Router for configuring routes and Redux for state management, providing an extensive set of tools to extend what React natively offers

- **Flexibility**: React allows developers to freely choose libraries and complementary tools based on their requirements instead of being limited by a rigid framework structure

- **Virtual DOM**: React's virtual DOM improves the performance of the application by reducing the amount of direct manipulation of the actual DOM, making it highly efficient for applications that require constant changes in UI rendering

- **Component-based architecture**: React has reusability at its core, focusing on reusable components and inspiring developers to follow good frontend development practices

Now, let's explore the main potential drawbacks that React can present in regular projects:

- **Learning curve for beginners**: New concepts in the React framework, such as React Hooks and the Context API, may be confusing and hard to learn for beginners who are used to working with class-based components

- **Boilerplate and configuration**: React requires additional configuration for things such as state management, form handling, and routing, leading to more boilerplate code than other frameworks

Now that you have an overview of the key strengths and drawbacks of React, let's do the same for Angular in the next section.

Angular analysis

As mentioned in the previous chapter, **Angular** is a framework that was developed and maintained by Google, making it a mature option for building large-scale applications. Angular uses TypeScript at its core, providing a strongly typed experience for frontend engineers. It also provides a set of tools to help development, such as dependency injection, two-way data binding, and **Reactive Extensions for JavaScript (RxJS)** for reactive programming.

Here are the key strengths of the Angular framework:

- **Dependency injection**: Angular has a native feature for dependency injection, which allows more testable and modular code

- **TypeScript support**: Angular has great support for TypeScript, improving tooling and ensuring type safety at compile time

- **Complete framework**: Angular provides a robust set of tools for routing, state management, HTTP client, and other features as part of the core of the framework

- **Powerful CLI**: Angular has one of the best CLIs compared to other frameworks, providing commands for generating services, components, and modules efficiently, facilitating the development process

Now, let's explore the main potential drawbacks that you can find when building applications with Angular:

- **Tough learning trajectory**: Angular is a complex framework with numerous concepts and tools involved, which can be difficult for beginners to learn

- **Bundle size**: It is well known that Angular applications often have larger bundle sizes than Vue. js and React, which can affect performance if not optimized

Now that you have an overview of the key strengths and drawbacks of Angular, let's do the same for Vue.js in the next section.

Vue.js analysis

Vue.js is well-known for its simplicity in terms of learning curve and maintenance, making it a good choice for developers who are new to frontend development. Vue.js offers robust features such as reactive data binding and an incremental approach to application design. Here are the key strengths of this framework:

- **Simplicity to learn**: Vue.js has a developer-friendly syntax and clear documentation, which facilitates adoption for new developers

- **Reactivity system**: Vue.js has a robust system for managing reactive data binding, making state management easy to maintain

- **Single-file components**: Vue.js supports the use of single-file components, keeping HTML, JavaScript, and CSS in the same file for self-contained components

- **Composition API**: It provides greater code reusability and flexibility, particularly for large applications

Now, let's explore the main potential drawbacks that you can find when building applications with Vue.js:

- **Ecosystem**: Despite the framework growing in terms of adoption, Vue's ecosystem and industry support are more limited than React or Angular, as fewer companies use Vue.js
- **Challenges of integrating into existing projects**: Transitioning old projects that use previous Vue.js versions or different technologies to Vue 3 can be quite effort-intensive

Now that you have an overview of the key strengths and drawbacks of Vue.js, let's discuss important aspects of defining the criteria for framework selection when building new projects.

Criteria for framework selection

When choosing a framework for a project, take the following criteria into account to make a well-informed choice:

- **Performance considerations**: Each of the three frameworks can achieve high performance. React is often noted for its virtual DOM and precise rendering control, while Vue.js provides strong reactivity and optimized rendering through its Composition API in Vue 3. Angular, too, can be highly performant, but optimizing it involves understanding its core principles and best practices, such as lazy loading and AOT compilation.
- **State management requirements**: If your application needs intricate state management, React provides powerful solutions such as Redux, Context API, and third-party libraries. Vue.js uses Vuex for state management, which is less complex than Redux and integrates smoothly with Vue.js. Angular employs RxJS and specific state management practices, but mastering them is tougher than Vuex or Redux.
- **Support from the community and ecosystem**: React has the most expansive ecosystem and community backing, providing numerous third-party libraries and tools. Vue.js is experiencing growth in its ecosystem and community, being especially popular in Asia and among developers seeking a simpler approach. Angular has robust support from Google and a well-organized ecosystem, though it is more structured than React and Vue.js.
- **Project dimensions and complexity**: For projects of small to medium scale, Vue.js and React offer adaptable and user-friendly solutions without unnecessary bulk. For extensive, enterprise-grade applications requiring strong architectural foundations and maintainability, Angular is typically a better option due to its full-fledged framework.
- **Team background and learning curve**: If your team is already skilled with a specific framework or library, it might be more efficient to continue using it. Vue.js and React offer a gentler learning curve and easier integration, ideal for teams with less frontend experience. Angular, while powerful, involves a steeper learning curve and may need more training.

Choosing the most suitable framework involves considering multiple factors, such as project requirements, team skill level, flexibility needs, and ongoing maintenance. Vue.js is great for those who want a progressive, easy-to-learn framework with extensive flexibility. React is suitable for developers who require a highly flexible and efficient library with a vast ecosystem. Angular is most suitable for teams working on large-scale enterprise applications requiring a comprehensive, structured framework with strong typing and dependency injection.

By evaluating these factors carefully and understanding the pros and cons of Vue.js, React, and Angular, you can make an informed decision that aligns with your project goals and development environment.

Summary

In this chapter, we took a deep dive into Vue.js, exploring important features such as the reactivity system and the **Composition API**. Understanding these basic concepts helps you create maintainable and efficient components, particularly in large-scale applications. We then covered state management in Vue.js, discussing both component-level and centralized state management systems using **Vuex** and the Composition API. Understanding state management correctly is crucial for ensuring that your applications remain predictable and organized as they grow in complexity and size.

We also covered routing and navigation in Vue.js using Vue Router, which allows you to define dynamic paths for your SPAs with user-friendly routes. Learning how to properly configure routes enables good navigation flows and user experience. Finally, we concluded the chapter with a detailed comparison of Vue.js, Angular, and React, highlighting the strengths and weaknesses of each JavaScript framework, and providing you with the information needed to define selection criteria for deciding which framework is the right one to meet your project's requirements.

This chapter's content is invaluable for developers aiming to enhance their expertise in creating modern web applications. Recognizing when and how to apply each framework gives you the adaptability to select different frameworks according to different demands.

In the next chapter, we will explore how to integrate Vue.js with ASP.NET Core. You will learn how to build full-stack applications that have both frontend and backend systems connected, giving you a holistic overview of modern web development.

Get This Book's PDF Version and Exclusive Extras

UNLOCK NOW

Scan the QR code (or go to `packtpub.com/unlock`). Search for this book by name, confirm the edition, and then follow the steps on the page.

Note: Keep your invoice handly. Purchase made directly from packt don't require one.

12

Integrating Vue.js with ASP.NET Core

Integrating Vue.js with ASP.NET Core presents a robust approach to building modern, full-stack applications. This chapter covers the main aspects of combining Vue.js, a lightweight frontend framework already explored in previous chapters, with ASP.NET Core, a high-performing backend framework, to create scalable and ultra-efficient applications. In this chapter, we will learn how to configure the integration between these two technologies and explore how to optimize the performance of our full-stack applications.

By the end of this chapter, you will have a clear understanding of how to handle data flow between the frontend and backend and implement secure authentication and authorization. Furthermore, we will learn important strategies to ensure our application stays updated and performs effectively.

In this chapter, we are going to cover the following main topics:

- Vue.js and ASP.NET core integration
- Performance considerations in full-stack applications

Technical requirements

As mentioned in the previous chapter, to effectively use Vue.js, you need Node.js installed on your machine, as it provides the runtime environment to execute and run your applications. Node.js is also required for package management, which has tools, such as npm, for managing dependencies and packages required to develop your applications locally. The most recent version of these tools is sufficient to prepare you for the practical examples in this chapter for the Vue.js application, assuming you have already installed **Visual Studio Code** (**VS Code**), which was required in the previous chapters of this book.

Additionally, we will create a .NET 9 application in this chapter. Therefore, you must have this version of the .NET SDK installed on your machine along with VS Code or Visual Studio. If you already have the most recent version of Visual Studio installed on your machine, you do not need to worry about any further .NET installation.

The code files required for you to follow along with this chapter can be found at: `https://github.com/PacktPublishing/Modern-Full-Stack-Web-Development-with-ASP.NET-Core/tree/main/Chapter12`.

Vue.js and ASP.NET core integration

Integrating Vue.js with ASP.NET Core represents an excellent option for building full-stack applications where the frontend brings all the reactive aspects of Vue.js, while the backend uses a scalable and high-performing technology, such as ASP.NET Core. In this section, we will configure a backend application in ASP.NET Core, integrate it to serve the Vue application, create Vue components to call the backend endpoints, and configure routing in Vue.js.

To demonstrate the integration, we will use a hypothetical scenario where a logistics application is built. This involves creating CRUD endpoints in an ASP.NET Core web API project and a Vue.js frontend that will call the backend endpoints, step by step, starting with the creation of the domain model in the following section.

Creating the domain model

A **domain model** in C# is a representation of the principal entities, concepts, and rules within a business domain. This model defines the structure and behavior of data and logic associated with the domain, incorporating business rules, validations, and connections between entities. Typically, it consists of classes that depict real-life objects, with their respective properties, methods, and interactions.

Follow these steps to create the domain model of the example in this chapter:

1. In Visual Studio, create a new project using the ASP.NET Core web API template, as shown in *Figure 12.1*:

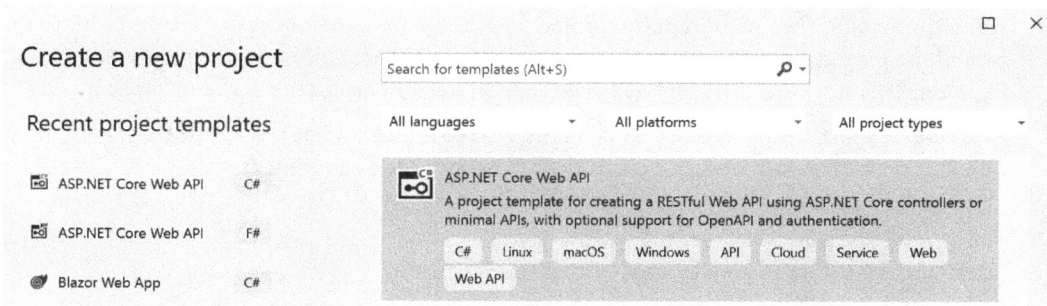

Figure 12.1: ASP.NET Core web API template

2. After giving a name to the project, check the **Place solution and project in the same directory**, **Do not use top-level statements**, and **Use controllers** options, as shown in *Figure 12.2*:

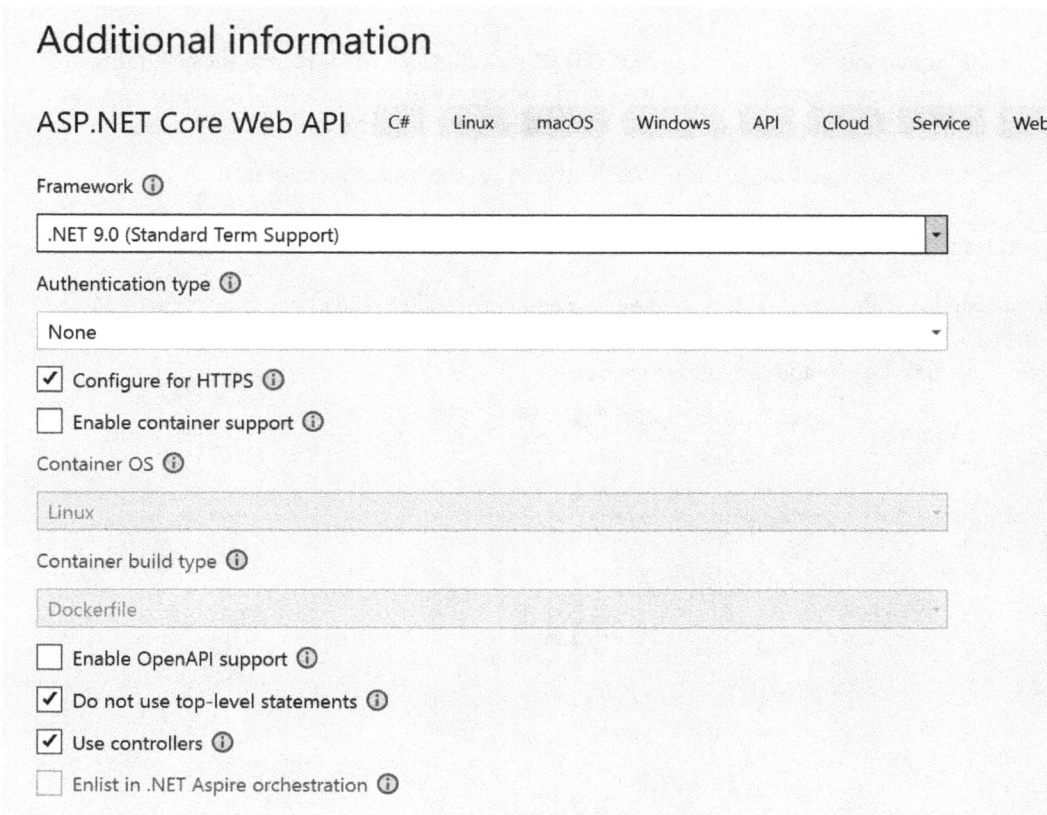

Figure 12.2: ASP.NET Core web API configuration

3. After confirming the creation of the project, create a new directory called Models in the root of the project by right-clicking on the name of the project in the Visual Studio Solution Explorer. This Models directory will centralize all the models for the backend application.

4. Next, create a new file by right-clicking on the Models folder, then add a class to create a file called LogisticItem.cs and insert the following code as its content:

```
namespace Chapter12.Models
{
    public class LogisticItem
    {
        public int Id { get; set; }
        public string ItemName { get; set; }
        public int Quantity { get; set; }
        public string Location { get; set; }
    }
}
```

In this code snippet, the namespace is Chapter12.Models, as seen at the beginning of the file. Remember to replace it with your own namespace in your project. This class represents a logistics item with properties for Id, ItemName, Quantity, and Location.

In the next section, we will create the actual controller for the backend endpoints.

Creating the controller

In Visual Studio, within your project, create a new empty controller called LogisticController. cs in the /Controllers folder to manage the CRUD operations for the logistics items. After creating the file, you can add the following code:

```
using Microsoft.AspNetCore.Mvc;
using Chapter12.Models;

namespace Chapter12.Controllers
{
    [Route("api/[controller]")]
    [ApiController]
    public class LogisticsController : ControllerBase
    {
        private static List<LogisticsItem> logisticsItems =
        new List<LogisticsItem>
        {
            new LogisticsItem
            {
                Id = 1,
                ItemName = "Pallet of cotton seeds",
                Quantity = 50,
```

```
                Location = "Warehouse A"
            },
            new LogisticsItem
            {
                Id = 2,
                ItemName = "Box of electronics",
                Quantity = 200,
                Location = "Warehouse B"
            }
    };

    [HttpGet]
    public ActionResult<IEnumerable<LogisticsItem>>
        GetItems()
    {
        return Ok(logisticsItems);
    }

    [HttpGet("{id}")]
    public ActionResult<LogisticsItem>
        GetItem(int id)
    {
        var item =
            logisticsItems.Find(i => i.Id == id);
        if (item == null)
            return NotFound();
        return Ok(item);
    }

    [HttpPost]
    public ActionResult<LogisticsItem>
        CreateItem(LogisticsItem item)
    {
        item.Id = logisticsItems.Count + 1;
        logisticsItems.Add(item);
        return CreatedAtAction(
            nameof(GetItem),
            new { id = item.Id },
            item
        );
    }

    [HttpPut("{id}")]
    public IActionResult
        UpdateItem(int id, LogisticsItem updatedItem)
    {
```

```
        var item =
            logisticsItems.Find(i => i.Id == id);
        if (item == null)
            return NotFound();
        item.ItemName = updatedItem.ItemName;
        item.Quantity = updatedItem.Quantity;
        item.Location = updatedItem.Location;
        return NoContent();
    }

    [HttpDelete("{id}")]
    public IActionResult DeleteItem(int id)
    {
        var item =
            logisticsItems.Find(i => i.Id == id);
        if (item == null)
            return NotFound();
        logisticsItems.Remove(item);
        return NoContent();
    }
    }
}
```

Note that you may need to replace the Chapter12.Controllers namespace with your own namespace based on the configuration in your project. Also, the reference to the models in using Chapter12.Models may need to be replaced in your code with your own reference path.

LogisticsController provides CRUD operations to handle logistics items, including creating, deleting, fetching details, and updating items. These endpoints will be consumed later by the Vue.js frontend.

In the next section, we will configure the web API to serve the Vue.js application.

Configuring ASP.NET Core to serve the Vue.js application

To configure the Vue.js application to be served within the ASP.NET Core project, you need to use the SpaServices.Extensions package. Within your project, using the Package Manager Console in Visual Studio, install the following package by executing the following command:

```
dotnet add package Microsoft.AspNetCore.SpaServices.Extensions
```

After installing the package, update the Program.cs file of your project to configure ASP.NET Core to serve the Vue.js application, as shown in the following code block:

```
namespace Chapter12
{
```

```
    public class Program
    {
        public static void Main(string[] args)
        {
            var builder =
                WebApplication.CreateBuilder(args);

            // Add services to the container.

            builder.Services.AddControllers();

            builder.Services.AddSpaStaticFiles(
                configuration =>
            {
#if DEBUG
                configuration.RootPath = "ClientApp";
#else
                configuration.RootPath =
                    "ClientApp/dist/spa";
#endif
            });

            builder.Services.AddCors(options =>
            {
                options.AddPolicy(
                    "AllowLocalDevelopmentOrigin",
                    policy => policy
                        .WithOrigins(
                            http://localhost:8080
                        )
                        .AllowAnyMethod()
                        .AllowAnyHeader()
                        .AllowCredentials());
            });

            var app = builder.Build();
            app.UseStaticFiles();
            app.UseSpaStaticFiles();

            app.UseSpa(spa =>
            {
                spa.Options.SourcePath = "ClientApp";
            });
```

```
            app.UseCors("AllowLocalDevelopmentOrigin");

            app.MapControllers();

            app.Run();
        }
    }
}
```

In this code, remember to replace `Chapter12` with your own namespace. The `AddSpaStaticFiles` method is called to configure the app to serve static files for the **Single-Page Application** (**SPA**), which is the Vue.js application that will be created later. The `RootPath` setting determines the root folder where the static files are located in the project. The code below the `#if DEBUG` statement runs when the application is in `DEBUG` mode, usually during development. This part serves files directly from the `ClientApp` folder; the `#else` clause is used to determine the configuration for the production mode or non-`DEBUG` environment, with the following block determining `RootPath` for the production environment.

Regarding **Cross-Origin Resource Sharing** (**CORS**) configuration, the `AddCors` method is used to configure CORS services for the application. CORS allows the server to specify which domains are permitted to access resources. In this case, the localhost URL for the Vue frontend app is specified within the `AllowLocalDevelopmentOrigin` policy. The `app.UseCors` method applies the `AllowLocalDevelopmentOrigin` CORS policy to incoming HTTP requests. This ensures that only allowed origins can interact with the backend API.

The use of the `UseStaticFiles` method enables the application to serve static files (such as images, CSS, and JavaScript) from the `wwwroot` directory by default. The `UseSpaStaticFiles` method allows serving static files specifically configured for the SPA. Finally, the `app.UseSpa()` method configures the app to use an SPA. `SourcePath` is set to `ClientApp`, which is the folder where the SPA's source files are located.

Now that you have the ASP.NET web API configured, let's create the Vue.js application in the next section.

Creating the Vue.js application

Follow these steps to create a Vue.js application:

1. In Visual Studio, open the developer command prompt and create the Vue application by executing the following command in the root of your ASP.NET web API project:

    ```
    vue create clientapp
    ```

    The preceding command generates a `clientapp` folder with all the initial files for the Vue application.

2. Next, navigate to the `clientapp` folder using `cd clientapp` on the terminal and install the Axios library by running the following command:

```
npm install axios
```

Axios will be used to make API calls from the frontend.

3. After installing Axios, create a new folder called `services` within the `ClientApp/src` directory and create a file called `logisticsService.js`. This file will centralize all the API calls made to the backend application. After creating the file, add the following code to it:

```
import axios from 'axios';

const apiClient = axios.create({
  baseURL: 'http://localhost:5161/api', // Adjust
                                        // based on
                                        // your
                                        // backend URL
  headers: {
    'Content-Type': 'application/json',
  },
});

export default {
  getLogisticsItems() {
    return apiClient.get('/logistic');
  },
  getLogisticsItem(id) {
    return apiClient.get(`/logistic/${id}`);
  },
  addLogisticsItem(item) {
    return apiClient.post('/logistics', item);
  },
  updateLogisticsItem(id, item) {
    return apiClient.put(`/logistic/${id}`, item);
  },
  deleteLogisticsItem(id) {
    return apiClient.delete(`/logistic/${id}`);
  },
};
```

The preceding code sets up an Axios service for handling HTTP requests to the backend API, calling the endpoints that we specified previously. This service file (`logisticsService.js`) centralizes all API interactions. By using this service, the code becomes more organized and reusable across different components in the Vue application.

The `import axios from 'axios'` line imports the actual Axios library and the `axios.create` method is used to create a new Axios instance with custom configurations:

- `BaseURL`: This is the base URL for all HTTP requests made with this Axios instance. It points to the backend API server running locally on `http://localhost:5181/api`. You can adjust this URL based on your local development environment.

- `Headers`: This sets default headers for all requests made with this Axios instance. Here, `Content-Type` is set to `application/json`, indicating that the requests will send and receive data in JSON format.

Finally, the logisticsService.js implementation exposes methods to interact with logistic items, specifying `GET`, `POST`, `PUT`, and `DELETE` methods according to the CRUD operations created previously in the ASP.NET Core web API.

With the service already configured, the next section contains details on each Vue component that needs to be created.

Creating the Vue components

Based on the models that were previously created in the ASP.NET web API, to enable the actual CRUD operations in the frontend, we need to create three specific components:

- `LogisticsList.vue`: This is to list the logistic items from the API

- `LogisticsForm.vue`: This is to allow the creation of new logistics items via a form

- `LogisticsDetails.vue`: This is to display the details of a logistics item in the Vue application

All the UI components in the context of this section will use Bootstrap as the UI framework to facilitate styling. Let's get started with the steps:

1. Install Bootstrap in your Vue application by executing the following command in Visual Studio (the **Developer Command Prompt** window) within the root of your project (the `ClientApp` directory):

    ```
    npm install bootstrap bootstrap-vue-3
    ```

2. After the installation, you need to register the use of Bootstrap globally in your application. You can achieve this by adapting the `main.js` file of your Vue application, as highlighted in the following code:

    ```
    import { createApp } from 'vue'
    import App from './App.vue'
    import BootstrapVue3 from 'bootstrap-vue-3';
    import 'bootstrap/dist/css/bootstrap.css';
    ```

```
import 'bootstrap-vue-3/dist/bootstrap-vue-3.css';

const app = createApp(App);

app.use(BootstrapVue3);

app.mount('#app');
```

3. With Bootstrap already registered, create a new component called `LogisticsList.vue` within the `src/components` folder of your Vue application. After that, specify the following code:

```
<template>
  <b-container>
    <b-card>
      <h1 class="card-title">Logistics Items</h1>
        <b-button
          variant="primary"
          @click="fetchLogisticsItems"
          class="mb-3"
        >
          Refresh
        </b-button>

        <b-table
          :items="logisticsItems"
          :fields="fields" hover bordered
        >
          <template #cell(actions)="data">
            <b-button
              size="sm"
              variant="info"
              @click="viewDetails(data.item.id)"
            >
              View Details
            </b-button>
            <b-button
              size="sm"
              variant="danger"
              @click="deleteItem(data.item.id)"
            >
              Delete
            </b-button>
```

```
        </template>
      </b-table>

      <router-link to="/logistics/add">
        <b-button
          variant="success"
          class="mt-3">
          Add New Item
        </b-button>
      </router-link>
    </b-card>
  </b-container>
</template>

<script>
import logisticsService
  from '../services/logisticsService';

export default {
  data() {
    return {
      logisticsItems: [],
      fields: [
        { key: 'id', label: 'ID' },
        { key: 'itemName', label: 'Item Name' },
        { key: 'quantity', label: 'Quantity' },
        { key: 'location', label: 'Location' },
        {
          key: 'actions',
          label: 'Actions',
          sortable: false
        },
      ],
    };
  },
  methods: {
    fetchLogisticsItems() {
      logisticsService.getLogisticsItems().then(
    . (response) => {
        this.logisticsItems = response.data;
      });
    },
```

```
    viewDetails(id) {
      this.$router.push(`/logistics/${id}`);
    },
    deleteItem(id) {
      logisticsService.deleteLogisticsItem(id).then(
      () => {
        this.fetchLogisticsItems();
      });
    },
  },
  created() {
    this.fetchLogisticsItems();
  },
};
</script>

<style scoped>
.card-title {
  margin-bottom: 20px;
}
</style>
```

This Vue component displays a list of logistics items in a Bootstrap-styled table using `b-table` from `BootstrapVue`. It provides buttons to refresh the list, view details, and delete items, as well as a link to add a new item. The `fetchLogisticsItems` method retrieves the logistics data from the backend via the API service (`logisticsService`), while `viewDetails` navigates to the details page, and `deleteItem` removes an item from the list.

The component uses Vue's data function to define the state (`logisticsItems` and table fields) and the life cycle hook created to fetch data when the component is initialized. The template includes `BootstrapVue` components such as `b-container`, `b-card`, `b-button`, and `b-table` to create a responsive and user-friendly interface for managing logistics data.

4. Next, create the second component called `LogisticsForm.vue` within the `src/components` folder, and specify the following code:

```
<template>
  <b-container>
    <b-card>
      <h1 class="card-title">
        {{ isEditMode ? 'Edit' : 'Add' }}
        Logistics Item
      </h1>
        <b-form @submit.prevent="saveItem">
```

```
<b-form-group
  label="Item Name:"
  label-for="itemName"
>
  <b-form-input
    id="itemName"
    v-model="logisticsItem.itemName"
    required
  ></b-form-input>
</b-form-group>

<b-form-group
  label="Quantity:"
  label-for="quantity"
>
  <b-form-input
    id="quantity"
    type="number"
    v-model="logisticsItem.quantity"
    required
  ></b-form-input>
</b-form-group>

<b-form-group
  label="Location:"
  label-for="location"
>
  <b-form-input
    id="location"
    v-model="logisticsItem.location"
    required
  ></b-form-input>
</b-form-group>

<b-button
  type="submit"
  variant="success">
  {{ isEditMode ? 'Update' : 'Add' }}
</b-button>
<router-link to="/logistics">
  <b-button
    variant="danger"
    class="ml-2">
```

```
                    Cancel
                  </b-button>
                </router-link>
              </b-form>
            </b-card>
          </b-container>
        </template>

<script>
import logisticsService
  from '../services/logisticsService';

export default {
  data() {
    return {
      logisticsItem: {
        itemName: '',
        quantity: 0,
        location: '',
      },
      isEditMode: false,
    };
  },
  methods: {
    saveItem() {
      if (this.isEditMode) {
        logisticsService.updateLogisticsItem(
        this.$route.params.id,
        this.logisticsItem).then(() => {
          this.$router.push('/logistics');
        });
      } else {
        logisticsService.addLogisticsItem(
        this.logisticsItem).then(() => {
          this.$router.push('/logistics');
        });
      }
    },
    fetchLogisticsItem() {
      if (this.isEditMode) {
        logisticsService.getLogisticsItem(
        this.$route.params.id).then((response) => {
```

```
                    this.logisticsItem = response.data;
                });
            }
        },
    },
    created() {
        this.isEditMode = !!this.$route.params.id;
        this.fetchLogisticsItem();
    },
};
</script>

<style scoped>
.card-title {
    margin-bottom: 20px;
}
</style>
```

This Vue component, LogisticsForm.vue, provides a form for adding or editing logistics items using BootstrapVue components, such as b-form, b-form-group, and b-form-input. Depending on the isEditMode state, the form's title and button labels dynamically change to *Add* or *Edit*. The form collects data for the item's name, quantity, and location, and on submission, it either creates a new item or updates an existing one by calling appropriate methods from logisticsService.

The component uses Vue Router to determine if it is in edit mode by checking for a route parameter (id). If in edit mode, it fetches the existing item details using the fetchLogisticsItem method. The saveItem method handles form submission, calling the API to either update or create an item, and then redirects the user back to the logistics list view. Vue Router must be installed in your application, which can be achieved, as explained in the previous chapter, by running the following command in the root of your Vue application:

```
npm install vue-router
```

After the installation, you need to register Vue Router in the application globally, which can be achieved by modifying your main.js file, as highlighted in the following code:

```
import { createApp } from 'vue'
import App from './App.vue'
import router from './router';
import BootstrapVue3 from 'bootstrap-vue-3';
import 'bootstrap/dist/css/bootstrap.css';
import 'bootstrap-vue-3/dist/bootstrap-vue-3.css';
```

```
const app = createApp(App);

app.use(router);
app.use(BootstrapVue3);

app.mount('#app');
```

5. The next step is to create the `LogisticsDetails.vue` component within the `src/components` directory, specifying the following code:

```
<template>
  <b-container>
    <b-card>
      <h1
        class="card-title">
        Logistics Item Details
      </h1>
        <div v-if="logisticsItem">
          <p>
            <strong>Name:</strong>
            {{ logisticsItem.itemName }}
          </p>
          <p>
            <strong>
            Quantity:</strong>
            {{ logisticsItem.quantity }}
          </p>
          <p>
            <strong>Location:</strong>
            {{ logisticsItem.location }}
          </p>
          <router-link to="/logistics">
            <b-button
              variant="primary"
              class="mt-3"
            >
              Back to List
            </b-button>
          </router-link>
        </div>
    </b-card>
  </b-container>
</template>
```

```
<script>
import logisticsService
  from '../services/logisticsService';

export default {
  data() {
    return {
      logisticsItem: null,
    };
  },
  methods: {
    fetchLogisticsItem() {
      const id = this.$route.params.id;
      logisticsService.getLogisticsItem(id).then((
      response) => {
        this.logisticsItem = response.data;
      });
    },
  },
  created() {
    this.fetchLogisticsItem();
  },
};
</script>

<style scoped>
.card-title {
  margin-bottom: 20px;
}
</style>
```

The `LogisticsDetails.vue` component displays detailed information about a specific logistics item using `BootstrapVue` components, such as `b-card` and `b-button`. When the component is created, it retrieves the logistics item data from the backend API based on the `id` parameter from the route using the `fetchLogisticsItem` method. If the item exists, it shows its name, quantity, and location.

The component provides a *Back to List* button, allowing the user to navigate back to the logistics items list view using Vue Router's `router-link`. The template is styled with `BootstrapVue` classes to create a visually consistent UI.

6. The next step to have the Vue application ready to run is to modify the App.vue file to include navigation links to the components that were created. Adapt your App.vue file to have the following code:

```
<template>
  <div id="app">
    <b-navbar
      toggleable="lg"
      type="dark"
      variant="primary"
    >
      <b-container>
        <b-navbar-brand href="#">
          Logistics Management System
        </b-navbar-brand>
        <b-navbar-toggle target="nav-collapse">
        </b-navbar-toggle>
        <b-collapse id="nav-collapse" is-nav>
          <b-navbar-nav>
            <b-nav-item
              to="/logistics"
              class="nav-link"
            >
              Logistics Items List
            </b-nav-item>
            <b-nav-item
              to="/logistics/add"
              class="nav-link"
            >
              Add New Logistics Item
            </b-nav-item>
          </b-navbar-nav>
        </b-collapse>
      </b-container>
    </b-navbar>

    <b-container class="mt-4">
      <router-view />
    </b-container>
  </div>
</template>

<script>
export default {
```

```
   name: 'App',
};
</script>

<style>
.nav-link {
  cursor: pointer;
}
</style>
```

The preceding code defines a Vue component that uses BootstrapVue to create a navigation bar (b-navbar) for a logistics management system with links to view and add logistics items. The b-navbar component provides a responsive layout with toggle functionality for small screens, while router-view is used to render different components based on the current route. The navigation links are styled with a cursor pointer to enhance user experience.

Finally, you need to configure the actual routes of the application to point to the Vue components.

7. Create a folder called router in the src directory.

8. After that, create an index.js file within the router folder and specify the routes to the components, as shown in the following code:

```
import {
  createRouter, createWebHistory
} from 'vue-router';
import LogisticsList
  from '../components/LogisticsList.vue';
import LogisticsDetails
  from '../components/LogisticsDetails.vue';
import LogisticsForm
  from '../components/LogisticsForm.vue';

const routes = [
  {
    path: '/logistics',
    name: 'LogisticsList',
    component: LogisticsList,
  },
  {
    path: '/logistics/:id',
    name: 'LogisticsDetails',
    component: LogisticsDetails,
  },
```

```
    {
      path: '/logistics/add',
      name: 'AddLogisticsItem',
      component: LogisticsForm,
    },
    {
      path: '/logistics/edit/:id',
      name: 'EditLogisticsItem',
      component: LogisticsForm,
    },
    {
      path: '/',
      redirect: '/logistics',
    },
  ];

  const router = createRouter({
    history: createWebHistory(process.env.BASE_URL),
    routes,
  });

  export default router;
```

The preceding code sets up Vue Router for the Vue application by defining routes for viewing a list of logistics items (`LogisticsList`), viewing details (`LogisticsDetails`), and adding or editing logistics items (`LogisticsForm`). It uses `createRouter` with `createWebHistory` for clean URLs and includes a redirect from the root path (`/`) to the logistics items list (`/logistics`). The routes link to their respective components, enabling navigation within the application.

Now that the frontend and backend applications are complete, in the next section, we will run the application and see the results.

Running the logistics application

To run the Vue.js (frontend) and the ASP.NET web API (backend) applications and see the results, you can use the play button in Visual Studio to run the backend. For the frontend application, you can use the **Developer Command Prompt** window in Visual Studio and execute the following command within the `ClientApp` path:

```
npm run serve
```

You can open the URL displayed in the output of the prompt window in Visual Studio, which is usually `http://localhost:8080` for Vue applications. This should display the `LogisticsList.vue` component configured for the / path in the router, as seen in *Figure 12.3*:

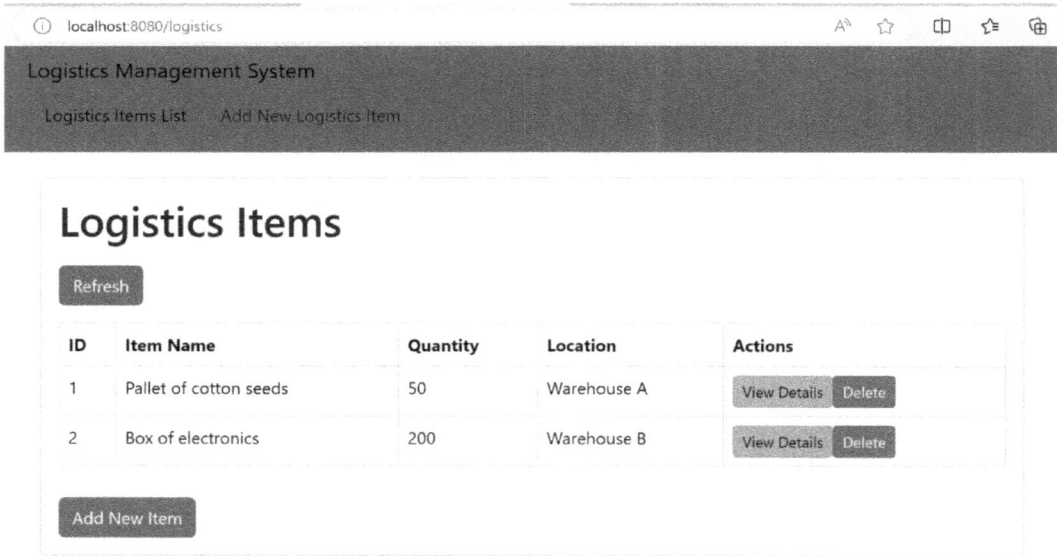

Figure 12.3: The LogisticsList.vue component

This page displays the list of logistics items returned as a response by the ASP.NET Core web API. If you click on the **Add New Item** button, it opens the `LogisticsForm.vue` component, as seen in *Figure 12.4*:

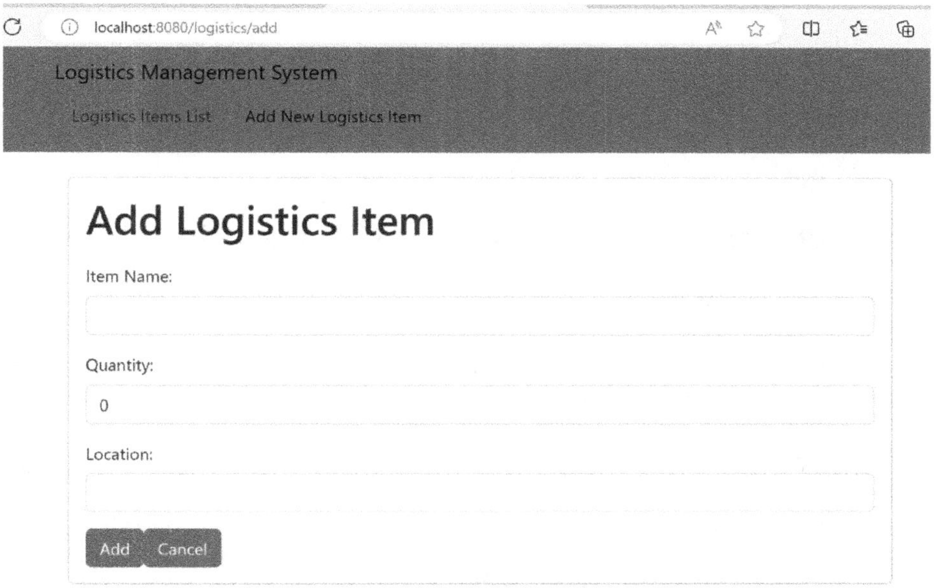

Figure 12.4: The LogisticsForm.vue component

Finally, if you click on the **View Details** button in the `LogisticsList.vue` component, you can see information about the selected item on the screen, as seen in *Figure 12.5*:

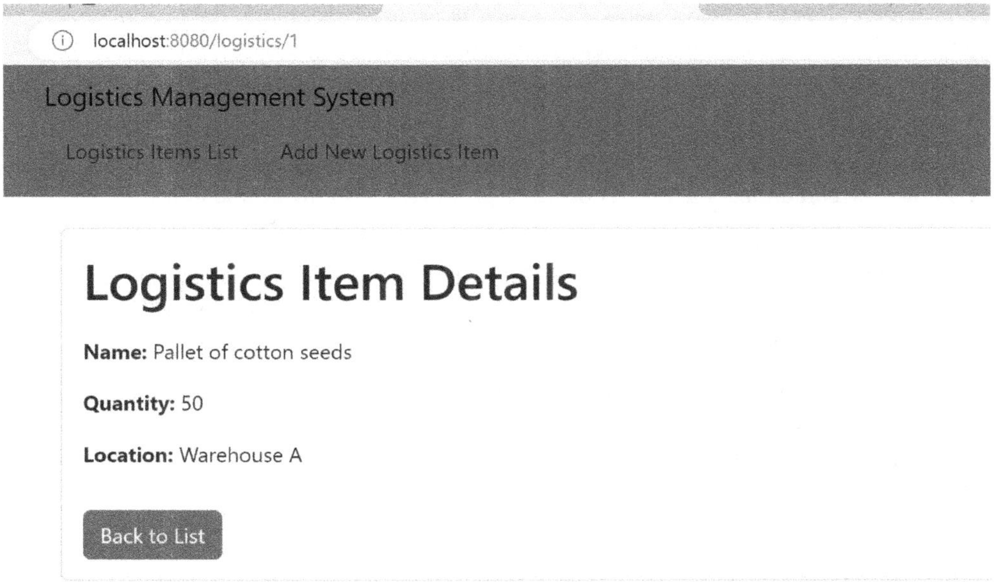

Figure 12.5: The LogisticsDetails.vue component

Feel free to create new logistic items to see the results. Additionally, you can try to apply UI modifications on these components and create new similar endpoints, to play with the integration between Vue and ASP.NET Core web API projects.

In the next section, you will find some advice on performance considerations for full-stack applications, which is crucial when integrating Vue.js with ASP.NET web API projects.

Performance considerations in full-stack applications

Building full-stack applications with Vue 3 as the frontend and ASP.NET Core web API as the backend requires careful performance optimization to provide a smooth and responsive user experience. The effectiveness of such applications is based on optimizing both the client side (Vue 3) and the server side (ASP.NET Core). This section highlights crucial methods for improving performance in this stack:

Frontend performance enhancement with Vue 3

Vue 3 provides various features and techniques to enhance the performance of client-side applications:

- **Eliminating unused code and dynamic loading**: Vue 3's build tools (such as Vite and Webpack) facilitate tree-shaking, reducing the overall bundle size. Tree-shaking is a method in JavaScript bundling that removes any unused or "dead" code from the final application bundle.

- Utilizing code splitting to load only the essential parts of the application, applying dynamic imports for components to boost initial load performance.

- **On-demand loading and Suspense API**: Use Vue 3's native capabilities for lazy loading along with the Suspense API to load components only when necessary. This method stops the browser from fetching all components initially, reducing the **time to interactive** (TTI).

- **Improving state management efficiency**: Leverage Vue 3's reactive and ref for optimal state management. Pinia (Vuex 5) provides a simpler and more efficient alternative to Vuex 3/4, cutting down on unnecessary re-renders and promoting smooth UI updates.

- **Optimizing virtual DOM and re-renders**: Vue 3's virtual DOM offers greater efficiency than its earlier versions, but developers should be cautious of excessive reactivity that may lead to redundant component updates. Leverage v-memo to optimize components that don't need frequent re-rendering.

- **Cache management and local storage optimization**: Use Vue's keep-alive component to cache frequently used data and store less dynamic data in local storage or Indexed Database API. This helps lower the number of API requests to the backend, speeding up data retrieval and making the UI more responsive.

Backend performance optimization with ASP.NET Core web API

ASP.NET Core web API offers comprehensive tools for developing scalable and high-performance backend services. Here are important techniques for improving backend performance:

- **Optimizing data fetching with async/await**: Use `async/await` for handling I/O-bound tasks without blocking threads. This method allows the server to handle more simultaneous requests, increasing overall responsiveness.

- **Use effective caching methods**: Employ in-memory caching (e.g., `IMemoryCache`) for high-frequency data and distributed caching (e.g., Redis) to support scaling over multiple servers. This approach reduces database stress and enhances response times for frequent queries.

- **Improve database efficiency with Entity Framework Core**: When employing Entity Framework Core, make use of query optimization, eager loading, and batching techniques to cut down on the number of database interactions. For critical queries, consider leveraging stored procedures or raw SQL.

- **Apply compression to API responses**: Enable Gzip or Brotli compression in ASP.NET Core to cut down the size of API responses. Reduced response sizes mean faster transmission across the network, leading to better-perceived performance on the client side.

- **Rate limit and throttle requests**: Implement rate limiting and throttling to restrict the number of requests a user or service can make within a defined time period. This prevents API abuse and promotes fair resource allocation.

Optimizing the performance of a full-stack application developed with Vue 3 and ASP.NET Core web API demands a thorough approach, addressing both frontend and backend optimization tactics. By making the most of the strengths of each technology stack, employing caching strategies, improving data fetching, and maintaining continuous performance monitoring, developers can ensure a high-speed, scalable, and responsive application that offers a top-tier user experience.

Summary

In this chapter, we explored how to integrate Vue.js with ASP.NET Core to build a modern full-stack application that combines a reactive frontend with a scalable backend. We started by setting up a .NET 9 web API project and configuring it to serve a Vue.js application, covering everything from creating domain models and controllers to configuring the frontend with Vue Router and `BootstrapVue` for UI components. We also created service files to handle API calls and developed components to perform CRUD operations, allowing seamless interaction between the frontend and backend.

We delved into the performance considerations necessary for optimizing full-stack applications built with Vue 3 and ASP.NET Core web API. We discussed frontend strategies, such as tree-shaking, lazy loading, and efficient state management, along with backend techniques, such as caching, asynchronous programming, and optimizing database queries. By applying these strategies, we can ensure that our application remains responsive, efficient, and scalable. In the next chapter, we will focus on securing full-stack applications, including implementing authentication and authorization, which is the next logical step to safeguarding your optimized application.

We will shift our focus to integrating Angular with ASP.NET Core, providing another approach to full-stack development. We will cover how to set up Angular with ASP.NET Core, manage communication between the frontend and backend, and apply the best architectural practices for building robust and scalable applications. This will provide a broader perspective on integrating popular JavaScript frameworks with .NET backends, enhancing your full-stack development toolkit.

Get This Book's PDF Version and Exclusive Extras

UNLOCK NOW

Scan the QR code (or go to `packtpub.com/unlock`). Search for this book by name, confirm the edition, and then follow the steps on the page.

Note: Keep your invoice handly. Purchase made directly from packt don't require one.

13

Integrating Angular with ASP.NET Core

Integrating Angular with ASP.NET Core provides a powerful toolkit for developing scalable full-stack applications. Angular works seamlessly with ASP.NET Core to build dynamic web applications. This chapter will walk through the steps to configure Angular with ASP.NET Core, facilitating the creation of high-performance and efficient full-stack applications. We will learn how to make API calls between Angular and ASP.NET Core applications, implementing secure and efficient communication between these two powerful frameworks.

By the end of this chapter, you will have a solid understanding of how to develop an Angular application that interacts with an ASP.NET Core backend while following good software development practices. You will also learn how to optimize both frontend and backend performance to ensure a responsive user experience. These skills are crucial for software engineers looking to create and design scalable applications using the most modern stack available in the market.

In this chapter, we are going to cover the following main topics:

- Setting up Angular with ASP.NET Core
- Building a sample application

This structure will help you navigate the key concepts in a practical way, giving you a strong foundation to understand the integration aspects between Angular and ASP.NET Core.

Technical requirements

As mentioned in *Chapter 10*, to effectively use Angular, you need Node.js installed on your machine, as it provides the runtime environment to execute and run your applications. Node.js is also required for package management. Along with Node.js, you need **Node Package Manager** (**npm**) installed, which is a tool for managing dependencies and packages required to develop your applications locally. The most recent version of these tools is sufficient to prepare you for the practical examples in this chapter for the Angular application, assuming you have already installed VS Code, which was required in the previous chapters of this book.

Additionally, we will create a .NET 9 application in this chapter. Therefore, you must have this version of the .NET SDK installed on your machine. If you already have the most recent version of Visual Studio installed on your machine, you do not need to worry about any further .NET installation.

The code files required for you to follow along with this chapter can be found at: `https://github. com/PacktPublishing/Modern-Full-Stack-Web-Development-with-ASP. NET-Core/tree/main/Chapter13`.

Setting up Angular with ASP.NET Core

In this section, we will set up a development environment for integrating Angular with ASP.NET Core, configure ASP.NET Core to serve an Angular application, and create the basic structure of an Angular project to get started.

Assuming that you already have Node.js and npm installed on your machine based on the practical exercise of the previous chapter, to work with Angular, you must have the Angular CLI installed as well. This provides a powerful set of tools to manage Angular applications during development. To install it globally, you can run the following command using a regular **Command Prompt (CMD)**:

```
npm install -g @angular/cli
```

Now, with everything installed correctly, we can proceed to create the ASP.NET Core Web API project in the next section.

Creating an ASP.NET Core Web API project

To create an ASP.NET Core Web API project, follow these steps:

1. Open Visual Studio and create a new project by selecting the **ASP.NET Core Web API** template, as shown in *Figure 13.1*:

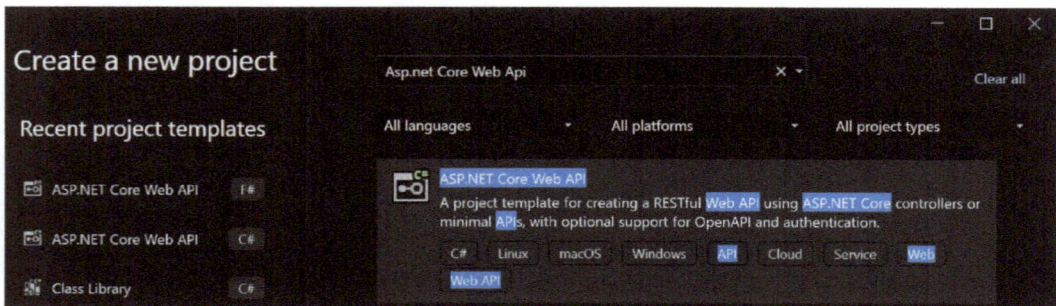

Figure 13.1: ASP.NET Core Web API template

2. After selecting the **ASP.NET Core Web API** template, make sure to select the .NET 9 version and choose to use controllers without top-level statements in the final screen, as shown in *Figure 13.2*:

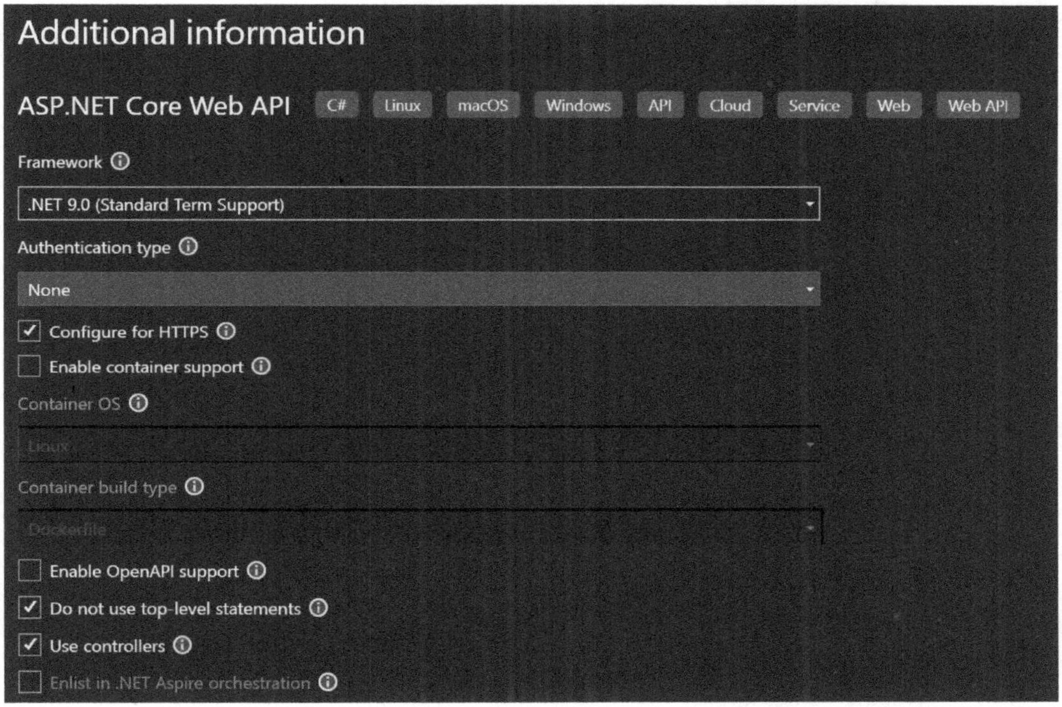

Figure 13.2: ASP.NET Core Web API configuration

After creating the ASP.NET Core Web API project, you need to install the SPAServices. Extensions package, which will be used to configure the ASP.NET Core project to serve the Angular application.

3. To install the package, right-click on your newly created project in **Solution Explorer** and choose the **Manage NuGet Packages…** option as shown in *Figure 13.3*:

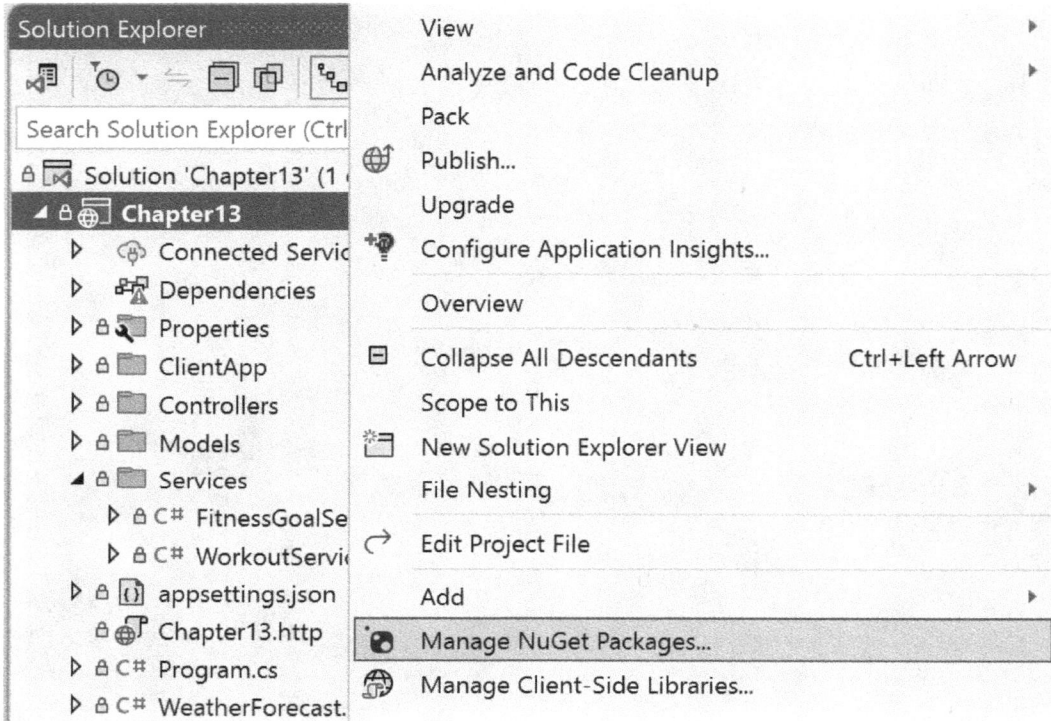

Figure 13.3: Manage NuGet Packages… option

4. In the **NuGet Package Management** window, select the **Browse** option, search for the `Microsoft.AspNetCore.SpaServices.Extensions` package, and confirm the installation, as shown in *Figure 13.4*:

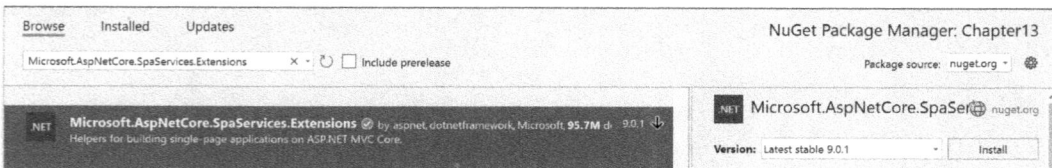

Figure 13.4: SPAServices.Extensions installation

5. After that, you have to make some changes to the `Program.cs` file to configure ASP.NET Core to serve the Angular application. Modify the `Program.cs` file as follows:

```
namespace Chapter13
{
    public class Program
    {
        public static void Main(string[] args)
        {
            var builder =
                WebApplication.CreateBuilder(args);

            builder.Services.AddControllers();
            builder.Services.AddSpaStaticFiles(
                configuration =>
            {
                configuration.RootPath =
                    "ClientApp/dist";
            });

            var app = builder.Build();

            app.UseStaticFiles();
            app.UseSpaStaticFiles();

            app.UseAuthorization();


            app.MapControllers();

            app.Run();
        }
    }
}
```

In this configuration, `AddSpaStaticFiles` is used to serve the static files for the Angular application. `RootPath` is configured to the `ClientApp/dist` folder, which is where the production build of the Angular application will be placed.

The ASP.NET Core application is now set up to serve the Angular application, which we will create later in this chapter using a step-by-step approach. In the following section, we will build a sample application by extending the ASP.NET Core Web API project developed in this section.

Building a sample application

In this section, we will build a **Fitness Tracker** application, a simple tool that allows users to monitor their workouts and fitness goals. The application will include CRUD operations, enabling users to log their daily exercises, track their progress over time, and set specific fitness goals. For the backend of the application, the ASP.NET Core Web API project created in the previous section will be used to define the endpoints that will be called by the frontend. Additionally, we will build an Angular application from scratch, configuring aspects of the data communication between the frontend and backend, including the necessary **User Interface (UI)** elements.

From a technical standpoint, this app will leverage key concepts such as RESTful API development (we talked about RESTful APIs in *Chapters 8* and *9*) and an in-memory database for interactions, just for demonstration purposes. Additionally, we will use built-in Angular features such as routing and an HTTP client, and we will also use TypeScript interfaces to maintain a consistent data flow between the Angular application and the ASP.NET Core Web API projects. By the end of this section, you will have a basic understanding of how to integrate Angular with ASP.NET Core, following a step-by-step approach.

In the next section, you will find details on the domain models that need to be created in the backend for the **Fitness Tracker** app.

Creating the domain model

In this section, we will define the core domain model for the **Fitness Tracker** application. The domain model defines the key entities that encapsulate the business logic and data structure of the application. For our app, the primary entities are `Workout` and `Fitness Goal`.

We will store these entities in memory in the ASP.NET Core backend, allowing us to simulate data storage without needing an actual database. This setup is ideal for rapid development and testing, enabling us to quickly prototype the application. In a real production environment, you would use an actual database with Entity Framework Core or another framework to handle interactions between the backend and the database.

However, even though we are storing the entities in memory, it is still crucial to define them properly in the backend so they can be used effectively by our in-memory storage system. Let's get started with the steps:

1. In your ASP.NET Core Web API project, create a folder called `Models` in the root of the project using **Solution Explorer** in Visual Studio.

2. After that, create a `Workout.cs` file, which will contain the specifications for the Workout model. After creating the file, add the following code:

    ```
    namespace Chapter13.Models
    {
    ```

```
public class Workout
{
    public int Id { get; set; }
    public string Exercise { get; set; }
    public int Duration { get; set; }
    public DateTime Date { get; set; }
    public string Notes { get; set; }
}
}
```

You can replace the namespace with the one from your own project, which is applicable to all C# examples in this chapter. This model contains the basic properties for a regular workout session to be recorded in the **Fitness Tracker** app, such as Id, Exercise, Duration, Date, and Notes.

3. The next model is FitnessGoal, which also contains basic properties. This can be defined by creating a FitnessGoal.cs file within the Models folder. After that, you can add the following code:

```
namespace Chapter13.Models
{
    public class FitnessGoal
    {
        public int Id { get; set; }
        public string GoalName { get; set; }
        public string Description { get; set; }
        public DateTime TargetDate { get; set; }
    }
}
```

The FitnessGoal model allows users to specify fitness-related goals, such as achieving a certain number of workouts or hitting a specific fitness milestone by a target date. This entity helps track goals over time and determine whether they have been achieved.

With the models already created, the next section focuses on the creation of in-memory repositories for the models.

Creating the backend services

To store the Workout and FitnessGoal entities in memory, we will use an in-memory list in the ASP.NET Core backend. This approach will simulate a database, allowing us to perform CRUD operations without needing to set up an actual database locally.

To configure the in-memory storage, create a `Services` folder in the root of your project, at the same level as the `Models` folder, and create a `WorkoutService.cs` file within the `Services` folder containing the following code:

```csharp
using Chapter13.Models;

namespace Chapter13.Services
{
    public class WorkoutService
    {
        private readonly List<Workout> _workouts =
            new List<Workout>();

        public IEnumerable<Workout> GetWorkouts() =>
            _workouts;

        public Workout GetWorkoutById(int id) =>
            _workouts.FirstOrDefault(w => w.Id == id);

        public void AddWorkout(Workout workout)
        {
            workout.Id = _workouts.Count + 1;
            _workouts.Add(workout);
        }

        public void UpdateWorkout(
            int id, Workout updatedWorkout)
        {
            var workout =
                _workouts.FirstOrDefault(w => w.Id == id);
            if (workout != null)
            {
                workout.Exercise = updatedWorkout.Exercise;
                workout.Duration = updatedWorkout.Duration;
                workout.Date = updatedWorkout.Date;
                workout.Notes = updatedWorkout.Notes;
            }
        }

        public void DeleteWorkout(int id)
        {
            var workout =
                _workouts.FirstOrDefault(w => w.Id == id);
            if (workout != null)
```

```
            {
                _workouts.Remove(workout);
            }
        }
    }
}
```

The `WorkoutService` class is responsible for managing all the workout data in memory. It provides methods for creating, reading, updating, and deleting workout records, simulating a data repository that could later be replaced with a database. Here's an explanation of each method:

- `GetWorkouts`: This method retrieves all workouts stored in memory. It returns `IEnumerable<Workout>`, allowing the calling function to access the list of workouts.

- `GetWorkoutById(int id)`: This method returns a specific workout based on the provided ID. It uses LINQ to find the workout with a matching ID, and if no workout is found with the given ID, it returns `null`.

- `AddWorkout(Workout workout)`: This method adds a new workout to the in-memory list. The workout ID is auto-generated by simply incrementing the count of the workouts already present in the list. The method simulates the behavior of an auto-incrementing primary key in a database.

- `UpdateWorkout(int id, Workout updatedWorkout)`: This method updates the details of an existing workout. It first retrieves the workout by ID and, if found, updates its properties. In a real-world application, this would involve an update query in the database or an update operation using Entity Framework.

- `DeleteWorkout(int id)`: This method removes a workout from the in-memory list. It retrieves the workout by ID and, if one is found, removes it from the list. In a full application, this would involve a `DELETE` operation on a database table.

Now that you have the `WorkoutService` class completed, there is a need to create a service class for the `FitnessGoal` entity as well. Create a new file called `FitnessGoalService.cs` within the `Services` folder, and add the following code in the new file:

```
using Chapter13.Models;

namespace Chapter13.Services
{
    public class FitnessGoalService
    {
        private readonly List<FitnessGoal> _goals =
            new List<FitnessGoal>();
```

```
    public IEnumerable<FitnessGoal> GetGoals() =>
        _goals;

    public FitnessGoal GetGoalById(int id) =>
        _goals.FirstOrDefault(g => g.Id == id);

    public void AddGoal(FitnessGoal goal)
    {
        goal.Id = _goals.Count + 1;
        _goals.Add(goal);
    }

    public void UpdateGoal(
        int id, FitnessGoal updatedGoal)
    {
        var goal =
            _goals.FirstOrDefault(g => g.Id == id);
        if (goal != null)
        {
            goal.GoalName = updatedGoal.GoalName;
            goal.Description = updatedGoal.Description;
            goal.TargetDate = updatedGoal.TargetDate;
        }
    }

    public void DeleteGoal(int id)
    {
        var goal =
            _goals.FirstOrDefault(g => g.Id == id);
        if (goal != null)
        {
            _goals.Remove(goal);
        }
    }
    }

}
```

The `FitnessGoalService` class manages all operations related to fitness goals in memory. Just like `WorkoutService`, it provides methods for creating, reading, updating, and deleting fitness goals, simulating what a repository would do with a persistent database. Here's an explanation of each method in the service:

- `GetGoals()`: This method retrieves all fitness goals stored in memory. It returns `IEnumerable<FitnessGoal>`, which is a collection of all fitness goals. In a real-world system, this would involve querying a database for all goal records.

- `GetGoalById(int id)`: This method retrieves a specific fitness goal by its ID. It uses LINQ to search the in-memory list for the goal with a matching ID. If the goal is not found, it returns `null`.

- `AddGoal(FitnessGoal goal)`: This method adds a new fitness goal to the in-memory list. Similar to `AddWorkout`, it auto-generates the goal's ID by incrementing the count of the existing goals. This process simulates how a database might auto-increment primary keys for new records.

- `UpdateGoal(int id, FitnessGoal updateGoal)`: This method updates the details of an existing fitness goal. It retrieves the goal by its ID and updates its properties. In a real-world application, this method would correspond to an `UPDATE` query in a database.

- `DeleteGoal(int id)`: This method removes a fitness goal from the in-memory list. It finds the goal by its ID and, if found, removes it from the list. In a persistent storage system, this would correspond to a `DELETE` operation in a database.

Just like `WorkoutService`, `FitnessGoalService` provides full CRUD functionality but stores the data in memory. This setup is highly useful for fast prototyping and development before committing to a more complex database integration.

In the next section, we will be creating the controllers for the `Workout` and `FitnessGoal` entities.

Creating the controller

To properly implement the backend API for managing workouts in our **Fitness Tracker** app, the underlying controllers need to be created in the ASP.NET Core project to expose APIs that will be integrated with the Angular app later. The first controller is `WorkoutsController`, which is responsible for exposing the necessary API endpoints for performing CRUD operations on workout data. Using ASP.NET Core's Web API capabilities, the controller will act as the intermediary between the frontend and backend logic, ensuring that HTTP requests such as GET, POST, PUT, and DELETE are handled properly. By creating this controller, you establish the API routes that will allow users to interact with the workouts in the system, utilizing the underlying service layer to perform the necessary operations.

In your ASP.NET Core project, create a file called `WorkoutsController.cs` within the `Controllers` folder, specifying the following code:

```
using Chapter13.Models;
using Chapter13.Services;
using Microsoft.AspNetCore.Mvc;

namespace Chapter13.Controllers
{
    [Route("api/[controller]")]
```

```csharp
[ApiController]
public class WorkoutsController : ControllerBase
{
    private readonly WorkoutService _workoutService;

    public WorkoutsController(
        WorkoutService workoutService)
    {
        _workoutService = workoutService;
    }

    [HttpGet]
    public ActionResult<IEnumerable<Workout>>
        GetWorkouts()
    {
        return Ok(_workoutService.GetWorkouts());
    }

    [HttpGet("{id}")]
    public ActionResult<Workout> GetWorkout(int id)
    {
        var workout =
            _workoutService.GetWorkoutById(id);

        if (workout == null)
            return NotFound();
        return Ok(workout);
    }

    [HttpPost]
    public ActionResult<Workout> CreateWorkout(
        Workout workout)
    {
        _workoutService.AddWorkout(workout);

        return NoContent();
    }

    [HttpPut("{id}")]
    public IActionResult UpdateWorkout(
        int id, Workout updatedWorkout)
    {
        var workout =
```

```
        _workoutService.GetWorkoutById(id);

        if (workout == null)
            return NotFound();

        _workoutService.UpdateWorkout(
            id, updatedWorkout);

        return NoContent();
    }

    [HttpDelete("{id}")]
    public IActionResult DeleteWorkout(int id)
    {
        var workout =
            _workoutService.GetWorkoutById(id);


        if (workout == null)
            return NotFound();

        _workoutService.DeleteWorkout(id);

        return NoContent();
    }
  }
}
```

In this controller, the constructor injects an instance of WorkoutService using dependency injection. By injecting WorkoutService, the controller can interact with the in-memory list of workouts. This approach improves testability and decouples the controller from the service, making it easier to replace the service with a different implementation if needed. Here's an explanation of each API endpoint:

- GetWorkouts: This action retrieves all the workouts from the service using the GetWorkouts method. The result is returned with an HTTP 200 OK status, indicating the successful retrieval of data. The Ok() method automatically serializes the list of workouts into JSON for the Angular app to consume.

- GetWorkout(int id): This action retrieves a specific workout based on the provided ID. If the workout is found, it returns an HTTP 200 OK status with the workout data. If no workout is found with the given ID, the method returns HTTP 404 Not Found, indicating that the resource does not exist.

- `CreateWorkout(Workout workout)`: The `CreateWorkout` action is responsible for adding a new workout. It takes a `Workout` object as input, which is passed to the `AddWorkout()` method in the service to store it in memory. The method returns an `HTTP 204 No Content` status to indicate that the creation was successful but without any content in the response body.

- `UpdateWorkout(int id, Workout updatedWorkout)`: This action updates an existing workout. It first retrieves the workout by ID, and if the workout is found, the `UpdateWorkout` method of the service is called to apply the changes. If the workout is not found, the method returns `HTTP 404 Not Found`. If the update is successful, it returns `HTTP 204 No Content`.

- `DeleteWorkout(int id)`: The `DeleteWorkout` action handles the deletion of a workout by its ID. It first checks whether the workout exists. If it does, it deletes the workout using the `DeleteWorkout()` method in the service. If the workout does not exist, the action returns `HTTP 404 Not Found`. A successful deletion returns `HTTP 204 No Content`.

Now that we have the controller for the Workout model created, let's create a similar controller for the `FitnessGoal` model. Create a new file called `FitnessGoalController.cs` within the `Controllers` folder, specifying the following code:

```
using Chapter13.Models;
using Chapter13.Services;
using Microsoft.AspNetCore.Mvc;

namespace Chapter13.Controllers
{
    [Route("api/[controller]")]
    [ApiController]
    public class FitnessGoalsController : ControllerBase
    {

        private readonly FitnessGoalService
            _fitnessGoalService;

        public FitnessGoalsController(
            FitnessGoalService fitnessGoalService)
        {
            _fitnessGoalService = fitnessGoalService;
        }

        [HttpGet]
        public ActionResult<IEnumerable<FitnessGoal>>
            GetGoals()
        {
```

```csharp
        return Ok(_fitnessGoalService.GetGoals());
}

[HttpGet("{id}")]
public ActionResult<FitnessGoal> GetGoal(int id)
{
    var goal = _fitnessGoalService.GetGoalById(id);

    if (goal == null)
        return NotFound();
    return Ok(goal);
}

[HttpPost]
public ActionResult<FitnessGoal>
    CreateGoal(FitnessGoal goal)
{
    _fitnessGoalService.AddGoal(goal);

    return NoContent();
}

[HttpPut("{id}")]
public IActionResult UpdateGoal(
    int id, FitnessGoal updatedGoal)
{
    var goal = _fitnessGoalService.GetGoalById(id);

    if (goal == null)
        return NotFound();

    _fitnessGoalService.UpdateGoal(
        id, updatedGoal);

    return NoContent();
}

[HttpDelete("{id}")]
public IActionResult DeleteGoal(int id)
{
    var goal = _fitnessGoalService.GetGoalById(id);
```

```
            if (goal == null)
                return NotFound();


            _fitnessGoalService.DeleteGoal(id);


            return NoContent();
        }
    }
}
```

The controller's constructor uses dependency injection to receive an instance of `FitnessGoalService`. Here's a detailed explanation for each controller action present in `FitnessGoalController`:

- `GetGoals`: This action handles HTTP GET requests to retrieve all fitness goals stored in the system. It calls the `GetGoals()` method from the service to return a list of fitness goals, wrapping the result in an HTTP 200 OK response, which serializes the list into JSON.

- `GetGoal(int id)`: This method retrieves a specific fitness goal based on the provided ID. If the goal exists, it is returned along with an HTTP 200 OK response. If the goal is not found, the method returns HTTP 404 Not Found.

- `CreateGoal(FitnessGoal goal)`: This action allows clients to create a new fitness goal by sending a POST request with the goal data. The goal is added to the in-memory list using the `AddGoal()` method from the service. A successful creation returns an HTTP 204 No Content status, indicating that the request was successful but does not return any content in the response body.

- `UpdateGoal(int id, FitnessGoal updatedGoal)`: The PUT method allows the update of an existing fitness goal by providing the ID of the goal and the updated data. If the goal exists, it is updated with the new data, and an HTTP 204 No Content status is returned. If the goal does not exist, HTTP 404 Not Found is returned.

- `DeleteGoal(int id)`: This action deletes a fitness goal from the system based on its ID. It first checks whether the goal exists by using the `GetGoalById()` method. If the goal is found, it is deleted, and the action returns HTTP 204 No Content. If the goal is not found, it returns HTTP 404 Not Found.

The last step is to register the underlying `Workout` and `FitnessGoal` services in the application using the Singleton scope. You can register the services by adding the lines highlighted in the following code to your `Program.cs` file:

```
using Chapter13.Services;


namespace Chapter13
{
    public class Program
```

```
{
    public static void Main(string[] args)
    {
        var builder =
            WebApplication.CreateBuilder(args);

        builder.Services.AddControllers();
        builder.Services.AddSpaStaticFiles(
            configuration =>
        {
            configuration.RootPath = "ClientApp/dist";
        });

        builder.Services.AddCors(options =>
        {
            options.AddPolicy("AllowAllOrigins",
                policy => policy.AllowAnyOrigin()
                                .AllowAnyMethod()
                                .AllowAnyHeader());
        });

        builder.Services
            .AddSingleton<WorkoutService>();
        builder.Services
            .AddSingleton<FitnessGoalService>();

        var app = builder.Build();

        app.UseStaticFiles();
        app.UseSpaStaticFiles();

        app.UseAuthorization();

        app.UseCors("AllowAllOrigins");

        app.MapControllers();

        app.Run();
    }
}
}
```

`FitnessGoalController` and `WorkoutsController` provide the full set of CRUD operations for managing workouts and fitness goals in the **Fitness Tracker** application. They expose the necessary API endpoints that allow the frontend to interact with the fitness goals stored in memory. By using dependency injection, the controllers communicate with the underlying services (`WorkoutService` and `FitnessGoalService`) to perform data operations. This structure ensures a clean separation of concerns, allowing the controller to focus on handling HTTP requests while the service manages the business logic and data storage. The controllers adhere to RESTful principles, making it easy to integrate with client-side applications such as Angular.

In the next section, we are going to create the Angular application that will be used to consume the backend service.

Creating the Angular application

In this section, we will focus on setting up the Angular frontend for our **Fitness Tracker** application. This application will enable users to interact with the backend we've built in the previous sections to manage their workouts and fitness goals. By the end of this section, you will have a fully functioning Angular application that communicates with the backend services to fetch, display, create, update, and delete workout and fitness goal data.

Take the following steps to create the Angular project:

1. First, open a new **Developer Command Prompt** window in Visual Studio, targeting the root of your ASP.NET Core project.

2. Then, create a new app called `ClientApp` by executing the following command:

    ```
    ng new ClientApp
    ```

3. When prompted, choose **CSS** as the stylesheet format that you would like to use. After that, navigate to the root of your newly created app by executing the following command:

    ```
    cd clientapp
    ```

4. To enhance the UI, we will use Bootstrap for responsive design and styling. Install Bootstrap and its dependencies by running the following command:

    ```
    npm install bootstrap
    ```

5. Once installed, you will need to add Bootstrap's CSS file to your `angular.json` configuration file, which is located in the root of your Angular project within the `ClientApp` folder. In this file, add the lines highlighted in the following code under the styles array:

    ```
    {
      „$schema":
       „./node_modules/@angular/cli/lib/config/
    ```

```
      schema.json",
  "version": 1,
  "newProjectRoot": "projects",
  "projects": {
    "ClientApp": {
      "projectType": "application",
      "schematics": {},
      "root": "",
      "sourceRoot": "src",
      "prefix": "app",
      "architect": {
        "build": {
          "builder": "@angular-devkit/
            build-angular:application",
          "options": {
            "outputPath": "dist/client-app",
            "index": "src/index.html",
            "browser": "src/main.ts",
            "polyfills": [
              "zone.js"
            ],
            "tsConfig": "tsconfig.app.json",
            "assets": [
              {
                "glob": "**/*",
                "input": "public"
              }
            ],
            "styles": [
              "src/styles.css",
              "node_modules/bootstrap/dist/css/
                bootstrap.min.css"
            ],
            "scripts": [
              "node_modules/bootstrap/dist/js/
              bootstrap.bundle.min.js"

            ]
          },
          "configurations": {
            "production": {
              "budgets": [
                {
```

```
                "type": "initial",
                "maximumWarning": "500kB",
                "maximumError": "1MB"
            },
            {
                "type": "anyComponentStyle",
                "maximumWarning": "2kB",
                "maximumError": "4kB"
            }
        ],
        "outputHashing": "all"
    },
    "development": {
        "optimization": false,
        "extractLicenses": false,
        "sourceMap": true
    }
},
"defaultConfiguration": "production"
},
"serve": {
    "builder": "@angular-devkit/
    build-angular:dev-server",
    "configurations": {
        "production": {
            "buildTarget":
                "ClientApp:build:production"
        },
        "development": {
            "buildTarget":
                "ClientApp:build:development"
        }
    },
    "defaultConfiguration": "development"
},
"extract-i18n": {
    "builder": "@angular-devkit/
    build-angular:extract-i18n"
},
"test": {
    "builder": "@angular-devkit/
    build-angular:karma",
    «options»: {
```

```
        «polyfills»: [
          «zone.js»,
          «zone.js/testing»
        ],
        «tsConfig»: «tsconfig.spec.json»,
        «assets»: [
          {
            «glob»: «**/*»,
            «input»: «public»
          }
        ],
        «styles»: [
          «src/styles.css»
        ],
        «scripts»: []
      }
    }
  }
  }
  }
}
```

Now, Bootstrap styles will be available throughout your Angular project. In the next section, we will set up the services for integration with the backend services.

Creating the services for HTTP requests

To interact withcreating for HTTP requests" the ASP.NET Core backend, we will create two services: one for workouts and one for fitness goals. These services will use `HttpClient` to communicate with the API endpoints. Let's get started with the steps:

1. First, create a folder called `services` within the `src/app` directory and create a file called `workout.service.ts`, which will contain the necessary logic to make API requests to the backend for the Workout endpoints. After creating the file, specify the following code:

```
import { Injectable } from '@angular/core';
import { HttpClient } from '@angular/common/http';
import { Observable } from 'rxjs';

export interface Workout {
  id: number;
  exercise: string;
  duration: number;
  date: Date;
```

```
  notes: string;
}

@Injectable({
  providedIn: 'root',
})
export class WorkoutService {
  private apiUrl =
    'http://localhost:5124/api/workouts';

  constructor(private http: HttpClient) {}

  getWorkouts(): Observable<Workout[]> {
    return this.http.get<Workout[]>(this.apiUrl);
  }

  getWorkout(id: number): Observable<Workout> {
    return this.http.get<Workout>(
      `${this.apiUrl}/${id}`
    );
  }

  createWorkout(workout: Workout): Observable<Workout>
  {
    return this.http.post<Workout>(
      this.apiUrl, workout
    );
  }

  updateWorkout(id: number, workout: Workout):
  Observable<void> {
    return this.http.put<void>(
      `${this.apiUrl}/${id}`, workout
    );
  }

  deleteWorkout(id: number): Observable<void> {
    return this.http.delete<void>(
      `${this.apiUrl}/${id}`
    );
  }
}
```

The preceding code defines an Angular service called `WorkoutService` that manages the communication between the Angular frontend and the backend API for handling workout data. The service uses `HttpClient` to make HTTP requests to the API.

The `Workout` interface creating for HTTP requests" defines the structure of a workout object, with the same fields that are returned by the backend API. The `WorkoutService` class is decorated with `@Injectable({ providedIn: 'root' })`, making it a Singleton that can be injected anywhere in the application. Here's a further explanation about `WorkoutService`:

- `apiUrl`: The base URL for the backend API
- `getWorkouts()`: Fetches a list of all workouts from the API
- `getWorkout(id: number)`: Retrieves a specific workout by its ID
- `createWorkout(workout: Workout)`: Sends a POST request to create a new workout
- `updateWorkout(id: number, workout: Workout)`: Sends a PUT request to update an existing workout based on its ID
- `deleteWorkout(id: number)`: Sends a DELETE request to remove a workout by its ID

This service provides the necessary methods for performing CRUD operations on workouts via HTTP requests.

2. Next, create a new file called `goal.service.ts` within the same services folder, which will accommodate the logic to handle API requests related to the Fitness Goal operations. After creating the file, add in the following code:

```
import { Injectable } from '@angular/core';
import { HttpClient } from '@angular/common/http';
import { Observable } from 'rxjs';

export interface FitnessGoal {
  id: number;
  goalName: string;
  description: string;
  targetDate: Date;
}

@Injectable({
  providedIn: 'root',
})
export class GoalService {
  private apiUrl =
    'http://localhost:5124/api/fitnessgoals';
```

```
constructor(private http: HttpClient) {}

getGoals(): Observable<FitnessGoal[]> {
  return this.http.get<FitnessGoal[]>(this.apiUrl);
}

getGoal(id: number): Observable<FitnessGoal> {
  return this.http.get<FitnessGoal>(
    `${this.apiUrl}/${id}`
  );
}

createGoal(goal: FitnessGoal):
Observable<FitnessGoal> {
  return this.http.post<FitnessGoal>(
    this.apiUrl, goal
  );
}

updateGoal(id: number, goal: FitnessGoal):
Observable<void> {
  return this.http.put<void>(
    `${this.apiUrl}/${id}`, goal
  );
}

deleteGoal(id: number): Observable<void> {
  return this.http.delete<void>(
    `${this.apiUrl}/${id}`
  );
}
}
```

The preceding codecreating for HTTP requests" defines an Angular service called `GoalService` that manages communication between the Angular frontend and the backend API for handling `FitnessGoal` data. Similar to the previous `WorkoutService`, it uses `HttpClient` to perform HTTP requests to interact with the API. The `FitnessGoal` interface outlines the structure of a fitness goal object, with similar properties specified in the backend.

Here's a detailed explanation of all methods and properties of the `GoalService` class:

- `apiUrl`: The base URL for interacting with the fitness goals API

- `getGoals()`: Retrieves all fitness goals from the API

- `getGoal(id: number)`: Fetches a specific fitness goal based on its ID

- `createGoal(goal: FitnessGoal)`: Sends a POST request to create a new fitness goal

- `updateGoal(id: number, goal: FitnessGoal)`: Sends a PUT request to update an existing fitness goal

- `deleteGoal(id: number)`: Sends a DELETE request to remove a fitness goal by its ID

This service creating for HTTP requests" contains all the necessary methods for performing CRUD operations on fitness goals via HTTP requests, facilitating interaction with the backend API.

In the next section, we will learn which of the Angular components need to be created for the **Fitness Tracker** application.

Creating the Angular components

In this section, we will focus on creating the essential Angular components for our **Fitness Tracker** application. By creating separate components for workouts and fitness goals, we will organize the application into reusable pieces. These components will allow users to view lists, add new entries, and edit or delete existing workouts and fitness goals. Throughout this process, we will also integrate Bootstrap to ensure a responsive UI, starting with the Goal Form component in the following section.

Creating the Goal Form component

We will first create the Goal Form component, which will allow users to create and update fitness goals by providing a UI with standard form fields. To create the component, execute the following command:

```
ng generate component components/goal-form
```

The preceding command will create a `goal-form` folder within the `src/app/components` directory. After the directory is created with the default files for the Goal Form component, edit the `goal-form.component.ts` file with the following content:

```
import { Component, OnInit } from '@angular/core';
import { FormsModule } from '@angular/forms';
import {
  FitnessGoal, GoalService
} from '../../services/goal.service';
import {
  ActivatedRoute, Router, RouterModule
} from '@angular/router';

@Component({
  selector: 'app-goal-form',
  standalone: true,
  templateUrl: './goal-form.component.html',
  imports: [FormsModule, RouterModule]
```

```typescript
})
export class GoalFormComponent implements OnInit {
  goal: FitnessGoal =
    {
      id: 0,
      goalName: '',
      description: '',
      targetDate: new Date()
    };
  isEditMode: boolean = false;

  constructor(
    private goalService: GoalService,
    private router: Router,
    private route: ActivatedRoute
  ) {}

  ngOnInit(): void {
    const id = this.route.snapshot.paramMap.get('id');
    if (id) {
      this.isEditMode = true;
      this.goalService.getGoal(Number(id)).subscribe(
      data => {
        this.goal = data;
      });
    }
  }

  saveGoal(): void {
    if (this.isEditMode) {
      this.goalService.updateGoal(
      this.goal.id, this.goal).subscribe(() => {
        this.router.navigate(['/goals']);
      });
    } else {
      this.goalService.createGoal(this.goal).subscribe(
      () => {
        this.router.navigate(['/goals']);
      });
    }
  }
}
```

This code defines GoalFormComponent, an Angular component responsible for handling the creation and editing of fitness goals. It uses FormsModule to manage user input and RouterModule to handle navigation between routes.

The component is declared as standalone, meaning it does not rely on Angular's NgModule system. It imports both FormsModule (for handling form inputs) and RouterModule (for navigation).

Regarding the component properties, goal represents a fitness goal, initialized with default values. The isEditMode property is a Boolean flag used to differentiate between creating a new goal and editing an existing one.

In terms of dependency injection, the component injects GoalService (to handle backend communication), Router (to navigate after form submission), and ActivatedRoute (to retrieve route parameters like ID).

On ngOnInit, when the component initializes, it checks whether an ID is present in the route parameters. If so, the component switches to edit mode and fetches the corresponding goal from the service. Otherwise, it remains in create mode.

The saveGoal method handles saving the goal. It either calls updateGoal (if in edit mode) or createGoal (if in create mode). After successfully saving the goal, the user is navigated back to the list of fitness goals.

This component enables users to create new fitness goals or edit existing ones, making it a core part of the goal management functionality in the application.

Now that the logic of the component is already created, it is time to define the HTML part of the component to display the necessary fields in the UI. To achieve that, edit the goal-form.component.html file with the following code:

```html
<div class="container mt-4">
  <h2>
    {{ isEditMode ? 'Edit Goal' : 'Add New Goal' }}
  </h2>

  <form (ngSubmit)="saveGoal()">
    <div class="form-group">
      <label for="goalName">Goal Name</label>
      <input
        type="text"
        id="goalName"
        class="form-control"
        [(ngModel)]="goal.goalName"
        name="goalName" required
      >
```

```
      </div>
      <div class="form-group">
        <label for="description">Description</label>
        <textarea
          id="description"
          class="form-control"
          [(ngModel)]="goal.description"
          name="description" required
        ></textarea>
      </div>

      <div class="form-group">
        <label for="targetDate">Target Date</label>
        <input
          type="date"
          id="targetDate"
          class="form-control"
          [(ngModel)]="goal.targetDate"
          name="targetDate" required
        >
      </div>
      <br>
      <button
        type="submit"
        class="btn btn-success">
        {{ isEditMode ? 'Update' : 'Add' }}
        Goal
      </button>
      <a
        class="btn btn-secondary ml-2"
        [routerLink]="['/goals']">
        Cancel
      </a>
    </form>
  </div>
```

This HTML code defines the structure of a form for creating and editing fitness goals in the **Fitness Tracker** application. The form adjusts dynamically based on the value of the isEditMode flag, which determines whether the user is adding a new goal or editing an existing one. The form includes fields for the goal's name, description, and target date, all of which are bound to the corresponding properties in the Angular component through two-way data binding using ngModel. This ensures that any changes made by the user are immediately reflected in the component's goal object.

When the form is submitted, the `saveGoal()` function in the Angular component is triggered, handling either goal creation or updating based on the current mode. The form also includes a **Cancel** button, which navigates back to the list of fitness goals without submitting any changes. Bootstrap classes are used to style the form, ensuring a clean and responsive layout, while the `ngSubmit` directive is used to capture form submission. This form is an essential part of the goal management functionality in the application, providing a user-friendly interface for interacting with fitness goals.

With the Goal Form component created, it is time to create the component to list the fitness goals in the following section.

Creating the Goal List component

We will create the `Goal List` component, which will allow users to view a list of registered goals, giving them the ability to edit or delete goals. To create the component, execute the following command:

```
ng generate component components/goal-list
```

This command will create a `goal-list` folder within the `src/app/components` directory. After the directory is created with the default files for the `Goal List` component, edit the `goal-list.component.ts` file with the following content:

```
import { Component, OnInit } from '@angular/core';
import { CommonModule } from '@angular/common';
import { Router } from '@angular/router';
import {
  GoalService, FitnessGoal
} from '../../services/goal.service';

@Component({
  selector: 'app-goal-list',
  standalone: true,
  templateUrl: './goal-list.component.html',
  imports: [CommonModule],
})
export class GoalListComponent implements OnInit {
  goals: FitnessGoal[] = [];

  constructor(private goalService:
    GoalService, private router: Router) {}

  ngOnInit(): void {
    this.loadGoals();
  }
```

```
loadGoals(): void {
  this.goalService.getGoals().subscribe(data => {
    this.goals = data;
  });
}

goToAddGoal(): void {
  this.router.navigate(['/add-goal']);
}

goToEditGoal(id: number): void {
  this.router.navigate([`/edit-goal/${id}`]);
}

deleteGoal(id: number): void {
  if (confirm(
  'Are you sure you want to delete this goal?')) {
    this.goalService.deleteGoal(id).subscribe(() => {
      this.loadGoals();
    });
  }
}
}
```

The preceding code defines GoalListComponent, an Angular component responsible for displaying a list of fitness goals and providing actions to add, edit, or delete goals. The component is set as standalone, meaning it imports its dependencies directly rather than through Angular modules. It uses GoalService to fetch and manipulate the data, and Router to handle navigation between different pages.

In the ngOnInit() life cycle method, the loadGoals() function is called, which subscribes to the getGoals() method of the service to retrieve the list of fitness goals. The component includes methods for navigating to forms for adding or editing a goal (goToAddGoal() and goToEditGoal()), as well as a deleteGoal() function that confirms the action with the user before calling the service to delete the goal. After deletion, the list of goals is reloaded to reflect the changes. This component provides the main interface for managing fitness goals in the **Fitness Tracker** application.

Now that the logic of the Goal List component is done, it is possible to define the presentation part of the component to display the list of goals. Edit the goal-list.component.html file with the following code:

```
<div class="container mt-4">
  <h2 class="text-center">Fitness Goals</h2>
  <button
```

```
      class="btn btn-primary mb-3" (click)="goToAddGoal()">
      Add New Goal
  </button>

  <table class="table table-hover">
    <thead>
      <tr>
        <th>Goal Name</th>
        <th>Description</th>
        <th>Target Date</th>
        <th>Actions</th>
      </tr>
    </thead>
      <tbody>
        <tr *ngFor="let goal of goals">
        <td>{{ goal.goalName }}</td>
        <td>{{ goal.description }}</td>
        <td>{{ goal.targetDate | date }}</td>
        <td>
          <button class="btn btn-warning"
            (click)="goToEditGoal(goal.id)">Edit</button>
          <button class="btn btn-danger ml-2"
            (click)="deleteGoal(goal.id)">Delete</button>
        </td>
      </tr>
    </tbody>
  </table>
</div>
```

The preceding HTML template is used for displaying the list of fitness goals in the `Goal List` component. It uses Bootstrap for styling, which facilitates the responsiveness of the UI interface. The container starts with a heading (`Fitness Goals`) and a button labeled `Add New Goal`, which triggers the `goToAddGoal()` method to navigate to the form for creating a new goal.

The table structure organizes the data with headers for the goal's name, description, target date, and available actions (`Edit` and `Delete`). Using Angular's `*ngFor` directive, the template iterates through the list of goals, displaying each goal's details in the respective table row. The **Edit** button calls `goToEditGoal()` to allow the user to modify the selected goal, while the **Delete** button triggers `deleteGoal()` to remove the goal from the list. The target date is formatted using Angular's date pipe for a user-friendly display. This template provides a clear and interactive way for users to manage their fitness goals.

With the `Goal List` component created, it is time to create the component that allows users to create and edit workout data.

Creating the Workout Form component

In this section, we will create the Workout Form component, which will allow users to create and update workouts by providing a UI with standard form fields. To create the component, execute the following command:

```
ng generate component components/workout-form
```

The preceding command will create a workout-form folder within the src/app/components directory. After the directory is created with the default files for the Workout Form component, edit the workout-form.component.ts file with the following content:

```
import { Component, OnInit } from '@angular/core';
import { FormsModule } from '@angular/forms';
import {
  WorkoutService, Workout
} from '../../services/workout.service'
import {
  ActivatedRoute, Router, RouterModule
} from '@angular/router';   // Import RouterModule

@Component({
  selector: 'app-workout-form',
  standalone: true,
  templateUrl: './workout-form.component.html',
  imports: [FormsModule, RouterModule],   // Add
                                          // RouterModule to
                                          // imports
})
export class WorkoutFormComponent implements OnInit {
  workout: Workout =
    {
      id: 0,
      exercise: '',
      duration: 0,
      date: new Date(),
      notes: ''
    };
  isEditMode: boolean = false;

  constructor(
    private workoutService: WorkoutService,
    private router: Router,
    private route: ActivatedRoute
```

```
) {}

ngOnInit(): void {
  const id = this.route.snapshot.paramMap.get('id');
  if (id) {
    this.isEditMode = true;
    this.workoutService.getWorkout(Number(id)).subscribe(
    data => {
      this.workout = data;
    });
  }
}

saveWorkout(): void {
  if (this.isEditMode) {
    this.workoutService.updateWorkout(
    this.workout.id, this.workout).subscribe(() => {
      this.router.navigate(['/workouts']);
    });
  } else {
    this.workoutService.createWorkout(this.workout)
    .subscribe(() => {
      this.router.navigate(['/workouts']);
    });
  }
}
}
```

The preceding code defines `WorkoutFormComponent`, an Angular component responsible for creating and editing workout entries in the **Fitness Tracker** application. The component is standalone, meaning it imports the necessary modules (such as `FormsModule` for handling form inputs and `RouterModule` for managing routing) directly, rather than relying on a module declaration.

The component initializes with a default `Workout` object, which contains fields such as `id`, `exercise`, `duration`, `date`, and `notes`. The `ngOnInit` life cycle method checks whether there is an ID in the route parameters. If an ID is found, the component switches to edit mode and fetches the corresponding workout details from `WorkoutService`. If no ID is present, the component operates in create mode, allowing users to add a new workout. The `saveWorkout()` method handles both creation and updating based on the current mode, interacting with the service to send the data to the backend and then redirecting the user to the list of workouts once the operation is complete.

Now that the logic of the Workout Form component is done, it is possible to define the presentation part of the component to display the list of goals. Edit the workout-form.component.html file with the following code:

```html
<div class="container mt-4">
  <h2>
    {{ isEditMode ? 'Edit Workout' : 'Add New Workout' }}
  </h2>

  <form (ngSubmit)="saveWorkout()">
    <div class="form-group">
      <label for="exercise">Exercise</label>
      <input
        type="text"
        id="exercise"
        class="form-control"
        [(ngModel)]="workout.exercise"
        name="exercise" required
      >
    </div>
    <div class="form-group">
      <label for="duration">Duration (minutes)</label>
      <input
        type="number"
        id="duration"
        class="form-control"
        [(ngModel)]="workout.duration"
        name="duration" required
      >
    </div>

    <div class="form-group">
      <label for="date">Date</label>
      <input
        type="date"
        id="date"
        class="form-control"
        [(ngModel)]="workout.date"
        name="date" required
      >
    </div>

    <div class="form-group">
      <label for="notes">Notes</label>
```

```
      <textarea
        id="notes"
        class="form-control"
        [(ngModel)]="workout.notes"
        name="notes">
      </textarea>
    </div>
    <br>
    <button
      type="submit"
      class="btn btn-success">
      {{ isEditMode ? 'Update' : 'Add' }}
      Workout
    </button>
      <a
        class="btn btn-secondary ml-2"
        [routerLink]="['/workouts']">
        Cancel
      </a>
  </form>
</div>
```

The preceding code defines a form for adding or editing workout details in WorkoutFormComponent of the **Fitness Tracker** app. The form dynamically adjusts based on the isEditMode flag, showing either **Edit Workout** or **Add New Workout** as the heading, and similarly toggling between **Update** and **Add** on the submit type button. The form includes fields for exercise name, duration (in minutes), date, and notes, all of which are bound to the Workout object in the component using Angular's two-way data binding via ngModel.

The form triggers the saveWorkout() method when submitted, which either creates a new workout or updates an existing one depending on the mode. It also includes a Cancel button that navigates the user back to the workout list using the routerLink directive, without submitting the form. Bootstrap classes such as form-control, btn-success, and btn-secondary are used to style the form elements and buttons, ensuring a clean and responsive layout for the UI.

With the Workout Form component created, it is time to create the component that allows users to view the list of registered workouts.

Creating the Workout List component

We will create the Workout List component, which will allow users to view a list of registered workouts, giving them the ability to edit or delete workouts. To create the component, execute the following command:

```
ng generate component components/workout-list
```

This command will create a workout-list folder within the src/app/components directory. After the directory is created with the default files for the Workout List component, edit the workout-list.component.ts file with the following content:

```typescript
import { Component, OnInit } from '@angular/core';
import { CommonModule } from '@angular/common';
import { Router } from '@angular/router';
import {
  WorkoutService, Workout
} from '../../services/workout.service';

@Component({
  selector: 'app-workout-list',
  standalone: true,
  templateUrl: './workout-list.component.html',
  imports: [CommonModule],  // Add HttpClientModule here
})
export class WorkoutListComponent implements OnInit {
  workouts: Workout[] = [];

  constructor(private workoutService: WorkoutService,
    private router: Router) {}

  ngOnInit(): void {
    this.loadWorkouts();
  }

  loadWorkouts(): void {
    this.workoutService.getWorkouts().subscribe(data => {
      this.workouts = data;
    });
  }

  goToAddWorkout(): void {
    this.router.navigate(['/add-workout']);
  }

  goToEditWorkout(id: number): void {
    this.router.navigate([`/edit-workout/${id}`]);
  }

  deleteWorkout(id: number): void {
    if (confirm(
    'Are you sure you want to delete this workout?')) {
```

```
        this.workoutService.deleteWorkout(id).subscribe(() =>
        {
          this.loadWorkouts();
        });
      }
    }
  }
```

The preceding code defines `WorkoutListComponent`, an Angular component responsible for displaying a list of workouts and providing actions to add, edit, or delete them in the **Fitness Tracker** application. The component is standalone, meaning it directly imports its necessary dependencies, such as `CommonModule` for basic Angular directives. The component interacts with `WorkoutService` to fetch the list of workouts and uses `Router` to navigate between pages.

In the `ngOnInit()` life cycle method, the `loadWorkouts()` function is called to fetch the workouts from the backend using `WorkoutService`. The retrieved workout data is stored in the `workouts` array and displayed in the associated template. The component provides methods for navigating to forms for adding (`goToAddWorkout()`) or editing (`goToEditWorkout()`) a workout. The `deleteWorkout()` method prompts the user for confirmation before calling the service to delete the selected workout and reloads the list once the deletion is successful. This component provides essential functionality for managing workouts in the **Fitness Tracker**.

With the logic of the `Workout List` component complete, we can now define the presentation part of the component to display the goals list. Update the `workout-list.component.html` file with the following code:

```html
<div class="container mt-4">
  <h2 class="text-center">Workout List</h2>
  <button
    class=»btn btn-primary mb-3»
    (click)="goToAddWorkout()">
    Add New Workout
  </button>

  <table class="table table-hover">
    <thead>
      <tr>
        <th>Exercise</th>
        <th>Duration (minutes)</th>
        <th>Date</th>
        <th>Notes</th>
        <th>Actions</th>
      </tr>
    </thead>
```

```
<tbody>
  <tr *ngFor="let workout of workouts">
    <td>{{ workout.exercise }}</td>
    <td>{{ workout.duration }}</td>
    <td>{{ workout.date | date }}</td>
    <td>{{ workout.notes }}</td>
    <td>
      <button
        class="btn btn-warning"
        (click)="goToEditWorkout(workout.id)">
        Edit
      </button>
      <button
        class="btn btn-danger ml-2"
        (click)="deleteWorkout(workout.id)">
        Delete
      </button>
    </td>
  </tr>
</tbody>
</table>
</div>
```

The preceding HTML template defines the structure for displaying the workout list in WorkoutListComponent of the **Fitness Tracker** application. It starts with a container that contains a heading (**Workout List**) and a button labeled **Add New Workout** that triggers the goToAddWorkout() method, allowing users to navigate to the form for adding a new workout.

The table in the component organizes the workout data, with headers for exercise name, duration, date, notes, and actions. The *ngFor directive is used to loop through the workouts array, displaying each workout's data in its own table row. The **Edit** button triggers the goToEditWorkout() method, allowing users to navigate to the form for editing a selected workout, while the **Delete** button calls deleteWorkout() to remove a workout from the list after confirmation. The workout's date is formatted using Angular's date pipe to ensure a user-friendly display. Bootstrap classes are applied to ensure a responsive, clean layout for the workout list.

Considering we have all the necessary components for workouts and fitness goals created at this point, the next section will show you how to adapt the main App component to include links for the new pages and to display the components based on the router configuration.

Adapting the app component

To allow navigation between all the workout and fitness goals components that were created, it is important to define a component that will contain links to these components and display details for the selected components. To achieve that, you can adapt the app.component.html file of your project within the src/app directory, adding the following code:

```
<style>
  body, html {
    margin: 0;
    padding: 0;
    font-family: Arial, sans-serif;
    background-color: #f4f4f9;
  }

  .container {
    text-align: center;
    padding: 2rem;
  }

  h1 {
    font-size: 2.5rem;
    color: #333;
  }

  p {
    color: #666;
    font-size: 1.2rem;
    margin-bottom: 2rem;
  }

  .nav-links {
    display: flex;
    justify-content: center;
    gap: 2rem;
  }

  .nav-link {
    display: inline-block;
    padding: 1rem 2rem;
    background-color: #4a90e2;
    color: white;
    border-radius: 50px;
```

```
      text-decoration: none;
      font-size: 1.1rem;
      transition: background-color 0.3s ease;
    }

    .nav-link:hover {
      background-color: #357ab8;
    }

    .footer {
      margin-top: 3rem;
      color: #aaa;
    }
</style>

<div class="container">
  <h1>Fitness Tracker App - Packt Book</h1>
  <p>
    Track your workouts and fitness goals to stay on top of
    your progress!
  </p>

  <div class="nav-links">
    <a routerLink="/workouts" class="nav-link">Workouts</a>
    <a routerLink="/goals" class="nav-link">
      Fitness Goals
    </a>
  </div>

  <div class="footer">
    <p>&copy; Fitness Tracker. All rights reserved.</p>
  </div>
</div>

<router-outlet></router-outlet>
```

The preceding code provides the styling and layout for the home page of the **Fitness Tracker** application. The CSS defines the appearance of the page, ensuring a clean, modern design with a responsive layout. The `body` and `html` elements have no margins or padding to eliminate default browser spacing, and the Arial font is used throughout for readability. The background color of the page is set to a light shade of gray (#f4f4f9), creating a soft, neutral backdrop. The `.container` class centers the content on the page, and the `h1` and `p` elements define the title and introductory text for the app, styled with appropriate font sizes and colors for contrast.

The navigation section, styled with the `.nav-links` class, displays two buttons: **Workouts** and **Fitness Goals**, which are aligned in the center using **flexbox**. Each button is styled with padding, a blue background color, white text, and rounded corners, giving them a polished, button-like appearance. The hover effect on the `.nav-link` class darkens the background color when the user hovers over the links, enhancing interactivity.

Considering we have the main page configured already, it is time to configure the actual routes of the application and test the application in the following section.

Configuring routes

In this section, we will configure the routing for our **Fitness Tracker** application to navigate between different components. Angular's `RouterModule` allows us to map URLs to components, providing users with a great experience as they move between views such as the workout list, workout form, goal list, and goal form.

To set up routing, we need to define the routes in the `app.routes.ts` file, located within the `src/app` directory. Each route is associated with a component that will be rendered when a user navigates to a corresponding URL. For example, we will have routes for displaying a list of workouts, adding a new workout, and editing an existing workout, as well as similar routes for fitness goals. Here's how the routes need to be configured in the `app.routes.ts` file:

```
import { Routes } from '@angular/router';
import {
  WorkoutListComponent
} from './components/workout-list/workout-list.component';
import {
  WorkoutFormComponent
} from './components/workout-form/workout-form.component';
import {
  GoalListComponent
} from './components/goal-list/goal-list.component';
import {
  GoalFormComponent
} from './components/goal-form/goal-form.component';

export const routes: Routes = [
  { path: 'workouts', component: WorkoutListComponent },
  { path: 'add-workout', component: WorkoutFormComponent },
  {
    path: 'edit-workout/:id',
    component: WorkoutFormComponent
  },
```

```
  { path: 'goals', component: GoalListComponent },
  { path: 'add-goal', component: GoalFormComponent },
  { path: 'edit-goal/:id', component: GoalFormComponent },
  { path: '', redirectTo: '/workouts', pathMatch: 'full' },
];
```

Each route is defined with a path and its corresponding component. For example, when the user navigates to the /workouts path, it renders WorkoutListComponent, which displays the list of workouts. Similarly, the /add-workout path displays WorkoutFormComponent, allowing users to create a new workout. The dynamic /edit-workout/:id route includes a parameter (:id), which refers to the ID of the workout to be edited. This pattern is followed for fitness goals as well, with paths such as /goals for listing goals, /add-goal for adding a new goal, and /edit-goal/:id for editing an existing goal.

The final route in the array is a redirect route. When the application is accessed at the base URL ('' '), it automatically redirects the user to /workouts, which shows the workout list by default. This ensures that users have a clear entry point when opening the application. Overall, this routing setup provides the essential navigation structure for users to manage both workouts and fitness goals.

With everything already configured, it is time to run both the Angular and the ASP.NET Core Web API applications.

Running the demo application

In this section, we will go through the steps to run both the ASP.NET Core backend and the Angular frontend of the **Fitness Tracker** application using Visual Studio. Since the application is a full-stack solution, you will need both parts running at the same time to fully test the application. Let's get started with these steps:

1. First of all, click the **Run** button in Visual Studio (or press *F5*). This will start the backend, which will usually run on http://localhost:5124 by default. You can verify that the API is running by navigating to the URL in your browser.

2. After that, you need to run the frontend alongside the backend. To achieve that, open a new terminal or CMD window in Visual Studio, navigate to the root directory of your Angular project (the ClientApp folder), and execute the following command:

   ```
   ng serve
   ```

   This will start the Angular development server, usually on http://localhost:4200.

3.   Open your browser and go to `http://localhost:4200` to view the application. The Angular frontend will communicate with the backend API running at `http://localhost:5124`. With both the backend and frontend running, you should see the initial page of the **Fitness Tracker** application in the browser, as seen in *Figure 13.5*:

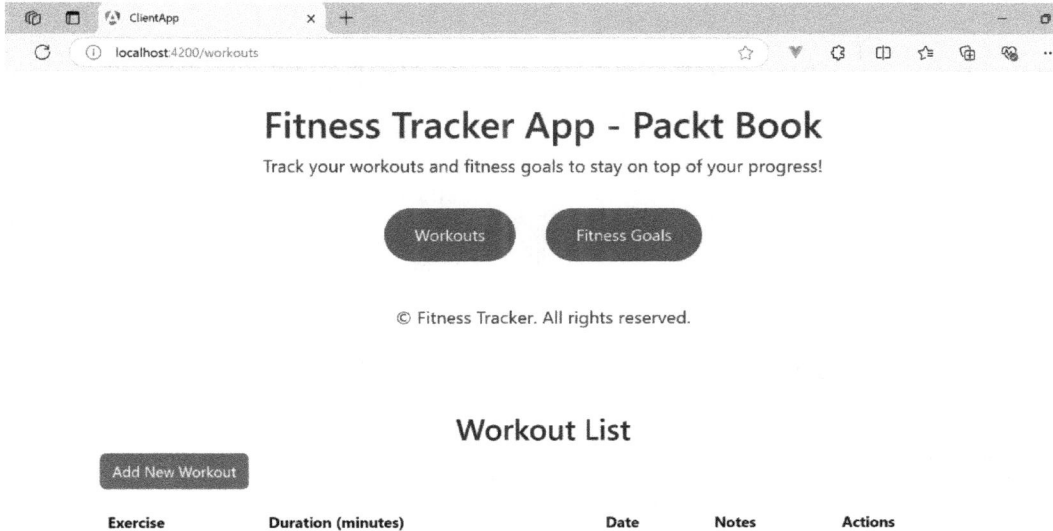

Figure 13.5: Home page of the Fitness Tracker app

The home page displays a table at the bottom with the list of registered workouts and, at the top, links to the **Workouts** and **Fitness Goals** pages. `WorkoutListComponent` is displayed because the routing was configured to show it when the root of the application is accessed.

If you click on the **Add New Workout** button, it will redirect you to the *Workout Form*, as seen in *Figure 13.6*:

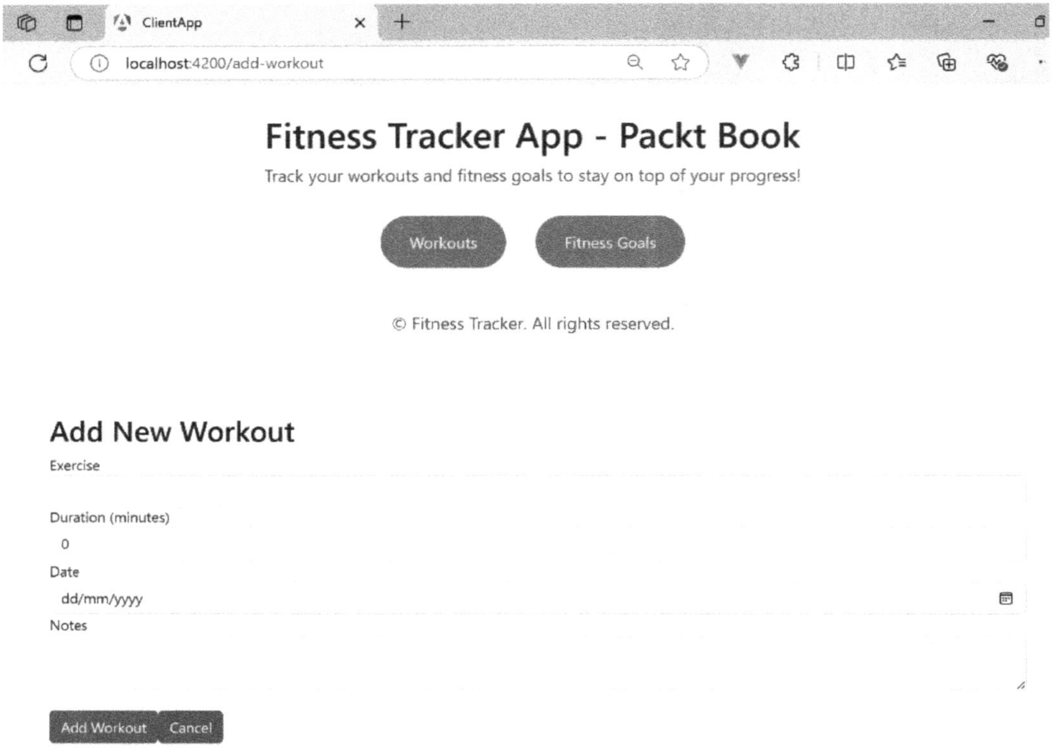

Figure 13.6: Workout form

After filling out the form with any test data, you can save it by clicking on the **Add Workout** button. After that, it will redirect you to the **Workout List** page, displaying the newly created workout, exactly as configured in WorkoutFormComponent previously. This can be seen in *Figure 13.7*:

Fitness Tracker App - Packt Book

Track your workouts and fitness goals to stay on top of your progress!

Workouts   Fitness Goals

© Fitness Tracker. All rights reserved.

Workout List

Add New Workout

Exercise	Duration (minutes)	Date	Notes	Actions
Workout test	60	Sep 30, 2024	Notes test	Edit Delete

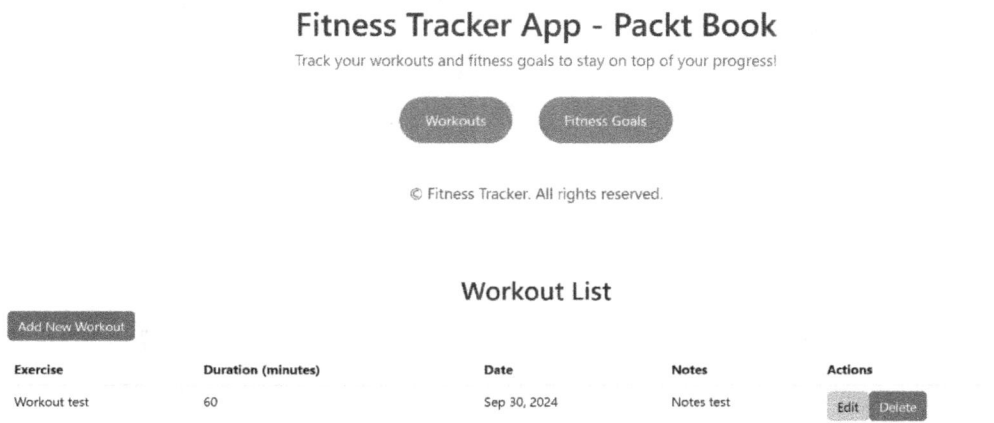

Figure 13.7: Workout List

As you can see on the **Workout List** page, the newly added workout is displayed in the table, with the **Edit** and **Delete** options available. You can try it out for the **Fitness Goals** options as well and check the results.

By running the backend and frontend simultaneously, you can see the full potential of the **Fitness Tracker** application in action. We integrated essential tools and features in Angular and ASP.NET Core to provide both a functional and visually appealing solution, using routing, two-way data binding, an HTTP client, Bootstrap, and standalone Angular components. We also created controllers to define API endpoints to handle HTTP requests and used ASP.NET Core's built-in dependency injection to inject services such as `WorkoutService` and `FitnessGoalService` into the controllers.

You've learned how to integrate Angular and ASP.NET Core, configuring everything necessary for a day-to-day full-stack application.

Summary

In this chapter, we constructed a full-stack **Fitness Tracker** application, combining ASP.NET Core on the backend and Angular on the frontend. We began by developing a strong API using ASP.NET Core, with controllers and services to manage workout and fitness goal data. On the frontend, we created Angular components that enabled users to interact with the API, employing features such as routing, two-way data binding, and HTTP client services to manage entries. Furthermore, we explored styling with Bootstrap and seamless navigation using Angular's `RouterModule`.

These skills are key to developing modern full-stack applications, allowing developers to offer smooth user experiences while maintaining reliable backend services. Understanding how to link a frontend framework such as Angular with an ASP.NET Core backend forms the basis for scalable, maintainable applications that manage data effectively.

Next, we will apply the skills learned so far to integrate React with ASP.NET Core, continuing our journey through how different JavaScript frameworks can be leveraged in full-stack development. The next chapter will expand on your existing knowledge, bringing in React-specific ideas and enhancing your capability in frontend-backend integration.

Get This Book's PDF Version and Exclusive Extras

UNLOCK NOW

Scan the QR code (or go to packtpub.com/unlock). Search for this book by name, confirm the edition, and then follow the steps on the page.

Note: Keep your invoice handly. Purchase made directly from packt don't require one.

14

Integrating React with ASP.NET Core

Integrating React with ASP.NET Core provides a robust approach for developing scalable full-stack applications. React works seamlessly with ASP.NET Core to build dynamic, responsive web applications. This chapter will guide you through the steps needed to configure React with ASP.NET Core, making it easier to create high-performance and efficient full-stack applications. You will learn how to make API calls between React and ASP.NET Core, ensuring efficient communication between these two powerful technologies.

You will also learn how to optimize both the frontend and backend to deliver a responsive user experience, taking full advantage of both technologies. These skills are essential for developers aiming to build modern web applications using the most recent versions of technology stacks available in the market.

In this chapter, we will cover the following key topics:

- Setting up React with ASP.NET Core
- Building an online polling and voting system

By the end of this chapter, you will have a grasp of how to develop React applications that interact with an ASP.NET Core backend, following good practices of software development.

Technical requirements

As mentioned in *Chapter 10*, to effectively use React, you need Node.js installed on your machine, as it provides the runtime environment to execute and run your applications. Node.js is also essential for managing dependencies. Along with Node.js, you'll need **Node Package Manager** (**npm**), which helps manage the libraries and packages required to develop your React applications locally. The most recent versions of these tools are sufficient for the practical examples in this chapter, assuming you already have Visual Studio Code installed, as discussed in previous chapters of this book.

In addition, we will be creating a .NET 9 application in this chapter. Therefore, you should have this version of the .NET SDK installed on your machine. If you already have the most recent version of Visual Studio installed, no additional .NET setup will be necessary.

The code files required for you to follow along with this chapter can be found at: `https://github.com/PacktPublishing/Modern-Full-Stack-Web-Development-with-ASP.NET-Core/tree/main/Chapter14`.

Setting up React with ASP.NET Core

In this section, we will set up a development environment for integrating React with ASP.NET Core, configure ASP.NET Core to serve a React application, and create the basic structure of a React project to get started.

Assuming that you already have Node.js and npm installed based on the practical exercise from the previous chapter, to work with React, you will need the `create-react-app` tool, which provides a streamlined setup for React applications. This tool helps manage the React development environment and create a basic project structure. You can install it globally using the following command in a regular command prompt:

```
npm install -g create-react-app
```

With everything installed correctly, we can proceed to create the ASP.NET Core Web API project in the next section.

Creating an ASP.NET Core Web API project

The creation of the ASP.NET Core Web API project is very similar to the steps followed in the previous chapter, but we will go through them once more. To create the project, follow these steps:

1. Open Visual Studio and create a new project by selecting the **ASP.NET Core Web API** template, as shown in *Figure 14.1*:

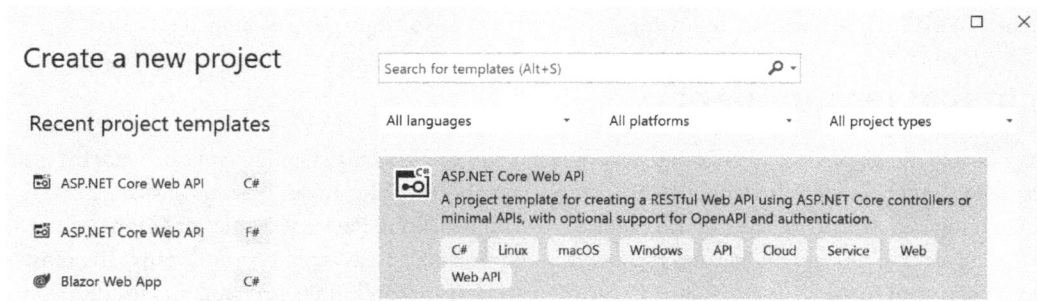

Figure 14.1: ASP.NET Core Web API template

2. After selecting the **ASP.NET Core Web API** template, define a location and a name for the project, as seen in *Figure 14.2*:

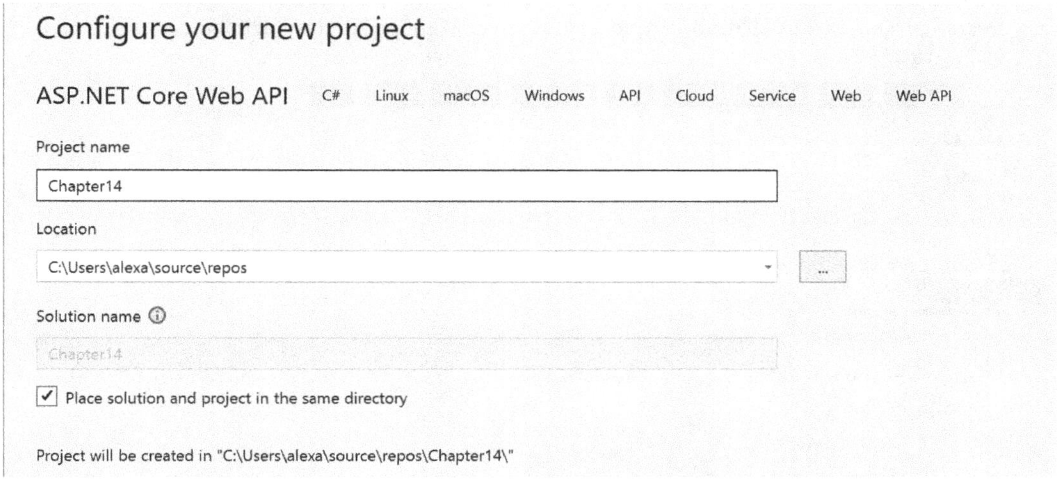

Configure your new project

ASP.NET Core Web API   C#   Linux   macOS   Windows   API   Cloud   Service   Web   Web API

Project name

Chapter14

Location

C:\Users\alexa\source\repos

Solution name ⓘ

Chapter14

☑ Place solution and project in the same directory

Project will be created in "C:\Users\alexa\source\repos\Chapter14\"

Figure 14.2: Web API project name and location

3. After defining a location and a name for the project, choose the .NET 9 version and opt to use controllers without top-level statements, as shown in *Figure 14.3*:

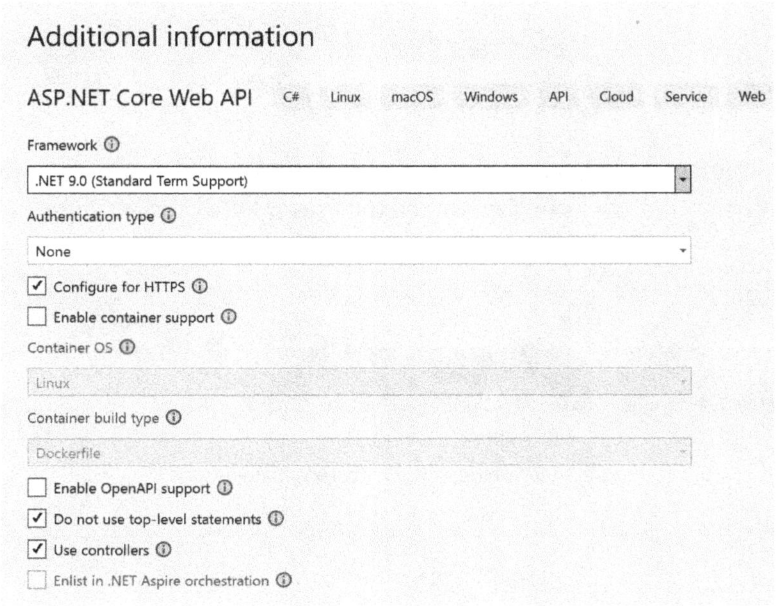

Additional information

ASP.NET Core Web API   C#   Linux   macOS   Windows   API   Cloud   Service   Web

Framework ⓘ

.NET 9.0 (Standard Term Support)

Authentication type ⓘ

None

☑ Configure for HTTPS ⓘ

☐ Enable container support ⓘ

Container OS ⓘ

Linux

Container build type ⓘ

Dockerfile

☐ Enable OpenAPI support ⓘ

☑ Do not use top-level statements ⓘ

☑ Use controllers ⓘ

☐ Enlist in .NET Aspire orchestration ⓘ

Figure 14.3: ASP.NET Core Web API configuration

4. Following the creation of the ASP.NET Core Web API project, you will need to install the SPAServices.Extensions package, which will be utilized to configure the ASP.NET Core project for serving the React application. To install the package, right-click on your newly created project in Visual Studio Explorer and select **Manage NuGet Packages…**, as shown in *Figure 14.4*:

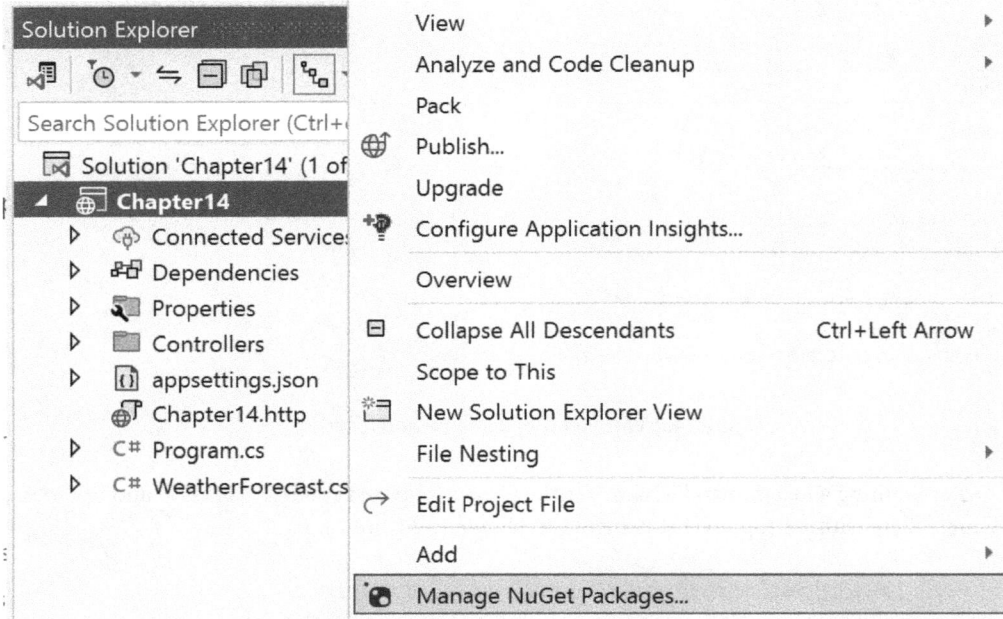

Figure 14.4: Manage NuGet Packages… option

In the **NuGet Package Manager** window, search for the Microsoft.AspNetCore.SpaServices.Extensions package and confirm the installation, as shown in *Figure 14.5*:

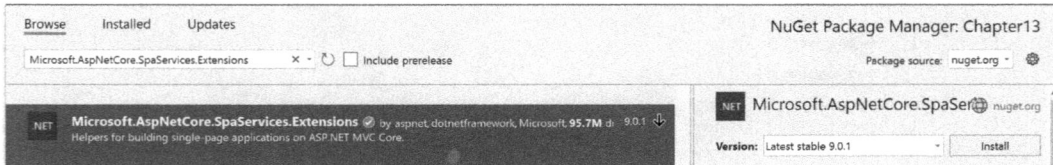

Figure 14.5: SpaServices.Extensions installation

After that, you have to make some changes to the `Program.cs` file to configure ASP.NET Core to serve the Angular application. Modify the `Program.cs` file as follows (shown with the highlighted code lines):

```
namespace Chapter14
{
    public class Program
    {
        public static void Main(string[] args)
        {
            var builder =
                WebApplication.CreateBuilder(args);

            builder.Services.AddControllers();

            builder.Services.AddSpaStaticFiles(
                configuration =>
            {
                configuration.RootPath =
                    "ClientApp/dist";
            });

            var app = builder.Build();

            app.UseStaticFiles();
            app.UseSpaStaticFiles();
            app.UseAuthorization();

            app.MapControllers();
            app.Run();
        }
    }
}
```

In this configuration, `AddSpaStaticFiles` is used to serve the static files for the Angular application. `RootPath` is configured to the `ClientApp/dist` folder, which is where the production build of the React application will be placed.

The ASP.NET Core application is now set up to serve the React application, which we will create later in this chapter using a step-by-step approach. In the following section, we will build a sample application by extending the ASP.NET Core Web API project developed in this section.

Building an online polling and voting system

In this section, we will build an online polling and voting system, a tool that allows users to create polls and vote on them, with real-time updates on the voting results using SignalR, which is a library developed by Microsoft to simplify real-time communication between server and client applications. The application will include basic CRUD operations, enabling users to create new polls with multiple options, submit their votes, and view the results in real time. For the backend of the application, the ASP.NET Core Web API project created earlier will be used to define the endpoints that will be called by the frontend. Additionally, we will build a React application from scratch, configuring the data communication between the frontend and backend and incorporating real-time functionality via SignalR.

From a technical standpoint, this app will leverage key concepts such as **RESTful** API development, real-time communication using SignalR, and an in-memory database for interactions, just for demonstration purposes. Additionally, we will use built-in React features such as routing and state management and implement SignalR in the frontend to enable real-time voting updates. By using **JavaScript** and **Hooks**, we will maintain a consistent data flow between the React application and the ASP.NET Core Web API project. By the end of this section, you will have a clear understanding of how to integrate React with ASP.NET Core, including real-time features with SignalR, following a step-by-step approach.

Next, we'll find details on the domain models that need to be created in the backend for the online polling and voting system.

Creating the domain model

In this section, we will define the core domain models for the online polling and voting system. The domain models define the key entities that encapsulate the business logic and data structure of the application. For our app, the primary entities are `Poll`, `Option`, `Vote`, and a few request models, such as `CreatePollRequest`, `VoteRequest`, and `UpdatePollRequest`.

We will store these entities in memory in the ASP.NET Core backend, allowing us to simulate data storage without needing an actual database. This setup is ideal for rapid development and testing, enabling us to quickly prototype the application. In a real production environment, you would typically use a database with **Entity Framework Core (EF Core)** or another **object-relational mapper (ORM)** to handle interactions between the backend and the database. EF Core is Microsoft's modern ORM for .NET, allowing developers to integrate applications with databases using C# objects rather than SQL queries.

Even though we are storing the entities in memory, it is still crucial to define them properly in the backend so they can be used effectively by our in-memory storage system.

To create the necessary models for your project, follow these steps:

1. In your ASP.NET Core Web API project, create a folder called `Models` in the root of the project using the Solution Explorer in Visual Studio.

2. In your `Models` folder, create a file called `Option.cs` and add the following code:

```
namespace Chapter14.Models
{
    public class Option
    {
        public int Id { get; set; }
        public string Text { get; set; }
        public int PollId { get; set; }
        public int Votes { get; set; } = 0;
    }
}
```

In the preceding code snippet, the namespace is `Chapter14.Models`. Remember to change the namespace according to your project name. The same applies to all code samples in this chapter.

The `Option` model represents an individual voting choice within a poll. Each option includes properties such as a unique ID, the text describing the option, the number of votes it has received, and a reference to the poll it belongs to via `PollId`. This allows each option to be distinctly identified and associated with the correct poll.

3. Next, in your `Models` folder, create a file called `Poll.cs` and add the following code:

```
namespace Chapter14.Models
{
    public class Poll
    {
        public int Id { get; set; }
        public string Question { get; set; }
        public List<Option> Options { get; set; } =
            new List<Option>();
        public DateTime CreatedAt { get; set; }
        public DateTime ExpiresAt { get; set; }
    }
}
```

The `Poll` model is the central entity of the system, representing a poll that contains multiple voting options. It has an ID for identification, a question that users vote on, and a list of options. `Poll` also includes timestamps for when it was created (`CreatedAt`) and when it will expire (`ExpiresAt`). These timestamps are essential for managing the life cycle of the poll.

4. In your `Models` folder, create a file called `Vote.cs` and add the following code:

```
namespace Chapter14.Models
{
    public class Vote
    {
        public int Id { get; set; }
        public int PollId { get; set; }
        public int OptionId { get; set; }
        public string UserId { get; set; }
        public DateTime VotedAt { get; set; }
    }
}
```

The `Vote` model is used to record each individual vote cast by users. A vote consists of an `Id` value, a reference to the `PollId` and `OptionId` values it is related to, and an optional `UserId` value that can be stored for tracking purposes. It also records when the vote was cast using the `VotedAt` timestamp. Although we are allowing users to vote multiple times in this system, `UserId` can still be useful for analytics or tracking purposes.

5. In your `Models` folder, create a file called `CreatePollRequest.cs` and add the following code:

```
namespace Chapter14.Models
{
    public class CreatePollRequest
    {
        public string Question { get; set; }
        public List<string> Options { get; set; }
        public DateTime ExpiresAt { get; set; }
    }
}
```

The `CreatePollRequest` model will be used to create new polls. This model contains the question for the poll, a list of options, and the `ExpiresAt` timestamp to define when the poll will end. This structure allows the frontend to submit new polls to the backend for creation.

6. In your `Models` folder, create a file called `UpdatePollRequest.cs` and add the following code:

```
namespace Chapter14.Models
{
    public class UpdatePollRequest
    {
```

```
        public DateTime ExpiresAt { get; set; }
    }
}
```

Similarly, the `UpdatePollRequest` model is used to modify certain attributes of an existing poll, specifically the `ExpiresAt` property, which allows for extending or adjusting the poll's expiration date.

7. In your `Models` folder, create a file called `VoteRequest.cs` and add the following code:

```
namespace Chapter14.Models
{
    public class VoteRequest
    {
        public string UserId { get; set; }
        public int OptionId { get; set; }
    }
}
```

Finally, the `VoteRequest` model is used to submit votes. It contains the `UserId` value (optional) and the `OptionId` value for the option that the user is voting for. This request model ensures that the backend receives the necessary information to register the vote for the correct poll and option.

These domain models will be stored in memory in the ASP.NET Core backend, simulating data storage without requiring a database. This setup is ideal for quick prototyping and testing, while in production, you would typically integrate with a persistent database using a tool such as EF Core. With the models now defined, we can move forward to setting up in-memory repositories to manage these entities effectively.

Creating the pool service and vote hub

To build the online polling and voting system, we need to manage polls and votes on the backend and provide real-time updates to the frontend. This is where **SignalR** and **WebSockets** come into play. WebSockets provides a two-way communication channel over a single connection, allowing servers to send data to connected clients at any time, making it ideal for applications requiring real-time interaction. SignalR is a library that simplifies the implementation of real-time web features in applications. It abstracts WebSockets and utilizes fallback methods (such as long polling) when WebSockets is unavailable, ensuring a consistent solution for real-time communication.

To implement real-time voting updates, we will start by creating a SignalR hub that will handle broadcasting the updated vote counts to all connected clients as soon as a vote is cast. A SignalR hub serves as the central class for real-time two-way communication between the server and connected clients, allowing direct server calls to client-side functions for seamless updates and interaction.

Follow these steps to create a SignalR hub:

1. First, create a Hubs folder in your project, at the same level as the Models folder. Inside this folder, create a file named VoteHub.cs and include the following code:

```
using Chapter14.Models;
using Microsoft.AspNetCore.SignalR;

namespace Chapter14.Hubs
{
    public class VoteHub : Hub
    {
        public async Task BroadcastVoteUpdate(
            int pollId,
            List<Option> options
        )
        {
        await Clients.All.SendAsync(
            "ReceiveVoteUpdate", pollId, options
        );
        }
    }
}
```

The VoteHub class is a SignalR hub that facilitates communication between the server and the clients. The BroadcastVoteUpdate method will send real-time vote updates to all connected clients, ensuring they always have the latest poll results without having to refresh the page.

2. Next, we will create PollService to manage polls and votes in the system. This service will handle operations such as creating new polls, recording votes, and broadcasting the results via VoteHub.

In your project, create a Services folder at the same level as Models and Hubs. Inside the Services folder, create a file named PollService.cs and include the following code:

```
using Chapter14.Hubs;
using Chapter14.Models;
using Microsoft.AspNetCore.SignalR;

namespace Chapter14.Services
{
    public class PollService
    {
        private readonly List<Poll> _polls = new();
        private readonly List<Vote> _votes = new();
```

```
private readonly IHubContext<VoteHub>
    _hubContext;

public PollService(
    IHubContext<VoteHub> hubContext
)
{

    _hubContext = hubContext;
}

public List<Poll> GetPolls()
{
    return _polls;
}

public Poll GetPoll(int pollId)
{
    return _polls.FirstOrDefault(
        p => p.Id == pollId
    );
}

public Poll CreatePoll(
    string question,
    List<string> options,
    DateTime expiresAt
)
{
    var newPoll = new Poll
    {
        Id = _polls.Count > 0
            ? _polls.Max(p => p.Id) + 1
            : 1,
        Question = question,
        CreatedAt = DateTime.UtcNow,
        ExpiresAt = expiresAt
    };

    foreach (var optionText in options)
    {
        newPoll.Options.Add(new Option
        {
            Id = newPoll.Options.Count > 0
```

```
                        ? newPoll.Options.Max(
                          o => o.Id) + 1 : 1,
                    Text = optionText,
                    PollId = newPoll.Id
                });
        }

        _polls.Add(newPoll);
        return newPoll;
    }

    public bool Vote(
        int pollId,
        int optionId,
        string userId
    )
    {
        var poll = GetPoll(pollId);

        if (poll == null || poll.ExpiresAt <
            DateTime.UtcNow
        )
        {
            return false;
        }

        var option = poll.Options.FirstOrDefault(
            o => o.Id == optionId
        );
        if (option == null)
        {
            return false;
        }


        option.Votes++;
        _votes.Add(new Vote
        {
            Id = _votes.Count > 0 ? _votes.Max(
                v => v.Id) + 1 : 1,
            PollId = pollId,
            OptionId = optionId,
            UserId = userId,
```

```
                VotedAt = DateTime.UtcNow
        });


        _hubContext.Clients.All.SendAsync(
            "ReceiveVoteUpdate",
            pollId,
            poll.Options
        );

        return true;
    }

    public List<Option> GetPollResults(int pollId)
    {
        var poll = GetPoll(pollId);
        return poll?.Options ??
            new List<Option>();
    }
  }
}
```

Let's break down the preceding code block:

- The `PollService` class is the core of the online polling and voting system, responsible for managing the polls and voting functionality in memory. It performs key tasks such as creating polls, registering votes, and broadcasting real-time voting results through SignalR. This service is designed to handle all operations related to polls and their associated voting options. At the heart of `PollService` is a simple in-memory storage solution, using two lists: one for `Poll` objects and another for `Vote` objects. These lists simulate database tables but operate entirely in memory, making the development process faster and easier without the need to set up a database. The `_polls` list stores the polls, each containing a question and a set of options. The `_votes` list stores individual votes, which allows tracking user choices.

- The service starts with its constructor, which accepts an instance of `IHubContext<VoteHub>`. This object is part of SignalR and is responsible for broadcasting real-time messages to all connected clients. SignalR provides real-time communication by abstracting WebSockets (or fallback techniques) to send data from the server to the client without the need for the client to explicitly request updates. In this context, `VoteHub` is used to send vote count updates as soon as votes are registered. One of the main functionalities of this service is retrieving all polls through the `GetPolls` method. This method simply returns a list of all polls stored in memory. The `GetPoll` method retrieves a specific poll by its ID, using LINQ to search through the in-memory collection.

- The `CreatePoll` method allows for the creation of a new poll. This method accepts parameters such as the poll question, a list of options, and the expiration date of the poll. The poll's ID is auto-generated by incrementing from the highest existing ID, simulating an auto-incrementing primary key like those found in relational databases. Each option for the poll is also given a unique ID and is linked to the poll via a foreign key relationship (`PollId`). Once created, the new poll is added to the `_polls` list.

- Voting is handled by the `Vote` method, which is a critical part of the service. This method first retrieves the relevant poll using its ID. It ensures the poll is still valid by checking whether it has expired. If the poll exists and is valid, the method then checks whether the selected voting option exists within the poll. If both conditions are met, the vote is registered by incrementing the `Votes` count for the chosen option. The vote itself is also stored in the `_votes` list, allowing for further analysis or audit trails if needed, even though the system doesn't limit users from voting multiple times.

- Once a vote is registered, the real-time aspect of the application comes into play. Using SignalR's hub context (`_hubContext`), the service broadcasts the updated vote counts to all connected clients. This is done via the `SendAsync` method, which calls the `ReceiveVoteUpdate` event on the client side, passing the updated poll options as parameters. This allows the frontend to display the new results instantly, without any need for the user to refresh the page or manually request the updated data.

- The service also includes a method called `GetPollResults`, which retrieves the current vote counts for a specific poll by returning its list of options, each containing the number of votes it has received. This method ensures that even users who join later, after votes have already been cast, can see the current results of the poll.

In summary, `PollService` not only manages CRUD operations for polls but also integrates with SignalR to broadcast real-time vote updates. It simulates a complete voting system by storing data in memory, registering votes, and updating all clients simultaneously whenever new votes are cast. The integration with SignalR ensures that the system provides immediate feedback to users, creating a dynamic and interactive voting experience. This design effectively demonstrates the use of in-memory data storage, real-time communication with SignalR, and the practical application of managing polls and votes within an ASP.NET Core application.

3. Finally, to properly integrate the online polling and voting system and ensure it functions with real-time updates and cross-origin requests, some important changes are required in the `Program.cs` file, as highlighted in the following code:

```
using Chapter14.Hubs;
using Chapter14.Services;

namespace Chapter14
{
    public class Program
```

```
{
    public static void Main(string[] args)
    {
        var builder =
            WebApplication.CreateBuilder(args);

        builder.Services.AddControllers();
        builder.Services.AddSignalR();
        builder.Services
            .AddSingleton<PollService>();

        builder.Services
            .AddSpaStaticFiles(configuration =>
            {

            configuration.RootPath =
                "ClientApp/dist";

        });

        builder.Services.AddCors(options =>

        {

            options.AddPolicy(
                "AllowSpecificOrigins", policy =>
                {
                    policy.WithOrigins(
                        "http://localhost:3000")
                        .AllowAnyMethod()
                        .AllowAnyHeader()
                        .AllowCredentials();
                });

        });

        var app = builder.Build();

        app.UseStaticFiles();
        app.UseSpaStaticFiles();

        app.UseAuthorization();
```

```
app.UseCors("AllowSpecificOrigins");

app.MapControllers();
app.MapHub<VoteHub>("/voteHub");

app.Run();
        }
    }
}
```

In this configuration of the Program.cs file, specific adjustments are necessary to support real-time communication with SignalR, allow **cross-origin resource sharing** (**CORS**) between the frontend and backend, and register the in-memory PollService that handles poll and voting operations.

Let's break down the preceding code block:

- The first change is the addition of SignalR using the app.MapHub<VoteHub>("/voteHub"); method. This maps VoteHub to the /voteHub endpoint, enabling clients to establish real-time connections with the backend. Whenever a vote is cast, SignalR will broadcast updated poll results to all connected clients through this hub. This endpoint must be correctly referenced in the frontend, ensuring the React application can connect to it and receive updates without refreshing the page.

- Next, the CORS policy is configured to allow the React frontend, which is running on http://localhost:3000, to interact with the ASP.NET Core backend. The builder.Services.AddCors() method sets up a policy named AllowSpecificOrigins, allowing requests from http://localhost:3000. This ensures that the frontend can make requests to the backend for tasks such as submitting votes, retrieving polls, and connecting to the SignalR hub. The AllowCredentials() method is necessary for SignalR to function properly, as it requires the ability to handle authentication cookies or headers during WebSocket connections.

- Finally, PollService is registered as a singleton using builder.Services.AddSingleton<PollService>();. This service handles the core logic of the polling system, such as creating polls, registering votes, and retrieving poll results. By registering it as a singleton, the same instance of PollService is shared across the entire application, ensuring that the in-memory data remains consistent across multiple requests and SignalR broadcasts. This is critical for maintaining the state of polls and vote counts in memory with each client interaction.

In this section, we added the necessary backend services that will support the use of the SignalR hub to establish real-time communication between the client and server applications. We also created PoolService, which contains all the necessary CRUD operations in the in-memory database. In the next section, we will be creating the controller for the Poll and Vote entities, which will allow us to handle API requests for creating polls, casting votes, and retrieving poll results.

Creating the controller

To properly implement the backend API for managing polls in our online polling and voting system, we need to create the necessary controllers in the ASP.NET Core project to expose APIs that the frontend (React app) will interact with. The first controller is `PoolsController`, which is responsible for exposing the required API endpoints for performing operations on poll data, such as creating polls, submitting votes, and retrieving poll results. Using ASP.NET Core's Web API capabilities, the controller will act as the intermediary between the frontend and backend logic, ensuring that HTTP requests such as GET, POST, and PUT are handled properly. By creating this controller, you will establish the API routes that allow users to interact with polls in the system, leveraging the underlying service layer (`PollService`) to execute the necessary operations.

To create controllers for your ASP.NET Core application, in your ASP.NET Core project, create a file called `PoolsController.cs` within the `Controllers` folder and specify the following code:

```
using Chapter14.Models;
using Chapter14.Services;
using Microsoft.AspNetCore.Mvc;

namespace Chapter14.Controllers
{
    [ApiController]
    [Route("api/[controller]")]
    public class PollsController : ControllerBase
    {
        private readonly PollService _pollService;

        public PollsController(PollService pollService)
        {
            _pollService = pollService;
        }

        [HttpGet]
        public ActionResult<List<Poll>> GetAllPolls()
        {
            var polls = _pollService.GetPolls();
            return Ok(polls);
        }

        [HttpGet("{pollId}")]
        public ActionResult<Poll> GetPoll(int pollId)
        {
            var poll = _pollService.GetPoll(pollId);
            if (poll == null)
```

```csharp
    {
        return NotFound(new
        {
            Message = "Poll not found"
        });
    }
    return Ok(poll);
}


[HttpPost]
public ActionResult<Poll> CreatePoll(
    [FromBody] CreatePollRequest request)
{
    if (string.IsNullOrEmpty(request.Question) ||
        request.Options == null ||
        request.Options.Count < 2)
    {
        return BadRequest(new
        {
            Message = "Invalid poll data. A poll
            must have a question and at least two
            options."
        });
    }

    var poll = _pollService.CreatePoll(
        request.Question,
        request.Options,
        request.ExpiresAt
    );
    return CreatedAtAction(
        nameof(GetPoll),
        new { pollId = poll.Id },
        poll
    );
}


[HttpPost("{pollId}/vote")]
public ActionResult SubmitVote(
    int pollId,
    [FromBody] VoteRequest request
)
{
```

```csharp
        if (string.IsNullOrEmpty(request.UserId) ||
            request.OptionId <= 0
        )
        {
            return BadRequest(new
            {
                Message = "Invalid vote data. UserId
                and OptionId are required."
            });
        }

        var result = _pollService.Vote(
            pollId,
            request.OptionId,
            request.UserId
        );
        if (!result)
        {
            return BadRequest(new
            {
                Message = "Unable to cast vote. Either
                the poll has expired, the option is
                invalid, or the user has already
                voted."
            });
        }

        return Ok(new
        {
            Message = "Vote successfully cast."
        });
    }

[HttpGet("{pollId}/results")]
public ActionResult<List<Option>>
    GetPollResults(int pollId)
{
    var results =
        _pollService.GetPollResults(pollId);
    if (results == null || results.Count == 0)
    {
        return NotFound(new
```

```
                    {
                        Message = "Poll not found or no votes
                        have been cast yet."
                    });
                }
                return Ok(results);
        }


        [HttpPut("{pollId}")]
        public ActionResult UpdatePoll(
            int pollId,
            [FromBody] UpdatePollRequest request
        )
        {
            var poll = _pollService.GetPoll(pollId);
            if (poll == null)
            {
                return NotFound(new
                {
                    Message = "Poll not found."
                });
            }

            poll.ExpiresAt = request.ExpiresAt;
            return Ok(poll);
        }
    }
}
```

In PollsController, the constructor injects an instance of PollService using dependency injection. This design allows the controller to interact with the poll management logic, which is stored in memory for this application. By using dependency injection, the controller is decoupled from the service, making it easier to test and swap out services if needed in the future. The controller is responsible for handling API requests for creating, updating, voting, and retrieving poll data, as well as broadcasting real-time updates via the service.

The GetAllPolls method retrieves all the polls from the system by calling the GetPolls method of PollService. The result is returned with an HTTP 200 OK status, meaning the data retrieval was successful. The Ok() method automatically serializes the list of polls into JSON, which can be consumed by the frontend (e.g., a React application).

The GetPoll method retrieves a specific poll based on its pollId. If the poll exists, it returns HTTP 200 OK along with the poll data. If no poll is found with the provided ID, the controller returns an HTTP 404 Not Found status along with an error message.

The `CreatePoll` method is responsible for creating a new poll. It takes a `CreatePollRequest` object as input, which includes the poll question, options, and expiration date. The method first checks that the poll data is valid (i.e., a question and at least two options are provided). If the data is invalid, it returns `HTTP 400 Bad Request` with a descriptive error message. If the data is valid, the poll is created using the `CreatePoll` method of the service and is returned with an `HTTP 201 Created` status, along with the URL to the new poll.

The `SubmitVote` method handles vote submissions for a specific poll. It accepts a `pollId` value and a `VoteRequest` object, which contains the `UserId` and `OptionId` values for the vote. The method checks whether the vote data is valid, ensuring both `UserId` and `OptionId` are provided. If the data is invalid, it returns `HTTP 400 Bad Request` with an appropriate error message. If the vote is successfully cast (i.e., the poll is valid, has not expired, and the option exists), the method returns `HTTP 200 OK` with a success message. If there are any issues with the vote (e.g., the poll has expired or the option is invalid), it returns `HTTP 400 Bad Request`.

The `GetPollResults` method retrieves the current results for a specific poll. It uses `pollId` to find the relevant poll and its options. If the poll exists and has results, the method returns `HTTP 200 OK` with the options and their vote counts. If the poll does not exist or no votes have been cast yet, it returns an `HTTP 404 Not Found` status along with an appropriate error message.

Finally, the `UpdatePoll` method allows updating an existing poll's expiration date. It takes a `pollId` value and an `UpdatePollRequest` object containing the new expiration date. If the poll exists, its expiration date is updated, and the poll is returned with an `HTTP 200 OK` status. If the poll is not found, the method returns an `HTTP 404 Not Found` error. This action allows extending or modifying a poll's lifespan if needed.

Now that we have the backend fully completed, in the next section, we are going to create the React application that will be used to consume the backend service.

Creating the React application

In this section, we will focus on setting up the React frontend for our online polling and voting system. This application will allow users to interact with the backend we've built in the previous sections to create polls, cast votes, and view live poll results. By the end of this section, you will have a fully functioning React application that communicates with the backend services to fetch, display, create, update, and manage poll data in real time using SignalR.

First, open a new terminal on Visual Studio, navigate to the root of your ASP.NET Core project, and create a new React app called `clientapp` by executing the following command:

```
npx create-react-app clientapp
```

This will generate a new React project in the `ClientApp` folder. Once the app is generated, you can proceed with configuring it to interact with the backend API and implement the features for creating polls, submitting votes, and retrieving real-time poll results using SignalR.

To ensure our React frontend can effectively communicate with the backend, handle real-time updates, and provide a user-friendly interface, we need to install several essential packages.

The first package we need is @microsoft/signalr, which will allow the React application to connect to the SignalR hub on the backend for real-time communication. This is crucial for features such as live voting updates, as SignalR enables bidirectional communication between the server and the client, pushing updates to the frontend as soon as votes are cast. To install it, navigate to the root of the ClientApp folder via the terminal on Visual Studio and run the following command:

```
npm install @microsoft/signalr
```

Next, for a responsive and visually appealing UI, we will use **Bootstrap** and react-bootstrap. Bootstrap is a popular **CSS** framework that helps you create responsive layouts with minimal effort, while react-bootstrap provides a set of Bootstrap components designed specifically for React. This integration allows you to easily implement buttons, forms, modals, and other UI elements in the React app. You can install both Bootstrap and react-bootstrap by running the following:

```
npm install bootstrap react-bootstrap
```

Additionally, to ensure that the frontend application has proper navigation and routing, we will use react-router-dom. This package allows us to define different routes in the application, enabling navigation between pages such as creating a poll, viewing poll results, and submitting votes. **React Router** ensures the frontend has a seamless and dynamic experience when interacting with different components. To install it, run the following:

```
npm install react-router-dom
```

With these packages installed, the React app will be fully equipped to handle real-time updates through SignalR, provide a polished UI using Bootstrap, and manage routing for a smooth user experience.

To ensure that Bootstrap styles are available throughout your React application, you need to import the Bootstrap CSS file in the entry point of your application, which is typically src/index.js, as highlighted in the following code:

```
import React from 'react';
import ReactDOM from 'react-dom/client';
import './index.css';
import App from './App';
import reportWebVitals from './reportWebVitals';
import 'bootstrap/dist/css/bootstrap.min.css';


const root =
  ReactDOM.createRoot(document.getElementById('root'));
root.render(
```

```
  <React.StrictMode>
    <App />
  </React.StrictMode>
);


reportWebVitals();
```

By adding the `'bootstrap/dist/css/bootstrap.min.css'`; line import, you are globally importing Bootstrap's styles, making them accessible across all components in your project. This allows you to use Bootstrap's responsive grid system and pre-styled components such as buttons, forms, and modals without manually including the CSS in every file.

If you don't include this import, your components will lack access to Bootstrap's styling, causing you to miss out on the consistent, responsive design that Bootstrap offers. This single line guarantees that Bootstrap styles are applied universally throughout your app, simplifying the development process and enabling you to create professional-looking UI elements swiftly and effectively.

In the next section, we will focus on building the essential components for our online polling and voting system. These components will handle various tasks, such as creating polls, submitting votes, and displaying real-time poll results. By breaking the interface into manageable and reusable components, we will create a dynamic and user-friendly React application that seamlessly interacts with the backend services we've set up.

Creating the React components

In this section, we will focus on creating the essential React components for our online polling and voting system. By breaking the application into separate components for creating polls, submitting votes, and viewing real-time poll results, we will organize the application into reusable and maintainable pieces. These components will allow users to interact with the system by creating new polls, casting their votes, and viewing updated poll results dynamically. Throughout this process, we will also integrate Bootstrap to ensure a responsive and polished UI, starting with the `CreatePoll` component in the following section.

Creating the CreatePoll component

The `CreatePoll` component is an important part of our online polling and voting system, allowing users to create new polls by entering a question and several voting options. Before proceeding, you must set up a `components` folder inside the `src` folder of your React application. This folder will hold all the components we will be creating. The component also needs to communicate with the backend API running on localhost. Ensure that your backend API is running correctly at the specified URL, or adjust the URL accordingly to match your local environment.

To begin, navigate to the `components` folder and create a file called `CreatePoll.js`. This component manages user input, validates the data, and interacts with the backend API by sending a POST request to the `/api/polls` endpoint to create a new poll. Here is the complete code for the component:

```javascript
import React, { useState } from 'react';
import { Form, Button } from 'react-bootstrap';
import { useNavigate } from 'react-router-dom';

const CreatePoll = () => {
  const [question, setQuestion] = useState('');
  const [options, setOptions] = useState(['', '']);
  const [error, setError] = useState(null);
  const navigate = useNavigate();

  const handleSubmit = async () => {

    if (!question || options.some(
    option => option.trim() === '')) {
      setError('Please fill in the question and all
        options.');
      return;
    }

    const newPoll = {
      question,
      options,
      expiresAt: new Date(
        Date.now() + 7 * 24 * 60 * 60 * 1000
      )
    };

    try {
      const response =
        await fetch('http://localhost:5261/api/polls', {
          method: 'POST',
          headers: {
            'Content-Type': 'application/json',
          },
          body: JSON.stringify(newPoll),
        });

      if (response.ok) {
        console.log('Poll created successfully');
```

```
      navigate('/polls');
    } else {
      const errorData = await response.json();
      setError(`Failed to create poll:
        ${errorData.message}`);
    }
  } catch (err) {
    setError('Error connecting to the server. Please try
      again later.');
  }
};

const addOption = () => {
  setOptions([...options, '']);
};

return (
  <div className="container">
    <h2>Create a New Poll</h2>
    {error && <div className="alert alert-danger">
      {error}
    </div>}
    <Form>
      <Form.Group controlId="formQuestion">
        <Form.Label>Poll Question</Form.Label>
        <Form.Control
          type="text"
          placeholder="Enter poll question"
          value={question}
          onChange={(e) => setQuestion(e.target.value)}
        />
      </Form.Group>

      {options.map((option, index) => (
        <Form.Group key=
          {index} controlId={`formOption${index}`}>
          <Form.Label>Option {index + 1}</Form.Label>
          <Form.Control
            type="text"
            placeholder={`Option ${index + 1}`}
            value={option}
            onChange={(e) => {
              const newOptions = [...options];
```

```
                    newOptions[index] = e.target.value;
                    setOptions(newOptions);
                  }}
                />
              </Form.Group>
          ))}

          <Button
            variant="secondary"
            className="m-2"
            onClick={addOption}
          >
            Add Another Option
          </Button>

          <Button
            variant="primary"
            className="m-2"
            onClick={handleSubmit}
          >
            Create Poll
          </Button>
        </Form>
      </div>
    );
};

export default CreatePoll;
```

Let's break down the code block:

- The component starts by using React's useState hook to manage three key pieces of state: question, options, and error. The question state stores the poll's question, while the options state is an array that holds the possible voting options. The error state is used to handle any form validation issues or errors encountered when communicating with the backend API.

- When the user submits the form by clicking the **Create Poll** button, the handleSubmit function is triggered. This function first validates that the question and options fields are filled in. If any field is empty, an error message is displayed and the form submission is halted. Once the validation passes, a newPoll object is created, containing the question, the list of options, and an expiration date set to seven days from the current date. The poll data is sent to the backend via a POST request to the /api/polls endpoint, which should be the exact localhost URL of your ASP.NET Core Web API, such as http://localhost:5261/api/polls. If the request is successful, the user is redirected to the poll list using React Router's useNavigate. If there's an error (e.g., a network issue or invalid API response), an error message is displayed.

- Another key feature of the `CreatePoll` component is the ability to dynamically add new voting options. The **Add Another Option** button calls the `addOption` function, which appends a new empty option to the `options` array. This allows users to add as many voting options as they need, starting with a minimum of two.

- Additionally, error handling is incorporated into the form. If there's an issue, such as a missing field or a problem communicating with the backend, the `error` state is updated with an appropriate message, which is then displayed to the user at the top of the form.

Now that we have the `CreatePoll` component created, let's create the `PollList` component to show the list of registered polls.

Creating the PollList component

The `PollList` component is another essential part of our online polling and voting system, allowing users to view a list of all available polls. This component communicates with the backend API to fetch existing polls and display them in a user-friendly format. Similar to the `CreatePoll` component, you must set up a `components` folder inside the `src` folder of your React application, where all components, including `PollList`, will reside. Additionally, ensure that your backend API is running correctly on localhost, or adjust the URL in the component to match your local setup.

To begin, navigate to the `components` folder and create a file called `PollList.js`. This component will make a GET request to the `/api/polls` endpoint to retrieve a list of all polls and render them in a table or list format for users to view. Here is the complete code for the component:

```
import React, { useEffect, useState } from 'react';
import { Link } from 'react-router-dom';
import { Button, Card } from 'react-bootstrap';

const PollList = () => {
  const [polls, setPolls] = useState([]);

  useEffect(() => {
    fetch('http://localhost:5261/api/polls')
      .then(response => response.json())
      .then(data => setPolls(data))
      .catch(error => console.error('Error fetching
        polls:', error));
  }, []);

  return (
    <div className="container">
      <h2>Available Polls</h2>
      <div className="row">
        {polls.map(poll => (
```

```
                <div className="col-md-4 mb-3" key={poll.id}>
                  <Card>
                    <Card.Body>
                      <Card.Title>{poll.question}</Card.Title>

                      {/* Button to vote on the poll */}
                      <Link to={`/poll/${poll.id}`}>
                        <Button
                          variant="primary"
                          className="m-2"
                        >
                          Vote
                        </Button>
                      </Link>

                      {/* Button to view poll results */}
                      <Link to={`/poll/${poll.id}/results`}>
                        <Button
                          variant="info"
                          className="m-2"
                        >
                          View Results
                        </Button>
                      </Link>
                    </Card.Body>
                  </Card>
                </div>
            ))}
          </div>
        </div>
      );
    };

export default PollList;
```

The PollList component is designed to fetch and display a list of available polls from the backend. It starts by using React's useState hook to initialize the poll state, which will store the poll data once retrieved. Initially, the poll state is set to an empty array, as the component hasn't fetched any data yet.

The useEffect hook is utilized to handle the side effect of fetching the poll data from the backend when the component is first mounted. The fetch request is made to the /api/polls endpoint on http://localhost:5261, which corresponds to the backend service. Once the response is received and converted to JSON format, the data is stored in the poll state using the setPolls function. If there's an error during the fetch operation, it is caught and logged to the console.

Once the poll data is successfully retrieved, the component maps through the `polls` array to dynamically create a card for each poll. Inside each card, the poll's question is displayed as the card title. Each poll card contains two buttons: one for voting on the poll and another for viewing the poll results. These buttons are rendered using React Router's `Link` component, which allows users to navigate to specific routes. The **Vote** button links to the voting page for the poll, while the **View Results** button links to the results page.

The cards are styled using `react-bootstrap`'s `Card` and `Button` components, ensuring a clean, responsive layout. Each poll is rendered within a `col-md-4` column to create a responsive grid layout with a bottom margin of 3 units between the cards, making the layout visually appealing and easy to navigate.

In summary, the `PollList` component fetches poll data from the backend, displays it in a grid of cards, and provides users with links to vote on or view the results of each poll. The use of React hooks for state and side effects, along with `react-bootstrap` for styling, creates an efficient and user-friendly component.

Now that we have the `PollList` component created, let's create the `PollDetails` component, which allows users to register votes for the poll.

Creating the PollDetails component

The `PollDetails` component is another critical part of our online polling and voting system, enabling users to view the details of a specific poll and cast their vote. Similar to the `PollList` component, it interacts with the backend API to fetch the poll's details, including the question and voting options, and displays them in an intuitive format. Users will be able to choose one of the options and submit their vote. Like the previous components, you need to ensure that a `components` folder is created inside the `src` folder of your React application to store the `PollDetails` component and other components. Also, confirm that the backend API is correctly configured to run on localhost or adjust the API URL in the component to match your environment.

To begin, navigate to the `components` folder and create a file called `PollDetails.js`. This component will make a GET request to the `/api/polls/{pollId}` endpoint to retrieve the specific poll details and allow the user to vote. Here is the complete code for the component:

```
import React, { useEffect, useState } from 'react';
import { useParams, useNavigate } from 'react-router-dom';
import { Button, ListGroup } from 'react-bootstrap';

const PollDetails = () => {
  const { pollId } = useParams();
  const [poll, setPoll] = useState(null);
  const [selectedOption, setSelectedOption] =
    useState(null);
```

```javascript
const navigate = useNavigate();

useEffect(() => {
  fetch(`http://localhost:5261/api/polls/${pollId}`)
    .then(response => response.json())
    .then(data => setPoll(data))
    .catch(error => console.error(
      'Error fetching poll:',
      error
    ));
}, [pollId]);

const submitVote = () => {
  if (!selectedOption) {
    alert('Please select an option to vote.');
    return;
  }

  fetch(`http://localhost:5261/api/polls/${pollId}/vote`,
  {
    method: 'POST',
    headers: { 'Content-Type': 'application/json' },
    body: JSON.stringify({
      userId: 'user123',
      optionId: selectedOption
    })
  })
    .then(response => {
      if (response.ok) {
        navigate(`/poll/${pollId}/results`);
      } else {
        alert('Error submitting vote.');
      }
    })
    .catch(error => console.error(
      'Error submitting vote:',
      error
    ));
};

return poll ? (
  <div className="container">
    <h2>{poll.question}</h2>
```

```
        <ListGroup>
          {poll.options.map(option => (
            <ListGroup.Item
              key={option.id}
              action
              onClick={() => setSelectedOption(option.id)}
              active={selectedOption === option.id}
            >
              {option.text}
            </ListGroup.Item>
          ))}
        </ListGroup>
        <Button
          className="mt-3"
          variant="success"
          onClick={submitVote}
        >
          Submit Vote
        </Button>
      </div>
    ) : (
      <div>Loading...</div>
    );
};

export default PollDetails;
```

Let's break down the code block:

- The `PollDetails` component is responsible for displaying the details of a specific poll and allowing users to cast their votes. It retrieves the poll data from the backend and presents the voting options to the user, who can then select one and submit their vote. The component makes use of React's `useState` and `useEffect` and React Router's `useParams` and `useNavigate` hooks to manage state, handle side effects, and facilitate navigation within the application.

- At the beginning of the component, `useParams` is used to extract the `pollId` value from the URL, which allows the component to request the details of the specific poll. The `useState` hook manages two key pieces of state: `poll`, which holds the poll data once fetched, and `selectedOption`, which stores the option that the user selects when voting. The `useEffect` hook is used to fetch the poll data from the backend when the component first loads. The API request is made to `http://localhost:5261/api/polls/${pollId}`, and once the response is received, the poll data is stored in the poll state. If any errors occur during the fetch process, they are caught and logged to the console.

- The main section of the component renders the poll's question and options once the data is available. If the poll state is still null (i.e., the data is still being fetched), a loading message is displayed. When the data is ready, the poll question is displayed as a heading, and the options are presented as clickable items using `react-bootstrap`'s `ListGroup`. Each option is clickable, and when clicked, the `selectedOption` state is updated with the corresponding option's ID. The selected option is visually indicated by the active state, which highlights the selected item in the list.

- The **Submit Vote** button allows the user to submit their vote. When clicked, the `submitVote` function checks whether an option has been selected. If no option is selected, an alert prompts the user to select one. Once an option is selected, the function sends a POST request to the backend at `http://localhost:5261/api/polls/${pollId}/vote` with `userId` and `optionId` as the payload. If the vote is successfully submitted, the user is redirected to the poll results page using `useNavigate`. If there's an error during the vote submission process, an alert is displayed to notify the user.

In summary, the `PollDetails` component fetches and displays poll details, allows users to select an option, and submits the vote to the backend. It uses React hooks for state management, side effects, and navigation, while `react-bootstrap` provides a clean and responsive UI for displaying the poll options. This component ensures that users can interact with polls seamlessly and participate in voting.

Now that we have the `PollDetails` component created, let's create the `PollResults` component, which displays the poll results, taking advantage of SignalR to show vote results in real time.

Creating the PollResults component

In this section, we will focus on creating the `PollResults` component, which allows users to view the real-time results of a poll. This component will fetch the initial results from the backend and then use SignalR to receive live updates as votes are cast, ensuring that users can see the vote counts change dynamically without needing to refresh the page. By integrating React hooks and SignalR, we will enable seamless real-time communication between the frontend and backend, ensuring that the displayed poll results are always up to date. Additionally, this component will be styled using `react-bootstrap` components to provide a clean, responsive UI.

To begin, navigate to the `components` folder inside the `src` directory of your React application, and create a new file called `PollResults.js`. This component will retrieve the poll results from the backend API, display them as a list, and use a progress bar to visually represent the number of votes each option has received. Furthermore, SignalR will handle live updates to ensure the poll results stay current. Here is the complete code for the component:

```
import React, { useEffect, useState } from 'react';
import * as signalR from '@microsoft/signalr';
import { useParams } from 'react-router-dom';
import {
  Card, ListGroup, ProgressBar, Container
```

```
} from 'react-bootstrap';

const PollResults = () => {
  const { pollId } = useParams();
  const [options, setOptions] = useState([]);


  useEffect(() => {
    if (!pollId) return;

    const fetchInitialResults = async () => {
      try {
        const response = await fetch(
          `http://localhost:5261/api/polls/${pollId}/
          results`
        );
        if (response.ok) {
          const data = await response.json();
          setOptions(data);
        } else {
          console.error(
            'Failed to fetch initial poll results.'
          );
        }
      } catch (error) {
        console.error(
          'Error fetching poll results:',
          Error
        );
      }
    };

    fetchInitialResults();


    const connection = new signalR.HubConnectionBuilder()
      .withUrl("http://localhost:5261/voteHub")
      .configureLogging(signalR.LogLevel.Information)
      .build();

    connection.start()
      .then(() => {
```

```
      console.log('Connected to the SignalR hub');


      connection.on("ReceiveVoteUpdate", (updatedPollId,
      updatedOptions) => {
        if (updatedPollId === parseInt(pollId)) {
          setOptions(updatedOptions);
        }
      });
    })
    .catch(err => console.error(
      'Error connecting to SignalR hub:', err
    ));

  return () => {

    connection.stop();
  };
}, [pollId]);

return (
  <Container className="mt-4">
    <h2 className="mb-4">Poll Results</h2>
    <Card>
      <Card.Body>
        <ListGroup>
          {options.map(option => (
            <ListGroup.Item key={option.id}>
              <div
                className=
                "d-flex justify-content-between"
              >
                <span>{option.text}</span>
                <span>{option.votes} votes</span>
              </div>
              <ProgressBar
                now={(option.votes / Math.max(
                  ...options.map(o => o.votes))) * 100}
                label={`${option.votes}`}
              />
            </ListGroup.Item>
          ))}
        </ListGroup>
```

```
            </Card.Body>
          </Card>
      </Container>
   );
};


export default PollResults;
```

Let's break down the code block:

- The `PollResults` component starts by utilizing React's `useState` and `useEffect` hooks to manage the state and handle side effects, such as fetching the poll results and connecting to the SignalR hub. The component uses the `useParams` hook from React Router to extract the `pollId` value from the URL, which is necessary to fetch the specific poll's results and subscribe to real-time updates.

- Upon loading, the `useEffect` hook makes an initial API call to fetch the poll's current results from the `/api/polls/{pollId}/results` endpoint. The fetched data, which includes the poll's options and their corresponding vote counts, is then stored in the `options` state using `setOptions`. This ensures that the initial vote counts are displayed to the user right after the component mounts.

- Once the initial results are fetched, the component establishes a SignalR connection to `voteHub` using `@microsoft/signalr`. The `HubConnectionBuilder` instance type is used to build and start the connection. Upon successfully connecting to the hub, the component listens for updates from the `ReceiveVoteUpdate` event. When new votes are cast, the backend triggers this event and sends the updated vote counts, which are then reflected in the UI by updating the `options` state. This ensures that users can see the vote counts change dynamically as others cast their votes.

- The `return` block of the component renders the poll results using `react-bootstrap`'s `Card`, `ListGroup`, and `ProgressBar` components. Each poll option is displayed in `ListGroup.Item` along with its current vote count. `ProgressBar` is used to visually represent the proportion of votes that each option has received, with the length of the progress bar reflecting the relative number of votes for that option. `ProgressBar` is updated in real time as the `options` state is modified by the incoming data from the SignalR connection.

- Finally, the `useEffect` hook cleans up the SignalR connection when the component unmounts by calling `connection.stop()`, ensuring that the connection is closed properly to avoid memory leaks or unnecessary network traffic.

In summary, the `PollResults` component efficiently handles the display and live updating of poll results using React hooks and SignalR. It provides a dynamic and responsive UI where users can watch the votes update in real time, ensuring a seamless experience. This component plays a crucial role in delivering real-time feedback to users, allowing them to monitor how a poll evolves as more participants cast their votes.

Now that we have all the main components created, in the next section, we will create a home page component to allow the user to navigate to the different components of the application in a centralized way.

Creating the Home component

The `Home` component serves as the landing page for the online polling and voting system, offering users an introduction to the application and quick access to key functionalities. It provides a simple and user-friendly interface with two main options: viewing all available polls or creating a new poll. This component acts as the central navigation hub of the system, making it easy for users to start interacting with the polling features. Using React Router's `Link` and `react-bootstrap` components, this page is visually appealing and provides a seamless experience for users as they navigate through the application.

To implement this, navigate to the `components` folder and create a file called `Home.js`. This component will serve as the entry point to the polling system, allowing users to either view the list of all available polls or create a new one. Here is the complete code for the component:

```
import React from 'react';
import { Link } from 'react-router-dom';
import { Button } from 'react-bootstrap';

const Home = () => {
  return (
    <div className="container text-center">
      <h1>Welcome to the Online Polling System</h1>
      <p>Select an option below to get started:</p>

      <Link to="/polls">
        <Button
          variant="primary"
          className="m-2"
        >
          View All Polls
        </Button>
      </Link>

      <Link to="/create-poll">
        <Button
```

```
            variant="success"
            className="m-2"
          >
            Create a New Poll
          </Button>
        </Link>
      </div>
    );
  };

export default Home;
```

The Home component is a functional component that uses react-bootstrap for styling and React Router's Link for navigation. At the top of the component, a welcome message, saying **Welcome to the Online Polling System**, is displayed as an h1 heading, setting the tone for the UI. Below the heading is a brief description (<p>) instructing users to select an option to get started with the system.

The component features two main buttons that allow the user to navigate to different sections of the application. The first button, labeled **View All Polls**, is wrapped in a React Router Link component that directs the user to the /polls route when clicked. This route takes the user to the page where all available polls are listed. The button is styled using react-bootstrap's Button component with a variant="primary" style, giving it a prominent and professional look.

The second button, labeled **Create a New Poll**, is also wrapped in a Link component, but this one navigates to the /create-poll route, leading users to the poll creation page. This button is styled with a variant="success" style, making it stand out as the action to create new content. Both buttons include margin classes (m-2) to ensure proper spacing between them, providing a clean and organized layout.

The entire content is wrapped in a div block with the container and text-center classes to centralize the content within the page and maintain a responsive layout. The use of react-bootstrap and React Router makes this component not only visually appealing but also highly functional, giving users a clear and intuitive way to navigate the system's core features.

Considering that we now have all the components ready for the React application, let's take the final step of configuring the routes of the application in the next section.

Configuring routes

In this section, we will focus on configuring routes for our online polling and voting system using React Router. Routing is a crucial part of any React application as it defines how users navigate between different pages. In our app, we utilize React Router to define routes that allow users to view all available polls, view poll details, create new polls, and see real-time results for a specific poll.

In the App.js file, routes are set up using React Router's Router, Routes, and Route components. The Router component wraps the entire application, enabling navigation. Inside Router, the Routes component holds individual Route elements that map specific paths to corresponding components, ensuring that the correct component is rendered when users visit a certain URL.

Here's the code for configuring the routes in App.js:

```js
import './App.css';
import {
  BrowserRouter as Router, Route, Routes
} from 'react-router-dom';
import PollList from './components/PollList';
import PollDetails from './components/PollDetails';
import PollResults from './components/PollResults';
import Home from './components/Home';
import CreatePoll from './components/CreatePoll';


function App() {
  return (
    <Router>
      <Routes>
        <Route path="/" element={<Home />} /> {}
        <Route path="/polls" element={<PollList />} /> {}
        <Route path=
          "/poll/:pollId" element={<PollDetails />}
        /> {}
        <Route path=
          "/poll/:pollId/results" element={<PollResults />}
        /> {}
        <Route path=
          "/create-poll" element={<CreatePoll />}
        /> {}
      </Routes>
    </Router>
  );
}

export default App;
```

In the `App.js` file, we configure the main routing system for the online polling and voting system using React Router. Routing is fundamental for enabling users to move between different parts of the application without needing to reload the entire page. The routing system defines which components are displayed based on the URL the user navigates to. In this configuration, we use React Router's `Router`, `Routes`, and `Route` components to define how the app behaves when users visit specific routes.

The `Router` component wraps the entire application and enables navigation throughout the app. Inside `Router`, we use the `Routes` component, which serves as a container for all the `Route` elements. Each `Route` specifies a path and the component that should render when the user visits that path. This structure allows us to map various URLs to their corresponding pages or features within the app, ensuring that users can easily navigate between viewing polls, casting votes, and creating new polls.

The first route defined in the application is the root route (`/`), which leads to the `Home` component. This is the default landing page that users encounter when they first access the system. From the home page, users can either view all the available polls or create a new one. The `/polls` path is linked to the `PollList` component, which displays a list of all existing polls that users can participate in. By clicking on one of the polls, users are taken to the detailed voting page, accessed through the `/poll/:pollId` dynamic route, which renders the `PollDetails` component. The `:pollId` part of the route allows the app to display specific poll data based on the poll's ID.

Similarly, the `/poll/:pollId/results` route displays the real-time results of a specific poll using the `PollResults` component. This allows users to see how the voting is progressing in real time, leveraging SignalR for live updates. Finally, the `/create-poll` path links to the `CreatePoll` component, where users can create new polls by entering a question and multiple voting options. This component provides an intuitive form for poll creation, allowing users to engage with the system and contribute new content.

Through this routing configuration, the `App.js` file establishes a seamless navigation experience, making it easy for users to interact with the polling system, whether they're creating polls, voting, or viewing results. The use of dynamic routes allows for flexible and efficient handling of specific poll data, ensuring that the app remains user-friendly and easy to navigate.

With everything configured, it is time to run both the React and ASP.NET Core Web API applications.

Running the demo application

In this section, we will go through the steps to run both the ASP.NET Core backend and the React frontend of the online polling and voting system using Visual Studio. Since the application is a full-stack solution, you will need both parts to be running at the same time to fully test the application.

To run the application correctly and view the results, follow these steps:

1. First of all, click the **Run** button in Visual Studio (or press *F5*). This will start the backend, which will usually run on `http://localhost:5124` by default. You can verify that the API is running by navigating to the URL in your browser.

2. After that, you need to run the frontend alongside the backend. To achieve that, open a new terminal or command prompt window in Visual Studio, navigate to the root directory of your React project (the `ClientApp` folder), and execute the following command:

    ```
    npm start
    ```

    This will start the React development server, usually on `http://localhost:3000`. Open your browser and go to `http://localhost:3000` to view the application. The React frontend will communicate with the backend API running at `http://localhost:5124`. With both the backend and frontend running, you should see the initial page of the online polling and voting system application in the browser, as seen in *Figure 14.6*:

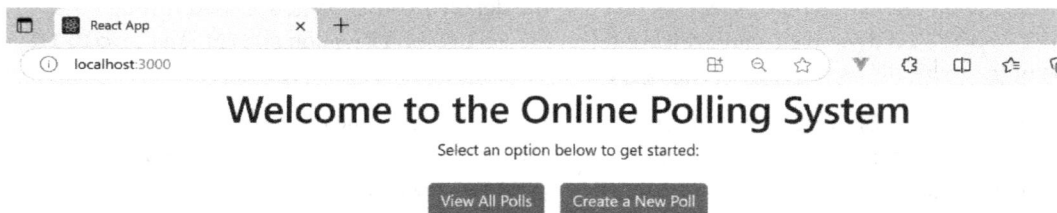

Figure 14.6: Online polling system home page

The home page of the online polling and voting system features a clean and simple layout, offering users two main actions at the top: viewing all available polls and creating a new poll. At the center of the page, users are greeted with a brief introduction and two buttons that lead them to the system's core features.

3. When users click on the **View All Polls** button, they are redirected to the list of existing polls where they can browse and participate in active polls. Alternatively, by clicking the **Create a New Poll** button, users are taken to the poll creation form, allowing them to create a new poll with a custom question and voting options. This structure ensures easy navigation and quick access to both poll creation and voting, offering a straightforward and user-friendly interface for engaging with the polling system.

If you click on the **Create a New Poll** button, it will redirect you to the poll form, as seen in *Figure 14.7*:

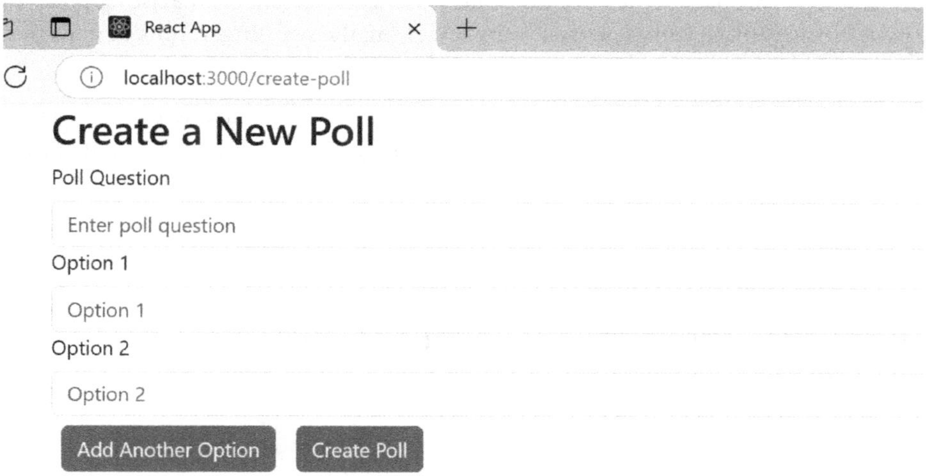

Figure 14.7: Poll form

4. After filling out the poll creation form with your desired question and options, you can save it by clicking on the **Create Poll** button. Once the poll is successfully created, you will be redirected to the poll list page, where the newly created poll will be displayed alongside existing polls. This behavior is configured within the `CreatePoll` component, ensuring that users can seamlessly create new polls and immediately see them listed for voting. After the creation of the poll, here's what the list of poll components looks like:

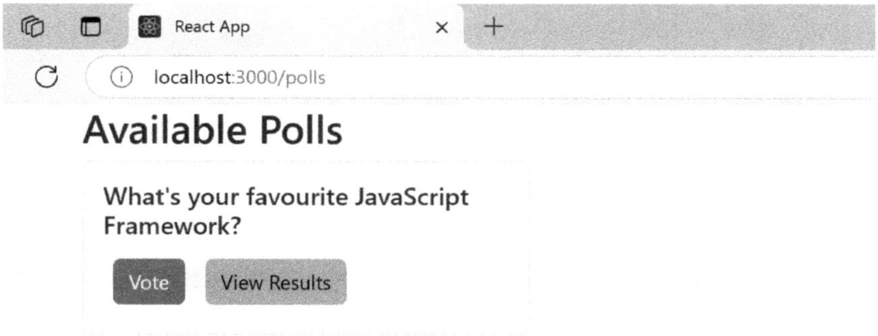

Figure 14.8: Poll list component

On the poll list page, users are presented with a list of all available polls. Each poll is displayed with its associated question, and users are given two primary actions for each poll: **Vote** and **View Results**. This page serves as a hub where users can engage with existing polls, either by participating in the voting process or by reviewing the real-time results of polls that are already underway.

5. When a user clicks the **Vote** button on a specific poll, they are redirected to the poll details page. On this page, the poll question is displayed along with the available voting options, as seen in *Figure 14.9*:

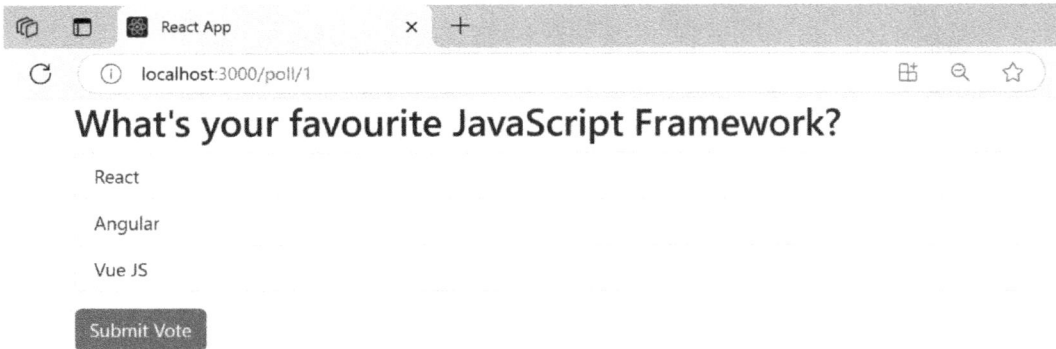

Figure 14.9: Vote page

6. The user can select one of the options and submit their vote. After voting, the application displays a confirmation message that their vote was successfully submitted and redirects the user to the **Poll Results** page, as seen in *Figure 14.10*:

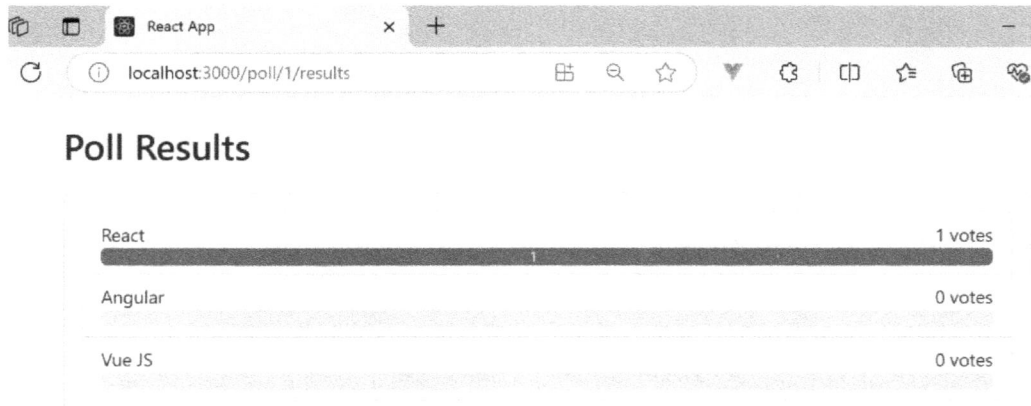

Figure 14.10: Poll results

Alternatively, when a user clicks the **View Results** button on the poll list page, they are taken to the **Poll Results** page as well, where they can see a live update of the vote counts for each option in the poll. The results are displayed with a progress bar representing the number of votes each option has received, and this data is updated in real time using SignalR. This allows users to monitor how the poll is evolving as new votes are cast, offering an engaging and dynamic experience.

By following the steps in this section, you were able to have both the ASP.NET Core backend and React frontend running concurrently. This setup allows you to experience the complete functionality of the online polling and voting system, where users can create, participate in, and view poll results in real time. Testing both components together demonstrates the power of full-stack integration, ensuring a seamless user experience and reliable backend data handling. With your environment properly configured, you're ready to dive deeper into each feature and make further enhancements to the application as needed.

Summary

In this chapter, we constructed a full-stack online polling and voting system, combining ASP.NET Core on the backend and React on the frontend. We began by developing a robust API using ASP.NET Core, with controllers and services to manage poll creation, voting, and results. On the frontend, we created React components that enabled users to interact with the API, employing features such as routing, state management, and HTTP requests to handle poll-related data. We also incorporated styling with Bootstrap and ensured smooth navigation using React Router.

These skills are essential for developing modern full-stack applications, allowing developers to provide smooth and responsive user experiences while maintaining reliable backend services. Understanding how to link a frontend framework such as React with an ASP.NET Core backend forms the foundation for scalable, maintainable applications that effectively manage data and real-time communication.

In the next chapter, we will apply the skills learned so far to further explore how to efficiently plan and structure full-stack applications. This will enhance your understanding of how different JavaScript frameworks can be integrated with ASP.NET Core and guide you in developing well-organized, scalable projects.

Part 3:
Good Practices for
Full-Stack Projects

In this part, you will focus on the essential practices for planning, structuring, and optimizing full-stack web projects. You will learn how to design scalable architectures, ensure maintainability, and implement performance optimization techniques. This section also covers strategies for effective project management, deployment, and the ongoing maintenance required to keep your applications running smoothly in production environments.

This part includes the following chapters:

- *Chapter 15, Planning and Structuring Full-Stack Projects*
- *Chapter 16, Performance, Deployment, and Maintenance*

15
Planning and Structuring Full-Stack Projects

Planning and organizing full-stack projects is a vital step in achieving success for any web application. In this chapter, we will delve into the key principles and best practices that guide full-stack development, from initial planning to deployment. Whether you are working alone or in collaboration with others, having a structured approach guarantees that both frontend and backend components align smoothly.

In this chapter, we will discover how to establish clear project objectives, design scalable architectures, and apply version control strategies that maintain an organized code base. Furthermore, we'll examine how Agile methodologies can enhance collaboration and project management, allowing you to work more effectively across teams.

By the end of this chapter, you'll be equipped to plan and structure full-stack web projects effectively, create scalable and maintainable architectures, and manage team collaboration for efficient project delivery. You will also understand how to implement version control and deployment strategies to ensure your applications are production-ready.

In this chapter, we're going to cover the following main topics:

- Project planning and design principles
- Architectural considerations for full-stack projects
- Team collaboration and Agile methodologies

Project planning and design principles

Effective project planning is one of the most important aspects of a successful full-stack development process. It defines a clear roadmap that guides the engineering team through various stages of project development, from conception to release to production. Without a solid and clear plan, any project can fail to meet its actual objectives, either due to quality issues or failure to meet the user's needs. Full-stack projects require a robust planning process because they involve multiple factors such as business logic implementation, **user interface** (**UI**), databases, integration points, and architecture decisions, among others. Each of these factors needs to work together; a great planning process can address these requirements effectively.

A good planning process starts with the definition of clear objectives. These must be measurable, describing what the project aims to achieve, primarily in terms of solving a problem for the user. When planning a project, it is important to ask some questions, such as the following:

- Do we need to consider scalability?

- Do users need real-time data for analysis?

- Should we choose a technology based on the technical specifications, or based on how easy it is to hire someone who knows this technology?

These questions are just examples, but a clear definition of objectives should consider many aspects of the ecosystem that a software project involves business implications, opportunities, the team's skills, and others. Each objective must be actionable, specific, and correctly aligned with the broader goals proposed by the business in which the project operates. Once the objectives are set, the next step is to define user stories. User stories are short, simple descriptions of features told from the perspective of the end user. Their purpose is to form the foundation for a basic understanding of what the user needs. For example, "*As a user, I want to be able to log in using my social media accounts.*" These stories, in this format, help ensure that the development process remains user-centric, aligning better with the primary goals of a software project.

Along with user stories, functional requirements should be comprehensively documented. These requirements specify the particular functions of a system, including how the application will handle user interactions, authentication, and other components. Collectively, clear objectives, user stories, and functional requirements provide a coherent framework to initiate a project successfully.

In the next section, we will discuss some aspects of scope definition for projects in general.

Defining the scope of the project

Defining a clear scope for a project is one of the fundamental aspects of the planning process. The scope defines what will and will not be included in the project, affecting many factors, such as timelines, resource allocation, and client expectations. The scope must be adequately set, avoiding the extremes of being too broad or too specific. A project with too wide a scope risks experiencing scope creep—when extra features and tasks are incorporated during the development process without sufficient evaluation, leading to budget excesses and delayed timelines. Conversely, a scope that is too limited may not fully address the needs of the business or end users.

An effective way to avoid issues in scope management is to break the project down into smaller tasks. These tasks should be related to the user stories and functional requirements defined earlier. In Agile methodologies, for instance, this breakdown usually happens in the form of a product backlog, where tasks are prioritized based on the value they represent for the business or user. An important part of scoping is identifying the core features that are critical to the project. These are the "must-haves" that, if not included in the project, would cause frustration for users. Non-essential features, or "nice-to-haves," can be included in future iterations of the development cycles with lower priority.

Imagine an e-commerce platform. Core functionalities could include product listings, a shopping cart, user authentication, and payment processing. These are the fundamental elements that users expect to work seamlessly from the outset. In contrast, features such as product reviews, wish lists, personalized recommendations, or multi-currency support may be considered secondary and implemented in later updates.

Through effective scoping, the team can concentrate on delivering the core functionalities in a **Minimum Viable Product** (**MVP**) that aligns with customer expectations, allowing the platform to launch sooner. This iterative approach mitigates risks, as it enables the team to collect early user feedback to guide future enhancements. Moreover, it helps align the objectives of developers, UX/UI designers, and business stakeholders, ensuring that all parties have a mutual understanding of the project and prioritize what is most essential in the initial phases.

Furthermore, a clearly defined scope leads to more accurate estimates regarding development timelines and resource requirements. This, in turn, assists project managers in balancing workloads, setting achievable deadlines, and managing stakeholder expectations. For example, using tools such as the **Must Have, Should Have, Could Have, Won't Have** (**MoSCoW**) method allows teams to prioritize features systematically, ensuring that they concentrate on delivering the most valuable components of the project first. Additionally, considering future enhancements during the early stages can provide long-term benefits. For instance, while a timeline feature may not be essential for an MVP, planning to store the necessary data upfront ensures smoother implementation later. Striking a balance between the effort required to prepare for potential future changes and the immediate resource constraints is the key to building adaptable solutions.

In the next section, we are going to discuss aspects of UI/**user experience** (**UX**) that need to be considered when planning a full-stack application.

UI/UX considerations

In the context of full-stack development, **UI** and **UX** are critical in determining an application's success. Regardless of how strong the backend architecture may be, if the frontend does not offer a seamless, intuitive UX, the project risks losing user engagement. Full-stack developers should work closely with UI/UX designers from the beginning to ensure that the user journey is carefully planned and aligned with the technical abilities of the system.

Creating an effective UI/UX necessitates a user-centered approach, which means that every design choice is made with the end user in focus. This includes outlining user personas, user journeys, and flow diagrams that depict how users will engage with the application. By comprehending the needs, challenges, and expectations of users, developers and designers can develop interfaces that are both functional and enjoyable to use.

For full-stack developers, factoring in cross-platform usability is crucial, ensuring that the application performs equally well on various devices and screen sizes. Frontend frameworks such as Vue, React, and Angular provide extensive capabilities for developing responsive interfaces, but the planning phase should involve careful consideration of how features such as navigation, input forms, and interactions will function across desktop, tablet, and mobile environments.

Wireframing and prototyping are essential tools in this process. Wireframes serve as a visual guide that illustrates the foundational structure of the application. Tools such as Figma, Sketch, or Adobe XD enable teams to create interactive prototypes that simulate UX without writing code. These prototypes help identify potential usability issues early, long before development commences. A well-executed prototype can act as a blueprint for developers, ensuring they are aligned with the design goals and preventing costly redesigns later in the development cycle.

A key consideration in UI/UX planning is accessibility. Modern applications must adhere to accessibility standards, ensuring that users with disabilities can navigate the application with assistive technologies such as screen readers. Best practices for accessibility involve the appropriate use of HTML semantic elements, implementation of **Accessible Rich Internet Applications (ARIA)** roles, and provision of alternatives to non-text content, all of which should be planned during the design phase.

In the next section, we will discuss important aspects of good software design, providing a brief overview of SOLID principles in the context of projects.

Principles of good software design

In the context of architecture decisions for full-stack projects, it is always recommended to adopt the well-known software design principles widely used in the market. Full-stack development is a complex process, where both the frontend and backend parts of a solution need to interact well, which requires using design principles to ensure that the code base remains maintainable and can support scalability in the future. These principles have proven to be effective strategies for improving code quality.

In the realm of good software development practices, the SOLID principles, originally documented by Robert C. Martin, provide guidelines for projects that use the object-oriented paradigm. Each principle is focused on reducing complexity and making applications easier to extend and modify. Here's a brief overview of each SOLID principle:

- **Single Responsibility Principle (SRP):** This principle states that a class or module should only have one reason to change. In full-stack development, this means distinguishing concerns such as data access, business logic, and UI components. For instance, a component that is responsible for rendering a user's profile should not simultaneously manage database interactions for updating that profile. Adhering to the SRP helps decrease complexity and makes individual parts of the system more straightforward to test and maintain.

- **Open-Closed Principle (OCP)**: This principle emphasizes that software entities (such as classes, modules, and functions) should be open for enhancement while being closed for changes. Practically, this means you should be able to add new features without altering existing code. This principle is crucial in full-stack projects, where introducing a new functionality (such as a new payment provider) should not require making modifications to the core systems.

- **Liskov Substitution Principle (LSP)**: This principle states that objects of a superclass should be replaceable by objects of a subclass without affecting the system's functionality. In full-stack systems, this principle is particularly valuable when designing APIs that leverage polymorphism. For example, a payment processor interface could be enhanced by various payment gateway implementations, ensuring that any new gateway fits seamlessly into the existing architecture.

- **Interface Segregation Principle (ISP)**: This principle asserts that no client should be required to rely on methods it does not utilize. The ISP advocates for designing small, focused interfaces rather than large monolithic ones. In full-stack development, this principle is particularly crucial in API design, where frontend clients should only interact with the endpoints necessary for their function, ensuring a clear division of concerns.

- **Dependency Inversion Principle (DIP)**: This principle ensures that high-level modules rely on abstractions rather than low-level modules. This is critical in full-stack development, where business logic should depend on interfaces or abstractions rather than on data access or service classes, providing the flexibility needed for future adjustments or integrations.

Along with SOLID principles, the **Don't Repeat Yourself** (**DRY**) principle is vital in preventing unnecessary repetition in code. In a full-stack project, this means leveraging components, services, and logic wherever appropriate. For instance, if form validation logic is implemented in both the frontend (React, Angular, or Vue.js) and the backend (ASP.NET Core), it's better to unify that logic into shared services to avoid redundancy. DRY leads to easier maintenance, fewer bugs, and a more organized code base.

By following these design principles, developers can build systems that are efficient in the short term and scalable in the long run. Full-stack applications often evolve over time, and adhering to these principles ensures they remain adaptable and free from technical debt accumulation.

Now that we've discussed the importance of project planning, scoping, and design principles, we can shift our attention to one of the most essential elements of full-stack development: architecture. A well-thought-out architecture ensures that your application is scalable, maintainable, and flexible enough to handle future needs. In this section, we'll explore the key architectural considerations that full-stack developers need to account for, such as selecting the right patterns, balancing frontend and backend responsibilities, and understanding the trade-offs between different architectural options. This foundation will help you structure your projects for long-term growth and reliability.

Architectural considerations for full-stack projects

Full-stack development involves more than writing frontend and backend code. It requires structuring your application to ensure scalability, maintainability, and ease of integration. Selecting the right architecture is critical to building robust applications that can scale and evolve over time. In this section, we'll explore various architectural patterns and choices, beginning with a comparison between monolithic and microservices architectures, then moving into an introduction to three-tier architecture, and then taking a close look at **RESTful** services versus **GraphQL** for API design. We will also cover effective ways to manage state and data flow between the client and server for a smooth UX.

Monolithic versus microservices architectures

At the beginning of a full-stack project, one of the most important choices is whether to adopt a monolithic or microservices architecture. Both come with their advantages and disadvantages, and the most suitable choice is determined by the project's complexity, scale, and future ambitions.

A monolithic architecture involves building an application as a single unit where all components, including the UI, backend, and database model, are integrated and released together. This approach has less complexity in terms of development and deployment, making it a great option for projects with a small scope. For instance, if you are developing a quick project to get market validation before its final version, a monolithic architecture can help you deliver this quickly without having to deal with all the complexity of a distributed architecture.

Here are some advantages of using a monolithic architecture:

- Simpler to develop, test, iterate, and deploy, as it does not have multiple components in terms of infrastructure
- Better integration between the components, as they reside in the same code base
- Ideal for teams with limited resources or no experience with microservices architecture

In contrast, in some scenarios, the use of the monolithic architecture might not be ideal. Here are some reasons why:

- Since the project has everything deployed on the same infrastructure, scalability presents a challenge, with no possibility of scaling components independently
- Each deployment or new release requires delivering the entire application, which might increase application downtime
- Maintaining a monolithic code base can become challenging as the application grows in complexity, considering the components tend to become more dependent on each other over time

Alternatively, microservices architecture splits an application into small, autonomous services, with each service dedicated to a particular function. These independent services communicate with each other via APIs, allowing for greater flexibility. Microservices are suitable for larger, more complex applications where individual components need to scale or be updated independently.

Here are some advantages of using a microservices architecture:

- If one service or component fails, it does not impact the entire system, only the affected service
- It allows for better code organization, as different services can be built by separate teams with clear boundaries in terms of the scope of the service
- Each service can be deployed and built separately, allowing for high flexibility in terms of new releases

In contrast, in some scenarios, the use of the microservices architecture might not be ideal. Here are some reasons why:

- Much higher infrastructure costs, as this architecture requires maintaining several services running
- Requires maturity and experience from multiple teams in terms of deployment strategies
- Higher complexity in terms of release management and testing

For full-stack projects, starting with a monolithic architecture might be sufficient in the initial stages, especially for simplicity and rapid development. However, as the application evolves, transitioning to a microservices architecture could become essential to ensure scalability and flexibility. This shift is often best approached incrementally, breaking the monolith into microservices in steps rather than attempting an all-at-once transformation. Following the principles outlined in resources such as Martin Fowler's *Monolith First*, it's crucial to design the monolithic architecture as modularly as possible. A well-structured monolith not only supports growth but also simplifies the transition to microservices by isolating responsibilities and minimizing interdependencies. While there isn't a universal consensus on the timing of such a shift, careful planning during the initial stages can significantly ease future architectural changes, especially if the application's growth trajectory indicates microservices as the ideal long-term path.

In the next section, we will explore the three-tier architecture approach, a common pattern used in full-stack applications.

Three-tier architecture

Regardless of whether you select a monolithic or microservices approach, three-tier architecture is a common pattern used in full-stack applications to appropriately separate concerns and improve aspects of maintainability. A three-tier architecture divides the application into three clear logical layers:

1. **Frontend**: Representing the user-facing part of the application, this layer is where frameworks such as Vue, React, or Angular are used to build the UI. The frontend is built such that, despite integrations with the backend, it can function independently.

2. **Business logic layer (backend)**: This layer is responsible for handling the core logic of the application, which usually includes business rules and data validation. In the context of full-stack applications, this is represented by the backend of the solution. The business logic layer directly interacts with the data access layer to update information in databases and exposes API endpoints to the frontend layer.

3. **Data access layer (database)**: This layer handles the database operations of the application. In the context of ASP.NET Core backends, it means that Entity Framework Core can be used to abstract the database integration and provide an object-oriented approach for data manipulation.

By splitting the application architecture into these three layers, software engineers can build modular systems that are easier to maintain and extend. Updates in one layer can be made without interfering with other layers. For instance, adding a new feature or changing the data access layer to use ADO. NET instead of Entity Framework Core will not necessarily affect the frontend and logic layers if the interfaces for integration are well established.

The next section covers the basic conceptual differences between RESTful and GraphQL APIs.

RESTful versus GraphQL

When defining the architecture and design of any modern full-stack application, you have two common options for API services to explore: RESTful or GraphQL APIs. Each has its strengths and can be better suited for different scenarios.

RESTful APIs are based on standard HTTP methods (`GET`, `POST`, `PUT`, and `DELETE`) and work around the concept of resources (e.g., `/products` or `/shipments`). This technique is simple to implement and widely adopted in the market, making it the preferred choice for the majority of software engineers. Here are some advantages of using RESTful services:

- Uses a standard approach with HTTP verbs and known status codes

- Easy to maintain and includes cache capabilities, as the endpoints are tied to specific resources

- Simple to integrate with the frontend, with an extensive range of available tools

On the other hand, there are some disadvantages in specific scenarios:

- Problems with over-fetching, depending on the design of the API, which may result in unused fields being included in the response, potentially causing performance issues
- Versioning is often a challenge, as it can be difficult to maintain conditionals in the same version of the API endpoint for different types of responses

As an alternative to the RESTful approach, there is the GraphQL technique. GraphQL is a query language for APIs that allows API consumers to request only the specific data they need. It offers more flexibility compared to the REST approach, especially in applications where the frontend requires different data views. Here are some advantages of GraphQL:

- API consumers can request only the data they need, preventing over-fetching issues
- The backend can maintain a single endpoint for all queries and mutations
- It simplifies integration with TypeScript, as GraphQL uses a strongly typed schema

In specific scenarios, the use of GraphQL may also present some disadvantages:

- Maintaining the backend becomes more complex over time due to the need to support dynamic queries
- Since the frontend defines which fields the endpoints return, caching becomes more difficult, as responses can vary depending on the request parameters

Here's an example of the differences between RESTful and GraphQL endpoints, starting with the RESTful API response for a list of objects:

```
GET /api/users
Response:
{
  "users": [
    {
      "id": 1,
      "name": "User 1",
      "email": user1@test.com
    },
    {
      "id": 2,
      "name": "User 2",
      "email": user2@test.com
    },
  ]
}
```

Note that the response returns a list of users with the `id`, `name`, and `email` properties. Now, here's an example of a GraphQL query:

```
query {
  users {
    name
  }
}
```

This GraphQL query allows the client to request only the `name` field, whereas the RESTful API mandatorily returns all fields from the `user` object.

Generally, the use of RESTful APIs is recommended when working with well-defined operations, allowing for caching and standard HTTP features. In contrast, the use of GraphQL is strongly recommended in cases where the frontend needs flexibility with numerous variations.

In the next section, we will discuss state management and data flow for full-stack applications.

State management and data flow

An effective state management strategy for full-stack applications is essential to ensure scalability and maintainability. Deciding whether state management should be handled on the frontend or backend is always a critical decision.

Here are some options for managing state on the client side in full-stack applications:

- Frontend features such as Redux, Vuex, and NgRx provide a centralized store for managing the application state, ensuring that all components have access to a single version of the data. For instance, in a healthcare system, patient data across different views can be managed in one place and consistently available throughout the application, avoiding synchronization issues.

- The state is usually kept in sync with the server via API calls, maintaining consistency between the frontend and backend information.

Apart from the strategy of keeping state management on the frontend, it is also possible to delegate this responsibility to the backend. Here are some examples:

- Store the state in an in-memory database for caching. Additionally, features such as session management and authentication can be used to manage the state between user interactions.

- ASP.NET Core provides native tools for managing state, such as **JSON Web Tokens (JWTs)** for authentication, and integrates well with caching tools such as Redis.

In a full-stack application, it is essential to decide on a state management strategy that suits the context of the application, ensuring seamless integration between the frontend and backend to keep data synchronized and consistent.

Now that we've covered some important aspects regarding architecture decisions for full-stack applications, let's explore the key aspects of a full-stack project that are not necessarily related to technical decisions. In the next section, we will discuss important points on team collaboration and Agile methodologies.

Team collaboration and Agile methodologies

Constructing a full-stack application typically involves a diverse group, including frontend and backend developers, UI/UX designers, project managers, and stakeholders. Successful projects rely on effective collaboration among these roles. Agile methodologies have become the standard in the industry for promoting team collaboration and improving productivity and adaptability, as well as the quality of deliverables. This section will explore Agile methodologies, including Scrum and Kanban, delve into approaches for encouraging collaboration between frontend and backend teams, and discuss tools and best practices to enhance team efficiency and alignment.

Agile methodologies

Agile methodologies offer a software development approach that concentrates on incremental progress, ongoing feedback, and team collaboration. Agile methodologies emphasize adaptability, allowing teams to accommodate changes and deliver value step by step, rather than following rigid, up-front planning.

The Agile Manifesto, introduced in 2001, highlighted essential principles for Agile practices, such as emphasizing individuals and interactions over processes and tools, focusing on working software over detailed documentation, and valuing responsiveness to change over strict adherence to a plan. These principles strive to cut down on waste, boost productivity, and provide a framework where development teams can rapidly adjust to changing requirements. Agile methodologies enable teams to align with business objectives and end user needs, making them particularly useful in full-stack projects where priorities might shift during development.

Among Agile methodologies, Scrum and Kanban are widely recognized:

*   **Scrum** is a framework that structures development into set-duration cycles called *sprints* (commonly lasting 2-4 weeks). Every sprint has defined goals, making it possible for teams to deliver functional software on a consistent schedule. Scrum encourages daily stand-ups, sprint planning, and retrospectives, giving team members a chance to evaluate progress, address issues, and improve processes. Within a full-stack team, a Scrum sprint might focus on building an integrated feature, such as a new registration process that incorporates both frontend forms and backend data handling.

- **Kanban** is designed around continuous delivery and flexibility, avoiding fixed-length iterations. On a Kanban board, work is visualized as tasks progress through columns that signify different workflow stages (e.g., **To Do**, **In Progress**, **Review**, and **Done**). Team members can pick up new tasks as they complete others, supporting a stable, manageable workflow. Kanban is ideal for situations where priorities shift frequently or where the project doesn't need strict iteration cycles, letting team members work on tasks as they arise.

Agile methodologies empower full-stack teams to promptly respond to user feedback, adjust to changes, and release features in small, iterative cycles, which is critical for aligning with project objectives and enhancing the UX.

Collaboration between frontend and backend teams

In full-stack development, establishing strong collaboration between frontend and backend teams is critical for developing cohesive and efficient applications. With the differences between frontend and backend workflows, effective communication and coordination are essential to prevent delays and ensure features function properly throughout the stack.

Effective practices to improve collaboration include the following:

- **API contract definition**: Creating an API contract early in the project allows frontend and backend teams to work independently while remaining aligned. An API contract explains the layout of requests and responses, specifying endpoints, data formats, and anticipated behaviors. As an example, a user registration feature contract might outline that the API will accept a JSON object with fields such as `id`, `name`, and `login`, and return a response indicating success or an error code. This early setup allows both teams to develop and test independently, reducing dependencies and minimizing communication needs.

- **Documentation and prototyping**: Detailed documentation helps link the frontend and backend teams. Documenting APIs, data structures, and workflows enables both teams to grasp each other's requirements. Additionally, prototyping tools such as Swagger and Postman enable the frontend team to simulate backend interactions and test implementations ahead of the full API build.

- **Shared development environments**: A synchronized development environment enables both teams to test features in real time and catch integration issues early. Using containerization tools such as Docker allows both frontend and backend environments to run on aligned setups, reducing environmental differences and facilitating debugging.

Strong collaboration between frontend and backend teams ensures that the application's UI and core logic are well integrated, minimizing rework and enhancing the quality of the final product.

Using tools for team collaboration

To enable effective collaboration, modern development teams rely on a collection of collaboration tools for communication, task organization, and code review. Here are some important tools and their roles within a full-stack development context:

- **Communication platforms**: Tools such as Slack, Microsoft Teams, or Discord provide real-time communication, allowing teams to address queries or share updates promptly. Creating specific channels for different teams or projects enables focused discussions, reducing irrelevant chatter and improving conversation relevance.

- **Project management tools**: Platforms such as Jira, Trello, and Asana support teams in organizing tasks, setting deadlines, and monitoring progress. Jira offers Agile teams robust Scrum and Kanban boards for sprint planning, backlog management, and tracking in a structured, visual format, helping teams meet deliverables, reduce bottlenecks, and improve transparency.

- **Version control and code review**: Git, along with services such as GitHub, GitLab, or Bitbucket, is crucial for managing code collaboratively. Git allows developers to work on different branches, merge changes, and maintain code versions effectively. A code review process ensures that all updates are reviewed for quality and consistency. Pull requests allow team members to propose changes and receive feedback before merging, improving code quality and encouraging knowledge sharing within the team.

- **Continuous Integration/Continuous Deployment (CI/CD)**: CI/CD tools, including Jenkins, GitHub Actions, and Azure DevOps, automate the processes of testing, building, and deployment. In a CI/CD pipeline, each code change initiates automated tests and deployments, ensuring every commit is verified against the system before going live. For instance, each push to the repository might trigger an ASP.NET Core backend build and deploy updates to a test server where the frontend and backend are tested together.

The use of these tools enhances collaboration, allowing team members to stay focused on their roles while ensuring visible progress and timely task completion.

Agile practices for team efficiency

Agile practices aim to improve team efficiency by promoting ongoing improvement and aligning development efforts with business objectives. Besides Scrum and Kanban methodologies, Agile provides various practices that are particularly valuable for full-stack development:

- **Daily stand-ups**: These are brief daily meetings where team members discuss their progress, upcoming tasks, and any challenges they have encountered. This ensures team alignment and allows issues to be addressed early.

- **Sprint planning**: In Scrum, sprint planning meetings help the team select tasks from the backlog and outline goals for the coming sprint. Full-stack teams use these sessions to distribute frontend and backend tasks, keeping both teams focused on the same goal.

- **Retrospectives**: After every sprint, retrospectives give teams a chance to assess successes, challenges, and ways to improve processes. This feedback cycle helps teams address issues quickly, supporting ongoing improvement.

- **User feedback loops**: Agile methodologies emphasize the role of regular user feedback in directing development. Involving stakeholders and end users allows full-stack teams to gather insights that refine features, set priorities, and ensure alignment with actual user requirements.

These practices, along with tools that facilitate Agile workflows, keep teams efficient, flexible, and aligned with project objectives. Agile methodologies encourage iterative progress and adaptability, allowing full-stack teams to respond to changing requirements and consistently deliver value.

Incorporating Agile methodologies and collaborative strategies in your full-stack project helps team members remain aligned, efficient, and responsive to changes. Through structured frameworks, collaborative tools, and Agile practices, you can create a unified, adaptable team environment that drives successful project delivery.

Summary

In this chapter, we explored the foundational aspects of planning and structuring full-stack projects. We began by understanding the importance of well-defined project objectives, user stories, and functional requirements, emphasizing how thoughtful project planning can set up a development team for success. We also examined effective strategies for defining project scope, ensuring that critical features are prioritized, and using scoping techniques to better manage resources and timelines.

Next, we delved into architectural considerations, covering monolithic and microservices architectures, along with three-tier architecture, to provide insights into choosing the right structure based on project needs. Additionally, we reviewed RESTful and GraphQL API options, assessing how each fits into different use cases and technical requirements. The chapter also addressed client and server-side state management strategies, highlighting how tools such as Redux, Vuex, and NgRx support consistent data flow in full-stack applications.

On the collaborative front, we examined Agile methodologies such as Scrum and Kanban, exploring how these frameworks facilitate teamwork, continuous improvement, and iterative development. We discussed key practices for improving communication between frontend and backend teams and the tools that support smooth collaboration.

These lessons are essential for building well-architected, scalable, and adaptable full-stack applications. By mastering these foundational planning and collaboration skills, you will be better prepared to tackle the complexities of full-stack development in an organized and efficient way.

In the next chapter, we'll focus on critical aspects of optimizing, deploying, and maintaining ASP.NET Core applications. This natural progression will build on the architectural foundations covered in this chapter, guiding you through how to make your applications not only functional but also efficient, scalable, and easy to maintain in live environments.

Get This Book's PDF Version and Exclusive Extras

UNLOCK NOW

Scan the QR code (or go to `packtpub.com/unlock`). Search for this book by name, confirm the edition, and then follow the steps on the page.

Note: Keep your invoice handly. Purchase made directly from packt don't require one.

16
Performance, Deployment, and Maintenance

In this chapter, we will discuss three essential aspects of full-stack development for web applications: performance considerations, deployment strategies, and maintenance. As applications grow in complexity and need to scale properly, adopting a solid strategy to maintain the project using good software engineering practices is crucial for any full-stack developer aiming to succeed in their career. This chapter will help you understand techniques and strategies to keep your ASP.NET Core application reliable.

You will learn techniques for optimizing performance in ASP.NET Core applications to support high-traffic demands and understand how to use monitoring practices to identify and resolve issues that your application may present over time.

In this chapter, we will cover the following main topics:

- Performance optimization techniques
- Deployment strategies for web applications
- Maintenance and monitoring of live applications
- Scaling applications for high traffic

Performance optimization techniques

Improving the performance of an ASP.NET Core application is fundamental to delivering projects that meet quality standards in terms of user experience. This section covers essential strategies and techniques to enhance the efficiency and scalability of your applications, focusing on areas applicable to typical ASP.NET Core projects. The first approach we will discuss involves server-side optimizations to improve the response time of your applications in the next section.

Server-side optimizations

Server-side performance typically has the greatest impact on the overall performance of a web application. Some important optimizations include the following:

- **Minimizing Middleware and Pipeline Requests**: Remove all unnecessary middleware components that affect request processing time. Carefully examine the middleware pipeline of your ASP.NET Core applications, ensuring components are in the correct order and removing any that are unnecessary.

- **Asynchronous Programming**: ASP.NET Core and C# support asynchronous operations that free up server resources during operations that need to wait for external processes, such as I/O operations, increasing the server's ability to handle concurrent requests.

- **Compression for Response Optimization**: It is possible to compress HTTP responses using tools such as Gzip, reducing the size of the data payload in backend responses.

By focusing on standard server-side optimizations, you can improve server response times. A combination of asynchronous programming and efficient middleware usage allows the server to handle a heavier load, enhancing scalability. Response compression also has a significant impact, especially in cases where the end user has limited bandwidth. In the next section, we will discuss caching strategies that can further boost performance for your ASP.NET Core applications in most cases.

Caching strategies

Caching can have a significant positive impact by reducing server load and improving response times by serving data from a source that is typically faster than regular databases. ASP.NET Core provides several caching options:

- **Output Caching**: Entire pages or partial content can be cached to avoid re-rendering. This is helpful for applications that need to handle heavy content as part of each request.

- **In-Memory Caching**: This option works well for small datasets that can be stored in memory, especially for data that doesn't change frequently.

- **Distributed Caching**: Ideal for applications hosted on multiple servers that require scalable caching. When multiple instances of the application are present on different servers, they can share the same cached data. This is achievable using distributed caching solutions such as Redis.

The adoption of an effective caching strategy minimizes the need to generate the same data multiple times, freeing up server resources for other operations. In-memory caching is recommended for small datasets, while distributed caching is essential in more complex scenarios where cached data needs to be shared across multiple servers. Applying these caching strategies in appropriate scenarios is crucial for creating responsive ASP.NET Core applications. In the next section, we will discuss techniques for database optimization.

Database performance optimization

Fast database interactions are essential for the performance of any ASP.NET Core application. Some recommended practices include the following:

- **Database Indexing**: Index commonly queried columns to accelerate search and retrieval, but avoid over-indexing, as it can degrade insert and update performance

- **Entity Framework (EF) Core Optimizations**: When using EF Core, apply techniques such as eager loading for related data retrieval and batch querying to minimize database calls

- **Optimizing Queries and Leveraging Stored Procedures**: Develop efficient queries, remove unnecessary columns, and use stored procedures when feasible to optimize complex database tasks

Efficient database operations reduce server load and ensure faster response times for end users. By optimizing queries, applying indexing, and using effective techniques with EF Core, you can significantly enhance application performance in scenarios requiring scalability and high usage demand. In the next section, we will focus on theoretical aspects related to refining the code within your application for better performance and maintainability.

Code efficiency and refactoring

Following good coding practices is essential for enhancing the performance of your applications. Here are some tips and coding techniques that can make your ASP.NET Core applications more efficient:

- **Remove Redundant Code**: Frequently review code to remove redundancies, eliminate unnecessary dependencies, and improve the code where necessary. Smaller code bases are easier to maintain and tend to perform better over time.

- **Use Dependency Injection Correctly**: ASP.NET Core has native support for dependency injection, which helps manage resources effectively, keeping them in memory only when needed. Configure the lifetime scope of injected objects carefully and correctly.

- **Reduce Resource-Intensive Operations**: Avoid operations that make intensive use of the server's CPU. Create separate services using asynchronous patterns for these tasks.

Maintaining clean code improves application performance and efficiency, as well as maintainability and scalability. Regular refactoring ensures that your code follows best practices and remains less vulnerable to errors. In the next section, we will discuss optimizations that can be applied on the client side, particularly in Blazor applications.

Client-side optimization for Blazor applications

Blazor applications can also be optimized on the client side by following these recommendations:

- **Minimizing Payload Size**: Bundle JavaScript and CSS files and eliminate unused libraries to reduce the size of the payload downloaded by users when they access the application

- **Optimizing JavaScript Interoperability**: For Blazor WebAssembly applications, reduce the number of JavaScript interactions to avoid a negative impact on performance

- **Lazy Loading Components**: Ensure that the application only loads the necessary components with each user interaction, reducing initial load time and providing users with a better experience

Applying these techniques on the client side for Blazor applications increases responsiveness and provides users with a better experience when accessing complex web applications with high usage demands. In the final section on performance, we will cover important aspects of monitoring to continuously apply performance improvements and optimizations for ASP.NET Core applications.

Monitoring and continuous optimization

Enhancing performance is a continuous process. Deploy monitoring tools to identify bottlenecks and analyze how the application behaves under heavy load. Here are two useful tips to apply as an engineering practice in your projects:

- **Constant Load Testing and Performance Benchmarking**: Frequently execute load tests to simulate critical traffic scenarios. Use well-known tools such as Apache JMeter to measure application performance with detailed benchmarking reports to identify areas for improvement. In terms of performance, there is always room for optimization.

- **Application Insights and Logging**: Use Application Insights by Microsoft or similar logging services to record performance data, request-response times, and other metrics that help you understand how your application behaves in different scenarios. Data from monitoring tools will guide you in identifying areas that need attention for performance optimization.

Constantly monitoring your application ensures that it maintains acceptable performance. Applying continuous optimization techniques keeps you one step ahead in preventing bottlenecks and slowdowns.

In the next section, we will transition to discussing deployment strategies that help ensure the smooth releases of your application in production environments.

Deployment strategies for web applications

Following effective deployment strategies is essential for delivering new releases of ASP.NET Core applications without disrupting service for users. In this section, we will explore important deployment strategies that can help you deliver ASP.NET Core applications smoothly. These deployment techniques cover a wide range of scenarios, from single-server deployments to distributed deployments in cloud-based environments, providing insights for choosing the right approach for your particular case.

Following a scale of complexity, we will start with single-server deployment in the next section.

Single-server deployment

Single-server deployment is a straightforward solution recommended for scenarios where applications are small or in testing environments. Here are some common aspects of this strategy:

- **Manual Updates or Scripts**: The application can be updated on the server by simply replacing files or deploying from a **continuous integration / continuous delivery (CI/CD)** pipeline

- **Deploying Locally or On-Premises**: Deploy your application on a single server (physical or virtual), handling the deployment manually or with simple automation scripts

While single-server deployment is simple and cost-effective, it is not a scalable model for larger applications. This approach is more suitable for development and testing environments or applications with low traffic demand where high performance is not required. In the next section, we will explore CI/CD pipelines, a valuable tool for automating deployment processes.

CI/CD pipelines for automated deployment

CI/CD pipelines automate deployment, lowering the chance of errors and boosting the efficiency of update rollouts. CI/CD pipelines do the following:

- **Automate Testing and Build Processes**: CI/CD pipelines take care of unit and integration tests along with building the application, validating code quality before deployment

- **Automate Deployments**: Once tests are complete, CI/CD can deploy the application automatically to the preferred environment—whether on-premises, in a cloud infrastructure, or on a staging server for final testing

Effectively using CI/CD pipeline tools, such as Azure DevOps and GitHub Actions, is essential for reliable deployments, as it enables automated testing and ensures that your deployment process follows a regular, repeatable workflow, making the release process predictable. In the next section, we will discuss containerization, an important strategy for packaging applications consistently, regardless of the environment.

Containerization with Docker

Containerization packages applications and dependencies in isolated containers, allowing for consistent deployments in varied environments. Docker's primary benefits include the following:

- **Environment Consistency**: Containers allow for consistent application execution in development, staging, and production, reducing deployment issues tied to environment discrepancies

- **Scalability and Isolation**: Containers make scaling easier by running multiple instances and maintain application isolation, lowering the risk of conflicts

Docker is particularly useful in microservices setups and cloud deployments, supporting the seamless functioning of multiple components. By using containers to isolate applications, you gain scalability and flexibility, simplifying complex deployment management. The next section will look at blue-green deployments, a technique that supports zero-downtime updates by using two distinct environments for continuous transition.

Blue-green deployment

Blue-green deployment is a strategy focused on minimizing downtime by keeping two duplicate environments—one live (blue) and one dormant (green). Here's how it functions:

- **Switching Environments**: For a new version deployment, start by deploying it to the idle (green) environment. After testing is complete, redirect users from the live environment (blue) to the updated environment (green).

- **Instant Rollback**: When issues arise, you can swiftly revert to the previous environment, limiting both downtime and user impact.

This deployment strategy is ideal for applications with critical high-availability needs. Blue-green deployment supports instant rollbacks and reduces downtime during updates, making it perfect for production environments with high user activity. In the following section, we'll look at canary releases, a technique for gradually introducing updates while assessing user response prior to full deployment.

Canary releases

A canary release involves deploying updates or new features to a small user group initially, before wider deployment. This approach helps with the following:

- **Early Problem Identification**: By deploying updates to a limited user segment, you can uncover and fix issues before they affect the entire audience

- **Collecting Feedback Phased**: Observe user responses and performance in the canary group, applying necessary adjustments before the full release

Canary releases decrease the risk of large-scale updates by facilitating staged rollouts. This approach is ideal for applications with heavy user traffic or when deploying experimental capabilities. In the following section, we'll look into rolling deployments, a strategy that allows updates to be deployed gradually across your infrastructure for a seamless transition.

Rolling deployments

In rolling deployments, your application is incrementally updated across your servers. This deployment strategy allows you to do the following:

- **Group Deployment**: Instead of deploying across all servers at once, rolling deployments update batches of servers, minimizing the effect of potential issues

- **Maintain Service Availability**: Rolling deployments impact only sections of your infrastructure sequentially, allowing continuous service through updates

Rolling deployments support a smooth process, making them ideal for large, distributed applications aimed at minimizing user disturbance. By deploying in portions, you can stop deployment swiftly when issues arise, simplifying problem-solving while minimizing impact on the user base. In the next section, we'll delve into cloud-based deployments and the benefits they provide for scalability and global distribution.

Cloud-based deployment

Cloud-based deployment delivers flexibility, scalability, and resilience by leveraging services from Azure, AWS, or Google Cloud. The benefits are as follows:

- **Dynamic Scaling**: Cloud platforms allow your application to scale according to demand, making sure resources are utilized efficiently

- **Global User Reach**: Deploying on cloud platforms allows your application to reach users internationally by taking advantage of data centers across the globe

- **Built-In Solutions and Services**: Cloud providers offer monitoring, security, and backup solutions, making deployment and maintenance easier

Cloud-based deployment is essential for contemporary web applications, especially those with an international reach or variable traffic patterns. With cloud services, you gain access to automatic scalability, dependable availability, and worldwide reach, simplifying the upkeep and growth of your application.

With these deployment strategies implemented, you're equipped to determine the ideal approach for your application's needs and user requirements. The next section will focus on maintenance and monitoring, essential for preserving the stability and performance of live applications over time.

Maintenance and monitoring of live applications

Once your ASP.NET Core application is deployed, safeguarding its stability, performance, and security is essential. With monitoring, issues can be identified proactively before affecting users, while routine maintenance sustains smooth operations as your application grows. This section details fundamental tools and methods for tracking application health, monitoring performance, and establishing maintenance routines to ensure reliability and responsiveness.

Application monitoring tools

Monitoring solutions offer live insights into application health, facilitating quick issue management. Essential tools and methods include the following:

- **Application Insights**: Microsoft's tool connects smoothly with ASP.NET Core, offering response time data, error rates, dependency tracking, and insights into user behavior.

- **Logging and Alerts**: Frameworks such as Serilog and NLog capture structured logs that can be aggregated and analyzed. Set alerts for critical metrics, such as error rates or slow responses, to be notified when performance thresholds are hit.

With observation tools, such as App Analytics, you gain a thorough insight into your application's stability and operational patterns. Instant alerts keep you updated on essential issues, while comprehensive logs supply the information necessary for thorough analysis. In the upcoming section, we'll delve into performance indicators and methods to assess them for enhancing your application.

Analyzing performance metrics

Evaluating performance indicators allows you to comprehend how your application functions under varying loads and usage trends. Essential indicators to monitor include the following:

- **Response Times**: Observing average and maximum response times can uncover code sections or queries that require improvement

- **CPU and Memory Consumption**: Elevated CPU or memory consumption may signal inefficiencies within your code or infrastructure

- **Failure Rates**: Monitor failure rates, especially HTTP 500 errors or any unhandled exceptions that could impact user experience

Consistently reviewing these indicators allows you to detect performance constraints and allocate resources efficiently. For instance, if you observe heightened response times during high demand, you might consider restructuring code, refining queries, or expanding resources. Regular metric evaluation is essential for sustaining a well-performing application. In the following section, we will cover approaches to incident management, ensuring you're equipped to address issues promptly as they occur.

Incident management and alerts

Incident response equips your team to manage unforeseen problems swiftly and efficiently. A clearly outlined incident response process includes the following:

- **Establishing Severity Levels**: Classify incidents based on severity to prioritize responses. For instance, high-priority incidents could involve outages or significant performance issues impacting user experience, whereas lower-priority incidents might encompass minor bugs.

- **Configuring Alerts and Notification Systems**: Leverage monitoring tools to establish alerts for urgent incidents. Make sure notifications are directed to the relevant team members or channels, such as Slack or email, to enable quick action.

Implementing a structured incident response process enables you to uphold user trust by addressing issues promptly and effectively. Alerts keep you notified as soon as an issue emerges, while severity levels assist in prioritizing and optimizing responses. In the upcoming section, we'll discuss automated testing as a proactive strategy to avert issues before they arise.

Automated testing for ongoing quality assurance

Automated testing guarantees that updates to your code base don't cause regressions or performance problems. Essential testing approaches include the following:

- **Unit and Integration Testing**: Develop unit tests to verify individual functions and integration tests to assess the interactions among various components of your application.

- **Load Testing and Stress Testing**: Emulate high-traffic conditions to evaluate application performance and durability. Tools such as Apache JMeter or Azure Load Testing enable you to analyze how your application behaves under pressure.

Executing automated tests helps identify issues before they reach production, making it a critical component of continuous maintenance. By integrating load and stress tests, you can evaluate your application's robustness under various conditions, ensuring a consistent user experience even as demand grows. In the following section, we'll examine routine maintenance tasks that keep your application current and secure over the long term.

Routine maintenance tasks

Ongoing maintenance is essential for sustaining the long-term health of your application. Typical maintenance activities include the following:

- **Dependency Updates**: Regularly update libraries, packages, and framework versions to leverage performance enhancements, security fixes, and new functionality

- **Database Maintenance**: Conduct regular database cleanups, including purging outdated data, refreshing indexes, and executing optimizations to maintain fast query performance

- **Security Audits**: Routinely assess security configurations, examine access controls, and verify that sensitive information is safeguarded, especially if your application is subject to regulatory or security standards

Regular upkeep minimizes technical debt, lowers vulnerability risks, and boosts performance. By routinely updating dependencies, managing the database, and conducting security audits, you help ensure your application stays robust and secure. In the upcoming section, we'll cover data backups and disaster recovery—vital elements for protecting your application data and maintaining business continuity.

Data backup and disaster recovery

Data backups and disaster recovery planning are essential for ensuring your application can bounce back from unforeseen data loss or system failures. Important practices include the following:

- **Automated Backups**: Set up periodic backups of your databases and file storage, utilizing cloud services or external servers for added redundancy

- **Disaster Recovery Plan**: Create and document a recovery strategy outlining the steps for data restoration, resolving system failures, and reducing downtime

An all-encompassing backup and recovery strategy safeguards against data loss and establishes a clear recovery protocol. By automating backups and implementing a thoroughly tested recovery plan, you can greatly minimize downtime and preserve user confidence in the event of a system failure. In the concluding section, we'll explore monitoring feedback loops and their importance in the ongoing enhancement of your application.

Monitoring feedback loops for continuous improvement

Monitoring feedback loops encompasses collecting and assessing user feedback and performance metrics to make well-informed improvement decisions. Suggested strategies include the following:

- **User Feedback Collection**: Gather and evaluate user feedback to identify pain points, frequently requested features, and areas needing improvement

- **Performance Evaluations and Iterations**: Periodically assess performance metrics and feedback to uncover patterns or recurring problems, implementing iterative enhancements to the application

Feedback loops ensure that your application evolves based on user needs and performance data. By consistently evaluating and responding to this information, you can proactively improve user experience, resolve frequent issues, and optimize application performance over time.

With these maintenance and monitoring strategies implemented, you'll be equipped to keep your application operating seamlessly, detect potential problems before they affect users, and respond efficiently when issues occur. In the next section, we'll discuss scaling strategies to help your application handle high traffic and demanding workloads while maintaining performance.

Scaling applications for high traffic

As your ASP.NET Core application gains popularity, effectively managing increased traffic becomes crucial for sustaining a high-quality user experience. Scaling methods enable you to adjust resources dynamically according to demand, ensuring consistent application performance even during heavy loads. This section examines strategies for scaling applications, including horizontal and vertical scaling, load balancing, and autoscaling within cloud environments.

Vertical scaling (scaling up)

Vertical scaling, also known as scaling up, entails boosting a single server's capacity by adding more resources, such as CPU, memory, or storage. Advantages of vertical scaling include the following:

- **Easier Implementation**: Scaling up is comparatively simple and doesn't necessitate major modifications to the application architecture
- **Temporary Solution for High Demand**: Vertical scaling can temporarily alleviate performance issues for applications experiencing sudden traffic surges or seasonal demand fluctuations

While vertical scaling works well for moderate growth, it does have limitations. The resources that can be added to a single server are limited, and as demand increases, it becomes less economical. Vertical scaling is ideal for applications with infrequent traffic surges or as a preliminary measure before adopting more advanced scaling strategies. In the following section, we'll cover horizontal scaling, a more resilient solution for sustainable growth.

Horizontal scaling (scaling out)

Horizontal scaling, also known as scaling out, entails adding additional instances or servers to manage increased traffic. ASP.NET Core facilitates horizontal scaling via load balancing and distributed architectures:

- **Adding Server Instances**: Spread traffic across multiple server instances to boost capacity, enabling the application to support more simultaneous users
- **Database Sharding or Replication**: Distribute database workloads by partitioning data (sharding) or replicating it across several databases to alleviate the load on a single database server

Horizontal scaling is optimal for applications that require consistent support for high traffic. It offers flexibility by enabling you to add or remove instances according to demand and is especially effective with cloud providers that supply load balancing and automated scaling options. In the upcoming section, we'll examine load balancing, a crucial method for efficiently distributing traffic across multiple servers.

Load balancing

Load balancing evenly allocates incoming traffic across multiple servers to avoid any single server becoming a bottleneck. ASP.NET Core applications can take advantage of the following:

- **Hardware or Software Load Balancers**: Hardware load balancers (e.g., F5 or Citrix) and software solutions (such as NGINX or HAProxy) efficiently distribute traffic

- **Cloud-Based Load Balancing**: Cloud providers, such as Azure and AWS, offer integrated load-balancing services that automatically distribute requests across multiple instances, scaling as required

Load balancing enhances reliability and response times by dispersing requests, ensuring that no individual server becomes overloaded. It also boosts fault tolerance, allowing the application to keep serving users even if one instance goes down. Well-configured load balancing is crucial for applications with high or variable traffic volumes. In the following section, we'll examine caching, an efficient technique for decreasing server load and enhancing response times.

Caching for high traffic

Caching alleviates server load by storing frequently requested data in memory, enabling quick access without repeated database queries. Effective caching approaches include the following:

- **Distributed Caching Solutions**: Utilize distributed caches, such as Redis or Memcached, to store cached data across several servers, allowing all instances to access the same cached content

- **Content Delivery Networks (CDNs)**: CDNs cache static assets, such as images, CSS, and JavaScript files, at multiple global locations, alleviating the main server load and enhancing load times for users across different geographic areas

Caching is an effective scaling method that decreases database load and accelerates response times, facilitating the efficient handling of high traffic volumes. By employing distributed caching and CDNs, your application can support more simultaneous users and enhance performance for a global audience. In the upcoming section, we'll discuss autoscaling in cloud environments, a contemporary method for dynamically scaling according to demand.

Autoscaling in cloud environments

Autoscaling is a cloud-based capability that automatically modifies the number of instances according to real-time demand. Cloud providers such as Azure and AWS provide autoscaling options:

- **Dynamic Scaling**: Automatically adjust resources up or down based on metrics, such as CPU usage, memory consumption, or request rates. This approach is perfect for managing sudden traffic surges or variable demand.

- **Scheduled Scaling**: Set up scaling adjustments based on anticipated patterns, such as daily traffic peaks or seasonal demand shifts, enabling your application to scale proactively.

Autoscaling optimizes resource utilization by ensuring you're only running the necessary number of instances at any time, cutting costs while offering the flexibility to manage peak loads. This method is particularly effective for applications with substantial traffic fluctuations, as it removes the need for continual manual adjustments. In the following section, we'll explore database scaling techniques, which are crucial for applications handling large data volumes and frequent data access.

Database scaling techniques

Database scaling is vital for supporting high-traffic applications, as it keeps data access quick and efficient. Effective methods include the following:

- **Read Replicas**: Configure read replicas for frequently accessed data, routing read requests to these replicas to lessen the load on the primary database.

- **Database Sharding**: Divide your database into smaller, more manageable segments and distribute these shards across multiple servers. This approach helps balance the load for large databases.

- **Caching Database Queries**: Store frequently requested data in a cache to minimize repetitive database queries and speed up response times.

Scaling your database ensures that heavy traffic doesn't impact data access speed or reliability. By utilizing read replicas, sharding, and caching, you can sustain optimal database performance even as demand grows.

Summary

In this chapter, we explored key strategies for optimizing, deploying, and maintaining ASP.NET Core applications, emphasizing the components necessary to ensure web applications operate smoothly and efficiently under heavy demand. We began with performance optimization techniques, discussing server-side improvements, caching strategies, database enhancements, and code efficiency. These methods are essential for delivering a quick, responsive application that offers a smooth user experience. We also examined client-side optimizations tailored for Blazor, highlighting their role in boosting an application's overall performance.

Next, we delved into deployment strategies, covering various options—from single-server setups and CI/CD pipelines to advanced approaches, such as containerization, blue-green deployments, and canary releases. Each deployment strategy provides developers with tools to efficiently handle application updates and scaling. We then concentrated on maintenance and monitoring, crucial for maintaining the stability and resilience of live applications. This section provided insights into monitoring tools, incident management, regular maintenance, and feedback loops for ongoing improvement. Finally, we examined scaling techniques, equipping readers to manage high traffic by applying solutions such as vertical and horizontal scaling, load balancing, caching, and cloud-based autoscaling.

These strategies are crucial for developing and sustaining dependable, high-performance ASP.NET Core applications that can scale and adapt to evolving user needs. By mastering these skills, readers are empowered to build applications that not only fulfill functional requirements but also provide efficiency, reliability, and a seamless user experience.

As you reach the final pages of this book, I want to take a moment to thank you for allowing me to be part of your journey. Writing this book has been more than just sharing technical knowledge—it has been about sharing the lessons, challenges, and insights I have gained over the years as a developer. I understand firsthand the excitement and frustrations that come with learning new technologies, building projects, and pushing ourselves to grow. I hope this book has not only provided you with the tools to succeed but also sparked the same passion for building that drives me every day.

In today's fast-paced world, being a full-stack developer is no small feat. It requires patience, determination, and a willingness to embrace continuous change. With ASP.NET Core and frameworks like React, Vue, and Angular, you now have the knowledge to bring your ideas to life and tackle projects with confidence. Beyond just writing code, always remember that the quality of your work truly matters. Whether it is for a client, an organization, or your own vision, your projects have the potential to drive meaningful impact, solve real challenges, and create connections in ways you may not yet foresee.

Finally, I want to encourage you to keep going and keep learning. Thank you for joining me on this journey. I wish you nothing but success and fulfillment as you write the next chapter of your software engineering career.

Get This Book's PDF Version and Exclusive Extras

17
Unlock Your Exclusive Benefits

Your copy of this book includes the following exclusive benefit:

- ☁ Next-gen Packt Reader
- 📄 DRM-free PDF/ePub downloads

Follow the guide below to unlock them. The process takes only a few minutes and needs to be completed once.

Unlock this Book's Free Benefits in 3 Easy Steps

Step 1

Keep your purchase invoice ready for *Step 3*. If you have a physical copy, scan it using your phone and save it as a PDF, JPG, or PNG.

For more help on finding your invoice, visit `https://www.packtpub.com/unlock-benefits/help`.

> **Note**
>
> If you bought this book directly from Packt, no invoice is required. After *Step 2*, you can access your exclusive content right away.

Step 2

Scan the QR code or go to `packtpub.com/unlock`.

On the page that opens (similar to *Figure 17.1* on desktop), search for this book by name and select the correct edition.

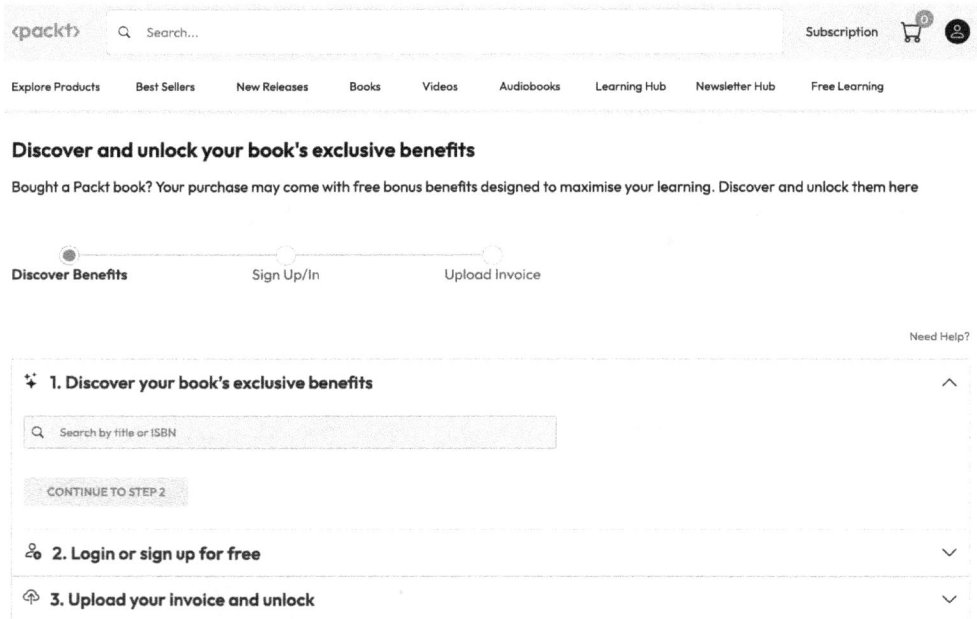

Figure 17.1: Packt unlock landing page on desktop

Step 3

After selecting your book, sign in to your Packt account or create one for free. Then upload your invoice (PDF, PNG, or JPG, up to 10 MB). Follow the on-screen instructions to finish the process.

Need help?

If you get stuck and need help, visit
`https://www.packtpub.com/unlock-benefits/help`
for a detailed FAQ on how to find your invoices and more. This QR
code will take you to the help page.

Note

If you are still facing issues, reach out to `customercare@packt.com`.

Index

<packt>

packtpub.com

Subscribe to our online digital library for full access to over 7,000 books and videos, as well as industry leading tools to help you plan your personal development and advance your career. For more information, please visit our website.

Why subscribe?

- Spend less time learning and more time coding with practical eBooks and Videos from over 4,000 industry professionals

- Improve your learning with Skill Plans built especially for you

- Get a free eBook or video every month

- Fully searchable for easy access to vital information

- Copy and paste, print, and bookmark content

Did you know that Packt offers eBook versions of every book published, with PDF and ePub files available? You can upgrade to the eBook version at packtpub.com and as a print book customer, you are entitled to a discount on the eBook copy. Get in touch with us at customercare@packtpub.com for more details.

At www.packtpub.com, you can also read a collection of free technical articles, sign up for a range of free newsletters, and receive exclusive discounts and offers on Packt books and eBooks.

Other Books You May Enjoy

If you enjoyed this book, you may be interested in these other books by Packt:

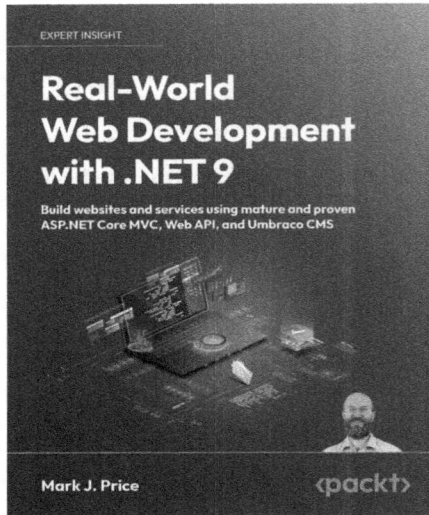

Real-World Web Development with .NET 9

Mark J. Price

ISBN: 978-1-83588-038-8

- Build web applications using ASP.NET Core MVC with well-structured, maintainable code
- Develop secure and scalable RESTful services using Web API and OData
- Implement authentication and authorization for your applications
- Test and containerize your .NET projects for smooth deployment
- Optimize application performance with caching and other techniques
- Learn how to use and implement Umbraco CMS

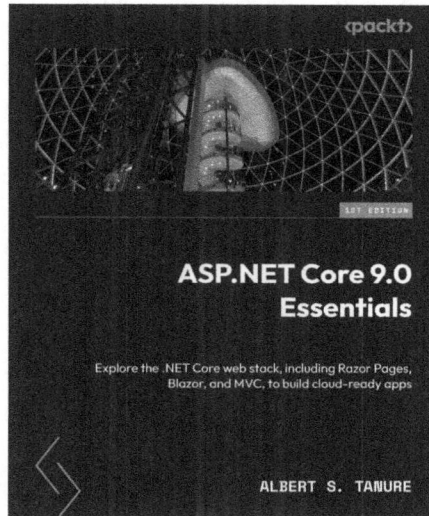

ASP.NET Core 9.0 Essentials

Albert S. Tanure

ISBN: 978-1-83546-906-4

- Deliver UI solutions using client-side, server-side, and hybrid model approaches with Razor Pages, MVC, and Blazor
- Implement real-time solutions and manage data streaming using SignalR
- Connect applications to a data persistence model using Entity Framework and Dapper
- Apply logging and monitoring strategies to maintain control over your applications
- Understand how .NET Aspire enhances your experience of building .NET cloud-native apps
- Find out how to test and debug your code effectively

Packt is searching for authors like you

If you're interested in becoming an author for Packt, please visit `authors.packtpub.com` and apply today. We have worked with thousands of developers and tech professionals, just like you, to help them share their insight with the global tech community. You can make a general application, apply for a specific hot topic that we are recruiting an author for, or submit your own idea.

Share Your Thoughts

Now you've finished *Modern Full-Stack Web Development with ASP.NET Core*, we'd love to hear your thoughts! Scan the QR code below to go straight to the Amazon review page for this book and share your feedback or leave a review on the site that you purchased it from.

`https://packt.link/r/1789132789`

Your review is important to us and the tech community and will help us make sure we're delivering excellent quality content.

www.ingramcontent.com/pod-product-compliance
Lightning Source LLC
Chambersburg PA
CBHW081225220326
41598CB00037B/6886